Border Interrogations

Remapping Cultural History
General Editor: Jo Labanyi, *Department of Spanish and Portuguese, New York University*

Published in association with the Institute of Germanic & Romance Studies, School of Advanced Study, University of London

This series challenges theoretical paradigms by exploring areas of culture that have previously received little attention. Preference is given to volumes that discuss parts of the world that do not easily fit within dominant northern European or North American theoretical models, or that make a significant contribution to rethinking the ways in which cultural history is theorised and narrated.

Volume 1
Cultural Encounters: European Travel Writing in the 1930s
Edited by Charles Burdett and Derek Duncan

Volume 2
Images of Power: Iconography, Culture and the State in Latin America
Edited by Jens Andermann and William Rowe

Volume 3
The Art of the Project: Projects and Experiments in Modern French Culture
Edited by Johnnie Gratton and Michael Sheringham

Volume 4
Locating Memory: Photographic Acts
Edited by Annette Kuhn and Kirsten Emiko McAllister

Volume 5
Intersecting Identities: Strategies of Visualization in 19th and 20th Century Mexico
Erica Segre

Volume 6
Fetishes and Monuments: Afro-Brazilian Art and Culture in the 20th Century
Roger Sansi

Volume 7
Journeys Through Fascism: Italian Travel-Writing between the Wars
Charles Burdett

Volume 8
Border Interrogations: Questioning Spanish Frontiers
Edited by Benita Sampedro Vizcaya and Simon Doubleday

Border Interrogations

Questioning Spanish Frontiers

Edited by
Benita Sampedro Vizcaya and Simon Doubleday

Berghahn Books
New York • Oxford

Published in 2008 by
Berghahn Books
www.berghahnbooks.com

©2008, 2012 Benita Sampedro Vizcaya and Simon Doubleday
First paperback edition published in 2012

All rights reserved. Except for the quotation of short passages for the purposes of criticism and review, no part of this book may be reproduced in any form or by any means, electronic or mechanical, including photocopying, recording, or any information storage and retrieval system now known or to be invented, without written permission of the publisher.

Library of Congress Cataloging-in-Publication Data

Border interrogations : questioning Spanish frontiers / edited by Benita Sampedro and Simon Doubleday.
   p. cm. -- (Remapping cultural history ; 8)
  ISBN 978-1-84545-434-0 (hbk) -- ISBN 978-0-85745-175-0 (pbk)
  1. Spain--Boundaries. 2. National characteristics, Spanish. 3. Minorities--Spain. 4. Spain--Foreign relations. I. Sampedro, Benita. II. Doubleday, Simon R.
  DP85.8.B67 2008
  303.48'24606--dc22
                    2008008098

British Library Cataloguing in Publication Data
A catalogue record for this book is available from the British Library

ISBN 978-0-85745-175-0 (paperback)
ISBN 978-0-85745-451-5 (ebook)

*For Beatriz, as she crosses the borders of childhood,
and Breogán, as he comes into his own.*

Contents

Acknowledgements   ix

   Introduction   1
   Benita Sampedro Vizcaya and Simon Doubleday

1. Europe's "Last" Wall: Contiguity, Exchange, and Heterotopia in Ceuta, the Confluence of Spain and North Africa   15
Parvati Nair

2. Migration, Gender, and Desire in Contemporary Spanish Cinema   42
H. Rosi Song

3. State Narcissism: Racism, Neoimperialism, and Spanish Opposition to Multiculturalism (On Mikel Azurmendi)   65
Joseba Gabilondo

4. Constructing *Convivencia*: Miquel Barceló, José Luis Guerín, and Spanish-African Solidarity   90
Susan Martin-Márquez

5. Galicia Beyond Galicia: "A man dos paíños" and the Ends of Territoriality   105
Cristina Moreiras-Menor

6. Foreignness and Vengeance: On Rizal's *El Filibusterismo*   120
Vicente L. Rafael

7. Through the Eyes of Strangers: Building Nation and Political Legitimacy in Eighteenth-Century Spain   147
Alberto Medina

8. On Imperial Archives and the Insular Vanishing Point: The Canary Islands in Viera y Clavijo's *Noticias*   165
Francisco-J. Hernández Adrián

9. Manso de Contreras' *Relación* of the Tehuantepec Rebellion
   (1660–1661): Violence, Counter-Insurgency Prose, and the
   Frontiers of Colonial Justice 188
   David Rojinsky

10. (The) *Patria* Besieged: Border-Crossing Paradoxes of
    National Identity in Cervantes's *Numancia* 204
    Michael Armstrong-Roche

11. Border Crossing and Identity Consciousness in the Jews
    of Medieval Spain 228
    Mariano Gómez Aranda

12. Seven Theses against Hispanism 246
    Eduardo Subirats

List of Contributors 260

Acknowledgements

Our initial questions about borders took place on the fringes of New York City. If some have associated the frontier with possibility, our first debt is to those colleagues at Hofstra University, and elsewhere, who provided us with the space and the stimulus to pursue its shifting dimensions. Among them are Stuart Rabinowitz, President of the University, Herman Berliner, Provost, Bernard J. Firestone, Dean of the College of Liberal Arts and Sciences, and Daniel Rubey, Dean of the Axinn Library. Jacques Berlinerblau, Stanislao Pugliese, Pellegrino D'Acierno, and Zilkia Janer offered valuable reflections on migration and exile. Discussions with Pepa Anastasio, Marta Bermúdez, Antonio Cao, Peter Caravetta, Marcelo Fiorini, Ben Heller, Mercedes Rodríguez, and Eduardo Subirats, directly and indirectly helped to galvanise this project. The Program for Cultural Cooperation Between Spain's Ministry of Culture & United States' Universities contributed generously to the individual and collective programs of research that inform the editors' approach.

A conversation with Jo Labanyi, as we walked through Washington Square, was the more immediate catalyst for this volume. It is Jo to whom we owe the initial suggestion of publishing with Berghahn Books, and we thank her as much for her intellectual inspiration as for her close and attentive reading of the manuscript. Michael Agnew, Fernando Gómez, Benjamin Liu, Ángel Loureiro, and Louise Vasvari offered fresh insights from a very early stage, and discussions with Román de la Campa, Joseba Gabilondo, Eyda Merediz, Walter Mignolo, Donato Ndongo-Bidyogo, David Rojinsky, and Michael Ugarte kept us conceptually alert to the fullest implications of interrogating the border. Parvati Nair's scholarly work was a source of continuing excitement, and from her husband Mark McGlynn, we received a number of haunting photographs of the cultural, human, and commercial traffic on the frontier between Ceuta and Morocco. Among the many who contributed unknowingly to the volume, special thanks are due to Teófilo Ruiz, Robert I. Burns, S.J., Angus MacKay, and Simon Barton, whose mutual concern with medieval border crossing, renegades, and turncoats has been invaluable in the urgent task of destabilizing nationalist fields of vision, and to Beverly Southgate, whose aspiration to a kind of scholarly writing that aims not for "closure," but for narratives that unsettle and invite further questioning, we deeply, and wholeheartedly, share.

Introduction

Benita Sampedro Vizcaya and Simon Doubleday

> ... we find ourselves in the moment of transit where space and time cross to produce complex figures of difference and identity, past and present, inside and outside, inclusion and exclusion.
> —Homi Bhabha, *The Location of Culture*

On one of the double perimeter fences at Melilla hang odd shoes and torn gloves, the ragged vestiges of an attempt by hundreds of sub-Saharan migrants to scale the walls of Fortress Europe. Many, but not all, have made it across into the legal limbo of this North African enclave. Six migrants have been shot and killed by Moroccan security forces, trigger-happy racism perhaps combining with the effects of pressure from the Spanish government and the European Union. Others who have made the journey across the great desert will be summarily returned and left to their fate, without food or water, a few days later. Some will be driven hundreds of miles south to another frontier, the border of the territory held by Polisario, with minimal rations and two bottles of water each, and instructed to leave through minefields towards another land of limbo: Birlehlu, in Western Sahara. A migrant from Ghana, interviewed by a British journalist near this southern frontier, reports that the "Moroccans are not Africans ... They call us black locusts." But it is the northern land border, fortified by its six meter double fences, that has captured the global imagination, graphically demarcating what President José Luis Rodríguez Zapatero has described as "the greatest difference in per-capita income between neighbouring countries in the world, a proportion of fifteen to one." It is here at Melilla—a disturbing legacy of fifteenth-century imperial ambitions—that the historical construct called "Spain" currently ends, and where, by virtue of the continuing relationship of inequality between the two, "Morocco" is consequently obliged to begin. The frontier is inscribed on the very skin of those who cross; the immigrant in Melilla wears dressings where the razor wire has sliced into his body. And it is at Ceuta, the sister enclave of Melilla, that we will begin this interrogation of, and on, Spanish borders; after all, as Parvati Nair reminds us in the opening essay of this volume, Ceuta "invites a questioning of such borders" by virtue of that overspill into the territory of the North African "other." But as her essay also suggests, a border is not always a barbed wire fence. The fences at Ceuta and Melilla cut deeply because they give torturously physical form to an accumulation of mutually reinforcing frontiers—political, legal, economic, religious, and, often but not exclusively, or even primarily, geographical.

At the outset, we might point out that one fundamental premise in this book is the conception—today quite commonplace—that borders need in no way be associated with literal geographical constructs; the primary understanding of the term under which our contributors are operating is not invariably concerned with the outer limits of territories. To the question "What is a border?", Étienne Balibar responded, nearly a decade ago, that we can not attribute to the border an essence which would be valid in all places and at all times, or which would be included in the same way in all individual and collective experiences (Balibar 2002, 75). Borders are dispersed, temporally as well as spatially, whenever and wherever the movement of information, people, and artifacts is controlled, patrolled and interrogated. The analysis of borders, in this sense, encompasses a challenge to disciplinary, chronological, and even academic practices and protocols. In conceiving this volume, our aim has been to embrace a wide understanding of the border, and its possibilities, defined as much as a site of contention and interrogation as a space from which the dynamics of subaltern and non-subaltern cultures and subjects are revisited and theorized. While our current academic interests (colonial territorial possessions in Africa and their representation in the Spanish imperial imaginary, and medieval Iberian cultural negotiations, respectively) are naturally suited to more direct participation in the debate, we have conceived our professional role, as editors of this volume, as facilitating the path for others to theorize while remaining at the conceptual edge. Our intention has been to encompass, in collaborative tension, a broad range of readings, engaging critically with a selection of paradigmatic moments from a number of different theoretical frameworks. The majority of the contributors approach the task by reassessing conceptual frontiers (and the discourses articulated in the liminality of the border), mostly understood as ambivalent spaces of negotiation and contestation. Each essay interrogates the border differently and uniquely, but there is a moment of convergence, almost unanimous and univocal, in their responses: their perception of the Spanish nation-space as a historical and ideological construct, continually experiencing mutations, transformations, and reformations. Frontiers are unhesitantly conceived as articulations, constitutively crossed and transgressed, and as fluid, porous, and multifaceted spaces of transition. Needless to say, frontier and fluidity are not contradictory and opposed, but complementary concepts. As contingent dividing lines, they may be acknowledged as thresholds of meaning that, as Homi Bhabha (1990) suggests, must be crossed, erased, and translated in the process of cultural production.

Under the current cartographies of globalism, where frontiers mutate, vacillate, and mark the contiguity of discourse, interrogating the border seems an urgent task. It is our conviction that intellectual responsibility must lead us to engage unblinkingly in the issues underlying current social and political tensions. It is precisely this sense that we must begin with the present—that the cardinal sin of "presentism" is not just inescapable but academically and ethically desirable—that has led us to organize the chapters in approximately reverse chronological order; and, while the opening contributions speak with greater immediacy to the present, the later essays have longer-term ramifications. Several chapters (those by Parvati Nair, Susan Martin-Márquez, and Joseba Gabilondo) are informed directly (although in different degrees) by a concern with Spanish-Moroccan relations. Others (including those by Rosi Song and Alberto Medina) respond to contemporary understandings of internationalism and globalization, phenomena that underline the contingency, artificiality, and inherently polemical nature of the nation-state. The volume also brings to bear distinct postcolonial perspectives, reflected variously in the chapters by Vicente Rafael, Francisco-J. Hernández Adrián, and David Rojinsky. Only with the range of subject matters and localities that this collection of essays addresses—Ceuta, the Caribbean, the Basque Country, North Africa, Galicia, the Philippines, Madrid, the Canary Islands, Mexico-Tehuantepec, Numancia, the medieval peninsular divides—will the volume maintain historical coherence; only within, and in-between, this complex web of localities can Spanish borders be fully interrogated and questioned.

In place of an aggressive assertion of *España como nación* (Real Academia de Historia, 2000), we will be concerned with Spain and its many frontiers as a deeply problematic and artificial construct (Epps and Fernández Cifuentes 2005), the single national adjective "Spanish" obscuring the complexity of realities. Despite the claim in the "Nota preliminar" of the Real Academia's collective volume that national sentiments are as legitimate as any others (2000, 11), it is quite clear that allegiance to nation has proved capable of immensely destructive consequences. As Gabilondo's contribution will reveal, there are in fact urgent moral grounds to condemn certain types of national sentiments, and the exaggerated notions of unity and frontier that underlie them, along with the misappropriation of history associated with narcissistic self-celebration. Neither the nation-state nor the territorial, legal, and economic frontiers that have underpinned it are concepts to which allegiance is self-evidently or invariably necessary. Indeed, loyalty to the nation as a primary form of allegiance is a relatively recent and almost certainly transient historical phenomenon, challenged in the twenty-first century by new forms of sub-state and supra-state identity that are, in certain respects, resonant of medieval precedent. Sovereignty has again become more fluid, cutting across the lines of nation-state and characterized by a plurality of overlapping power structures. While the state may be a useful and sometimes constructive mechanism for social and political organization, with the potential to facilitate, for instance, the equitable redistribution of wealth, this development is not necessarily to be lamented.

The lines of territorial, legal, and cultural relations, putatively distinguishing and demarcating from the alien and the other the realm of Spain (or, earlier, the loose and often internally hostile collective of medieval Christian kingdoms), are continually evolving, responding to changing forms, structures, and balances of power. "For borders have a history; the very notion of border has a history. And it is not the same everywhere and at every level" (Balibar 2002, 77). It is, perhaps, worth recalling here that the emergence of the notion of borders, in the Spanish context, can be traced quite specifically to the twelfth and thirteenth centuries. There had previously been little consciousness of frontiers of any kind, and a clear sense of "border" between Christianity and Islam had not yet crystallized (Christys 2002, 53). In general, the cultural and ideological frontier between Christianity and Islam appears to have been essentially a twelfth-century development associated with a more aggressive spirit of crusade brought by French immigrants, replacing an earlier dynamic of pragmatism. Even thereafter, it was constantly transgressed by Christian migrants to the north, mercenaries seeking their fortune in the south, and by Jewish merchants and those Jewish intellectuals that are the subject of Mariano Gómez Aranda's contribution to this volume (Chapter 11) (cf. Burns 1972; MacKay 1989; Fletcher 2000; Barton 2002). Any sense of Spanish unity was always complicated by the political and linguistic fragmentation of the changeable space occupied by the medieval Christian kingdoms, far more accentuated by 1250 than it had been in 750 (Fletcher 2000). In the Iberian Peninsula, the Roman notion of "Hispania" had survived largely as an ideal of *imperio,* rather than as a geopolitical entity with precise territorial borders; and across Western Europe, papal universalism remained paramount into the early thirteenth century (Abulafia 2002, 10–16). It is not until this point that we witness a shift towards a sharper sense of territorial boundaries in Iberia, corresponding in part to a new sense of political sovereignty.

If in the late medieval and early modern period, the peninsula witnessed increasingly rigorous attempts to raise the barriers of nation, law, morality, and ethnicity, almost inevitably bringing new, traumatic forms of exile (Abellán 2001, 17–25), not even in the sixteenth century did "Spain" exist as a legal entity. Furthermore, the project of cultural unification would be much slower than political-territorial demarcation. The strength of national sentiment in the sixteenth century continues to be a matter of debate. There was, as M. J. Rodríguez-Salgado has shown, a shift in the direction of communal association during this period, as a new sense of Spanish identity was negotiated through peninsular relationships with North Africa and the Americas. There emerged a "cosmopolitan, collective construct," she suggests (Rodríguez-Salgado 1998, 251); although given the proliferation of legal barriers against Jews, Muslims, *criollo* and *mestizo,* and "the need to present a united front against the Netherlanders, Germans and Italians," one might take issue with the first of these adjectives. On the other hand, she recognizes that Spanish society in the sixteenth century remained characterized by multiple layers of association, in which neither *patria* nor *nación* were terms exclusively applied to states. Indeed, the new "collective construct" of Spain coexisted at least as late as the eighteenth century with other powerful forms of allegiance: town, region, king, and universal church. As Michael Armstrong-Roche argues in "(The) *Patria* Besieged: Border-Crossing Paradoxes of National Identity in Cervantes's *Numancia*" (Chapter 10), the risks of projecting modern notions of "nation" onto the literature of the sixteenth century are legion.

Given the constructed nature of identity and frontier, it is striking that, as Parvati Nair observes in "Europe's 'Last' Wall: Contiguity, Exchange, and Heterotopia in Ceuta, the confluence of Spain and North Africa" (Chapter 1), adherence to the conspicuously artificial frontiers at Ceuta and Melilla is unchallenged today by even the most progressive Spanish political parties. The hegemonic form of patriotism, she states, "implies allegiance to an enclosed and static vision of Spain and her borders." In fact, adhesion to a conventional vision of Spain is present even in some surprising multicultural contexts, as Rosi Song shows in "Migration, Gender, and Desire in Contemporary Spanish Cinema" (Chapter 2). Here, she locates several unsettling dimensions in the construction of border crossing in modern Spanish cinema. The films she analyzes embody an idealized and highly problematic vision of assimilation, jarring with the harsher realities of immigrants' actual life experiences and tending to undercut the full possibilities of cultural diversity in Spain. This vision, informed by a neocolonial relationship between Spain and its former colonies in the Americas, rests in part on the films' surprisingly traditional set of gender values. Cultural anxiety, Song argues, is reflected in the directors' deployment of a range of ethnic and sexual stereotypes. Similarly, Joseba Gabilondo's "State Narcissism: Racism, Neoimperialism, and Spanish Opposition to Multiculturalism (On Mikel Azurmendi)" (Chapter 3) emphasizes the destabilizing effects of the Latin American "pseudo-other" on what he sees as the narcissistic, closeted, and a historical self-construction of the Spanish nation-state, a narcissism catalyzed by cultural anxieties associated with globalization. Latin America brings a "traumatic reminder of a failed colonial repression." In the case of the Basque anthropologist Mikel Azurmendi, an avowed enemy of the multicultural whose views respond to the "single State ideal ego, the nation," anxieties are compounded and shaped by the ongoing traumatic effect of Basque difference, leading to his complete neglect of the Latin American. Only the African, a fuller and more radically different "other," offers a useful object for Azurmendi's neoliberal ideology of assimilation—an ideology that implies crossing the divide to a morally superior, modern, Spanish culture.

In Chapter 4, "Constructing *Convivencia*: Miquel Barceló, José Luis Guerín, and Spanish-African Solidarity," Susan Martin-Márquez traces a deliberately positive and constructive conception of the relationship between Spain and Africa. The artist Miquel Barceló, she argues, "reverses the usual South-North flow" by successfully developing an intimate *convivencia* with the Dogon in Mali. She also invokes and redeploys Américo Castro's essentializing term, born of a now outdated preoccupation with defining Spanish national identity, to evoke the relationship between a Moroccan bricklayer and a *gallego* of the same profession in the documentary film *En Construcción*. The Galician coworker, Santiago, fails to live up to the reputation of his famous Moor-slaying namesake, establishing a close relationship with a Moroccan day laborer. The breakdown of *convivencia* in Yugoslavia, resonant of the medieval Spanish experience, forms an "insistent if subtle presence throughout the film," providing a counterpoint to the "construction of community out of diversity." In strikingly parallel terms, Cristina Moreiras-Menor traces what she calls "geographies under constant construction" in her essay "Galicia Beyond Galicia: 'A man dos países' and the Ends of Territoriality" (Chapter 5). Moreiras here leads us towards an understanding of the term "frontier" as a peripheral region, defined in relationship to a hegemonic national culture. The crucial question of how "nation-states founded historically on the premise of unity, commonality and sameness respond to the multiplicity of ethnicities and identities" (Fiona Allon 2002) becomes also an ethical issue. Through a close reading of Manuel Rivas' short story "A man dos países," Moreiras examines one of the peninsular cultures which, "because they are situated in the experience of the frontier ... question, resist and transgress" their relationship with the hegemonic and repressive national culture. As a frontier, Galicia marks a zone of contact, "constantly marked and unmarked as and when subjects are displaced and relocated." This incessant movement—between homeland and abroad, but also between life and death, and between past and present— is instrumental in forging cultural hybridity. Displacement, with accompanying memories of dislocation and violence, is so central to Galician identity, Moreiras concludes, that it undercuts the importance of territorial space and territorial boundary as markers of "home."

More than once, we see how attempts to impose unity on the complex human fabric of "Spain," or the Spanish-speaking world, give rise to the *haunting* of this artificial edifice. Just as Susan Martin-Márquez speaks of "spectral conversations" between Abdel and Santiago, Cristina Moreiras writes of the "ruptured, ghostly, space of the border," and of "a broad space of conflictive encounters and disencounters, lost and recovered memories, pointing from their deep wounds to the emergence of spectral presences." Her text echoes Jacques Derrida's evocation of ghosts as *revenants* of the improperly buried, the butchered, and of his observation that specters do not recognize borders: by definition, he says, they pass through walls, day and night (Derrida 1994, 30). Among the walls, then, are the walls of the *patria* and indeed of empire. Vicente Rafael, in "Foreignness and Vengeance: On Rizal's *El Filibusterismo*" (Chapter 6), will emphasize his subject's (ghostly) ability to cross the frontiers dictated by imperial relations. "He had a seemingly remarkable ability to cross geographical borders ... and linguistic differences": a form of transgression that is inevitably condemned by the Spanish authorities, criminalized and marked as *filibusterismo*, as a form of breaking and penetrating. Rizal himself, as Rafael remarks, explicitly refers to the *filibustero* as a "phantom" haunting the people; and the ghost of Crisóstomo Ibarra, enlightened protagonist of his first novel, hitherto missing, and presumed dead, will now return in his second novel, the *Fili,* to exact vengeance from the colonial authorities. All the more ironic, then, that the identity of modern Spain itself may be considered in large part the work of foreign elites (French and, in particular, Italian), breaking and entering into higher floors, the penthouse of the *patria.* The fluidity and instability of cultural frontiers during the eighteenth century lies at the heart of Alberto Medina's essay "Through the Eyes of Strangers: Building Nation and Political Legitimacy in Eighteenth-Century Spain" (Chapter 7) and problematizes the nature of inflections between national self and other. Medina's study of the cleansing of Habsburg attributes from Bourbon Spain, and the attempted "extinction of its own difference" resonates powerfully with Joseba Gabilondo's examination of the historical self-construction of the Spanish nation-state. The ideological context of this strategy also raises a number of interesting questions in relation to the current orthodoxy that "España no es diferente" (Doubleday 2003).

While the earlier essays in the volume directly address the contemporary, the following three chapters (8–10) help to constitute, in some sense, one of the cores of the issue at stake, articulating and theorizing challenges to the less traveled borders of empire, insularity, and violence. Border theory, after all, has been extensively developed in contemporary, modern, and even medieval Spanish studies, while early modern and imperial/colonial spaces have been strikingly under-theorized from this angle. It is precisely because of this historical divorce that the essays by Francisco-J. Hernández Adrián, Michael Armstrong-Roche, and David Rojinsky are indispensable. The three essays, read either individually or collectively, point towards the same conclusion: the Spanish empire can only imagine and legitimate itself through the border that establishes and then crosses with other subaltern subjects upon which it exerts its violence. They define imperial order and hegemony, then, as an act of border crossing and, perhaps more importantly, suggest that the border is not simply geopolitical, but also discursive and epistemological. With Hernández Adrián's "On Imperial Archives and the Insular Vanishing Point. The Canary Islands in Viera y Clavijo's *Noticias*" (Chapter 8), we pick up a thread that began in Vicente Rafael's chapter, and initiate a sequence of essays addressing the relationship between the written text and the highly contentious frontiers of empire. The author examines a critique from the margins: decentered history-making from an "insular" perspective that is anything *but* inward looking. History from the "vanishing point" of the Canary Islands, Hernández Adrián argues, resists colonial exploitation, both real and potential, and aims to rewrite the hegemonic reality on whose edges it stands. His essay brings new insight to one of the spaces in which the border of the empire is theorized and redeployed as a locus of contestation: the island, the ultimate paradigm of a border *per se.* The Canary Islands become the insular border where the Spanish Empire is always threatened with dissolution into an Atlantic space that other empires can dominate and rule. Thus, the insular border becomes a site for local subaltern subjects to find a new border identity, between the empire and the Atlantic, from which they affirm their border position and at the same time can contest those very borders of empire. The ideal of crossing (traversing) is central here: "Viera addresses the ever-present phenomenon of ethnographic and geographical objectification/subjectification traversing imperial geographies and modernities." Hernández

Adrián suggests how the theoretical location/perspective opened up by Viera contests the borders of the Spanish Empire and theorizes this border location as a scene of encounter and crossing. Viera's work may be perceived as "an important precedent in the theorization of a critical site, a multiple insular site where reality ... is reclaimed as local imagination and used to respond to the inhumanity of imperial sovereignty and the perpetual, perhaps constitutive crisis of territorial identification."

David Rojinsky's essay, "Manso de Contreras' *Relación* of the Tehuantepec Rebellion (1660–1661): Violence, Counter-Insurgency Prose and the Frontiers of Colonial Justice" (Chapter 9), deals with an episode in Mexican colonial history that might in certain senses be regarded as "peripheral" to a wider national history, a province geographically and culturally distant from Mexico City, the seat of Mexican political power. However, the episode allows the opportunity to present a subtle meditation on a whole range of pressing theoretical concerns. By tracing a genealogy between a seventeenth-century indigenous rebellion and the contemporary political mobilization of indigenous minorities against the current Mexican government's plan to exploit the region economically, the author undermines the first of a series of metaphorical "borders," "frontiers" or fixed demarcations: the opposition between *past* and *present* relations between centralized power in Mexico City and indigenous (minority) communities in the southern provinces. Having said that, it is clear that the first "border" with which the author is concerned is more conventional, relating to the territorial and administrative limits or frontiers of empire. The author of the *relación*, Manso de Contreras, regards the Zapotec rebellion of 1660 as a defiant challenge to those limits. Indeed, one of the principal motivations behind the writing of the *relación* is to impose those same limits discursively in a piece of prose that exemplifies the postcolonial notion of the "prose of counter-insurgency." And, if any consideration of "borders" (whether political, cultural, social or economic) relates inevitably, as Balibar (2002) argues, to the question of fixed identities, then it is also evident that Manso de Contreras responds to what he perceives as the disruption of colonial interpellations of indigenous subjectivities. He reasserts a series of dichotomies with regard to those same subjectivities: Indian/Spaniard; rebel/law-abiding Spaniard; violent Indian/peaceful Spaniard; treasonous Indian/loyal Spaniard. Given the fact that the rebellion was certainly not a *guerra de castas,* principally because indigenous élites enjoyed positions of power within the regional hierarchy, such dichotomies of course reduce the complexity of interethnic relationships in the region. Manso de Contreras struggles to inscribe the contours ("borders") of the essentialized and homogeneous identities constructed by colonial discourse.

Rojinsky's reading of Manso de Contreras' *relación* also lends itself to an analysis of the relationship between law, justice and violence as examined by Benjamin, Derrida, Agamben, and, most recently, Idelber Avelar. In this respect, he challenges Manso de Contreras' contention that the quashing of the rebellion served to exemplify how colonial law and justice might be regarded as isomorphic and, at the same time, as opposed to violence (the violence of the rebels). By drawing attention to the aesthetic of violence which characterizes the *relación*, and underscoring the law preserving nature of the indigenous rebellion, Rojinsky is able to challenge the metaphorical "border" which would separate the law from (discursive and material) violence. Ultimately, the colonial "frontier" between "justice/law" and "violence" (both material and discursive) is shown to be a site of contention rather than a natural barrier. To conclude, the essay brings to the forefront the use of writing as an instrument of violent *re-imposition* of hegemonic colonial authority after a presumed challenge to its territorial frontiers. The official and discursive violence of Manso de Contreras' *Relación,* Rojinsky argues, implies a self-serving and wholly artificial affirmation of a sharply demarcated moral frontier between legitimate (imperial) and illegitimate (indigenous) violence: a frontier that was, in reality, hotly contested and hopelessly blurred.

Michael Armstrong-Roche's study of "(The) *Patria* Besieged: Border-Crossing Paradoxes of National Identity in Cervantes's *Numancia*" (Chapter 10) rereads the play against the grain of conventional nationalist readings that tend to emphasize the divisive construction of borders, drawing attention to the dangers of appropriating history for political purposes, and—in particular—the retrospective construction of sharp moral or cultural frontiers to serve these purposes. Proposing that the Roman-Numantine border is intended as a staging of contemporary imperial frontiers, Armstrong traces in the play the interminable crossing of the Spanish imperial imagination between Rome and Numancia, and between empire and colony/Barbary. He rescues the original meaning of paradox (going around the *doxa*), as a means to highlight the "crossing" strategy of the play, traversing the border between *doxa* and non-accepted discourse. The play, which has been variously interpreted through the prism of presumed identifications (Spain-Rome, or Spain-Numancia) as a celebration of empire, or as a critique of it, was in fact intended to "unsettle facile appropriations"; Armstrong expands his imperial border theory to the broader canon of Golden Age literature through reference to *Don Quijote.* Far from positing a straightforward relationship between modern Spaniards and Numantines or Romans, the playwright blurs the lines between these enemies, Romanizing Numancia and demythologizing both, and posing the issue of national identity "as a question rather than a foreordained answer."

Questions of identity also lie at the heart of Chapter 11, "Border Crossing and Identity Consciousness in the Jews of Medieval Spain," in which Mariano Gómez Aranda examines the physical and geographical exile of three medieval Jewish intellectuals as a traumatic, but often intellectually productive process, generating new forms of identity consciousness. Moshe Ibn Ezra (d. 1135) leaves Al-Andalus under pressure from Almoravids; Abraham Ibn Ezra (d. 1160) leaves under the shadowy threat of Almohad occupation, perhaps in the face of more practical financial pressures; and Isaac Abravanel (d. 1508) departs as a result of the expulsions of 1492. Their mobility, from Muslim to Christian Spain, from Muslim Spain to Rome, and from Portugal to Castile, was followed, after the expulsion in 1492 and the partial reunification of the peninsula under the Catholic Monarchs, by further crossings to Naples, Corfu, Monopoli, and Venice. Yet in each case, the act of border crossing proves a catalyst, rechanneling the exiles' intellectual engagement, and galvanizing a new sense of identity. All three intellectuals and poets are conscious of displacement, longing, nostalgia, and resentment for lost status and comfort as central experiences in their lives. Such experience points to a certain sense of shifting identity, if not a loss of identity altogether, inherent to the idea of dislocation.

The contemporary resonance, and the dialogue between essays, becomes apparent. Just as Rojinsky, for instance, concludes his chapter by reflecting on the present day relevance of the recuperation of the Tehuantepec rebellion, suggesting that the putative frontier between justice and violence remains a site of contention in Mexico, and as Gabilondo reminds us of the dangers of imperial concepts from which academia itself is not exempt, so Gómez Aranda's dislocations of identity are not so far apart from those of the migrants analyzed by Rosi Song, Susan Martin-Márquez, and, to some degree, Cristina Moreiras-Menor. Indeed, while the more temporally distant essays in this volume cannot explain the *raisons d'etre* of the current border dilemmas addressed in the first seven chapters, they provide in some sense the historical and epistemological foundations on which these dilemmas lie. Parvati Nair's essay hearkens back to an imperial Castile and Aragon, covetous of Muslim territory in North Africa. Rosi Song's piece alludes to the Caribbean colonial and imperial legacies that also form an indisputable dimension of the present. Joseba Gabilondo engages directly with issues of Spanish imperialism both past and present, while the prominence given by Susan Martin-

Márquez to the word "convivencia" resonates immediately with medieval cultural, political, and territorial negotiations. The concerns of Cristina Moreiras' essay, in turn, are rooted in late medieval and early modern aspirations to territorial cohesion in the peninsula; Vicente Rafael's contribution can only be fully understood against the backdrop of Philip II's expansionist pretensions in Asia; and Alberto Medina's essay offers a bridge between old (Habsburg) imperial approaches and the more fluid but equally pervasive Bourbon attitudes toward empire.

The volume's complex historical and conceptual cartography finally encompasses Eduardo Subirats' "Seven Theses Against Hispanism" (Chapter 12): a call to arms, an appeal to the spirit of intellectual counterculture, to break down the repressive walls of our respective disciplines and to allow suppressed voices to speak. Subirats decries the violent imposition of ethno-national frontiers; the religious and philosophical constructs of the Christian west "fearsomely barricaded within the epistemological walls of its own immense powers of destruction"; and the passive orthodoxy of hybridity, multiculturalism (and other -*isms*), all ultimately serving neocolonial and neoliberal agendas. Few would disagree that Subirats not only represents—within the US, and in relation to Spanish academia in particular—a radical cultural critic, but also belongs to a singular genealogy in the history of Spanish criticism and radicalism that can be traced back to Blanco White in the nineteenth century, continuing through Américo Castro in the 1950s, and Juan Goytisolo in the 1970s. Readers are unlikely to search his work (any more than Goytisolo's) for bibliographical references to the innovative work being done by many other scholars in Spanish and Latin American Studies who have, like Subirats, been concerned precisely with challenging parochial and chauvinistic conceptions of "Spanish" culture. Notwithstanding, we propose that his attack on a Castilian-centric "Hispanism" which does not acknowledge "peripheries" or cultural plurality, represents a suitable form of *unclosure*; we underscore his plea for a more mobile form of Hispanism that would not only be transatlantic, but would also go beyond those resilient imperial borders by exploring the circulation of cultural traffic between the Spanish-speaking world and other cultures. We might add, in response to the taxi driver's interrogation of our first contributor, near the African border, that we have not just come for the windsurfing.

Bibliography

Abellán, José Luis. 2001. *El exilio como constante y como categoría*. Madrid: Biblioteca Nueva.
Abulafia, David. 2002. "Introduction: Seven Types of Ambiguity, c. 1100–c.1500." In David Abulafia and Nora Berend, eds, *Medieval Frontiers: Concepts and Practices*. Aldershot, England: Ashgate, 1–34.
Allon, Fiona. 2002. "Boundary Anxieties: Between Borders and Belongings." *Borderlands e-journal* 1, no. 2.
Balibar, Étienne. 2002. *Politics and the Other Scene*. London and New York: Verso.
Barton, Simon. 2002. "Traitors to the Faith? Christian Mercenaries in al-Andalus and the Maghreb, c.1100–1300." In Roger Collins and Anthony Goodman, eds, *Medieval Spain: Culture, Conflict and Coexistence. Studies in Honour of Angus MacKay*. New York: Palgrave Macmillan, 23–45.
Bhabha, Homi. 1990. *Nation and Narration*. New York: Routledge.
———. 1994. *The Location of Culture*. New York: Routledge.
Bishko, Charles Julian. 1980. *Studies in Medieval Spanish Frontier History*. London: Variorum.
Burns, Robert I. 1972. "Renegades, Adventurers and Sharp Businessmen: The Thirteenth-Century Spaniard in the Cause of Islam." *American Historical Review* 58, 341–366.
———. 1989. "The Significance of the Frontier in the Middle Ages." In Robert Bartlett and Angus MacKay, eds, *Medieval Frontier Societies*. Oxford: Clarendon Press, 307–330.
Christys, Ann. 2002. "Crossing the Frontier of Ninth-Century Hispania." In David Abulafia and Nora Berend, eds, *Medieval Frontiers: Concepts and Practices*. Aldershot, England: Ashgate, 35–53.
Derrida, Jacques. 1994. *Specters of Marx. The State of the Debt, the Work of Mourning, and the New International*. New York: Routledge.
Doubleday, Simon R. 2003. "English Hispanists and the Discourse of Empiricism." *The Journal of the Historical Society* 3, no. 2, 205–220.
———. 2004. "'O que foi passar a serra: Frontier-crossing and the thirteenth-century Castilian nobility in the *cantigas de escarnio e de maldizer*." In Martin Aurell, ed, *Le médiéviste et la monographie familiale: sources, méthodes et problematiques*. Turnhout: Brepols, 189–200.
Epps, Brad and Luis Fernández Cifuentes, eds. 2005. *Spain beyond Spain. Modernity, Literary History and National Identity*. Lewisburg: Bucknell University Press.
Filios, Denise K. 2005. *Performing Women in the Middle Ages. Sex, Gender, and the Iberian Lyric*. New York: Palgrave Macmillan.
Fletcher, Richard. 2000. "The Early Middle Ages." In Raymond Carr, ed, *Spain. A History*. Oxford: Oxford University Press, 63–89.
Liu, Benjamin. 1999. "'Affined to Love the Moor': Sexual Misalliance and Cultural Mixing in the *Cantigas d'escarnho e de mal dizer*." In Josaiah Blackmore and Gregory S. Hutcheson, eds, *Queer Iberia: Sexualities, Cultures and Crossings from the Middle Ages to the Renaissance*. Durham, NC: Duke University Press, 48–72.
MacKay, Angus. 1977. *Spain in the Middle Ages: from Frontier to Empire, 1000–1500*. New York: St. Martin's Press.
———. 1989. "Religion, Culture and Ideology on the Late Medieval Castilian-Granadan Frontier." In Robert Bartlett and Angus MacKay, eds, *Medieval Frontier Societies*. Oxford: Clarendon Press, 217–243.

Pratt, Mary Louise. 1992. *Imperial Eyes. Studies in Travel Writing and Transculturation.* New York: Routledge.
Real Academia de Historia, ed. 2000. *España como nación.* Barcelona: Planeta.
Rodríguez Salgado, María José. 1998. "Christians, Civilised and Spanish: Multiple Identities in Sixteenth-Century Spain." *Transactions of the Royal Historical Society,* sixth series, no. 8, 233–251.
Ruiz, Teófilo. 1997. "Fronteras: de la comunidad a la nación en la Castilla bajomedieval." *Anuario de Estudios Medievales* 27, 23–41.

Chapter 1

Europe's "Last" Wall:
Contiguity, Exchange, and Heterotopia in Ceuta, the Confluence of Spain and North Africa

Parvati Nair

As myth would have it, Hercules, in the course of performing his labors, marked the limits of the world as it was then known: the Pillars of Hercules, on the western shores of the Mediterranean, are located on the southern tip of Europe and on the northern tip of Africa. Here, where the Mediterranean spills out onto the wide Atlantic, Jebel Tariq, now better known as Gibraltar, and Jebel Musa on the Moroccan mainland, near the Spanish enclave of Ceuta, form an imaginary hang-line between the known world and the unknown. Present here since antiquity, therefore, has been the unsettling proposition of the unknown, the strange, the other. Jebel Musa, a promontory that slopes down to the sea, stretches out against the Mediterranean skyline, like a woman supine on her back. Known, thus, in Spanish as "La Mujer Muerta", or the dead woman, the sleeping body of Jebel Musa silently suggests a danger zone of alterity, challenged, nevertheless, by the unchecked flow of the waters below.

Ceuta, or Sebta as it is known in Morocco, is one of two Spanish enclaves in North Africa. A small port of no more than 18.5 square kilometers and a perimeter of 28 kilometers, it is surrounded to the north by the waters of the Straits of Gibraltar, themselves the line of slippage between the Mediterranean sea and the Atlantic ocean. The land around it belongs to Morocco and the nearest town is Tetuán. The physical location of Ceuta, both a part of Spain and separated from it, is weighted with geopolitical significance: at once a bastion of European presence in the region, anchored by the weight of colonial history, and an interrogation of Europe's relation to its North African "other," it remains a bone of contention between nations and governments that are neighbors, yet differentiated by degrees of wealth and empowerment. Similarly, the blue waters of Ceuta are a subject of litigation between Spain and Morocco, as fishing disputes continue to rage between the two countries. Ceuta, together with its sister city Melilla[1] near Nador in Morocco, marks Europe's southernmost border. Paradoxically, its location in the Maghreb looks northward "at Europe" even as it outshines its postcolonial neighbor with the lure of European economic might. As such, and in its physical isolation from the Spanish peninsula, it presents a fortified and intensified example of the border constructed to demarcate the European contours of the Western hegemony from the neighboring Third World. In its dangerous overspill into territories of alterity, Ceuta also invites a questioning of such borders and, by extension, of the means by which such hegemony is constructed and maintained.

This chapter will attempt an anthropology of the border as currently exemplified in Ceuta. It will explore the means by which cultural and social borders both subvert and bolster national or state borders; it will argue that border identities are shifting and contingent, at odds in their liminality with the state forces that seek to contain them. Such a contradictory context of obscure slippage in the face of enforced border controls inevitably poses a question mark around the liberal democracy that is a hallmark of the western hegemony. Democracy, a buzz word in post-Francoist Spain, inextricably tied to the ever-increasing ventures of late capitalism and reiterated politically as an ideological counterpoint to nearly four decades of dictatorship, stumbles across its own limits at those points where First World spills into Third. Here, where economic fault lines come into play, the urgency to reinforce borders is greatest, precisely to ensure the free circulation of the democratic project within the privileged spaces of the West. The theoretical line of analysis that I pursue will be drawn from the concepts of contiguity, as developed by Homi Bhabha and heterotopia, a term established by Michel Foucault and rethought by David Harvey. My claim is that Ceuta, at the interface of two nations, two continents and two levels of economic and political power, is at once a space of differentiation and a space of contestation, exchange, slippage. Ceuta's status as one of the seventeen regional autonomies of Spain elevates it to a status above that of its less affluent neighbor, Morocco. Nevertheless, the physical proximity of Morocco leads to close contact over and against border demarcations. If Ceuta is a part of Spain, then it is also intrinsically conjoined to Morocco, both through current social and cultural practices and through a history of interrelation. As such, Ceuta as border is also a bridge between First World and Third.

Like other border spaces, most especially the town of Tijuana on the United States-Mexico border, the city of Ceuta exemplifies the conflicting dynamics of border controls. A study of the politics of space and place in Ceuta cannot ignore the underground exchanges and dialectical relations that are ongoing between Ceuta and Morocco. Thus, a gap exists between official discourses, on the one hand, and social practices, on the other, which turn this border city into a "heterotopia," or space of numerous, fragmentary, contiguous, and contradictory worlds.

The research process for this analysis involved fieldwork in Ceuta. As such, and in the course of attempting to gain information on the city as a border space, I was acutely aware of the many borders that are perhaps impossible to cross and that must be borne in mind when conducting academic studies on immigration. In the first instance, I was only a visitor to the city. With limited resources and time at my disposal, the urge to collect information was constantly tempered by what appeared appropriate or possible. Equally, there was much that I discovered by chance. Secondly, interviews and conversations with "locals" or immigrants were inevitably framed by how they perceived me.[2] My key informant, Shamsul, a Bangladeshi immigrant, was forthcoming largely due to a racial, linguistic, and cultural commonality between himself and myself, whereas several undocumented African immigrants whom I met were unwilling to reveal their stories to me. Understandably, a sociopolitical divide separated the route of illicit migration that they had taken to reach Spain and the apparently "licit" nature of my enquiry and my presence there. Thirdly, there is the awareness of a chasm between the analysis of the academy, the production of discourses of knowledge and power, carried out within the safety of an institutional environment, and the harsh realities of immigrant experience. A certain discomfiture is in order, I believe, when academically approaching issues where human rights and human lives are at stake. Nevertheless, it is precisely such efforts that reveal the contingent frames surrounding academic discourse. Such issues of reflexivity have been raised in recent years by anthropologists, such as James Clifford (1997), Pierre Bourdieu (Bourdieu and Wacquant 1992), and others. In writing this chapter, I shall attempt to reflect the many voices and faces that I heard and saw on the border, in the hope that by so doing, and by self-consciously foregrounding the tenuous ground beneath studies of identity, the many more that I did not see or hear may gain a presence. I am aware too of the many frames and boundaries that I impose, unwittingly or not, in the translation or translocation of lived or narrated experience into written text. What became clear in the course of my efforts was that the border in this day and age is never unified, quantifiable or easily located. Borders overlap and become entangled with one another. They move in diverse directions and can be viewed from many angles. Most of all, there is a confounding coincidence of different spaces and times at the border.

Contiguity and Heterotopia

To state simply, then, that Ceuta is a border town between North and South, one that both bridges and divides two continents, is in many ways to elide the complexity of the counter-movements that are present there. Attempts to locate the border towns of Ceuta and Melilla in terms of either the First or Third World will inevitably fail: they are neither one nor the other, nor indeed the sum of their different parts. Instead, these frontier towns inhabit the ambivalence of the borderline, a contradictory and shifting space that presents varied perspectives. Furthermore, the diversities present in Ceuta defy the leveling and restrictive discourses of multiculturalism. The attempt to frame Ceuta, then, flounders, for the border space—ironically—refuses delimitation.

If, for historical reasons, Ceuta has long been a place of political and cultural complexity, then, in today's world, after 11 September 2001, it is all the more so. The ideals of law, citizenship, and human rights, those pillars of the modern nation-state as constructed by the European imagination, are put to the test at this point, when they come up against one of Fortress Europe's "last" walls. Late capitalism and globalization have led to a complex web of economic, political, and cultural connections between the global dominant powers and their postcolonial others. In his *The End of History and the Last Man* (1992), Francis Fukuyama famously announced "the end of history." By this, he meant that following the break-up of the Soviet Union, liberal democracy would become an all-encompassing ideological structure, unchallenged by any other. Furthermore, such liberal democracy was tied, in his view, to global market economics. This dependence on the marketplace in turn creates a rift between the ideology of liberal democracy and the realization of democracy in terms of lived practice as exercised by states and global alliances. This is poignantly in evidence in the context of global labor migration. In counter-movement to the extension of Western-centered capitalist enterprise across the world is the migration of persons to the Western metropole. Today, over 200 million persons are on the move around the globe, migrating northward from the impoverished South, often staking their lives to cross the global economic divide and the barbed gateways of border zones, such as Ceuta. Denied citizenship or legitimacy through illicit entry into Europe, such migrants nevertheless contribute both to the economic and cultural wealth of the host nations.

It is in this context of troubling and unfulfilled democracy that Homi Bhabha develops his notion of contiguity. He states that, "The contingencies and contiguities of the new cartography of globalism mutate and vacillate, mediate and morph …"(Bhabha 2002, 351). Rather than see current political, economic, and cultural practice as contradictions—a term that itself implies separate and contrary categories—Bhabha emphasizes the conflictual but communicative categories that comprise the global market economy and the impact upon other areas of lived practice. Borders, in such a context, both territorial and imagined, are double-edged, at once open and closed, at once mobile and controlled, wavering in the overall contingencies of global time and space. "Contiguity," he tells us, is "a way of dealing with the 'partial or incubational combination of old and new' (which) makes us attentive to the 'jurisdictional unsettlement' that marks the life-world of our times" (Bhabha 2002, 354). Hence the double horizon that he sees hovering over global discourse where the "national" persists, as the transnational or global predominates in a variety of spheres. It might be worth adding that regulating these contiguous discourses and connecting their apparent contradictions is the marketplace. That double horizon, the borderline between the national and the transnational, must be determined in line with market fluxes. Its effects too must be read in this light. Nowhere is this more in evidence than in the twilit edges of the First World. The open internal borders of the Schengen space—the free, unregulated circulation of currency, persons, and goods—are shut down at Ceuta. Here, the national asserts its old, historical self and claims the right to draw the line. Equally, such a line is daily challenged both by the processes of cultural intercourse with nearby Morocco and by the influx of migrants entering this policed space, spurred on by the ubiquitous migrant dream of "a better life."

The simultaneity and multiplicity of spaces that Ceuta presents can also be viewed in terms of Foucault's notion of heterotopia. Foucault first developed his notion of heterotopia in 1966, in his book *The Order of Things*. Here, his focus was on the heterotopia of discourse and the multiplicity of language. Later, in a lecture delivered in 1967 and published posthumously, "Des espaces autres," Foucault applies this same concept to space. He states that the nineteenth century focus on history has given way to a new concern with space. "We are," he tells us, "in the epoch of simultaneity, we are in the epoch of juxtaposition, the epoch of the near and far, of the side-by-side, of the dispersed." Foucault viewed this focus on space as itself a stage in history whereby a shift has taken place from a singularly diachronic paradigm to one which is determined by a spatial paradigm. What ensues is a double logic of shared space together with the simultaneous juxtaposition of different spaces: space, no longer lived in the singular or abstract but in terms of plurality. By extension, given that this shift has taken place within the larger paradigm of history, time too is lived in terms of plurality and simultaneity.

> The space in which we live, which draws us out of ourselves, in which the erosion of our lives our time and our history occurs, the space that claws and gnaws at us, is also, in itself, a heterogeneous space. In other words, we do not live in a kind of void, inside of which we could place individuals and things. We do not live inside a void that could be colored with diverse shades of light, we live inside a set of relations that delineates sites, which are irreducible to one another and absolutely not superimposable on one another. (Foucault 1986, 23)

This view of spatialization has a definite impact on questions of power and subjectivity. While Foucault wrote of space and time in the singular, his argument opens to the question of how this impacts a world of complex geopolitical, technological, and economic networks. The spatialized subject of late capitalism occupies numerous, possibly incompatible, sites or locations. Indeed, in an increasingly virtual world, many of these spaces may be disengaged from place. The time of place and the time of space may thus not coincide. Sites, whether virtual or not, may themselves not be self-contained and distinct units. The heterotopic subject treads numerous borderlines and the heterotopic city becomes a place of constant crossings.

Bearing in mind that Foucault's lecture was written nearly four decades ago, we come up against the need to reassess it in the context of late modernity. If heterotopia is a space of otherness or difference that allows for the production of "alternatives," as David Harvey suggests (2000, 184), then the complication of space and time that both constitutes and results from the socioeconomic and cultural configurations of late capitalism further scatter spatiality and complicate temporal experience. Foucault's heterotopia was a space of radical organization and practice, one that disrupts the normative and offers new perspectives. Harvey delineates the effects of late capitalism on this dialectic. In particular, he marks a tension that has arisen between space and place:

> The dialectical oppositions between place and space, between long- and short-term horizons, exist within a deeper framework of shifts in time-space dimensionality that are the product of underlying capitalist imperatives to accelerate turn-over times and to annihilate space by time. (Harvey 1996, 247)

This process, which he terms "time-space compression," is fundamentally tied to capitalism and calls for a new understanding of the dynamics and dialectics of contemporary life. Space, a constitutive frame of material life, must be viewed in terms, not only of organization, as suggested by Foucault, but also in terms of social practices. In this way, the geopolitics of spaces and places determined by the acquisitional thrusts of capitalism can find their dialectical and competing relation to one another and to time.

Once again, when viewed in terms of late capitalism and its sociocultural effects, the double horizon perceived by Bhabha resulting from the contiguity of current cultural processes comes into view. This time, though, when considered in terms of the tenuous junctures of today's spaces and times, it is seen to mark out a global landscape of difference, unevenness, injustice. In an overridingly capitalist world, the pitfalls of difference are most keenly felt and displayed in economic terms. The dynamics of contemporary life, issues of class relations or social justice, are mapped out in terms of an often unsituated and contingent geography of economic, and by extension political, difference. Hence, even as the dialectic of difference grows, so the gap between space and place, between the free floating and the embodied, between the mobile and the landlocked, between the winners and the losers of capitalist risk ventures, expands. The age of late capitalism spatializes difference and so threatens to dematerialize it; equally, it is an age where the periphery, the border, the margin, is ever more marked and more in evidence. If all existence is turned borderline, then, the border too becomes a space of contiguity and heterotopia. Multi-hued and radical in its proposition of difference, it is the frame within which otherness encounters its own alterities.

Border Spaces

To the naked eye the electronic fence seems almost aesthetic. There is something lace-like, diaphanous, in the intricacy of its appearance. There is no barbed wire here, no massive, stone wall. The filigree work glints in the Mediterranean sun. Yet, it is this fence, more than the difference in the uniforms of the guards or the passing of customs posts, that confirms to me that I am in Europe. There are as many men in djellabas on this side as on the other, perhaps even more. Rif women walk through the frontier posts as if there were no frontier at all. Unlike me, they do not wait for their passports to be stamped, for their visas to be scrutinized. The urchins approach me as I walk into Spain; they clutch my bag and offer to carry it. I know they will want a tip, but I cannot tip them all. They fight amongst one another for the little I give them. A frontier guard walks by and they scatter. The taxi driver chats as he takes me into the center of town. Have I come for windsurfing, he asks, for just a few days in the sun? The seafood restaurants are excellent, he tells me, and shopping is good.

This analysis of Ceuta embarks from a view of this small border city as a locus of difference. To think in terms of difference, as of the nation, the city or any other bounded space in the imaginary, is to think in terms of borders. The affirmation of collective identities and the play of power relations between such entities inevitably rely upon the construction of boundaries. The border, as a site of demarcation and as a point of contact and cultural exchange, selectively facilitates or obstructs passage. Located on the border are the symbols of power; in practice on the border is the exercise of the same. Thus, nation-states stress their lines of demarcation once these have been recognized by international law, as the modern drive to map the world in terms of nations or other legitimized spaces relies on the borderline as a marker of distinction. While state boundaries define the legal limits of sovereignty, these can nevertheless be subverted, challenged or reinforced, as the case may be, by cultural practices. Thus, the symbolic boundaries of culture seldom follow the spatial logic of state boundaries and can even force a refiguring of the latter through the impact of cultural practices on existing geopolitical mappings. The splintering of the former Yugoslavia through the assertion of ethnic differences is a case in point; so also the Partition of British India that resulted in the birth of independent India and Pakistan. This dynamic of contiguity between culture and the state turns borders into spaces of specific cultural and political relations, themselves contingent upon temporal and spatial processes arising from larger historical and global contexts. It could be argued thus that few spaces exemplify heterotopia more than the border.

While much theory related to borders can be applied to issues of identity, be these cultural, national or otherwise, such analysis relies upon the metaphorical imagination of the border as boundary of identity. As Gloria Anzaldúa's *Borderlands—La frontera: The New Mestiza* (1987) exemplifies, borderline identity is transgressive and marginal. To explore such identity is to encounter hybridity, the experience of culture performed and practiced as hyphenation. No doubt there is considerable overlap between such borders and territorial borders. Indeed, Anzaldúa's well-known work locates itself on the Mexico-US border, but then goes on to explore more general issues of border identities:

> The US-Mexico border *es una herida abierta* where the Third World grates against the first and bleeds. And before a scab forms it haemorrhages again, the lifeblood of two worlds merging to form a third country—a border culture. Borders are set up to define the places that are safe and unsafe, to distinguish *us* from *them*. (1987, 6)

For Anzaldúa, the specificities of the Mexican border open onto larger generalities about border identities and borderline experiences. The border, she states, is a space of transitionality, of crossing and being crossed, of bleeding and excess. Thus, border people engage in the ongoing practice of translation and translocation of selfhood and identity, a practice of cultural survival for heterotopic citizens, which imposes upon them a double time and a fractured space.

Nevertheless, it is also important to bear in mind for the purposes of this study that territorial frontiers, such as that of the US and Mexico or of Ceuta and Morocco, bring with them implications that are not only political and cultural but also juridical (Donnan and Wilson 1999, 1–17). Thus, state borders must be distinguished from other types of borders as they are policed zones, where the traffic of people and goods is controlled and monitored. To cross a state boundary illicitly is to violate international law. Furthermore, territorial borders are often determined by the history of the region, thus exemplifying the continuation of historical legacies of power and wealth. Just one such instance is the division of Middle Eastern territories, following the Sykes-Pycot agreement of 1916, into the modern nations-states of Jordan, Egypt, Syria, and Israel, the latter being constructed on Palestinian lands to the continuing detriment of the Palestinian people. The juridical dimension of territorial frontiers is complex and changeable. Despite the contingency of state law, this factor turns territorial and state frontiers into policed zones, where the passage of persons is monitored. Indeed, the juridical authority of the frontier zone sifts the documented migrant from the undocumented one. Hidden in the cracks between such opposed categories are the millions of stateless or undocumented migrants who slip across such policed borders and inhabit the blurred spaces and precarious times of non-recognition.

For these reasons, Henk Driessen rightly notes that: "since Spain's incorporation into the European Union, its southern border has been transformed into a *European* frontier—a frontier re-marked and reinforced. Central issues of border ethnography in nation-states are the politics, economics and symbolism of inclusion and exclusion of newcomers" (Donnan and Wilson 1998, 97). This is most certainly so, but there is a striking incongruity attached to border towns such as Ceuta and Melilla: they have the dual function of serving the nation they adhere to and, paradoxically, affirming the very continent they are geographically disconnected from. By consequence, they become the nerve centers where Europeanness is both most visibly constructed and most predictably challenged. The Spanish diplomat Máximo Cajal thus asks the question in his book *Ceuta, Melilla, Olivenza, Gibraltar* (2003): Where does Spain end? The borders of Ceuta have changed dramatically in the course of history. During the

Spanish Protectorate of northern Morocco, Cajal states, it blended in with its surroundings. Now, the city is increasingly fenced and rendered impenetrable to the undesired. Yet the crossings of precisely such groups into the fortified terrains of Europe via Ceuta continue.

As point of passage, the border is a place of transit. The border both proclaims the supposed fixity of the nation and is defined by the mobility, either chosen or forced, of those who travel through it. Borderline people are displaced and on the move, migrant in space and time. In the course of this migrancy, they find themselves driven, all too often, by global (im)balances of power, whereby they are drawn into the larger sweep of transnational interests. The border of Ceuta, for example, functions, like its sister city Melilla or like Tijuana in the American continent, as the nexus of First World and Third. The oddity, of course, is that in the case of Ceuta, its physical location in Africa contradicts its construction of identity as European. For this reason, the border is experienced differently from one side to another. As millions of hopeful *emigrés* in Morocco contemplate the crossing into Ceuta as a foray into an imagined European paradise, so Morocco is sold to Spaniards and other Europeans by the tourist industry as the nearby exotic. By the same token, the 2 million or more Moroccan immigrants in Europe cross the Straits of Gibraltar annually on their visits home. The diversity of uses that border spaces are put to includes the illicit trafficking of persons and goods, as transnational networks of traffickers smuggle immigrants and narcotics across boundaries of state, northward along routes into centers of capital in the First World. Thus, borders extend metaphorically, and well beyond their acknowledged lines, into the Western metropolis, whereby the urban spaces of the First World, the apparent centers of global power and wealth, become marked by the migrant presence of those who live on the margins of Western prosperity.[3] State boundaries thus extend in juridical and other ways beyond the physical demarcations of the frontier. Indeed, the provisionality of the migrant condition can itself be considered a border, if only because it reduces all experience to the transitional and the borderline. If Ceuta divides Spain from Morocco and Europe from Africa, then the border as point of crossing for many may begin in the backs of trucks of agricultural and other goods coming into Europe from Morocco. It may end in the warehouses where such goods are downloaded or in the ports of southern Spain, where ferries carrying vehicles from Morocco or Ceuta dock. The policing of the border extends, likewise, from port to metropolis, as dark-haired males, dressed in the familiar uniform of the immigrant—T-shirt, jeans, and trainers, all acceptable to Western eyes—are stopped in city centers and searched for documentation. Yet, such policing does little to stem the global flow of economic and political migrants moving daily toward and into Europe. In this jagged, unmapped line of crossing, Ceuta remains a nexus of possibility and challenge.

At dusk on the first day, I went down to the rocky shore. Ahead of me, to the north, was Gibraltar, Europe's southernmost point. A man, perhaps in his seventies, was clambering among the rocks, looking for octopus. "They come out at this time," he said. I told him to take care not to slip, as the tide was going out. He laughed. "I know this sea, I've lived here all my life," he replied. "The Mediterranean is the gentlest, most hospitable sea in the world."

Ceuta's position on the Mediterranean underlines its border role. The Mediterranean is itself a border region demarcating political, economic, and ideological differences. In the wake of 11 September 2001, it also divides the global hegemony of liberal democracies from the supposed lands of intolerance, religious fundamentalism, and terror. The Mediterranean divide has thus deepened greatly in the last two decades: firstly, since the opening up of internal state borders in Europe, ever since the fall of the Berlin Wall in 1989, and more recently, since the alliance of Western forces against fundamentalist Islam. In other words, the US-dominated quest for oil routes to the Gulf has led to current global configurations of capital and power, which impact upon the Mediterranean region, rendering it a space where the North-South divide is most keenly felt. If, during the Cold War, the enemy of Western capitalism was located in the east of Europe, then today, the enemy, now Islamic, is located across and beyond the Mediterranean sea. Concurrently, it is precisely from these very regions that immigration from Asia and Africa enters Europe. If economic migrants are by definition disadvantaged, then the Muslims who cross the Mediterranean are doubly so. Since 11 September 2001, several Muslim immigrants in Spain, mostly of Maghrebian origin, have been taken from their homes, detained, questioned, and then released for lack of evidence in the larger, global zeal to quell terror. To further the imbalance and in an ironic inversion of the North's political and economic domination over the South, the demography of the Maghreb far exceeds that of Europe. Thus, while Europe recedes increasingly into an ageing population, over 75 percent of Moroccans are under the age of twenty-five and the birth rate of the Maghreb region in general is over ten times that of Europe. Furthermore, and in a perhaps predictable reverberation of a US-led global culture of fear, the borders of the war on terror extend into the Maghreb, as the governments of Morocco and Tunisia wage the same fight against terror and fundamentalism within their frontiers: such eradication of terror, now part and parcel of liberal democracy as practiced in the West, has the added advantage of pleasing the powers that be. Hence the crackdown by Moroccan authorities in July 2003 on uncovered "terror" units in Tangiers (thought to have made their way into Morocco from Ceuta) and elsewhere, even as the economy increasingly fails to sustain its expanding population. Layered upon, and in counter-current to, the ideological borders of the war on terror, therefore, are the economic borders between the hopeful youth of countries such as Morocco and the apparent prosperity of the West. As a result, even as Islam becomes ever more suspect a religion in the West, the spaces and places of the latter become crossed by the presence of Muslim immigrants.

Located at this uncomfortable juncture, any monolithic perspective of Ceuta surely comes into question. A study of Ceuta throws up the imprecision that marks the demarcated juncture of nations and continents and reveals borders to be physical and ideological constructs of the state, whose implications extend not only into the body of the nation or continent, but into global arenas. Yet, it is precisely this complexity that marks Ceuta out as a point of crossing between two nations, two continents, and, most importantly, two very disparate levels of global power. In this paradigm of difference and contiguity, Ceuta presents an ambivalence or contradiction: the forces of globalization push toward a homogenization of Ceuta with the rest of Europe, in defiance of its African location, thus reinforcing a politics of identity aimed at maintaining and strengthening Western hegemony. Simultaneously, this apparent disregard for the physical embodiment of this piece of Europe in Africa can only take place through an overarching emphasis of Ceuta's border with Morocco. At play here is the flickering duality of the border, as point of crossing as well as line of control. It is thus precisely the proximity of otherness that Morocco presents that invests Ceuta with its political significance. Morocco, in its social problems and in its relative poverty, affords Ceuta its economic and political definitions, its borders of power. Multi-sited, heterotopic, and contiguous in its pluralities, this border defies its own restrictions.

Leïla, Perejil, Parsley Island ... In the summer of 2002, just as countless Europeans prepared to take off for the shores of the Mediterranean on their annual beach holidays, some shattering news broke out. "Ten Moroccan soldiers invade Spain," we were told. The reactions were vociferous. Around Europe, it was feared that, less than a year after the attack on the Twin Towers in New York and at a time when the righteous nations of the world were gathering together in order to combat terror, an Islamic nation had invaded European territory. The response from Brussels at the heart of the European Union was prompt: "Perejil is part of the territory of the European Union." Spain mobilized its defense forces, sent its Navy and Air Force to the region, and ousted the offending soldiers in a matter of days.

Located on the Straits of Gibraltar, Perejil, as it is known in Spanish or Leïla as it is called in Morocco, has a square area of just 500 meters by 300 meters. The minute size of this island, a mere dot off the coastline of Morocco, made the invasion, and the reaction it unleashed, seem absurd. Yet, for neither the Spaniards nor the Moroccans was it so. The Spaniards insisted that Perejil was theirs. The Moroccans, on the other hand, stressed that Leïla had been "liberated" and given over to Morocco when Spain signed over their Protectorate in 1956. Spain, backed by Europe, reiterated its control of this islet and accused the Moroccans of forcefully crossing borderlines. The Moroccans responded that their sole aim in entering the otherwise largely deserted Leïla was to set up an observation post in the fight against illicit migration, smuggling, and terrorism. This, they protested, was in total compliance with repeated European demands for tighter control of the border zones. Morocco was only attempting to carry out its duty to the International Community.

The Moroccan press, however, saw the events in a somewhat different light. Spain, in their view, was desperate to cling onto its foothold in the Maghreb. There were too many bones of contention between Spain and Morocco for Spain not to be anxious about maintaining its grip on the border region: the Moroccan failure to renew a fishing treaty allowing Spanish fishermen access to Moroccan waters, disagreements over the control of immigrant and drug traffickers, oil exploration in the region, and most thorny of all, the issue of the sovereignty of Ceuta and Melilla. Leïla was, as some contended, merely a cover for the larger issue of these enclaves. If Leïla were ceded to the Moroccans, then by extension, the Spanish hold on the two enclaves would weaken. In a historic reversal of colonial appropriation, Spain might then well lose the last vestiges of empire in Africa.

Ceuta

Ceuta remains one of the oldest cities in the region to be associated with the myth of Hercules. It is also a city with a history of diversity that is perhaps not surprising, given its location as a passageway to Europe. Babylonians, Phoenicians, Punics, and others are thought to have inhabited Ceuta. Occupied by the Romans in the first century, it was labeled *Civitas Romanorum*. The Vandals, who swept Spain prior to the Islamic invasion of the peninsula, occupied Ceuta and burnt it to the ground in 429. The Byzantine emperor Genserico took charge of Ceuta some hundred or so years later and in the eighth century, Ceuta acted as a launching pad for the Islamic invasion of the Spanish peninsula. During Islamic rule, Ceuta fell for a while under the control of the court of Córdoba and thus benefited from the superior levels of artistic and scientific endeavor that marked this court. By the fourteenth century, Ceuta had become an active Mediterranean port, regularly receiving sailors and ships from around the Mediterranean. The Christians reconquered Ceuta in 1309, after which it belonged to Spain, itself joined to Portugal for much of the sixteenth and early seventeenth centuries. As gateway to the Atlantic, Ceuta witnessed the passage of numerous ships, carrying slaves and merchandise, on their way to the Americas. When the two Iberian kingdoms separated again in 1640, Ceuta opted to remain as part of Spain, a choice that has endowed the city with an aura of patriotic fervor that is reiterated by the authorities to this day. Heightening Ceuta's affiliation to Spain was the siege laid on the city by Muley Ismael of Morocco, following the unification of the latter in 1672. Ceuta, an extremity of Spain, was at once the "most loyal and faithful" (as proclaimed by the city's motto) of its appendages.

By this very token, Ceuta, guardian of Europe's southernmost border, is charged with historical significance: since Spain's transition to democracy, it has simultaneously asserted Spain's integration into Europe in the wake of four decades of isolated dictatorship and also held symbolic significance for Spanish cultural memory. Most importantly, this affirmation of Spain in North Africa commemorates Spain's expulsion of the Moors in 1492 and the extension beyond the peninsula of a Spanish identity unified under the Catholic Church. Even more significantly, the *Guerra de África,* a war that ideologically united the otherwise deeply divided political factions of nineteenth-century Spain and that resulted in the successful procurement of a Protectorate by Spanish powers on Maghrebian lands, was launched from Ceuta. The first of the battles to be won by the Spaniards took place just outside Ceuta and the war ended with a peace accord being signed by the Sultan of Fez that confirmed Spanish control of hitherto Moroccan territories. Nor was this the only war that Ceuta is known for. In July 1936, the Movimiento Nacional launched the Civil War from Ceuta under the leadership of General Francisco Franco, himself experienced in quelling rebellion in colonized Moroccan territories, and rapidly took it northward across the country. He took with him from the port of Ceuta a sizeable convoy of Moroccan troops, who were to fight the Republicans on behalf of the Nationalists. For this reason, the *Virgen de África,* the Virgin of Ceuta, worshiped in the imposing cathedral on the *Plaza de África* in the center of the city, continued throughout the Francoist dictatorship to occupy a hallowed position amongst the patron saints revered by the Falangists.

As Cajal (2003) rightly stresses, the continued Spanish possession of Ceuta and Melilla is implicitly tied to the British control of Gibraltar. In the numerous exchanges that have taken place since the nineteenth century between the former colonial powers of Spain, Portugal, and Britain over the territories of Spanish-controlled Ceuta and Melilla, British-controlled Gibraltar, and Portuguese-controlled Olivenza (not to mention the small islands or islets of the Straits, such as Leïla), a dynamic has existed whereby their individual histories have persistently fallen into the larger history of colonial division of power and land. Thus, while the official Spanish position has been and continues to be that Ceuta will and should always belong to Spain, there is an awareness that should they gain control of Gibraltar, the Moroccans might well have good reason to claim Ceuta. At play in an intense and obvious manner here is the larger economic and political scenario.

The advertisements for Western Union urge us to send money to a loved one. The dissemination of global love, courtesy of the United States. At the Western Union office, the sole Spaniards are those behind the counter. Everyone else is black or brown. They speak Amazigh, some French, some Arabic, other languages. The Castilian that I hear is broken and incorrect. I see that for a small commission, Western Union throws a lifeline to the dispossessed. A young man collects his money. He has to show his photo documentation first. He counts the notes and leaves quickly. He crosses the road and goes to a kiosk to buy a phone card. He enters a supermarket and buys some beer, a large bag of potato crisps, some shaving cream. How many borders did his money cross? Or is the Western Union what it claims to be, a space without borders?

Meanwhile, a complex dynamic between appearance and reality continues to develop in Ceuta. Thus, in this city of colonial architecture, levels of prosperity rose sharply once the neighboring areas that had fallen under the Spanish Protectorate were signed over to Morocco in 1956. Even then, in the relatively harsh Francoist years, Ceuta could boast of a higher economic level than Morocco. Its role as a port afforded it the advantages of a duty-free zone with the added lure of shopping that this affords. Today, Ceuta is a haven for the purchase of domestic appliances, cosmetics, jewelry, and alcohol. With the neighboring regions now under Moroccan control, the frontiers of Spain beckon Moroccans most intensely at Ceuta. This is exacerbated by an agreement made for apparently historical reasons, whereby the inhabitants of the former Spanish Protectorate can legally enter Ceuta without recourse to the normal visa applications. Furthermore, such Moroccans from the Rif can also work in Ceuta. Thus, the border controls of the Schengen space are subject to a certain exception at this frontier, enabling Moroccans to freely enter and leave Ceuta without residence there.

For this reason, among others, Ceuta acts as a key juncture in the geopolitics of the Mediterranean region. Ceuta goes so far, in fact, as to claim four cultures on its diminutive territories: Christians from the Peninsula, Muslims from Morocco, Jews who settled at the time of the expulsion of Jews and Muslims from Catholic Spain, and Hindus, almost entirely merchants from Sind, who arrived on British ships following the Partition of India and Pakistan and have stayed on ever since. Given these aspects of Ceuta's cultural, political, and geographical identities, the city provides an intensified example of conflicting and interdependent, indeed contiguous, currents of difference. Laws and agreements that apply in a particular way in the mainland of Spain work differently here. This difference, especially the unexpected flexibility of the Schengen rules at this edge of Europe, is not present by accident nor indeed does it necessarily owe itself to reasons of historical alliance. There is a clear-cut economic advantage for Ceuta in maintaining such border flexibility at this point. The smuggling of goods from Ceuta to Morocco is a key source of income for the well-heeled citizens of Ceuta. On a daily basis, tens of thousands of Moroccans cross into Ceuta to do their shopping. They load their vehicles with goods and cross back to Morocco. Such contraband, legal on the Spanish side but illegal on the Moroccan side, is one of two main sources of income for the city. At night by the border, the Moroccans wait in their loaded cars for the change of guard at the gates, a moment generally reckoned to be good for passing through. Indeed, with corruption levels high on the Moroccan side, the guards may well benefit from turning a blind eye to the goings-on. The sea, too, serves as a means of smuggling. At night and in the half-light of dusk, Moroccan men can be seen wading through the water, as large loads are floated over from Ceuta onto neighboring Moroccan waters. A good location for doing this is at the foot of the promontory *Jebel Musa* or *La mujer muerta,* where Ceuta yields to Moroccan land. The Spanish police on guard often watch the proceedings but make no move to halt them.

Legal contraband of this sort is central to Ceuta's prosperity. Equally important in this context is the income derived from the illicit trafficking of goods and people across the Straits. As Juan Goytisolo states in his recent book *España y sus Ejidos* (2003, 141), the laundered money from such deals circulates freely in the city and keeps it buoyant. The wealth is glaringly in evidence to any visitor to Ceuta: this is a city without a Spanish working class, without run-down areas or neglected buildings. This is no typical metropolis; instead, it is a city laden with a multitude of shops and leisure facilities, which imports its workers on a daily basis from neighboring Morocco. The distinctions are clear even to the stranger's eye. Middle class Spanish women can often be seen shopping, their bags carried by Moroccan maids wearing headscarves. Of an evening, the prosperous locals can be seen taking a drive in their luxury cars along the sea front or socializing in their designer wear, smoking cigars in the bars of five star hotels, talking business or the politics of the right. While diversity is clearly present in Ceuta, the most significant difference that is discerned is that between those who apparently "belong" and those who do not. The many Moroccan working as domestics or in restaurants, bars, and building sites are transitory, dismissable, economically unprotected, even if waged. At the foot of *Jebel Musa,* facing the sea on the Spanish side, are large villas with private swimming pools. Pepe, one of my *ceutí* informants, confirmed that living in this exclusive neighborhood are the mafia kings of the Straits, those who reap their profits from the illicit and risk-laden transfer of deadly narcotics and hopeful, if petrified, humans across the Straits and into Spain and the rest of Europe.

Despite these complex connections between the practices that render Ceuta affluent and its supposed "others," and despite the reliance on exchange, the city itself belies relation or contiguity. Throughout the 1980s and 1990s, decades which witnessed a sharp escalation of immigration into Spain, Ceuta barricaded itself by constructing a wall of razor wire. This, however, did not deter those who managed to scale it and thus enter Europe. More recently, and with financial support from the European Union, Ceuta boasts of an electronic wall several meters long, which cost over $22 million to build. There are plans to extend it further now. However, as Goytisolo notes (2003, 138), neither the wall, with its sophisticated video cameras, halogen lights, and sensory system, nor the highway from Morocco that is constantly patrolled both by the Spanish Army and the Civil Guard, nor the barbed wire fencing off Ceuta can deter the entry of migrants into this European threshold. It would appear that the threat that Ceuta perceives to itself is that of the immigrant. In fact, the most vulnerable aspect of Ceuta's economic profile is its reliance on income from illicit trafficking. Furthermore, penetrating the social fabric of the city are the clandestine networks of such trafficking. Such facts, however, did not appear to pose a problem for the late, colorful Jesús Gil, not so long ago President of the Autonomous Region of Ceuta, or for his followers from the GIL (Liberal Independent Group) party. Formerly mayor of wealthy Marbella (resort to the King of Saudi Arabia, amongst others) and President of Madrid's Athletic Football Club,

Gil promised the citizens of Ceuta an even more glorious future. Gil himself had several court cases against him for corruption and was even imprisoned for some months on those grounds. Nor do the facts appear problematic to more recent changes in government, both in Ceuta and in Madrid. Plans are afoot to turn Ceuta into the Hong Kong of the Mediterranean, with a casino, an airport on the sea, and other marvels of capitalism. In other words, the aim of those in power is to turn Ceuta into the very El Dorado of the immigrant dream, whilst also keeping immigrants out. Furthermore, part of this venture to redesign and modernize Ceuta is the promised removal of the stains on this otherwise illustrious city's surface, namely those of narcotics and immigrants. An immediate aim is a city-wide "clean-up" that promises to remove the Moroccan minors, often ragged teenagers, who plague the streets and wander about without returning to their home towns across the border.

This culturally diverse city boasts four Muslims at present in its Legislative Assembly of twenty-five. Many of those who occupy these seats have been members of the Partido Popular and are clearly members of Spain's extreme right wing. Political affiliation, however, makes little difference. Indeed, across the range of political parties existing in democratic Spain, there is a consensus with regard to the issues of Ceuta and Melilla. Patriotism, which by extension implies allegiance to an enclosed and static vision of Spain and her borders, is seen by many to be part and parcel of Ceuta's traditions. As Goytisolo states (2003, 128), even the Spanish Communist Party, once the sole party to raise questions about whether Ceuta rightly belongs to Spain, now adheres to the view that Ceuta's borders must be tightened in order to affirm national and European coherence. Paramount in this stance of fixity are "current contexts and realities." It would be hard to argue that perhaps such contexts have less to do with a national feeling of being "harassed" or "blackmailed" by Morocco and more in fact to do with interests of capital. It goes without saying that the rhetoric of the reinforced border maintains the class distinctions between those who belong and those who do not. Equally, this same rhetoric masks the porosity of the border, whereby the affluence of those who belong is guaranteed by the continued presence of those who do not. Economic and political inequalities serve the interests of the empowered through a dynamic of growing difference.

The Other Ceutís

"Here they take the law into their own hands," Pepe said. "There are no guardias *here, just the* moros *who rule this bit. You wouldn't know you* were in Spain. Here it's an eye for an eye and a tooth for a tooth. We never come here and mess with them. Oh, no ... And it's always been like that, even before the Civil War. It's strange. Franco got rid of the Rojos from Spain, but he couldn't get rid of the moros."

To reach the Calle Real, one has to climb the steep incline going up from the port. Descending once again, but this time on the "other" side, an initially hidden face of the city comes into view. My Ceutí informant, Pepe, felt uneasy here, eager to move on. Away from the city center, we had come upon another dimension to Ceuta that dwells in apparently a different time and space. Here, however, Ceuta is most definitely known as Sebta. Príncipe Ildefonso is a locality somewhat removed from the Calle Real or the port, and resident here are the Muslims of Ceuta. Mint tea, hard to find in central Ceuta, is in plentiful offer here and men sit sipping it by the roadside for long stretches at a time. The posters and advertisements are in Arabic and modern Arabic music floats out from the shops. The shops themselves look as if they belonged in some Moroccan *medina* or *souk*. Five times a day, the call for *salaat* from the local mosque fills the air. There is nothing European about El Príncipe, as it is locally known, save its official denomination. The neighborhood serves as a keen reminder of Spain's colonial past, for at one time, during the Spanish Protectorate, El Príncipe would not have been that different from any of the nearby towns or villages. The Muslims here "belong" in a historical or chronological sense that perhaps does not apply to the Spaniards in authority. What El Príncipe does, more than anything else, is to throw up the bizarre contradiction between Ceuta's political affiliation and its undeniable embodiment on the North African coast. If the Spanishness of Ceuta has long been boasted of by the Spaniards, then there is a certain irony in this ethnic persistence of the Maghreb in the heart of this "Spanish" city. Seen in another light, the borders of Spain and Morocco, Europe and Africa, become indissoluble here, indissoluble but without integration. From yet another perspective, the sharp division of city space marks out the political and cultural antagonisms that mark the cultural memories and the present day practices of both Spain and the Maghreb, even as it marks their complex mutual implications.

The majority of the few Muslims who have seats in the Legislative Assembly are from this part of town. They inevitably belong either to the PDSC or the UDSC, both Ceutí parties set up by this community. The PDSC's founder is Mustafa Mezzian, whose brother is a much wanted trafficker sought by the Moroccan police. The apparent divisions of the city, therefore, might not apply to the circulation of money or power around Ceuta, and the links between communities are clearly strong but hard to fathom. Many believe that Gil in his time had struck deals with the mafia barons. Ironically, as the frontier tightens and grows more formidable, so the underground connections appear to proliferate.

CETI, Not Ceuta

"I have been here for nearly two years now. I have no work, nothing to do, only the meals to break up my day. Sometimes I do not know what day of the week it is."

"I feel as if I were in a shop which is open but which refuses to sell anything."

"The Spanish government says it does not like immigration. But they keep me here. I have been here for one year and four months now. Tell me, you say you study immigration. Why am I here?"

"Is this my punishment for being illegal or is the punishment only going to come? Nobody knows where people go when they leave CETI. Nobody knows what is next."

"I have no passport, no papers. Nothing. The mafia took my passport and threw it in the sea. I have nothing to say who I am."

"You want my story? This is not my story, this is everybody's story. This is HI-story!*" (Shamsul, aged 29, from Bangladesh, Ceuta 2003)*

The barefoot Moroccan children, many of whom can be seen wandering around the port area, are not the only "flaws" on this Mediterranean cityscape. Despite the show of wealth and comfort, a closer scrutiny of the city space reveals the fractures and disjuncture that are present. Public spaces, such as the square near the two main churches, playgrounds with benches, the wall running along the seafront, all host numerous young Africans who spend their days sitting idly in the sun. There is a wealth of human resource on display here, with nothing to do. Sub-Saharan immigration, which started as recently as in the 1990s, is at an all-time high in Ceuta. The enclave, already subject to immigration from the Maghreb, was ill prepared for this new influx. These Africans come from diverse countries, such as Mali (the last, major nexus point in Africa for migratory routes prior to reaching the Maghreb), Nigeria, Senegal, Zaire, Somalia and Liberia. Many of them will have covered tortuous routes in order to gain entry to European soil. Indeed, for sub-Saharan Africans, even entry into Morocco is a landmark event, as the crossing of the Sahara is in itself a life-threatening process. Thus it is that Morocco is a country of immigration as much as it is of emigration. The northward impetus of the sub-Saharan African takes him or her to the shores that face Europe, in an often harrowing journey that might take well over a couple of years or more. As Sirius Samura's documentary *Exodus* (2002) shows, the trek is long and costly, as migrants pass through routes established by networks of traffickers. The migrants stake their lives and savings largely to escape the conflicts and poverty that besiege their places of origin. For similar reasons, the Algerians enter Spain in large numbers. It is harder for immigrants to enter Ceuta now that the electronic fence has been built. Nevertheless, according to Pepe, the immigrants dig underground tunnels from Morocco to Spain or come in by sea. Just as the smuggling of goods to Morocco is often no more than a matter of wading through water, the passage of persons in the opposite direction can also take place undetected. Furthermore, many come in via the port. In the last five years or so, a further ethnic group has come into Ceuta. These are men from Asia, mostly Indians, Pakistanis, and Bangladeshis, as well as Kurds and Iraqis, who arrive by ship. They too will have taken a tortuous and costly route.

Such immigrants, whose own national borders are far removed from Spain, pose specific problems for the Spanish authorities. Unlike Moroccans, they cannot be taken to the border and left on Moroccan soil. Spain does not have repatriation agreements with most Third World countries. Furthermore, to return the increasing numbers of immigrants to their countries would result in severe financial repercussions. The vast majority of those entering Ceuta do not have passports or other documents of identity on them. They arrive as stateless citizens. This is a deliberate ploy on the part of traffickers, as European law forbids the expulsion of undocumented, stateless immigrants. Instead, they must be lodged and provided with legal assistance in order to file their petition for receiving rights to residence. The juridical process is lengthy and convoluted. If, in 1996, only 442 immigrants entered the two enclaves of Ceuta and Melilla, then today approximately three or four immigrants enter Ceuta alone per day. As Pietro Soddu states (2003, 101), the reinforcement of the land border via the expensive electronic fence has done nothing to reduce the numbers entering the city. By logical extension, it would seem that the tighter the border controls, the more reliant immigrants become on traffickers, who are able to find entry points into Europe via Ceuta. Given the reliance of Ceuta's economy on money obtained through trafficking, and given the prevalence of laundered money in the city, a corollary arises with regard to the possible profits to be derived from ever-stricter means of control. Indeed, it is interesting to note that the late Gil's one-time popularity coincided both with the rise in immigration in the 1990s and Ceuta's own escalating affluence in that decade.

CETI (Centro de Estancia Temporal de los Inmigrantes or Center for the Temporary Stay of Immigrants), on a hill away from the city center, provides yet another facet to this city. Built in 1999, following the disastrous and insalubrious accommodation offered to the steadily growing numbers of immigrants in the makeshift Camp Calamacorro, it is located in woodland and is fenced off. Its appearance is that of a borstal, at best drab. A police guard stands on duty and entry to visitors is by permit only. The immigrants are lodged there while their cases are processed; meanwhile, they can move around the city freely, but are not able to take up employment. They are provided with three meals a day and medical assistance. The court cases can take up to two years or more to be heard. Indeed, if delays for appeals are taken into account, then each immigrant could be in this position of limbo for many years. Consequently, the authorities in Ceuta, the office of the *Delegación del Gobierno,* who is responsible for CETI, would have to maintain these growing numbers for very long periods of time. The courts, which are located in the Peninsula, are heavily overburdened and delays are inevitable. Today, CETI too has collapsed. It is full to the brim with a predominantly male population (the Algerians are the only ones who have women and children among them) and over 380 immigrants have to camp out in tents in the nearby woods (Surdigital 27 January 2004). Thus, on the hillside away from CETI is a shantytown of blue plastic sheeting, where numerous Africans live. There are small streams running through the woods. The immigrants sometimes catch fish there and cook them on open fires. Between September and December of 2003, the authorities in Ceuta were obliged to "make room" in CETI by sending large numbers of immigrants into the Peninsula. The emptying out of the center was a desperate bid to contain numbers within the capacities of the place. Neither the center nor the courts can cope with the volume of names and numbers that they have to deal with. Nevertheless, the overflow continues and is on the rise.

Despite this grim reality, the people housed in CETI are already, in one sense, victors. These are people who have undertaken, in almost every instance, deeply risky ventures in order to make their way into the geopolitical heart of capitalism. Peripheral though they may be while in CETI, they are in some sense physically closer here to the fulfillment of that contiguous, half-lit dream of a better life. Some, certainly, might well be repatriated and have their illusions broken, such as the many Moroccans who are sent back. Others may have yet more hurdles to cross or may lose their dream along the way. Nevertheless, for these people, the stakes at play are their lives. In this context, it is important to remember that immigration into Morocco is not solely by those who wish to move on to Europe. There is another, much more tragic immigration into Morocco that takes place on a regular basis: the bodies of those who died at sea while attempting to cross. A regular system of "repatriation" is in place between Spain and Morocco for the return of those whose bodies have been found and identified. The unidentified are buried in mass graves, such as the ones in Málaga or in Tarifa. Even more tragic is the shadow that darkens Ceuta's double horizon and the seascape beneath it: the knowledge that in the waters of the Straits lie the bodies of thousands whose names are not known and whose faces cannot be remembered. For this reason, above all others, CETI must be seen as a place of survivors.

Shamsul's Story

My informant Shamsul is a graduate in Political Science from a university in Bangladesh. Faced with severe unemployment in his native country, he decided to venture forth to Europe. His aim was to come to England, the one part of Europe that had historical connections with his country. The travel "broker" he contacted put him in the hands of an international network of traffickers. His desire to reach England was overridden and, to his surprise, he was taken by ship to Ceuta. He realized that he was in Spain only when the Spanish police detained him at the port and took his fingerprints and other details. He did not know the language and they had to tell him where he was. Furthermore, he had never known that there was a Spanish city such as Ceuta on the tip of Africa. It was some time, he said, before he got to know where exactly on the world map he was. In the sixteen months that he had been at CETI, Shamsul had seen his lawyer a few times. He had received a letter of expulsion but his case was still going on. Meanwhile, Shamsul was free to walk around Ceuta, to sit in its park benches and to pass the time. Borders had formed inside CETI too. It was clear that people helped each other according to nationalities and cultural similarities. Racial and cultural divisions were strong and at times, according to Shamsul, antagonistic. As for local Ceutís, they had become inured to the sight of these "others" who roamed their city space. Only the mobile phone or the calling card allowed them to step outside their immediate setting and make contact across borders. Mobile phones were shared amongst men, those who were better off, courtesy of Western Union and other money transfer organizations, helping those without, such as Shamsul.

In a telephone interview (29 July 2003), Shamsul's lawyer, Enrique Martín-Herrera, explained his case—one among countless others. He said that there were indefinite delays in the hearings and that repatriation was the most likely legal outcome if his place of origin could be confirmed. This required willingness to cooperate between governments. Such agreements had only been forged as yet with Morocco and a few other countries, he said. According to Antonio Asenjo (2004,17), over 20 million euros were spent by Spain in 2003 for the repatriation of immigrants, mainly to African countries. This was over double the allocated budget. The cost of renting aircraft for short and long haul flights is exorbitant. Martín-Herrera could not tell me what the future held for Shamsul. It was clear that he, and the authorities in Ceuta, were coping as best as they could in the face of a legal and political system of that had long lost its equilibrium. As an immigration lawyer, he understood the larger global factors of economic push and pull that compelled people to violate international law. Equally, he himself was bound by the constrictions of the law as it stood.

I have kept in touch with Shamsul and am following the route of his migratory process. In autumn 2003, as part of the move to make space in CETI, he and all the other Bangladeshis in CETI whom I had met were given tickets to diverse parts of the mainland of Spain. Shamsul arrived in Barcelona, with no money and no one he knew. His legal case carries on unresolved, and the authorities in Ceuta sent him off with only his expulsion letter to show for himself. In his trajectory from near Dacca to the Catalan capital, Shamsul has crossed numerous national, juridical, economic, and cultural borders. The sense of enclosure that he experienced in CETI has accompanied him to Catalunya; so also, the uncertainty of where to turn next. In turn, Shamsul's location is nowhere but on the border, both tantalizingly near and removed from the "good life" that he seeks. This borderline position renders him vulnerable, open to flux, unable to determine his own moves.

Conclusion

"Why did I come? I came to make a good life. Is this the good life?"

Shamsul's story does indeed exceed the boundaries of the particular and claim its place in a larger history of our contemporary times. The hopeful dream of a better life propels the migrant and the space that he occupies, uncertain as it may be. Nevertheless such a hope or dream is in itself a manufactured product of capitalism. As such, it is a dream of taking risks and possibly losing the stakes. The space of hope that results from capitalist expansion and globalization is thus scarred by its repeated rejection of what it demarcates as other. Liberal democracy, tied to capitalism, encounters obstacles of its own making that prevent the practice of democracy. As David Harvey states, "the more free-market utopianism converges on the inequalities and unfreedoms of actually existing capitalism, the harder it becomes to change or even maintain its own trajectory" (2000, 185). A market-centered democracy is thus a contradiction in terms. The complications of late capitalism result in otherness being accompanied by inequalities of power, large risks, and deadly pitfalls. Even as global connectivity extends in web-like fashion, the power centers become strengthened and the margins are brought into sharp relief. Furthermore, such borders as are created are now subject to the spatial-temporal contiguities of a global system whereby the border persists in many guises well beyond its physical or geographical delineation. If as Bhabha suggests, the cultural logic of late capitalism is marked by contiguity, then such contiguous zones also embrace inequality. Ceuta today is a case in point. For many who find themselves there, this border city is a space of hope. Nevertheless, and although shaped by the same capitalist drive for self-expansion, the dreams differ, as do the contexts of different social classes and groups. In the half-light of Ceuta's many ambiguities and contradictions—its contiguities—and in the diversity of its border spaces, the other proliferates and struggles for recognition.

The ambiguities and contradictions of the border pose an interrogative that extends deep into the heart of national and European identity. Thus, though the border may vacillate, it does not disappear; on the contrary, it has become the object of a dual dynamic of reinforcement and contestation. Even as the European Union extends the technologically sophisticated electronic wall that blocks Africa from access to Europe at Ceuta, the trajectories of those such as Shamsul into the mainland of Europe from Ceuta trace the border onto the nation. The invention and maintenance of a Europeanized, pluralistic, and democratic Spain has thus been challenged throughout by the accompanying surge of otherness in the guise of the migrant. The collective refiguring of democratic Spanishness, imagined in terms of regional and other differences, flows over the Pyrenees into the free-floating Schengen space; it stops short, however, at the southern borders of Spain and Europe, revealing divisions that are historical, political, and economic. Challenging democracy in Spain, and by extension, in the West, therefore, are the many tributaries of this border that course across the nation, testing the ground beneath such fundamental rights as civic equality and the equal dignity of languages, classes, sexes, races, and religions. The border, as experienced in Ceuta, is confusing and complex. The imagination of Spanish democracy, exemplary in many ways of western liberal democracy at its most accepting and so central to the nation's membership of the First World hegemony, is faced with the limit of the border. Here, at the border, what comes into relief is the chasm that undermines the democratic projects of late capitalism, that between a professed politics of the social and a practiced politics of exclusion.

Notes

1. Many of the points discussed here in relation to Ceuta apply to Melilla. This is another border town on the Moroccan mainland, near Nador, whose economy is also boosted by exchanges with Morocco. While, in this chapter, I shall focus specifically on Ceuta, readers interested in Melilla might wish to view the documentary *Melillenses* (2004), directed by Moisés Salama.
2. My two main informants in Ceuta, Pepe (interviewed 17 to 24 July 2003) and Shamsul (22 July 2003), were both concerned that revealing information about illicit migration might perhaps lead to negative repercussions. Neither of them was entirely sure what use I would put to the information they gave me. For this reason, and in order to protect their identities, I have changed their names in this chapter. I acknowledge their assistance and am greatly indebted to them for their help.
3. Another good example of this is the locality of Lavapiés in Madrid. Home to numerous immigrants, many of them Moroccan, this was also the principal scene of the bomb blasts which shook the Spanish capital on 11 March 2004. In many ways, especially given the relative economic disempowerment of the residents of Lavapiés, their religious and ethnic alterity, and the emphasis on trade and exchange that marks this area (home to Madrid's rastro or flea market), Lavapiés exemplifies the incursions of the border into the urban spaces of the nation. Here, citizens uncomfortably rub shoulders with the displaced, the migrant, the other. In the context of the war on terror, the tragically proven vulnerability of the capital city is undeniably linked to the porosity of the borders of democracy. For those who followed the details of the terror attack of 11 March 2004, such democracy, tied to the global network and free flow of capital and communications, was ironically defied by the workings made possible by a commodity item that is, in many ways, iconic of this late capitalism of our times: the mobile phone.

Bibliography

Anzaldúa, Gloria. 1987. *Borderlands-La Frontera: The New Mestiza*. San Francisco: Aunt Lute Press.

Asenjo, Antonio. 2004. "Aviones privados contra las pateras." *La Clave* (January 9–15), 17–19.

Bhabha, Homi. 2002. "Democracy De-Realized." In Okwui Enwenzor, Carlos Basualdo, Ute Meta Bauer, Susanne Ghez, Sarat Maharaj, Mark Nash, Octavio Zaya, *Democracy Unrealized, Documenta 11_Platform 1*. Ostfildern-Ruit: Hatje Cantz Publishers.

Bourdieu, Pierre and Louis Wacquant. 1992. *An Invitation to Reflexive Sociology.* Chicago: Chicago University Press.
Cajal, Máximo. 2003. *Ceuta, Melilla, Olivenza, Gibraltar: ¿Dónde acaba España?.* Madrid: Siglo Veintiuno.
Clifford James. 1997. *Routes: Travel and Translation in the late Twentieth Century.* Boston: Harvard University Press.
Donnan, Hastings and Thomas Wilson. 1999. *Borders: Frontiers of Identity, Nation and State.* Oxford: Berg.
Driessen, Henk. 1998. "The 'new immigration' and the transformation of the European-African border." In Thomas Wilson and Hastings Donnan, eds, *Border Identities: nation and State at International Frontiers.* Cambridge: Cambridge University Press.
Foucault, Michel. 1986. "Of Other Spaces." *Diacritics* 16(1), 22–27.
Fukuyama, Francis. 1992. *The End of History and the Last Man.* London: Penguin.
Goytisolo, Juan. 2003. *España y sus Ejidos.* Madrid: Hijos de Muley Rubio.
Harvey, David. 1996. *Justice, Nature and the Geography of Difference.* Oxford: Blackwell.
———. 2000. *Spaces of Hope.* Edinburgh: Edinburgh University Press.
Salama, Moisés, dir. 2004. *Melillenses* [film].
Samura, Sirius, dir. 2002. *Exodus* [film].
Soddu, Pietro. 2003. "Ceuta y Melilla: etapas y metas de las nuevas rutas migratorias." In *Nación árabe,* Summer, no. 49, 89–108.
Surdigital (http://servicios.diariosur.es/pg040127).

Chapter 2

Migration, Gender, and Desire in Contemporary Spanish Cinema

H. Rosi Song

It is widely recognized that the notion of Spanish sociocultural uniformity enforced under Francisco Franco (1939–1975), already undercut by the transition to democracy, has faced new challenges in a wave of immigration that has given added urgency to debates concerning national, regional, and cultural identities as well as geographical borders.[1] While successive governments have attempted to negotiate legal and social parameters to this immigration, the media continually report the attempts of *pateras* [rafts]—often tragically unsuccessful—to reach the Canary Islands or the peninsula. There are, nonetheless, major discrepancies between popular perceptions and new patterns of immigration. One concerns the dimensions of the phenomenon. Whereas many Spaniards envision an image of Spain under siege, and vulnerable to foreigners, the report produced by the Secretaría de Estado de Inmigración y Emigración in late 2004 indicates that legal immigrants represent only 4.9 percent of Spain's population of more than 40 million.[2] By the same token, whereas the popular perception has often been that the largest number of immigrants come from Africa, are black, and work on farms or as street vendors—the presence of such immigrants has been met with a barrage of negative stereotypes—reality appears quite different. A study in the mid 1990s, for instance, concluded that 63 percent of legalized immigrants were white, came from other EU countries, and worked in the service sector (Izquierdo 1996, 279).[3] A second, little appreciated, feature of the recent wave of immigration is the markedly increased prominence of women.[4] New scholarship in this area has begun to improve our understanding of social relationships of inequality, including matters of socioeconomic visibility among the immigrant population and issues of gender discrimination for both natives and newcomers. As Carlota Solé and Sònia Parella have shown, since the mid 1980s, migratory flows into Spain have become increasingly female, coming to represent 48.2 percent of all migrants by 1998 (Solé and Parella 2003, 61).[5] Among them, women from Latin America represent the highest percentage; women from the Dominican Republic have been identified as the leading group in female migration to Spain (Gregorio Gil 1998; Izquierdo 1996). This article will focus on depictions of recent female migrants in the context of contemporary Spanish cinema.

The topic of immigration has become an important theme in Spanish filmmaking. *Cartas de Alou* (1990, dir. Montxo Armendáriz) and *Bwana* (1996, dir. Imanol Uribe) examined the problematic experience of African immigrants in Spain, and each received critical acclaim for addressing the difficulties of socio-economically and culturally displaced subjects, as well as the problems of racism and right-wing violence against racial minorities.[6] Peter Evans (1995, 326) echoes critical consensus when he writes that the disappearance of Francisco Franco had the effect of "re-politicizing film language" or, in other words, "to speak the unspeakable, confronting the realities of everyday living, acknowledging the inseparability of art from the frameworks of history and tradition." This turn meant, on the one hand, the production of numerous films dealing overtly with questions of sexuality and other topics considered taboo during the dictatorship. On the other hand, it also produced films dealing more directly with social and political issues that were in the past avoided or allegorized (Evans 1999, 1–4). For Barry Jordan and Rikki Morgan-Tamosunas, for instance, if there is one unifying characteristic of this critical gaze, it would be the preoccupation with questions of identity, not only of the individual, but also of groups and communities. Their study of Spanish cinema focuses on the ways it surfaces through the treatment of gender and sexuality (Jordan and Morgan-Tamosunas, 1998, 10–11).[7] In both *Cartas de Alou* and *Bwana,* the portrayal of foreigners from racially, ethnically, linguistically, and religiously different backgrounds as an encounter with the "other" revealed an understanding of difference that often relied on existing racial and cultural prejudices. As Isabel Santaolalla (1999) correctly argues, the representation of the other can be complicated when it fails to recognize the ways in which the very narrative strategies used to convey this otherness are problematic. Many of the recent Spanish films on immigration tend to focus on characters that are visibly distinct from Spaniards (for example, immigrants or refugees from North Africa, and lately from Asia) and are, therefore, easily presented as the other. Critics like Santaolalla have fruitfully applied postcolonialist perspectives to understand the remnants of past ideologies and colonialist projects that underpinned and shaped these perceptions (Martín-Cabrera 2000; Molina Gavilán and Di Salvo 2003). For many European countries, as Gisela Brinker-Gabler and Sidonie Smith point out (1997, 15), "now that the post-colonial encounter takes place 'at home' in the metropolitan centres," it is important to consider the weight this past exerts in the imagining of national identities. This encounter is not limited to those countries with a formal colonial relationship in the past, as a cursory look into studies on current immigration reveals. The migratory movement from what is generally thought of as the Third World to developed Western countries recalls colonial practice in the way the immigrant is treated and perceived as the other (Kofman 2000). The depiction of female migrants from Latin America in Spanish contemporary cinema, however, reveals a particularly compelling layer to this postcolonial encounter. The familiarity projected by the recently arrived subject becomes a significant element in the representation of her experiences in the metropolis. As natives of Spain's ex-colonies, these women (along with their male counterparts) share a substantial historical, cultural, and linguistic connection, as well as blood relations, with many Spaniards. Compared with the widespread cultural rejection of immigrants from cultural, racial, and religious backgrounds perceived as an "unknown" and as a threat to national homogeneity, issues of difference with Latin American immigrants are consequently more complicated to maneuver. The portrayal of female characters from Latin America in contemporary Spanish films simultaneously blurs and marks difference through a representation sustained by ethnic and racial stereotypes. I will argue in this essay that the use of these stereotypes redraws the boundaries of the cultural and historical legacy of the colonial experience for both Spain and its one-time colonial subjects, while raising questions regarding the understanding of this shared past.

Historically, various forms of nationalism have promoted and depended upon discourses that have invoked different forms of sexuality, and, sometimes, contradictory discourses of gender. Brinker-Gabler and Smith remind us of the different allegories that surround this narrative, from the nationalist fervor sustained by the rhetoric of masculinity under siege to the defeated body of the nation impregnated by the enemy (Brinker-Gabler and Smith 1997, 11–12).[8] This highly sexualized and destiny ridden nationalistic rhetoric is recovered when there are perceived threats to national stability. In this context, what is important to consider are the ways in which "these discourses of nationalism take up and deploy gender ideologies, figures of 'woman,' family likenesses, and sexualized scenarios" and the way they affect immigrant women (Brinker-Gabler and Smith 1997, 15). Thus, the examination of discrimination faced by migrant women not only contributes to the discussion of difference in relation to the boundaries and strategies of nationalist discourse, but also brings into light its negative consequences within contemporary global female migratory movements.

To navigate the discussion between gendered migration and the legacies of the colonial experience as it affects concepts of the Latin American other within Spanish society, I will focus on three recent films that portray the experience of immigration for women from the Dominican Republic and Cuba. The films in question are *Cosas que dejé en La Habana* (1998) [Things I Left in Havana], directed by Manuel Gutiérrez Aragón, *Flores de otro mundo* (1999) [Flowers from Another World], directed by Icíar Bollaín, and finally, Alfonso Albacete and David Menkes's *I Love You Baby* (2001).[9] On the one hand, the Latin American characters of these films complicate the notion of otherness, exposing simultaneously their connection to, and rejection by, Spanish society. On the other, these characters, willingly or unwillingly, through the lens of gender and racial discrimination, bring into the present memories of an uneven relationship between the *madre patria* (motherland) and its ex-colonies. Finally, the love interests that resolve these three films offer a troubling form of assimilationism. The narration that organizes these films, incorporating the new elements into the Spanish social pattern, actively erases marks of "difference" while preserving certain instances of otherness through the use of stereotypes, or what Homi Bhabha (1983, 29) would call a "fetishistic mode of representation" in colonial discourse and its construction of identity.

The currency of stereotypes when representing women immigrants, enhanced by a racialization of the "foreign" female body, is significant when considering existing discourses regarding the role envisioned for female immigrants as cultural intermediaries. This envisioned role, as pointed out by Jacqueline Andall (2003, 3), has played a part in the way some European governments conceived the function of ethnic minority women in their countries as mediators of integration and assimilation of immigrants into their societies. For instance, in France, "crises of national identity and conflicting laws concerning personal status have pushed women to the fore in political debates around issues of the wearing of the headscarf, polygamy and excision. This has been specially charged in a country such as France where women have turned into the 'vectors of integration'" (Kofman 2000, 18). In view of policies formulated from this perspective, it becomes important to study the historical use of concepts such as "culture" in nationalistic projects that have constructed women symbolically as "border guards of ethnic, national and racial difference." It also becomes pertinent to examine how cultural and racial boundaries become spaces of contestation and negotiation, especially when these discussions can be mediated by "assigning" or "defining" certain roles to and for women (Andall 2003, 3). While discussion of issues of female integration and assimilation of immigrants in Spain is in its earlier stages, it should be of interest to consider the topic of immigrant women in the future treatment of the social and cultural dimension of their experience. In the case of Latin American immigrants, the use of women as spaces of contestation for national identity will have to negotiate issues of gender and race, which will have to take into account the baggage of a shared colonial past.

The use of postcolonial perspective in studying Spanish films is, Isabel Santaolalla suggests, useful for "examining not only the poetics but also the politics governing the representation of ethnic minorities in contemporary Spain, whether or not their presence bears any relation to the country's remote colonial history" (Santaolalla 1999, 57). Taking a rather different approach, I would like to argue that the value of this critical perspective comes precisely from taking into account the bearing of the country's colonial history when examining the representation of Latin American immigrants in contemporary Spanish films. Even if Latin America's colonial past is different from that of other modern colonies where postcolonial theory has been central to the analysis of norms and practices of domination (Alva 1995, 245),[10] its colonial experience triggers specific experiences that complicate gender and racial issues. One instance of this specificity has to do the manner in which the articulation of difference and national identity is expressed in the representation of otherness. For Bhabha (1983, 19), for example, the construction of the colonial subject "demands an articulation of forms of difference, racial and sexual," which are important differences because they are inscribed in both "the economy of pleasure and desire and the economy of discourse, domination and power." Despite the historical distance of its colonial experience, the racial and sexual construction of the colonial subject—both biologically and discursively—was part of Spanish colonial history, in which *mestizaje* (or miscegenation) was widely practiced and later regulated. In addition, if we consider the fundamental linguistic and cultural similarities between Spain and Latin American countries, heralded by some modern Spanish politicians and intellectuals under the rhetoric of *hispanidad*—replacing imperial hegemony for a cultural one (Labanyi 2000, 63)[11]—the contestation of cultural and national boundaries is no longer a simple affair. From this perspective, the currency of stereotypes in the representation of Latin American women in contemporary Spanish films examined in this essay reveals the permanence of the prior construction of a colonial subject aided by a gendered discourse.[12]

A quick review of the plots of the three films mentioned earlier reveals the common thread that runs through them. Marisol, one of the main characters of *I Love You Baby,* is a Dominican immigrant living and working as a domestic help in Madrid. Hers is the typical case of the immigrant who has left her native country in search of better opportunities. Her story intersects with the ongoing romance between Daniel and Marcos, a Spaniard who has recently arrived in Madrid from his small village. This relationship is changed one night by a falling disco ball at a karaoke bar. As a consequence of the concussion he receives, Marcos becomes heterosexual and is responsive to the romantic advances of Marisol. Meanwhile, Daniel decides to disguise himself as a woman to seduce again his ex-lover. The situational comedy that ensues from these circumstances evolves into a discussion about sexuality, moral principles, and attainable relationships, ending with Marco's choosing of Marisol as his life partner. The topic of love relationships finds a similar treatment in the box office hit *Cosas que dejé en La Habana.* Three Cuban sisters, who have just arrived in Madrid in search of better economic and professional opportunities, find themselves at the mercy of their aunt María, who wants to save her struggling small business with their help. Part of her plan is an arranged marriage between the oldest sister and the homosexual son of María's business supplier. To keep up appearances, the mother wants to find a wife that might play the role of a traditional good Spanish wife for her son, Javier. However, he expresses his desire to marry the youngest of the sisters who, in turn, has fallen in love with Igor, another Cuban immigrant. When the marriage agreement falls through, the second sister, Ludmila de la Caridad, meets with Javier and is able to bring back the marriage proposal back to the table by turning him away from his homosexuality. Similarly, the forging of romantic ties between female immigrants and Spaniards—amid the harsh realities of the experience of immigration—is also explored by Icíar Bollaín in the critically acclaimed *Flores de otro mundo.* Based on the "Caravana de mujeres" (Caravan of Women) or "Caravana del amor" (Love Caravan), organized by single men from isolated Spanish farming villages who charter buses to invite single women to meet them, the film follows the story of a Dominican woman (Patricia) who marries a Spanish farmer (Damián) after one of these visits. Her story is narrated alongside that of a young Cuban woman, Milady, who has been chosen by one of the villagers, Carmelo, who rejects modernized Spanish women and seeks in the island his ideal sexual and life partner. The story of both women contrasts that of Marirrosi, a divorcée from Bilbao, who has also come with the caravan and starts a relationship with another resident, Alfonso. Despite the latter's failure in her relationship, her easy acceptance by the villagers highlights the struggles of both Patricia and Milady, who must fight to find their place as outsiders to both the village and the country.

The narratives that sustain these relationships are problematic in their propositions. First, the apparent ease with which the female characters (especially Marisol in *I Love You Baby* and Ludmila in *Cosas que dejé en La Habana*) are socially accepted and integrated into Spanish society contradicts the reality of the female immigrant experience. In most of the cases, immigrant women come from "Third World" locations that in terms of both geography and ethnoculture are already disadvantaged. This situation makes them vulnerable and their work is generally characterized by marginalization and invisibility in regard to labor hierarchy and social organization. Their marginalization perpetuates an uneven and gendered distribution of labor that increases the invisibility of migrant women, who are limited to jobs such as domestic service, cleaning services, and caring for the sick (Solé and Parella 2003, 63–65). Even if their disadvantaged situation is portrayed in the films through the hardships of the female characters, the relative facility with which these women are allowed to change their precarious social and financial position through romantic relationships undermines the hard reality of their situation. Second, a stereotypical discourse permeates the characterization of these female immigrants in the films, in terms of ethnically gendered and racialized difference. Finally, the conventional heterosexual narrative advanced in these films counteracts the reality of sexual liberation undergone in democratic Spain. The exploration of sex and sexual identity, which played a major role in the early films after the end of the dictatorship, and for which Spanish film was widely praised, gives way in these films to a narrative in which sexual desire, even if it overrides boundaries of both gender and orientation, ends up reinstating and sanctioning heterosexual social organization.[13]

In all three films, the leading female characters who find heterosexual love, stability, and eventual social acceptance in the arms of Spaniards are portrayed with specific physical and moral virtues. While these merits, easily identifiable, will not help them achieve success either financially or professionally in their new country, they will help them attain quick social acceptance and stability through personal relationships. In Gutiérrez Aragón's film, for instance, the aunt of the Cuban sisters describes her eldest niece Rosa as being nice, responsible, obedient, and self-sacrificing. These traits are desirable to the aunt's business provider, who wants to arrange a marriage for her homosexual son, Javier, to keep up appearances. This ideal recovers a traditional view of women in Spain and their role as spouses and mothers—recalling the traits promoted by National Catholic ideology under Franco's dictatorship—for which the newcomer seems better suited than the modernized (and liberated) Spanish woman (Morcillo Gómez 1999, 51–52). Even when Rosa is turned down by Javier, she is quickly replaced by her sister Ludmila, who, in addition to the same virtues that her older sister possesses, is young, physically attractive, and sexy. Her womanly qualities are so strong that she is even able convert Javier from his homosexuality during a brief but sexually charged encounter. This sexual conversion also appears in the movie *I Love You Baby*, where the male protagonist, Marcos, who first seems to responds to Marisol's advances only as a consequence of his accident with a falling karaoke disco ball, chooses her at the end as his partner over his lover Daniel, because of her virtues. Besides her physical charms, Marisol is a hardworking woman, with strong family values and dedication to her man, and she is also more culturally compatible with Marcos (like him, she loves football while Daniel prefers modern dance). These supposedly positive traits, both moral and physical, also appear in Bollaín's film. One of the main characters, Patricia, struggles to be accepted. While her physical attributes help her to quickly establish a relationship with her husband, she is ultimately only successful in her new life for the effort and sacrifice she makes to provide for her kids and her family. Despite her initial rejection, Damián's mother learns to appreciate her daughter-in-law for the love she demonstrates for her children, her selflessness, and hard work. And at the end, it is the mother who will encourage her son to keep his new family together.

The stereotypes through which the virtues of these female immigrants are portrayed in these films offer an opportunity, moving beyond the mere identification of positive or negative representation of these characters, to analyze the way the subject of the immigrant is constructed. As Homi Bhabha (1983, 18) has proposed, the study of stereotypes should focus on the "processes of subjectification that is made possible (and plausible)" by them: in other words, how the articulation of difference through stereotypes reflects the way the subject is perceived, varying depending on the power position he/she occupies. From this perspective, Barbara Creed points out how postcolonialist theory in film shifts from the study of "flawed" or "negative" images to understand "the filmic construction of the relationship between colonizer and colonized, the flow of power between the two, the part played by gender differences and the positioning of the spectator in relation to such representations" (Creed 2000, 85–86). Rey Chow explains that this "positioning" is favored in films because film narratives offer identity construction and influence the formation of subjectivity through their narration and technique (i.e., montage, panoramic shots, close-ups, etc.). The processes of introjection, projection or rejection that happens between the images and the narration of the film intersects with the "audiences' sense of self, place, history and pleasure" that reveals how "the fantasies, memories, and other unconscious experiences, as well as the gender roles imposed by the dominant culture at large, play important roles in mediating the impact of the spectacle" (Chow 2000, 168). Put differently, this intersection between the film's narrative and its reception by the audience hints at the ways in which one is rejected or resonates within the other, in the process of constructing or affirming existing identities.

The role of spectacle (or the nature of the screen/spectator relationship) in the process of identification and the formation of a subject, analyzed through psychoanalytical approaches and its emphasis on desire, is revisited by Homi Bhabha in order to reflect on colonial discourse and its ideological construction of otherness. He is interested in the ambivalence of stereotypes since it is what gives it currency, ensuring its continuity amid historical and discursive changes, informing its "strategies of individuation and marginalisation," producing the "effect of probabilistic truth and predictability which, for the stereotype, must always be in *excess* of what can be empirically proved or logically construed" (Chow 2000, 168). Bhabha (1983, 27) expands on this idea to establish a functional relationship between stereotypical discourse and fetishism, in which both rely on the contradictory play between the recognition of absence/presence that simultaneously recognizes difference while it disavows it. This play is constantly put into practice because it reactivates a primal fantasy, which in the case of colonial discourse, always returns to an "ideal ego that is white and whole." For this critic, this ideal that often refers to notions of origin as well as national unity or identity, depends on the visual and auditory imaginary as they work as sites of subjectification (through identification) where histories of societies are created and preserved. From this perspective, films as well as other cultural practices that rely on a scopic drive—they are there to see and to be seen—are important in sustaining structures of power. In the case of colonial discourse, they work on a double identification where the stereotype, "as a form of multiple and contradictory belief, gives knowledge of difference and simultaneously disavows or masks it" (Bhabha 1983, 29).

Homi Bhabha's reading of the purpose of stereotypical discourse and its efficiency in a visual medium reveals how the construction of the female characters in these three Spanish films can affect native audiences and the way they see the newcomers and themselves. What becomes clear is that the women immigrants appearing in these films are fragmented in different ways, which on the one hand create positive and thus acceptable identities, but on the other, expose them as outsiders and keep them marginalized from the local community. From this perspective, while it is obvious through the narrative of the films that what allows acceptance of these immigrant women is the similarity they share with other Spaniards, they are simultaneously portrayed through their differences. The visualization that keeps these women marginalized at the same time places the real success of their assimilation in question. The gaze that allows recognition of difference keeps them visualized through their particularities, despite the narrative effort to individualize their stories. In other words, despite the success of the female characters in assimilating to their new culture, they are always introduced in the film in scenarios and spaces explicitly differentiated by clichés associated with their place of origin.

From the very beginning of *I Love You Baby,* Marisol appears in marginalized social settings clearly intended for and attended by immigrants, whose presence always seems to trigger a salsa rhythm somewhere in the film soundtrack. In these places, like the beauty parlor or the small bar that she frequents, Marisol's friends appear as loud, physically large, colorfully or skimpily dressed, highlighting their foreignness with their accent, speech, and their interaction with each other. This visual marginalization also happens in the opening shots of *Flores de otro mundo,* which show Patricia and her friends laughing and speaking loudly while riding in the back of the bus to the village. Their behavior is looked upon suspiciously by the rest of the Spanish women who ride in the front of the bus and, one of them, at one point, comments with a hand gesture how the country is full of "them." These scenes effectively project the visual difference that exists between immigrants and natives—the camera lumps them all together, visualizing difference, ignoring the diversity that exists within the first group. That is, the easily recognizable and seemingly harmless stereotypes that are used in the films, such as the salsa rhythm, specific social settings or cultural behavior, reduces the immigrants to a collective without any distinctions, asserting quickly identifiable characterizations that also work to emphasize their foreignness in opposition to the native community and its own identity. When the three sisters in *Cosas que dejé en La Habana* are taken to a salsa dancing club on their first night out in their new country, their presence in the club does not serve as a space of meaningful interaction with the natives. Instead, the sisters, along with other immigrants, are showcased in the club to accentuate their palatable and colorful presence within Spanish society. Indeed, the Spaniards who patronize this social establishment engage willingly in a voyeuristic experience, with displayed exoticism as just another object of consumption. While the flaunting of visual and aural difference in these films work to make it more easily digestible or to distinguish one group from another, it is also symptomatic of uneven power relationships. Understanding or being conscious and accepting of diversity is one thing, but it is another when this difference is perceived to threaten existing social hierarchies. It is telling how, during the failed marriage agreement, even if Rosa is welcomed for her traditional Spanish womanly qualities—being responsible, docile, self-sacrificing—Javier's mother is quick to pull a prenuptial agreement that reminds both her and the viewer the precarious reality of her situation. As Bhabha (1983, 33–34) points out, the use of stereotypes is not just creating false images that can be exploited to justify discrimination. It serves as an "ambivalent text of projection and introjection, metaphoric and metonymic strategies, displacement, overdetermination, guilt, aggresivity; the masking and splitting of "official" and phantasmatic knowledges to construct the positionalities and oppositionalities" that reveal the workings of a discourse based on discrimination.

In addition to the focus of these films on ethnic gender stereotypes when portraying Latin American immigrants, there is also a clear emphasis on the visualization of racial difference in the shots that capture both immigrants and natives. Curiously, the question of racial difference in Latin American immigrants is only once explicitly addressed by one of the female protagonists. But as stereotypes are sustained by racial discourse, the subject cannot be ignored, especially when, as Sheelagh Ellwood documents, many Latin American immigrants are victims of racially motivated hate crimes, as are the immigrants from North Africa (Ellwood 1995, 154–155). In Bollaín's movie, it is difficult not to perceive the difference between Milady and Patricia, and between them both and the rest of the village, in racial terms. Even if the priorities between both women are clearly distinguished—Patricia is ready for financial and emotional stability for herself and her children and is willing to work hard while Milady wants to explore the world—the sexualized portrayal of the Cuban woman through her blackness dominates any narrative that surrounds her character. If Patricia is given the chance to demonstrate to her mother-in-law, her new husband, and the villagers that she has the right values and the right mindset to make her life successful in Spanish society, Milady is only further alienated by the way the film exploits her distinctiveness through the sexual and racial stereotypes applied to Caribbean women.

In her influential essay about cinematic gaze, Laura Mulvey (1990, 33–35) has argued that its construction of the viewer reflects the predominant social structures of gender and sexual desire. Her discussion of women in film as a passive and manipulated object of the voyeuristic gaze of the camera that adopts a "masculine" position drew much controversy about the agency of female spectators (Creed 2000, 81–82). The predominance of a male gaze is clearly present in *Flores de otro mundo,* where the portrayal of Milady focuses heavily on her sexuality, both in terms of her gender and race, overshadowing any attempt to understand her situation: the reason she left the island, her loneliness, or her desire. Her display as a sexual trophy, through close-ups and long shots that follow the gaze of the village men that never stops sexualizing her, hides the story of Milady's adversities. What drives her representation is her sexuality through a masculine gaze that vacillates between fear and fascination, with comments about her untamed sexuality (Martín-Cabrera 2000, 50–51; Camí-Vela 2000a, 180–183). The persistence of this male gaze in the film, despite the fact that it is directed by a woman, seems to attest to one of Mulvey's more widely debated observations, where she identifies female desire as adopting a "masculine position" as result of internalizing predominant sociocultural structures. Icíar Bollaín has expressed her pride that the film was made without exploiting any female body part; there is no explicit nudity in the film (Camí-Vela 2000b, 238–239). The male gaze that guides the director's camera work is explained in her own mind by her desire to document the natural reaction of the villagers where the movie was shot. She believes that the way the male characters talk and view Milady is authentic, and therefore good. The director even talks about "authenticity" in the context of the fact that the casting of the actress who plays Milady (Marilyn Torres) was done in Cuba to make the movie more "real." Unfortunately, the director never questions the old men's racialized sexual bias that their gaze and dialogue reveal. The male gaze that objectifies Milady, and which the director reproduces as a way to offer an authentic view, ultimately serves only to enforce racial and sexual prejudice. The lack of awareness from the director's part is indicative of the complexity of reading difference for Spaniards when it comes to Latin Americans.[14] It is interesting that the characters in her film, as racial minorities, appear to be more conscious of the role played by racial difference in the experience of immigration to Spain. When Milady talks about her original plans—first coming to see the village and then deciding whether or not to stay and marry Carmelo—Patricia reveals the reality of their situation: "That works if you're white and the police don't stop you in the street." While it is true that Milady takes advantage of the village men and manipulates them into offering her what she desires, the fact that she cannot be seen as anything but a sexual object undermines any effort on her part to adjust or improve her social standing in the village. Her departure from Santa Eulalia does not guarantee a better outcome and in fact, her future remains pessimistically uncertain at the end of the film. Ultimately, Bollaín's film still assumes a particular view of gender and racial qualities that serves the ideal of the predominant culture, whereby once immigrant women display certain acceptable virtues, they are easily integrated to maintain existing social and gender hierarchies.

The proposition advanced in the plot line of all three films is that for their female immigrant characters, their opportunity for success comes through their personal relationships, as long as they possess certain attributes that identifies them as ideal cohorts in a heterosexual partnership within the dominant society. The implication of this success is, of course, that these characters will be kept within the sphere of domesticity. Interestingly, the issue of gendered social space that arises from this narrative contrasts with the development seen in women's social roles after the end of the dictatorship. The changes experienced by women in post-Franco Spain have transformed their socioeconomic status and have deeply impacted their traditional ideal of female social passivity (Brooksbank Jones 1995, 387). The increased cultural presence and profile of Spanish women is well reflected in the country's contemporary cinema, where they are represented as complex, multidimensional, and thinking subjects. But as Jordan and Morgan-Tamosunas point out, their visibility hinges on class, professional category, and financial dependence, ignoring the complexity of social reality (Jordan and Morgan-Tamosunas 1998, 127–128). Patriarchal values and traditional expectations about the role of women in society still persist in lower social classes, and according to Solé and Parella (2003, 69), the situation of employment of migrant women in domestic services reveals the prejudice whereby immigrant women are seen as being capable of performing only "female" tasks. Stereotypes and prejudices intrinsic to the dominant belief system see these women as "traditional" and "underdeveloped" (in contrast to modern and emancipated European women). They "reinforce to an even greater degree the discrimination ... turning them into ideal candidates for carrying out tasks related to social reproduction, due to their 'docile' nature, their 'patience' and their submissiveness."[15]

The love interests that organize all three films also allude to a changed relationship between Spanish men and Spanish women and to the breakdown of a traditional, and desirable, social organization. The three Spanish women that appear in the films—Daniel's best friend Carmen, María's friend Azucena, and Alfonso's girlfriend Marirrosi—are middle-aged women who have failed in their love life and are longing for a cure to their loneliness. When Carmen talks about her romantic misfortunes, she implies that her sexual freedom has prevented her from committing to long-term relationships and has led her down the path of a sterile existence. Her last resort for companionship is adoption, for which she travels to Russia and brings back two orphan brothers. For her part, Azucena is quick to let Igor, a Cuban immigrant, into her bed and her life, clinging to an idealized relationship with a passionate Latin lover, one who satisfies her imagination by providing her with forged pictures of himself with Fidel Castro and other stereotyped images of the island's revolution. In the case of Marirrosi, even if she is able to briefly find romance with Alfonso, she is unwilling to give up her job and her lifestyle to go join her boyfriend in his village. Even if his refusal to move to the city with her can be seen as egotistic, it is arguably Marirrosi who is portrayed as selfish. After all, Alfonso left the city and has found his vocation living in the village, happily working for its improvement and missing one thing only: a romantic relationship. She, on the other hand, hates her job and her single life in Bilbao, but cannot let go of her urban way of life. In contrast to all these women, the loving and family oriented immigrant characters seem to better fulfill the ideal for a life or love companion. This contrast of values presented in the films, given the successful relationship between immigrant women and Spanish men, suggests an aspiration to social harmony and the preservation of traditional values. It could also be read as indicative of a trend observed by critics of Spanish cinema like Marsha Kinder (1997, 23), who has noted that after the end of the socialist government in the 1990s, the new films speak to a "growing disillusionment with the libertarian ethos and an attempt to recuperate conservative traditions."[16]

The return to conventionality is also seen in the treatment of homosexuality in the films *Cosas que dejé en La Habana* and *I Love You Baby,* where their male protagonists are ultimately denied any sexual identity that is not heterosexual. The apparent fluid treatment of sexuality in these films, reminiscent of the early post-Franco *movida,* serves to return desire within the traditional and predominant heterosexual structure: Marcos's sexual orientation is nothing but the consequence of his ambivalence induced by the novelty of the big city, and Javier's homosexuality is the result of a childhood trauma, after having seen his mother naked. The way in which homosexuality is presented in both films, either as a lifestyle choice or a mental sickness, becomes even more problematic when we consider how these two Spaniards are "sexually converted." They are changed when two Caribbean women, both with overflowing exotic sensuality and the right family values, are able to turn them from being two emasculated male characters—shy, effeminate, weak, quiet—into "real" men reinserting them into the traditional heterosexual social hierarchy. The sexual explosion that followed the end of the dictatorship and which had brought new visibility and an important political moment for homosexuals seems to be challenged in these films. The sexual freedom of post-Francoism is alluded to in the movie *I Love You Baby* when Daniel, on his first date with Marcos, wants to kiss him in a park in broad daylight. Marcos reacts with surprise and asks "Right now? In public?" to which Daniel responds: "This is Madrid." But this freedom does not carry much meaning in the film, as Marco's happiness does not depend on having the chance to explore his sexuality but rather, as his uncle keeps urging him, in finding the right woman. This conservatism is less surprising than it might seem, taking into consideration that, politically speaking, the freedom enjoyed by Marcos and Daniel to display their affection publicly did not amount to any significant advance in Spanish homosexual rights for a long period after the end of the dictatorship (Garlinger 2003, 83–88).[17] In legal terms, the Ley de Peligrosidad Social y Rehabilitación (Law against Social Danger and Rehabilitation) was not repealed until 1979, four years after the death of Franco. Even after that, its prohibition was exerted through the "figura de escándalo público" (public scandal), an ambiguous legal category used to police Spanish homosexuals.[18] The conservative backlash in the 1990s observed by Kinder seems appropriate to explain the return in these films of the predominance of heterosexual social order and the longstanding discrimination against homosexuality normalized under Francoism. While the recent return of the socialists to the government has meant that concrete progress has been achieved in terms of legislation to promote equal rights for homosexuals,[19] the existence of biased heterosexual perceptions like those narrated in the three films raises questions regarding the existing social tolerance toward different sexual identities.

In none of the three films, once the love interests are identified and engaged, is there any reference to the possibility of conflict between the female and male characters in terms of cultural or class differences. (The tribulation faced by Patricia and Damián because of the woman's lies to cover her past, for instance, never challenge the cultural or social compatibility between them). Gutiérrez Aragón, speaking about his film *Cosas que dejé en La Habana* and its commercial success, has reasoned that Spanish filmmakers, despite the increasing number of immigrants in Spain, do not make more movies about them because many of the immigrants, including those from Cuba, are not perceived as foreigners.[20] In this line of thinking, many Spaniards have blood relations with the people from the island and everybody feels like a big family. This assumed kinship seems to be the basic principle shaping the view that even when the portrayal of immigrants is anchored in their differences, the eventual integration into the host society by characters such as Marisol and Ludmila will not be a struggle. Or as in the case of Patricia, any obstacle can be overcome by determination and hard work. The success of this assimilation is, in fact, reaffirmed in the last scenes shown in all the movies: the wedding between Ludmila and Javier with the blessing of their families; Marisol and Marcos after five years of marriage with three kids and a fourth one on its way, a successful family restaurant, and yearly visits to relatives in the Dominican Republic; the picture of Patricia's new family at her daughter's first communion.

In light of Homi Bhabha's articulation of the ambivalence of stereotypical discourse and the way it speaks to existing colonial power relations, these films acquire more complexity. Bhabha refers to the effectiveness of the use of stereotypes within colonial discourse through visual and aural contexts, constantly enacting a primal fantasy, an idea of origin that may be linked to national identities in order to preserve structures of power. By extension, one could argue that the currency of stereotypes can be explained in relation to their allusion to ideals of a hegemonic past that still weighs heavily in the perception of an idealized national identity. The permanence of power relations related to colonial domination, despite its historical distance, can nevertheless be traced in a romanticized view of a past national hegemony. The relationship between Spain and its former colonies continued for many centuries to reveal the workings of a deeply embedded relationship of subordination. Those responsible for the process of nation building in the New World never ceased to look to the West (and to Spain) to replicate social establishments and cultural values in the belief that this model would bring progress in the newly created nations (Lander 2003, 13).[21] This conviction intersected with the racial policy of the new governments, which saw in the arrival of white immigrants from Europe a desirable social composition. As Jo Labanyi (2000, 57) writes: "Micegenation was thus regarded as 'normal' or even, with the influence of Darwinist theory in the post-independence period, as a way of 'improving the stock.'" The continuance of the rhetoric of the *hispanidad* today, an ideological bridge between Spanish-speaking countries, continues in similar fashion to locate Spain at the cultural forefront.[22] When considering the presence of Latin Americans in Spain, then, it seems essential to examine how the discrimination between the immigrant population and the natives—in terms of labor, socioeconomic, and cultural relations—becomes reminiscent of past colonial relationships of subordination. The visually identified positive traits that make Latin American immigrants appear less foreign than other newcomers—in terms of language, culture, religious beliefs, etc.—recover a colonial gaze that remains a relationship based on either assimilation or discrimination. This dual idea of familiarity and estrangement is clear in the very opening of the film *Cosas que dejé en La Habana*. Bárbaro, who arrives in Spain with his family to pick up the false passports that will allow him to enter the US, when confronted with the possibility of having been swindled, starts arguing with his wife, who asks him: "And now? What are you going to do with your daughter in a foreign country?" To which he snaps back: "Shut the fuck up. This is not a foreign country. This is the motherland (*madre patria*)." To this statement, his friend Igor responds with an expletive while he takes Bárbaro and his family out of the airport as soon as he sees the guards patrolling the airport asking for documentation. From this scene, the viewer realizes that the familiar motherland has become for them nothing more than, as Igor says, "the *puta madre* who gave birth to us." The hardships experienced by Igor and his friends in the film are testament to this changed relationship.

In these films, then, the narrative surrounding cultural affinity proposes a seamless integration into Spanish society and the eventual erasure of any marks of ethnic diversity, while at the same time hinging its representation on the visual difference between the newcomers and the local inhabitants. For instance, in *Cosas que dejé en La Habana,* the aunt, María, has lost her Cuban accent, changed her eating habits, and modified her manners to conform to the etiquette of her new country. But this transformation is problematic in the way it undermines her nieces, who are constantly being reminded about their bad manners. The message about the unruliness and disorder from the island is repeatedly compared to the operative ethics of a "civilized" society. When the aunt is seen hungrily devouring a Cuban dish made by one of her nieces in the middle of the night, her need to hide her craving speaks to the pressure of assimilation, apparently indicating that successful integration can occur only at the expense of turning away from one's own tradition. Equally, the happy family portraits and situations that end each film project a sense of unity deriving from having overcome issues of difference. However, what this resolution communicates is that this understanding emerges, not only because of the realization from both immigrant and native groups that they share many similarities, but also as a result of the women's recognition that they will not change, but only reinforce, existing social and cultural hierarchies. The rhetoric of acceptance for female immigrants happens only within the frame of socially acceptable arrangements. In the case of Nena, the youngest sister of *Cosas que dejé en La Habana* for example, the desire to pursue an acting career complicates her life and highlights her difficulties as an immigrant in Spain. At the end, she is unable to overcome bureaucracy with her talent only and has to work under a fake identity using falsified documentation. What the visualization of all the immigrant women in these films guarantees is that, despite their differences, they will help preserve the predominant social organization and its traditional ideals. From this perspective, these films do not explore the complexity of immigration but rather simplify its experience, projecting an idealized reality that never acknowledges the possibility of diversity, only its assimilation.

In the last scene of *I Love You Baby,* Marcos and a very pregnant Marisol, accompanied by their three children, bump into Daniel in the airport. As they exchange greetings, the spectator finds out that the latter has become a big movie star. As the camera zooms in, the tension between the characters becomes noticeable. Marisol is not very comfortable facing Daniel, who seems not to have totally forgotten his ex-lover. Marcos, for his part, looks at him with affection, and the viewer cannot but wonder about his heterosexual conversion. When Daniel's travel (and presumably sentimental) companion shows up—Boy George, the English pop star who, early in the film, Daniel and Marcos had made the witness of their relationship and the "saint" of all things gay—the viewer understands how different Marcos and Daniel's lives are and will be. Marcos will remain with his family, his children and his wife. He will stay in Madrid and live a traditional life. Daniel, who has embraced his homosexuality, ends up leaving Spain and now resides in London. His career and sexual orientation suggest he is no longer compatible with Spanish culture. After all, everybody surrounding Daniel has chosen a more traditional path: Marcos married Marisol, and Carmen, his best friend, adopted two kids and has now embraced her role as a mother. Daniel no longer seems to fit in this social organization, and by extension, in Madrid. The social organization portrayed in *I Love You Baby*—and repeated in the other two films—returns to a basic conception of heterosexual relationships anchoring the plot line. The reality of female immigration finds a narration that erases hardship while advancing a traditional narrative of romantic solutions. This narrative raises several important questions regarding the interaction between Spaniards and Latin Americans, recreating the unevenness of past interactions while projecting a social and national imaginary that becomes problematically assimilistic. This social organization evoked in the films seems to return Spain to its previous, coherent, and unified national identity. It is significant that Spain's own cultural and linguistic difference is never addressed, visually or verbally, conveying an idea of homogeneity whereby the only differences are those that can be visibly exposed in foreigners. As the number of immigrants grows and the fight for regional autonomy intensifies, it will be interesting to follow the ways in which certain differences will be preserved in Spain, while others will be pushed toward assimilation, and the way these negotiations will shape the future of Spain's national identity.

Notes

1. Upon joining the European Union and signing the Schengen agreement in 1991, Spain effectively became part of "fortress Europe" and took on the role of protecting its southern borders.
2. 1,977,291 legal immigrants, out of a population of more than 40 million (*extranjeros con tarjeta*).
3. The visibility of immigrants from Africa in media outlets and the existing rhetoric about immigration have resulted, observes Izquierdo, in the racialization of the immigrant population (1996, 281). African immigration, despite having increased in the past decade, is still smaller that those of European countries or Latin America.
4. The increase in female migration is a global phenomenon. An overview of studies in this area, and a useful bibliography, can be found in Kofman (2000). Recent attention to gender-related issues in migration has added new categories to its study, including labor (both legal and undocumented), family reunion and formation, marriage, prostitution, asylum seeker and refugees (Kofman 2000, 17).
5. Their data comes from the 1999 OPI (Observatorio permanente de la inmigración) report.
6. *Cartas de Alou* was nominated for eight Goya Awards (the Spanish national film award) and won two for Best Screenplay and Best Cinematography in 1991. It also won prizes at the San Sebastián International Film Festival and the Spanish Cinema Writers Circle Awards. Uribe's film was nominated for three Goyas in 1997 and won prizes at the San Sebastián International Film Festival and the Miami Hispanic Film Festival in 1996. Other films addressing ethnic issues in the Spanish context include *Lejos de África* (1996, dir. Cecilia M. Bartolomé); *Taxi* (1996, dir. Carlos Saura); *La sal de la vida* (1996, dir. Eugenio Martín); *En la puta calle* (1997, dir. Enrique Gabriel); *La fuente amarilla* (1998, dir. Miguel Santesmases); *Saïd* (1999, dir. Llorenç Soler); *En construcción* (2001, dir. José Luis Guerín); and *Salvajes* (2001, dir. Carlos Molinero).
7. The centrality of identity, as well as the treatment of the past, gender, and sexuality in post-Franco Spanish cinema, is also observed in the works of Marsha Kinder, Kathleen Vernon, and Paul Julian Smith, among others.
8. The allegories of the nation as a female that needs protection abound: "The land is there to be penetrated, explored and mapped, subdued, and then domesticated in service to nation ... Once the nation is founded and the land domesticated, the nation becomes 'motherland'" (Brinker-Gabler and Smith 1997, 12). The relationship between nationalism and issues of gender and sexuality is also explored in Parker (1992).
9. *Cosas que dejé en La Habana* was nominated for a Goya Award and won at the Valladolid International Film Award. Bollaín's film achieved greater critical recognition, including wins at the Cannes Film Festival and the Bordeaux International Festival of Women Cinema. *I Love You Baby* has had only one nomination (from the Torino International Gay and Lesbian Film Festival), but has a wider distribution.
10. I refer to this controversial essay because it takes as its starting point similarities between the colonizer and the colonized in terms of fundamental tenets of sociopolitical organization.

Migration, Gender, and Desire in Contemporary Spanish Cinema   61

11. Labanyi documents how the Franco regime encouraged the export of Spanish films to Spanish America as way to emphasize the country's cultural hegemony. The philosophical underpinning of this concept is laid out in Maeztu (1935).
12. The complexity of this relationship, however, seems to go undetected in contemporary Spanish discourse. Isabel Santaolalla (2002, 65) notes, for example, that in Spain, the growing number of immigrants from the Caribbean has resulted in the exoticization of black Latin Americans in media outlets as dark-skinned, voluptuous females. But while the conversion of Latin Americans into "exotic" material is part of the increasing international visibility of Latino culture, the "almost total indifference to the rules of political correctness in Spain … means that the stereotypical connection between the exotic, racialised body and the erotic … circulates practically unexamined and uncriticised."
13. Paul Julian Smith (2000, 3) writes that the fluid treatment of sexuality in post-Franco Spanish film, with its critique of identity and essence in terms of sexuality, as it appears in Almodóvar's films, would later become part of academic feminist, minority, and queer theory debates.
14. Given the reality of racism in Spain, the lack of awareness of racial discrimination faced by Latin American immigrants is surprising. An example of this apparent oversight is Bollaín's reaction to the comment made by Marilyn Torres, who plays the role of Milady. Torres made the comment that the actress realized she was black in Spain because the way people stared at her. The filmmaker quickly conflates her experience with the situation of being an attractive woman and people's perception of difference without ever considering the particularities of Torres's experience as a black woman from Latin America in Spain (Carmí-Vela 2000, 240).
15. One important aspect of this division of labor is that the social shift, which moved Spanish women to work outside of their homes, did not change the dynamics of housework (i.e., men in the house taking more responsibility for house chores, etc.). What it created was a perceived need for domestic help; in this case, from immigrant women who came to fulfil and replace the traditional role played by native women.
16. Or, as she writes, "it also makes us reconsider the moral price Spain paid for replacing matadors and militants with hookers and dopers as the nation's privileged cultural icons" (Kinder 1997, 20).
17. Garlinger explains that "the lack of a strong political movement for gay liberation in Spain is often interpreted in a positive light as a self-conscious refusal of identity politics by Spanish gays and lesbians" (2003, 85). Critics even praised this rejection and thought that the sexual fluidity implied in this dismissal would mean an advance in homosexual identity politics. But as he quickly clarifies, this sexual revolution, politically or socially, never happened in post-Franco Spain as it was perceived, and the truth was that the existing sexual tolerance was only superficial (2003, 86).
18. Aliaga and Cortés (1997, 28–33) note that it was not until 1988 that the "figura del escándalo público" disappeared from the Spanish penal code. This did not mean a *de facto* disappearance of allusion to lewdness allowing a conservative judge to rule against acts of homosexuality (Aliaga and Cortés 1997, 31).
19. The battle for homosexual rights has been a long and sometimes uphill political battle. The ousting in March 2004 of the conservative Partido Popular (PP), which during the 1990s worked to impose its traditional values, has improved the

outlook for gay activists in Spain. Within six months, the new socialist government, led by José Luis Rodríguez Zapatero, approved the legalization of gay marriage in Spain (*El País* 2004).
20. *Cosas que dejé en la Habana* official web site.
21. Lander bases her argument on the complicity between the nineteenth-century sentimental novel and the dominant ideology of the ruling class in the newly created societies, who used this literary model to educate its populations. Obviously, the composition of the ruling class guaranteed the continuance of a specifically European and Spanish cultural patron in the recently established nations.
22. Updated versions of Spain as a pioneer on the cultural front can be found in the coproductions being filmed which allow film companies to access the nearly 400 million Spanish speakers around the world (Santaolalla 2003, 49).

Bibliography

Albacete, Alfonso and David Menkes, dir. 2001. *I Love You Baby*. Madrid: Alquimia Cinema.
Aliaga, Juan Vicente and José Miguel G. Cortés. 1997. *Identidad y diferencia sobre la cultura gay en España*. Barcelona-Madrid: Editorial Gay y Lesbiana.
Andall, Jacqueline, ed. 2003. *Gender and Ethnicity in Contemporary Europe*. Oxford-New York: Berg.
Bhabha, Homi K. 1983. "The Other Question…" *Screen* 24, no. 6, 18–36.
Bollaín, Icíar, dir. 1999. *Flores de otro mundo*. Madrid: Alta Films.
Brinker-Gabler, Gisela and Sidonie Smith, eds. 1997. *Writing New Identities. Gender, Nation, and Immigration in Contemporary Europe*. Minneapolis and London: University of Minnesota Press.
Brooksbank Jones, Anny. 1995. "Work, Women, and the Family: A Critical Perspective." In Helen Graham and Jo Labanyi, eds, *Spanish Cultural Studies. An Introduction*. Oxford: Oxford University Press, 386–393.
Camí-Vela, María. 2000a. "*Flores de otro mundo:* una mirada negociadora." In George Cabello-Castellet, et al., eds, *Cine-Lit 2000. Essays on Hispanic Film and Fiction*. Portland: Oregon State University Press, 176–188.
———. 2000b. "Una entrevista con Icíar Bollaín." In George Cabello-Castellet, et al., eds, *Cine-Lit 2000. Essays on Hispanic Film and Fiction*. Portland: Oregon State University Press, 232–243.
Chow, Rey. 2000. "Film and Cultural Identity." In John Hill and Pamela Church Gibson, eds, *Film Studies. Critical Approaches*. Oxford: Oxford University Press, 167–173.
Cosas que dejé en La Habana. n.d. Official website of the film <http://www.tornasolfilms.com/peliculas/cosas_habana/texto.html>. Accessed on 6 November 2003.
Creed, Barbara. 2000. "Film and Psychoanalysis." In John Hill and Pamela Church Gibson, eds, *Film Studies. Critical Approaches*. Oxford: Oxford University Press, 75–88.
El País. 2003. "La inmigración en cifras." (Accessed from www.elpais.es). 25 October.
———. 2004. "El Gobierno incluye la adopción en la ley que legalizará el matrimonio gay." (Accessed online from www.elpais.es). 30 September.
Ellwood, Sheelagh. 1995. "'Spain is Different.'" In Alec G. Hargreaves and Jeremy Leaman, eds, *Racism, Ethnicity and Politics in Contemporary Europe*. Aldershot: Edward Elgar, 145–158.

Evans, Peter. 1995. "Back to the Future: Cinema and Democracy." In Helen Graham and Jo Labanyi, eds, *Spanish Cultural Studies. An Introduction.* Oxford: Oxford University Press, 326–331.
———, ed. 1999. *Spanish Cinema. The Auterist Tradition.* Oxford: Oxford University Press.
"Extranjeros con tarjeta o autorización de residencia en vigor a 31 de diciembre de 2004" (2004). Accessed from <http://dgei.mir.es/es/general/InformeEstadistico_Diciembre_04_completo.pdf>. 25 February 2005.
Garlinger, Patrick Paul. 2003. "Pleasurable Insurrections: Sexual Revolutions and the Anarchy of Writing in Lluís Fernàndez's *L'anarquista nu.*" *Bulletin of Hispanic Studies* 80, 83–104.
Gregorio Gil, Carmen. 1998. *Migración femenina. Su impacto en las relaciones de género.* Madrid: Narcea, S.A. de Ediciones.
Gutiérrez Aragón, Manuel, dir. 1999. *Cosas que dejé en La Habana.* Madrid: Sogetel.
Izquierdo, Antonio. 1996. *La inmigración inesperada. La población extranjera en España (1991–1995).* Madrid: Trotta.
Jordan, Barry and Rikki Morgan-Tamosunas. 1998. *Contemporary Spanish Cinema.* Manchester and New York: Manchester University Press.
Kinder, Marsha, ed. 1997. *Refiguring Spain. Cinema/Media/Representation.* Durham and London: Duke University Press.
Klor de Alva, J. Jorge. 1995. "The Postcolonization of the (Latin) American Experience: A Reconsideration of 'Colonialism,' 'Postcolonialism,' and 'Mestizaje.'" In Gyan Prakask, ed, *After Colonialism. Imperial Histories and Postcolonial Displacements.* Princeton: Princeton University Press, 241–275.
Kofman, Eleonore, et al., eds. 2000. *Gender and International Migration in Europe.* London and New York: Routledge.
"La inmigración en España." Accessed from <http://dgei.mir.es/es/general/inmigracion.html>. 14 September 2004.
Labanyi, Jo. 2000. "Miscegenation, Nation Formation and Cross-Racial Identifications in the Early Francoist Folkloric Film." In Avtar Brah and Annie Coombes, eds, *Hybridity and Its Discontents. Politics, Science, Culture.* London-New York: Routledge, 56–71.
Lander, María Fernanda. 2003. *Modelando corazones. Sentimentalismo y urbanidad en la novela hispanoamericana del siglo XIX.* Rosario, Argentina: Beatriz Viterbo.
Maeztu, Ramiro de. 1935. *Defensa de la hispanidad.* Madrid: Gráfica Universal.
Martín-Cabrera, Luis. 2000. "Post-Colonial Memories and Racial Violence in *Flores de otro mundo.*" *Journal of Spanish Cultural Studies* 3, no. 1, 43–55.
Molina Gavilán, Yolanda and Thomas J. Di Salvo. 2003. "Policing Spanish/European Borders: Xenophobia and Racism in Contemporary Spanish Cinema." *Ciberletras* 5. Accessed from <http://lehman.cuny.edu/ciberletras/v05/molina.html. 16 November 2003>.
Morcillo Gómez, Aurora. 1999. "Shaping True Catholic Womanhood." In Victoria Lorée Enders and Pamela Beth Radcliff, eds, *Constructing Spanish Womanhood. Female Identity in Modern Spain.* Albany: State University of New York Press, 51–69.
Mulvey, Laura. 1990. "Visual Pleasure and Narrative Cinema." In Patricia Erens, ed, *Issues in Feminist Film Criticism.* Bloomington: Indiana University Press, 28–40.
Parker, Andrew et al. 1992. *Nationalisms and Sexualities.* New York and London: Routledge.
Santaolalla, Isabel. 1999. "Close Encounters: Racial Otherness in Imanol Uribe's *Bwana.*" *Bulletin of Hispanic Studies* 76, 111–122.

———. 2002. "Ethnic and Racial Configurations in Contemporary Spanish Culture." In Jo Labanyi, ed, *Constructing Identity in Contemporary Spain*. Oxford: Oxford University Press, 55–71.

———. 2003. "The Representation of Ethnicity and 'Race' in Contemporary Spanish Cinema." *Cineaste* vol. 29, no. 1 (Winter), 44–49.

Smith, Paul Julian. 2000. *Desire Unlimited. The Cinema of Pedro Almodóvar*. London and New York: Verso.

Solé, Carlota and Sònia Parella. 2003. "Migrant Women in Spain: Class, Gender and Ethnicity." In J. Andall, ed, *Gender and Ethnicity in Contemporary Europe*. Oxford: Berg, 61–76.

Chapter 3

State Narcissism:
Racism, Neoimperialism, and Spanish Opposition to Multiculturalism (On Mikel Azurmendi)

Joseba Gabilondo

> To the car-window sociologist, to the man who seeks to understand and know the South by devoting the few leisure hours of a holiday trip to unraveling the snarls of centuries,— to such men very often the whole trouble with the black fieldhand may be summed up by Aunt Ophelia's word, "Shiftless!"
> WEB Dubois, *The Souls of Black Folk*

> Spanish tolerance was Muslim, not Christian.
> Américo Castro, *España en su historia*

At the turn of this millennium, a new globalized form of liberalism (neoliberalism) is being upheld in Europe and the United States as the only valid political future and as the sole prospect of salvation from "barbarism" (Fukuyama 1992, Sartori 2000). At the opposite end of the spectrum, post-Marxism is emphasizing capitalism's internal contradictions as the only other alternative to this barbarism, which, according to its theorists (Hardt and Negri 2000, Zizek 2001), is being generated by capitalism itself. Ultimately, the First World's difficult relationship with history and difference is at stake and, as I will argue below, this tension is negotiated and legitimized through a discursive structure I denominate "State narcissism,"[1] which neoliberalism and post-Marxism share. As I will develop in the following, "State narcissism" denominates the modern State's refusal to deal with different forms of otherness that globalization brings its way. Instead, the State chooses to articulate new forms of nationalism that force otherness to disappear under the pretence of "assimilation" and thus attempt to restore the original modern self of the

State. In this narcissistic maneuver, the State also discards and represses as barbaric forms of difference that resist assimilation.

In this context, the discussions on multiculturalism and immigration developed in Spain over the last few years and epitomized by the work of anthropologist and president of the governmental "Foro de la Inmigración," Mikel Azurmendi, shed new light on the problem of State narcissism as well as on the impasse reached by neoliberalism and post-Marxism vis-à-vis "barbarism" in the first world. Moreover, Spain's contradictory position in modern European history enables us to rethink this narcissistic impasse reached by First World states and ideologies in new productive ways.

Multiculturalism and State Narcissism

It is important to underscore first the fact that both neoliberalism and post-Marxism denounce multiculturalism as the theoretical harbinger of global barbarism, especially when it concerns issues of migration. Interestingly enough, these negative reactions to multiculturalism linger on barbarism and irrationality; they point to the underside of any theory that does not rethink globalization and social difference without unconsciously upholding the nation-state as the only possible political outcome. Here, I mean by multiculturalism the social differences and movements that the modern liberal State has not addressed satisfactorily and, therefore, challenge, through a politics of human rights, any narcissistic return to such (nation-) State.

In the post-Marxist camp, authors such as Zizek have denounced multiculturalism as the logic of late capitalism, thus equating it with neoliberalism:

> The much-praised postmodern 'proliferation of new political subjectivities,' the demise of every 'essentialist' fixation, the assertion of full contingency, occur against the background of a certain silent *renunciation* and acceptance: the renunciation of the idea of a global change in the fundamental relations in our society (who will seriously question capitalism, state and political democracy?) and, consequently, the *acceptance* of the liberal democratic capitalist framework which *remains the same,* the unquestioned background, in all the dynamic proliferation of the multitude of new subjectivities. (Butler, Laclau, and Zizek 2000, 321)

Zizek concludes that multiculturalism, "the mad dance" of identities, will generate its own Jacobinism and thus propounds thinking beyond capitalism *tout court*:

> Today's 'mad dance,' the dynamic proliferation of multiple shifting identities, also awaits its resolution in a new form of Terror. The only 'realistic' prospect is to ground a new political universality by opting for the *impossible,* fully assuming the place of the exception,

with no taboos, no a priori norms ('human rights,' 'democracy'), respect for which would prevent us also from 'resignifying' terror, the ruthless exercise of power, the spirit of sacrifice ... if this radical choice is decried by some bleeding-heart liberals as *Linksfaschismus*, so be it! (Butler, Laclau, and Zizek, 326)

What is interesting in Zizek's reaction is his preventive recourse to "fascism" to qualify his own position in the eyes of liberals. That is, Zizek himself accepts his own "barbarian" positioning vis-à-vis neoliberalism and multiculturalism, thus mirroring his previous characterization of multiculturalism as Jacobinist. The encounter yields the contraposition of fascism and Jacobinism as the only two possibilities of politics in globalization; his later attempt to rescue Lenin points in the same direction (Zizek 2001).[2] As I will elaborate below, this irrational upsurge in leftwing politics points to a form of narcissism that ultimately is enabled by the European state itself.

In defence of neoliberalism, intellectuals such as Giovanni Sartori attack multiculturalism while also emphasizing the Jacobinist *telos* of such politics. When pointing out the non-European formation of multiculturalism, which, according to him, migrates from British Marxism to the American academic milieus of feminism and race studies, Sartori concludes that multiculturalism is close to ethnic cleansing (2000, 112). In this context, interculturalism implies a neoliberal understanding of tolerance and pluralism, which ultimately are grounded on civil society and its traditional political parties rather than on newer social movements. Sartori clearly identifies the different histories of North America and Europe and concludes that the bases for the corresponding difference between multiculturalism and neoliberalism is migration (2000, 113).

However, since Sartori's analysis does not historically correlate European imperialism and postcolonial migration, he ends up using an "irrational" language to deal with the supposedly ahistorical and unprecedented novelty of immigration:

A foreign population of 10 percent might constitute a number that can be welcomed; one of 20 percent, most surely, would be strongly resisted. Does resistance constitute "racism"? It is admitted (but not granted) that it might be so, but the responsibility for this racism lies with those who have created it. (Sartori 2000, 106, my translation)

Ironically enough, Sartori does not have an answer for the historical agency that has "created" immigration: imperialism is not a component of his understanding of the European nation-state. Consequently, Sartori ends up advocating a very irrational scenario in which an anti-immigrational Europe could be justified on mere numerical grounds rather than on political ones, thus opening the gate for justifying racism even in our days. In Sartori's account, the ahistorical European nation-state, void of imperialist history, and the consequent novelty of immigration from the Third World, stripped of a colonial past, clash in a barbarian mirroring where the European state must be upheld against otherness.

In short, post-Marxism and neoliberalism share the same political unconscious structure, which ultimately relies on and is triggered by State narcissism.[3] State narcissism describes the European state's resistance to historical and global differences, which prompts the State to resort irrationally to ideas of sameness and assimilation in order to disavow and/or repress difference.

State Narcissism

As a first tentative elaboration, one could say that State narcissism refers to the State's new refusal to acknowledge an other that is so overwhelming that it forces the former to withdraw into itself. Freudian psychoanalysis denominates this regressive closure within oneself "secondary narcissism" and, thus, it is important to return to Freud and his description of individual narcissism in order to articulate its connection with State narcissism.

When commenting on the megalomaniac tendencies of psychotic individuals, Freud concludes that there is an originary narcissism in childhood: the earliest form of being. However, any new withdrawal from either the world or other subjects in a mature age represents a form of psychosis that Freud denominates secondary narcissism. In his words: "The libido that has been withdrawn from the external world has been directed to the ego and thus gives rise to an attitude which may be called narcissism ... This leads us to look upon the narcissism which arises through the drawing in of object-cathexes as a secondary one, superimposed upon a primary narcissism" (1953–74, 75). Although Freud only refers to individual narcissism, it is important to note that this psychoanalytical elaboration allows him to formulate the idea of the superego and, from this new instance, to sketch a hypothesis about mass behavior and social anxiety, that is, about the irrational and "barbarian" functioning of societies. Therefore, it is important to examine in detail Freud's theorization of narcissism, and specifically narcissism's secondary formation, in order to explain the cultural and social behavior of European states and ideologies, which at this point are marked by an irrationality and violence that is clearly narcissistic.

Freud locates the access of the infant to the social order precisely in a split of his primary narcissism. As the child interacts with parents and society, he renounces his original narcissism in which the infant himself is the only object of interest, but does not fully discard it. Instead, the child moves part of his narcissistic libido to the creation of an ideal ego. This split is explained by Freud in the following way: "This ideal ego is now the target of the self-love which was enjoyed in childhood by the actual ego ... What he projects before him as his ideal is the substitute for the lost narcissism of his childhood in which he was his own ideal" (1953–74, 94). Freud emphasizes that the formation of the ideal ego is directly connected with the infant's new access to the social: "For what prompted the subject to form an ego ideal, on whose behalf his conscience acts as watchman, arose from the critical influence of his parents (conveyed to him by the medium of the voice), to whom were added, as time went on, those who trained and taught him and the innumerable and indefinable host of all the other people in his environment—his fellow-men—and public opinion" (1953–74, 96). Therefore, the ideal ego, although a remnant of an original narcissism, it is also the source of consciousness and criticism, since such ideal ego absorbs parental and societal influence.

Yet, Freud emphasizes that the ideal ego has another function or, to be more precise, its formation is only successful as a result of a simultaneous action: repression. As Freud argues, "the formation of an ideal heightens the demands of the ego and is the most powerful factor favouring repression ... a special psychical agency [super-ego] which performs the task of seeing that narcissistic satisfaction from the ego ideal is ensured and which, with this end in view, constantly watches the actual ego and measures it by that ideal" (1953–74, 95). In the following, I will equate "ideal ego" and "super ego," and will not use the form "ego ideal," in the interest of brevity and consistency, although they are not technically the same in psychoanalysis.[4] Thus, the connection between ideal ego and repression is clearly established by Freud when discussing the way the ideal ego controls and regulates the ego's relations with others and the world in general: "The ego ideal has imposed severe conditions upon the satisfaction of libido through objects [including people]; for it causes some of them to be rejected by means of its censor, as being incompatible" (1953–74, 100).

The simultaneous articulation of narcissism and repression, in the form of an ideal ego, is for Freud at the core of the functioning of society, since the ideal ego is ultimately a narcissistic internalization of parental controls and societal rules. Consequently, and according to Freud, a severe rift in the body politics over the conventions and rules that govern the formation of the shared ideal ego has the effect of generating social anxiety and guilt:

> The ego ideal opens up an important avenue for the understanding of group psychology. In addition to its individual side, this ideal has a social side; it is also the common ideal of a family, a class or a nation ... The want of satisfaction which arises from the non-

fulfilment of this ideal liberates ... libido, and this is transformed into a sense of guilt (social anxiety). Originally this sense of guilt was a fear of punishment by the parents, or, more correctly, the fear of losing their love; later the parents are replaced by an indefinite number of fellow-men. (1953–74, 101–102)

As Freud states, the consequence of not being able to fulfill the ideal ego's expectations is guilt and anxiety, which produce further repression in the ego. Ultimately, this excessive repression is the origin of secondary narcissism. Incapable of relating to the outside world and to others according to the ideal ego, the individual's ego experiences excessive repression and thus withdraws into itself, avoiding any libidinal relationship, sexual or otherwise, with the outside world. At that point, the ego and the ideal ego almost coincide again, since the complete withdrawal from objects and the outside world is impossible, and therefore there is a regression to a narcissism that, nevertheless, is not original but secondary.

Although Freud does not refer to the uncanny effects of repression in his article on narcissism, he states elsewhere ("The Uncanny") that, when certain objects and subjects become destructive to the ego, but cannot be fully repressed by the ideal ego in secondary narcissism, they become uncanny: the Freudian Thing or, in Lacanian psychoanalysis, the Real. However, because repression also defines the ideal ego and its relationship to the ego, the Real is ultimately the instance that constitutes and upholds the entire psychic apparatus that defines the individual; it defines what the ideal ego cannot repress and thus shapes the ego's narcissistic relationship with the ideal ego as well.

In this sense, the European state constitutes the ultimate order and horizon of the modern individual and his/her politics. In the State, the ideal egos of the modern citizens come together and reach a social balance that, in return, regulates their respective individual egos. In this respect, the result of this balance can be understood as the State's own ideal ego. Moreover, the State, as the ultimate containment and horizon of the narcissistic bind between individual egos and their ideal egos, can also be considered a narcissistic institution endowed with its own ego. Although this is a departure from Freud's development, one can postulate that the institutions defining the State constitute its own ego. Furthermore and in the case of Europe, one could hypothesize that the (imperialist) nation is the ideal ego of the State and thus the functioning of its institutions, its ego, is regulated by this ideal ego, the (imperialist) nation.[5] In short, the State finds in the nation its ideal ego, and thus the nation-state constitutes the narcissistic bind that defines the State *qua* ideal nation.

Given the irrational attitudes of some European political theorists toward multiculturalism, as well as the European states' own irrational reaction to global migration, I want to defend, in this article, that the theorization of State narcissism is crucial to understanding the above scenarios. State narcissism—and more precisely State secondary narcissism—emerges when, in the face a threat such as immigrants, the national (imperialist) ideal ego represses the State ego so that the latter withdraws from the differential object of immigration and retreats into itself, giving rise, in turn, to social anxiety at the level of individual citizens. Therefore, I want to hypothesize that the State's secondary narcissism is a result of globalization and, thus, any political theorization must address State narcissism in order to resolve the irrationality and anxiety that define the European state and its theorists in the face of globalization.

Difference and Neoliberal Integration

The above authors and discussions have also generated specific but similar debates in Spain, one of the European countries most defined by the diversity of its immigrants (East Europe, Africa, Latin America, and Asia) and therefore a prime context in which to study State narcissism. More specifically, Mikel Azurmendi, a Basque anthropologist appointed by the right-wing party (the Partido Popular [PP], in power from 1996 to 2004) to direct the Forum for the Integration of Immigration (a branch of the Department of Immigration), generated quite a scandal when he declared that multiculturalism was a form of gangrene in the social body (Efe 2003). His ethnography of El Ejido (Azurmendi 2001), the town where some of the most violent incidents triggered by immigration took place in Spain and Europe in 2000, prompted more than sixty Spanish scholars to denounce his work publicly (Efe 2002). Furthermore, it is important to note that Azurmendi has previously written on Basque nationalism and terrorism, as well as on state violence toward Basque peasants in early modernity. During the late 1990s, he became the PP's government spokesperson in matters of immigration as well as the most decidedly neoliberal and anti-multiculturalist intellectual in Spain. No post-Marxist voice echoes Azurmendi's anti-multiculturalism within the Spanish state, which makes the study of his work all the more important. It is my contention that the analysis of Azurmendi's thought can shed important light on the interrelated issues of multiculturalism, neoliberal/post-Marxist "irrationality," and State narcissism. The diverse and complex relationship between Spain's imperialist history and the global flow of (postcolonial) migration can clarify the above "barbarian" impasse and debate while emphasizing the importance of understanding State narcissism.

In his *Estampas de El Ejido,* after introducing most of the Andalusian characters of his ethnography by resorting to Greek mythology—as if to separate their "Western origins" from any historical Muslim influence—Azurmendi inquires of the other, the immigrant, and especially of the most "intractable" one, the Maghrebian, the reasons why he/she does not wish to assimilate. Yet Azurmendi does not allow the other to speak. As Juan Goytisolo clearly notices in his review of Azurmendi's work, "Azurmendi's approach, covering over the voice of the people he interviews with his own at every step, in a kind of interior monologue in which the former is engulfed and absorbed en masse by the interviewer, gravely damages, if not killing, the anthropologist's project" (Goytisolo 2003, 45, my translation). Azurmendi's silencing of the other allows him to denounce multiculturalism and to issue a call favoring the immigrants' full integration into Spanish society. That is, Azurmendi propounds the erasure of otherness and difference as the solution to migration so that, as I will discuss below, the State's ego (the sum of its institutions) remains untarnished by globalization and, thus, continues to respond to the national ideal ego.

This approach allows him to affirm that there is no racism in southern Andalusia, in El Ejido, even though many residents rioted against immigrant settlements after three Spaniards were killed by immigrants in February 2000. In Azurmendi's words:

> Neither racism nor xenophobia are the problem in El Ejido, and I begin to be convinced that it is one of the places in the world not merely with less of the racism one might anticipate [*con menos racismo del previsible*] given the volume and rapidity of the concentration of illegal immigrants in the area, but also a laboratory, almost unique in our country, for resolving an assimilationist form of immigration with less of a price in racism [*con menos costo de racismo*]. (Azurmendi 2001, 287–288; all translations from Azurmendi are my own)

Azurmendi never addresses and evaluates what *racismo previsible* and *menos costo de racismo* mean and, furthermore, he does not elaborate a theory of racism, for ultimately his goal is to privilege the fully assimilative State in which difference and otherness disappear under the sway of the national ideal ego. Since State narcissism is at stake, it is important to analyze in detail the reasons for Azurmendi's discursive and ideological maneuver.

It must be noted, first, that Azurmendi speaks out against the Spanish and European media and faults the latter for labeling the population of El Ejido racist:

> The effect of the press and the media has been to isolate the population of western Almería from other Spaniards and to demonize them as a whole. The people in the western region have already realized that they have not been and are not treated like other Spaniards but as a marginal group of loathsome racists. (Azurmendi 2001, 338–339)

Azurmendi is quite correct in his assessment: the media has "othered" El Ejido as the most prominent site of racism and, as a result, they have absolved the remainder of the Spanish state and Europe from any charges of racism. However, Azurmendi's stand against the media does not explain why, instead of generalizing the accusation of racism to the entire Spanish state, he resorts to the opposite logic of absolving even the population of El Ejido, and thus, unconsciously the rest of Spain and Europe. Here, a different discourse and ideology appears in Azurmendi's writing, one that ultimately has little to do with discussing racism and very much with upholding State narcissism, so that the Spanish state continues to respond to the national ideal ego of the State.

In order to negate racism and uphold a State free of difference, Azurmendi first frames the divide between Spanish and Muslim cultures in terms of moral superiority, and he thereby creates a partition based on the Western idea of progress—one in which Spain is unproblematically aligned with the West and modernity. In this way, the difference between State and immigrant becomes a moral and, ultimately, natural difference derived from modernity's historical and teleological superiority. While addressing a social worker named Carmen, Azurmendi writes:

> I did not tell Carmen that I suspect that *our culture has progressed more in moral terms than Muslim culture* because it has detected that a person is someone who can be wounded and injured, someone who can be humiliated and suffer. That is precisely why the suffering of the immigrant makes us so indignant. Sometimes *even more than they are*. And that is why we are starting to be sensitive even towards animals and future generations. (Azurmendi 2001, 101, my emphasis)

Once he erects a moral divide between modernity's progress and the other's backwardness, Azurmendi moves on to uphold the West, and most specifically the Spanish state, as the *socium* of democracy and individuality. This is the founding discursive maneuver of Orientalism by which, as Edward Said states, "the difference between the familiar (Europe, the West, "us") and the strange (the Orient, the East, "them")" (Said 1979, 43) is established as a way to proclaim Western superiority. Yet the historical problems of upholding such a divide in the case of Spain are incommensurable: the origins of Spanish modernity are essentially Muslim (medieval) and French (Enlightenment); Spanish modernity itself is not capitalist and thus falls off the Marxist, Weberian, and—most importantly—the liberal understanding of modernity; although the debate continues, many authors still defend that Spain never consolidated as a nation-state in the nineteenth century (Pérez Garzón 2000, Riquer 1993); there was a civil war in the twentieth century; finally, Spain boasted its difference (*España es diferente*) in ethno-fundamentalist ways under Franco's forty-year dictatorship. Even in the post-dictatorial transition, when joining the European Community, Spanish society and government exploited their difference as sign of instantaneous hyper-modernity, as if a recently acquired modernity were still supplemental in its excess rather than constitutive in its "normalcy." The Spanish state's tendency to use violent and undemocratic means (most notably the Grupo Antiterrorista de Liberación,"GAL") calls into question its modernity (Woodworth 2001). Until the defeat of the PP by the Partido Socialista Obrero Español (PSOE) in the elections of 14 March 2004, the Spanish government sided with North American imperialism (and against European modernity) in the war against Muslim fundamentalist terrorism and in Iraq.

Furthermore, in order to defend a Spanish state where all its citizens are equal before the law, Azurmendi needs to attack the Spanish intellectual tradition that defends historical and cultural difference. It is important to note that a Basque anthropologist who spent but five months in Andalusia is able to dismiss local academics and their defense of cultural difference out of hand. After all, and unlike Azurmendi, Andalusian academics have dealt with and thought about this problem for years. Yet, Azurmendi disavows Andalusia of any intellectual authority: "I therefore consider unacceptable the conception, already virtual orthodoxy in Andalusian university departments, that cultural diversity has rights" (Azurmendi, 2001, 352). Furthermore, he makes no references to the problem of Andalusis (descendants of Medieval Spanish Muslims who live in the Maghreb) who suffer immigrational discrimination as voiced by Mohammed ibn Azzuz Hakim, the most important Moroccan Hispanist (Gibson 2002).

Once Azurmendi negates racism in Andalusia—and unconsciously in Spain and in Europe—and also asserts Spain's Western character and moral superiority over the dissenting, intellectual voice of Andalusian academics, he makes an unproblematic apology for a "democratic and modern Spanish state" and, thus, upholds "assimilation" (adaptation, integration) as the only path to moral progress and democracy:

> The process of cultural adaptation in a democratic society either exists on the individual level or it will not exist at all, and so it is each person who must respond, man to man, woman to woman, and take responsibility in the family sphere, in the school, at work. There does not exist, therefore, a supposed 'minority' culture that should adapt to ours, the receiving culture, supposedly considered the 'majority.' No: there exists here today a society with certain values, a society that can only receive other people insofar as they contribute to improving it. (Azurmendi, 2001, 353)

The fact that Azurmendi defends such Spanish individualism makes even more problematic the unmediated alignment of Spain with the West and its modern values. It will suffice to recall that Spain is a country run, until recently, according to patriarchal Catholic values. As a result, abortion, for example, is still not fully legal and, thus, a woman does not have full rights over her body. In short, the idea of individuality is not yet universal but remains gendered in Spain.

Azurmendi concludes by demonizing "multiculturalism," and thus any form of difference. Multiculturalism, in his discourse, becomes the real culprit of all the evils that happened in southern Spain. "Hence one of the great enemies of any attempt at assimilationist immigration in the region of Almería is multiculturalism or the leftist tenet of faith whereby all cultures are equal or equally respectable and should cohabit next to each other" (Azurmendi, 2001, 355–356). Consequently, Azurmendi disavows racism and avows the "integrative" modern Spanish state, void of non-modern Western history and difference, as the real subject of his ethnography. In short, he turns otherness and difference into the ultimate, real causes of racism, and in this new circular logic immigrants and their moral backwardness are to be blamed for racism, not a progressive democratic Spain. Immigrants are at fault in their resistance to assimilation.

Yet Azurmendi's integrative definition of a supposedly modern European Spain requires other discursive and political maneuvers so that all non-modern difference in Spanish history is repressed, for ultimately his anthropologist trajectory, unaware of its imperialist unconscious and narcissistic nationalism, marks his approach to immigration and racism. In a trend that begins with *Estampas de El Ejido* (2001) and continues with *Todos somos nosotros* (2003), Azurmendi theorizes neoliberal assimilation by always focusing on a single type of immigrant, the African. The reason is that the discourse of difference and assimilation only works against the African immigrant (Maghrebian or Sub-Saharan) but not against the Hispanic immigrant from Latin America (the second largest non-European immigrant group). In 2000, there were 199,964 Latin Americans in Spain (22 percent of all immigrants) compared to 261,385 Africans (29 percent of the total; Ortega Pérez 2004); yet Azurmendi ignores Latin America.[6]

This complete neglect of Latin Americans is due to the fact that this immigrant group does not reflect the perfect "other" that then can be repressed through assimilation, as is the case of many Maghrebian workers in El Ejido or Muslim Spaniards in Ceuta. The Latin American immigrant is a "pseudo-other" tainted by Spain's own imperialist history: they are natives or African Americans in many instances, but they are mainly Catholic and they also speak Spanish fluently either as their first or second language. This "pseudo-other" can be considered a historical abject, in the psychoanalytical sense (Kristeva 1982), since it questions the divide between self and other, difference and sameness. Therefore, the Latin American immigrant destabilizes the narcissistic balance between ego and ideal ego, since he/she cannot be either accepted or repressed by the ideal ego of the State. The reason for ignoring the unstable effects of Latin American immigration for the narcissistic balance between State ego and ideal ego lies in the fact that the neoliberal ideology of assimilation, represented by Azurmendi, needs to conflate many forms of social difference (economic, class, ethnic, sexual, racial, etc.) under a single one: race and its "darkest" or most negative representation, Africa. Only by emphasizing racial difference can Azurmendi's anthropological thrust make sense and repress the other under the ahistorical mirror of radical difference, so that the State's ideal ego is upheld and thereby the narcissistic relationship that defines the bind between ego and ideal ego, State and nation, is legitimized.[7]

The fact that an anthropologist upholds the State's ego and its ideal ego (the nation-state) is not a coincidence, since anthropology is historically founded precisely in the act of othering the colonial subject. A postcolonial subject, such as the Latin American, who remains other but at the same time is also Hispanic, must be repressed more than the African immigrant because he is a reminder of a failed repression. The immigrant hailing from Africa (who is taken to be radically different despite Spain's Muslim history and slavery) holds in his radical difference the promise and legitimization of a full assimilation, since he has not become the traumatic reminder of a failed colonial repression. The Latin American immigrant is the traumatic Real of Azurmendi's discourse, along with the Basques (as I will discuss later). In short, Spain's own imperialist and colonial history becomes Azurmendi's Real: the traumatic element that destabilizes the narcissistic balance between the State's ego and ideal ego in ways that the African immigrant, in his supposed "full otherness" and proof of his "moral inferiority," does not. The Latin American immigrant represents the return of a repressed other, which, in its return, signifies the traumatic failure of the State and its ideal ego to repress the colonial other during the period of imperialist expansion. The Hispanic immigrant represents both the return of repressed history and the failure of State repression.

Thus, once the "radical difference" of African immigration is articulated as a promise of full assimilation and the trauma of past Latin American colonialism is repressed once again, then history disappears and Western superiority appears to be as natural and self-evident as in any hegemonic ideology—hence Althusser's pertinent claim that ideology has no history (Althusser n.d., 159–162). Furthermore, only through this racial conflation of difference can the political alternatives of neoliberalism be narrowed down to a single choice: assimilation (indirect repression) or direct repression. In this way, the abjection of history and its scaling of differences and positions are eliminated. At the end of this ideological maneuver, the Spanish state appears as the only subject of politics and, consequently, the practice of assimilation by the Spanish neoliberal order also emerges as the only possible form of politics. Consequently, the narcissistic balance between the State's ego and ideal ego is ideologically restored and the Spanish state can be thought of again as a nation even in the midst of globalization. However, the fact that the immigrational presence does not go away and any attempt at assimilation fails only proves that the balance between State ego and ideal ego is reached temporarily. Ultimately, this balance points to an increasing secondary narcissism in which the State's ideal ego needs to further repress any form of otherness, thus increasing social anxiety and distress. This increasing form of repression creates a new form of nationalism that is defined by its ideological failure to repress the global immigrational other, which then prompts the State to narcissistically retreat within itself, thus slipping into secondary narcissism. In this sense, this new globalized nationalism, resulting from secondary narcissism, can be called "neonationalism" in order to differentiate it from traditional nationalism.[8]

The State's secondary narcissism also explains the ideological attack of authors such as Azurmendi upon multiculturalism. Only from a neonationalist, neoliberal viewpoint can multiculturalism be approached as a theory that upholds both the relativity and equality of all cultures and beliefs (with the pretended contradiction of having to respect fascism, racism, homophobia, or misogyny). Neonationalism cannot think difference historically but nationalistically, according to the State's ideal ego, and thus it assumes that any cultural difference is a radical difference without history that must be either assimilated or repressed nationalistically. It is this ontologized difference against which neonationalism imagines itself and represses any other form of difference. In this respect, neonationalism imagines multiculturalism as multinationalism and thus can only approach any other difference as national (fascism bad, democracy good) and think of subject formation as individuality (individual rights good, collective rights bad). In short, multiculturalism represents the traumatic symptom of the State's ideal ego, which shows the latter's necessity to repress any historical difference, because of its abjection, by first othering it as nationally different.

Instead, multiculturalism and especially its poststructuralist strand thinks of difference in historical terms through particularity and universality. These multicultural poststructuralist theorists emphasize the historicity of cultural difference, so that universality can only be attained when all cultural differences come dialectically together by claiming their particular universality and by determining one another. In short, what multiculturalism affirms is precisely that Western culture is not superior or teleologically the only one to which we are all irremediably bound, but rather that Western culture must still accept its particularity and continue to determine and be determined by other particular cultures. A "truly" historically global culture will emerge only when all cultures determine one another. Furthermore, the apparent universality of Western culture derives precisely from its determination by other cultures (medieval Muslim and Chinese cultures, native cultures of the modern colonial period, etc.) rather than from some inner epistemological or ontological trait or disposition. In this regard, it is important to emphasize that "democracy, human rights, and individualism" are not yet historically universal values and rights. They must determine and be determined by other non-Western cultures and values in so far as they are all affected by capitalism, which creates the possibility for universalism, as Marx had already foreseen.

Archaeology of State Difference: From Basque Conversion to Immigrant Integration

Yet, in order to understand the reasons for Azurmendi's use of African-Andalusian racial tensions as a narcissistic screen to project the moral progress of a putative democratic Spanish state and, thus, legitimize Spanish neonationalism through increased repression and secondary narcissism, it is important to look elsewhere in his texts: to his intermittent remarks about the Basque Country. The Basque Country, nationalism, and violence appear as a subtext in Azurmendi's ethnographic palimpsest on immigration. The Basque Country and its violence are the historically abject and traumatic instances that Azurmendi cannot successfully repress through the State's ideal ego. Furthermore, they sustain his entire discourse of ideological balance between the State's ego and ideal ego.

In *Estampas de El Ejido*, the two subtexts of the palimpsest, the immigrational-Andalusian and the Basque, intersect in one instance. In an ethnography where the immigrant other speaks very few times and the Andalusian natives' voices explain the whole conflict, Azurmendi nevertheless dismisses and represses both voices—the immigrant and the Basque—as precisely the marks of people who do not want to integrate. For Azurmendi, their refusal to integrate destabilizes the State's narcissistic balance and ultimately shows their "racist" nature:

> I was horrified by what Mohamed had told me ... of telling stories in the *ikastolas* [Basque schools]. He told me that he had come back struck by how bilingual the Basque children were. But surely you, poor Mohamed, must have been the only Spanish-speaker to have gone to tell stories in *castellano* in those schools. I told him this and he seemed

to understand me. Certainly, Mohamed recognized that in the Basque country he had not been treated as a Spaniard, despite being one and speaking Arabic. And without a shadow of doubt, Mohamed must appreciate not being compared here to the clowns and other storytellers [*payasos y otros contacuentos*] who go around the *ikastolas* in that region, where so many parents think that they belong to a pure race [*una pura raza*]. (Azurmendi, 2001, 226)

In short, the only instance of clear racism in Spain is the Basque Country. This is the kernel of the Real, the unwritable text of Azurmendi's ethnography: Andalusia and Spain are not racist, only the Basques are. When he is boasting against multiculturalism and Andalusian academia, and even when he dismisses the words of an immigrant, he is still speaking against a Basque Country that is ultimately racist *in toto*. The Basque Country is the land of *payasos y contacuentos* who believe they belong to *una raza pura*. In short, Azurmendi needs to dismiss a multicultural encounter such as the one taking place between Mohamed and the children of Basque schools, to uphold the integrationist non-differential Spanish state and its "democratic moral progress," because Basque difference is ultimately traumatic and therefore cannot be successfully repressed by the State's ideal ego.

Yet it is important to examine why the Spanish Basque Country and the conflicts that take place in that region are at the basis of Azurmendi's neoliberal reformulation of Spanish nationalism (a State ego endowed with a national ideal ego that represses global immigration). This examination is important especially if we consider that Azurmendi has dedicated most of his work to the Basque Country and has only recently shifted to the issue of immigration. It is even more disconcerting if one considers that his two most important previous works (Azurmendi 1993 and 2000) are dedicated precisely to the critique of State oppression against the Basque rural classes. Azurmendi's work is nationalist from its very inception and, thus, the continuity of this nationalist epistemology explains his similar approach to different realities. His work has shifted from the denunciation of State oppression against internal minorities in the past to the defense of State assimilation of external minorities in the present. As I will explain in the following, Azurmendi's anthropological othering of the Basque peasant classes as a single nationalist identity in his early work explains the continuity and coherence of his later work. Thanks to the nationalist epistemology underlying Azurmendi's work, the othering of Basque rural masses in the past lends itself to be written as the othering of global immigration in the present, so that, at the end, Azurmendi ends up upholding retroactively the State's national ideal ego (the nation-state). Yet, it is also important to explain that, because of his nationalist epistemology, Azurmendi's initial denunciation of State oppression ends up becoming a neoliberal defense of State assimilation, where labor exploitation is the main purpose and thus "oppression" still remains an operative term—as exemplified by the quota system implemented by the Spanish government in recent years (Ortega Pérez 2004). In short, there is a nationalist continuity in Azurmendi's conceptualization of the State from apparatus of oppression to institution of integration. Thus, it is not a coincidence if Goytisolo concludes his review of Azurmendi's *Estampas* by emphasizing the similarity between Basque nationalism's racism and Azurmendi's: "The invading immigrants from elsewhere in Spain [*maketos*] or the "Moors of Euskadi" as Sabino Arana called them, suffer from the same vices (idleness, lechery) as the Moors of El Ejido depicted by Azurmendi, and resemble each other extremely closely" (Goytisolo 2003, 47).

In his *Nombrar, embrujar* (1993), Azurmendi clearly expresses the thesis that the Inquisition terrorized the Basque peasant masses on both sides of the border between Spain and France, with the complicity of local élites, in order to enforce the masses' submission to the State. Azurmendi makes patent that this oppression was not only political but also cultural, since rural culture and language (Basque) were proscribed by the Inquisition under suspicion of witchcraft: "The truth here must therefore have something to do with understanding the strategy whereby the Basque social élite, in connivance with the central power of Spain, proscribed the system of popular signs, implanting in people's minds (and not exclusively through violence) another system more to their liking" (Azurmendi, 1993, 14). Azurmendi also states that the new repressed rural culture and landscape become the benign and utopian horizon for the idealizations of later political ideologies in the nineteenth century: Carlism, foralism, and nationalism.

Yet Azurmendi's anthropological approach collapses several historical realities into a single homogeneous other: the Basque peasant. This social group becomes, in Azurmendi's text, an other that mirrors narcissistically the absolutist State and turns unconsciously its ideal ego into a nationalist one—a contemporary State ideal ego, the nation. In three out of the five chapters that constitute the book, Azurmendi presents a straightforward analysis of contemporary Basque language, without many dialectological distinctions or historical references to the past, which then it is made to stand for "the" entire Basque rural cultural system. As a result, different areas of the Basque Country, which were disconnected at the time under different political systems, are treated homogeneously. Furthermore, the non-Basque speaking rural areas (parts of Álava and Navarre) are repressed from his analysis, so that rural culture and the Basque language are made to coincide. Conversely, his analysis also avoids the towns and cities in which Basque was spoken in order to disavow Basque speaking in non-rural areas and reify the identification between rural life and Basque language. The lack of a thorough historical analysis allows Azurmendi to avoid any reference to the different areas of the countryside and towns dedicated to industry (steel and ship construction), which, until the end of the eighteenth century, were the other important sector of the Basque economy, alongside agriculture. In short, the Basque Country is dehistorized and turned into an anthropological object that can be analyzed through language (expressions, etymology, mythology, etc.) in a study that nevertheless is not conducted linguistically—at least one of the etymologies Azurmendi propounds is clearly wrong.[9]

Toward the end of his book, Azurmendi further reduces Basque peasants to "the Basque-speaking peasants of the Spanish state" (thus excluding French, Navarrese, and Alavese peasants) and explains the subalternization of the Basque language in the following terms:

> In order to assert themselves collectively, the peasant community had no option but to go to church, since after the inquisitorial trials the doors of the provincial *juntas*, in which they had been accustomed to meeting to debate their problems and choose their representatives, were closed for good. At least from 1615, that is to say once the Grand Inquisitor had established that only Castilian was suitable for detecting malign and diabolical activity, the *juntas* demanded that in order to meet and talk about that more benign form of activity relating to the rural community, it was also necessary to speak and write in *castellano*. (Azurmendi 1993, 198)

In short, Azurmendi equates the repression of Spanish-Basque peasants and the outlawing of Basque language from two provincial parliaments with the blockage of the Basque Country from modernity, which, as he elaborates in the last chapter, becomes the foundation of Basque nationalism. However, it is Azurmendi's anthropological approach that is nativizing and ultimately nationalist; it responds to a contemporary State ideal ego that exerts repression in a nationalist way through intellectual history.

Consequently, as Azurmendi approaches the twentieth century at the end of his text, suddenly State oppression becomes secondary and Basque nationalism, which does not resonate with the State's ideal ego, becomes the only problem in the narcissistic othering logic that he himself constructs in the text. Yet Basque nationalism cannot be othered as nonnational and thus ultimately becomes traumatic and irrepressible. In short, at a time when the absolutist State has subjugated all minorities and, thus, has repressed any form of difference, the historical persistence of the Basque problem, now under the guise of nationalism, is unthinkable for Azurmendi. For him, this problem ends with the subjugation of the Basque peasant masses by the end of the 1600s. As a result, Basque nationalism returns in the text with the traumatic impetus generated by failed repression. In his next work, which deals with contemporary Spanish-Basque politics and terrorism, *La herida patriótica* (1998), Azurmendi adopts the historical conclusion of his previous work: only the Spanish state, *qua* modern and national, represents the political ideal ego of modernity and thus, the persistence of Basque nationalism and terrorism is a traumatic reality that must, nevertheless, be repressed. Hence, Azurmendi resorts to organic medical metaphors of wounding and injury in order to signify the asocial or natural character of this problem: it is beyond the State's ideal ego and its repression. Its uncanny appearance must be understood as coming from nature, as originating beyond society. Yet in this natural state of things Basque is also an affliction that must be treated by the doctor, who deals with human nature. Azurmendi concludes that Basque nationalism is an organic disorder that needs medical treatment and therapy. Basque nationalism is a pathology, which requires treatment for *natural* (self-evident and self-legitimizing) reasons: "nationalism is a patriotic wound, a permanent sore which harms the very depths of identity. *They have stolen from us what we should have been! We have lost what we should achieve!*" (Azurmendi 1998, 177). Thus, the State becomes the only solution to the problem of Basque nationalism: the State is the only healer that will bring the Basque Country back from nature and into society. In this way, the Basque problem is also legitimized as originating in nature, in a non-human state, and since it is impossible to solve by any social means, justifies inhuman remedies (violence, torture, etc.).

In sum, it is not contradictory but logical that Azurmendi moves from criticizing the State to becoming its apologist, since his understanding of Basque history is nationalist and ahistorical—it responds to a single State ideal ego, the nation. Azurmendi tends to nativize and anthropologize Basque history, so that the latter ends up caught in the only two alternatives that an imperialist nationalist State offers: othering (and consequent social assimilation) or traumatic repression (and consequent naturalization). The fact that a historical problem that should have disappeared at the end of the seventeenth or beginning of the eighteenth century still persists in our days and, moreover, has also taken the shape of a nationalist trauma that defies the State's national ego, prompts Azurmendi to connect both historical developments. In order to link them historically, Azurmendi needs to find a nationalist impulse already in the subjugation of the Basque peasant masses, which no longer is mainly conducted by the State, but rather by the local Basque ruling classes. As a result of this need for a historical connection, Azurmendi turns the Basque ruling classes into the new culprits of Basque nationalism's retrospective existence and articulation at the end of the ancient regime, precisely at the moment when the subjugation of the Basque peasant masses should have ended the Basque problem and when the absolutist State should have prevailed in its liberal and centralist refashioning.

In his most complex and comprehensive work on Basque history, *Y se limpie aquella tierra* (2000), Azurmendi moves away from an anthropological approach and shifts toward a more historically grounded analysis. Yet he does not abandon the nationalist approach to his new object of study: Basque ideological discourse. Not by coincidence does he find the origins of Basque nationalism at the end of the eighteenth century among Jesuits such as Manuel Larramendi and enlightened noblemen such as Xavier Munive. Here, nationalism results from an atrophy of an earlier Basque discourse, the Renaissance theories of *tubalismo,* which legitimized the Basques as the original inhabitants of Spain. Azurmendi denominates this atrophy "traditionalization":

> So it was that the old myth was sufficiently modified to sustain the legitimacy of the new and most radical claims of the Basque élite of the eighteenth century. We may refer to this process as the traditionalization of the myth ... If an older generation had founded their privileges on *tubalismo,* those of the eighteenth century founded them on the inalterability of *tubalismo,* introducing the will to deny new conditions and new social customs. (Azurmendi 2000, 313)

Azurmendi notes that, as a result of "traditionalization," authors such as Manuel de Larramendi and enlightened noblemen such as the "Caballeritos de Azcoitia" begin to develop, in different forms and degrees, projects and ideas that point to an independent Basque Country, one endowed with its own history. Furthermore, Azurmendi finds that the "othering" of the Spanish monarchy and state lies at the core of this traditionalization and independent-mindedness of the Basque Country (Azurmendi 2000, 320). As a result, the Basque enlightenment becomes the foundational—and thus also traumatic—moment that haunts Azurmendi's entire discourse. The first political subject to other the State according to an ideal ego, which does not correspond to the State's ideal ego, to nationalism, is the enlightened Spanish-Basque elite. This is a traumatic moment that, since it defies the modern State's narcissistic balance between ego and ideal ego, between State and nation, it also challenges the contemporary nation-state and its ideal ego. Azurmendi's discourse finds its traumatic kernel in this Basque historical moment, one that articulates an ideal ego that challenges the State, but nevertheless cannot be repressed in nationalist terms, for its political historicity is not nationalist, but imperialist.

Azurmendi's own traumatic denunciation of the supposed nationalist nature of the Basque Enlightenment, which nevertheless does not live up to the ideal ego of the modern State (it is not nationalist), points to the imperialist origins of the Basque enlightened discourse and ideology. The Basque Enlightenment reacts simultaneously to the decline of the Spanish empire and to the rise of an absolutist North European hegemony, which results in the triumph of the French royal house, the Bourbons, in Spain. The decadence of Spanish imperialism and the arrival of a new absolutist monarchy of French origin, which no longer favors Basque industry and economy, results in an agricultural refashioning of the Spanish Basque Country—hence its traditionalization. Yet, the Spanish Basque Country's ruralist reorganization cannot coincide with the project of the nation-state, since the latter is a result of the rise of industrial capitalism in countries such as England or France; it is rather an imperialist development.

As Emiliano Fernández de Pinedo adds in his recounting of popular uprisings in Europe during the 1600s and 1700s, the popular rebellions that occurred in the Basque Country against the ruling classes and the monarchy are not specifically Basque but European; their origins are not nationalist or anti-nationalist, as Azurmendi's analysis would require, but anti-absolutist. Furthermore, Fernández de Pinedo also recounts several attempts led by the nobility to generate independence in different parts of Spain, including areas lacking a previous political identity, such as Andalusia (Fernández de Pinedo, 75–76). Therefore, even the formation of an independent political identity, such as the Andalusian, does not yield a nationalist formation; it is rather a historical development internal to Spain's imperialist history and decadence. In the Basque case, and as the Spanish Basque Country's seaborne commerce and inland custom houses prove, its economy had been clearly Atlantic (Astigarraga 2003). When the Spanish monarchy began to lose its Atlantic hegemony, Spanish-Basque writers and ideologues noted this change, legitimized its results (the agricultural turn of the Basque Country), but sought to re-deploy this new economy in an Atlantic framework. For example, Azurmendi neglects to mention that the biggest success of the society founded by enlightened noblemen known as Caballeritos de Azcoitia, the Real Sociedad Vascongada de Amigos del País Vasco, was on the other side of the Atlantic, in colonial Latin America (Astigarraga 2003, 67–69), whence it derived the majority of the membership and economic support. In short, the Basque Enlightenment was, historically speaking, an Atlantic reaction to an Atlantic problem.

The fact that ultimately the Spanish monarchy and the church curtailed and destroyed this enlightened Basque project shows its non-nationalist nature. It is a modern and enlightened Basque response to an *ancien régime* crisis in the Spanish empire; it is only historically logical that the result did not follow the project of the nation-state. Yet it is also clear that, in the early nineteenth century, the Spanish monarchy did not manage to solve this Basque Atlantic problem, and, later on, Spanish liberalism also failed to assimilate it in its centralist project. The Basque Enlightenment marks the beginning of a Basque modernity that does not follow the project of the nation-state but attempts to give an Atlantic solution to the Spanish imperial problem of a shrinking economy that loses its industrial might, central to the Basque economy, and thus condemns the masses to a very new phenomenon: re-ruralization. It is this problem that then explodes with the Spanish civil conflicts of the nineteenth century known as the Carlist wars.

Azurmendi's nationalization of Basque history and its ideologies, his reading from the State ideal ego's position, explains why, when dealing with contemporary global immigration, he also resorts to a nationalist paradigm that disavows history, defends the State as the ultimate subject (ego) of history and politics, and thus ends up "othering" the immigrant as the State's other (thus ultimately justifying racism, violence, and social anxiety). The mirroring effect between State and immigrant other is perfect, not *despite* the fact that Azurmendi disavows the Basque problem, but precisely *because* he misconstructs Spanish and Basque history as nationalist problems. That original and traumatic misconstruction, which points to the status of Basque and colonial Latin American history as the "Real" in Azurmendi's discourse, supports and gives shape to his anti-multiculturalist defense of the State vis-à-vis the immigrant. Azurmendi also represses immigrant history and difference by forcing it into a nationalist history of assimilation.

Ironically enough, a very worrisome continuity emerges between the Inquisition's discourse of conversion and Azurmendi's discourse of integration. From conversion to integration, the State emerges retrospectively as the ahistorical ideal ego of politics, one that secures ideological continuity between inquisitors such as Avellaneda or Lancre and anthropologists such as Azurmendi. Michael Ugarte has incisively demonstrated that discourses, such as Azurmendi's, ultimately legitimize the ahistorical ideology of the Spanish state's ideal ego, traditionally summarized by the slogan "Spain is different." Given the Spanish state's lack of modernity and Azurmendi's own anthropological and nationalist treatment of Basque history and subalternity, it is only coherent that he go from joining ETA (Euskadi Ta Askatasuna) in the 1960s to upholding Spanish state power in the 1990s. Both alternatives respond to a nationalist understanding of Basque history, which ultimately represses Basque and immigrant reality and upholds the Spanish state. As Ugarte demonstrates, there is continuity between Unamuno and Fraga's ideology of Spanish difference ("Spain is different") and Azurmendi's defense of the integrative superiority of the Spanish state.

State Narcissism and the Denial of Multiculturalism

To conclude, I would like to emphasize that previous nationalist discourses on internal differences (such as the ethnic discourse on Basques) are being deployed in order to deal with new external differences such as global immigration. This redeployment toward external minorities, ironically enough, is exerted and legitimized by intellectuals, such as Azurmendi, who hail from one of those internal minorities historically repressed by the State. In this way, the Spanish state ensures a historical continuity in the way it exerts violence toward any form of subject formation and difference that does not comply with the existing State structures. Any difference is controlled by the State's ideal ego, and thus the State becomes the only beneficiary of any difference. The irony is that intellectuals like Azurmendi are precisely the ideologues who ensure a historical continuity that otherwise could have only been experienced as break or discontinuity.

The important ideological countereffect of State repression, which I must emphasize for the political advancement of multiculturalism, results from the fact that the attempt to ensure the continuity of the State's ideal ego over historical breaks, such as ancient regime/modernity, modernity/globalization, results in secondary narcissism: the State's withdrawal from contemporary global history into its ahistorical self. This secondary narcissism furthers the repression of otherness and difference, which, in turn, results in an upsurge of anxiety and irrationality among both masses and political theorists such as Zizek, Sartori or Azurmendi.

Confronted by a discourse that upholds State narcissism as a way to freeze the State's own historicity in times of globalization, my proposal for multiculturalism emphasizes the fact that the European state is also historical. Therefore, we have to underline the fact that the State's ideology of democracy, private property, and civil rights—which does not change even in the new European Union—is historical and must be rethought historically. The repression of new historical events, according to a nationalist articulation of the State's ideal ego (be it neoliberal or post-Marxist) can only further increase social anxiety; it will only lead to the radicalization of the State's secondary narcissism. Only the assumption of the historical particularity of the European state in globalization will allow us to move forward in search of universal forms of politics and interaction—forms that will allow us to look toward the future instead of folding back in a recessive secondary narcissism that freezes the European state in time.

Notes

1. In this chapter I will be using the word "State" capitalized in order to emphasize its transcendental character. When referring to a specific state, I will use it in lower characters: "Spanish state."
2. Hart and Negri (2000, 413) propound a return to Franciscanism as a model of activism in globalization at the end of their work. This semi-religious turn can also be considered a "barbarian" one in the sense that it rejects the rational matrix upon which Marxist philosophy has historically been built.
3. I have elaborated a theory of State melancholia elsewhere (Gabilondo 2002 and 2003). However, the relationship between State narcissism and melancholia, a complex relationship that might alter our understanding of both narcissism and melancholia, remains to be elaborated elsewhere.
4. Although in his later work Freud includes the ideal ego as part of the super ego, and therefore splits the narcissistic and repressive tasks of the super ego among its different sub-components, at the time he wrote his article on narcissism, he did not elaborate a theory of the super ego. Thus, I use "ideal ego" in its early formulation, and as also participating in repression. My use of ideal ego is closer to Freud's later use of superego.
5. Only some European nation-states have been, historically speaking, imperialist; this is why I write "imperialist" in parentheses. However, I would argue that, because of the "ideal" nature (prescriptive and critical) of the European nation, ultimately all European states are historically bound to imperialism, although some might not have the means to do so.
6. Europeans constitute the largest immigrant group: 361,437 or 40 percent (Ortega Pérez 2004).
7. He is also silent about internal Spanish migration in the 1960s and 1970s (South to North).
8. Furthermore, as a result of this discursive articulation, a new form of nationalism emerges, which is different from traditional nationalism in the sense that the Spanish community does not imagine itself (Anderson 1983), but imagines global others and, consequently, the Spanish community is imagined by this worldly reflection.
9. Azurmendi connects *sorho* (field) and *sorgin* (witch) (249). However, the etymological origin of *sorho/soro* is vulgar Latin *solu(m)* (from which the Spanish *suelo* derives), and therefore a recent connection between the two words is impossible, historically speaking.

Bibliography

Althusser, Louis. n.d. "Ideology and Ideological State Apparatuses." *Lenin and Philosophy and other Essays by Louis Althusser.* Trans. Ben Brewster. New York: Monthly Review Press, 127–186.

Anderson, Benedict. 1983. *Imagined Communities. Reflections on the Origin and Spread of Nationalism.* London: Verso.

Astigarraga, Jesús. 2003. *Los ilustrados vascos: ideas, instituciones y reformas económicas en España*. Barcelona: Crítica.
Azurmendi, Mikel. 1993. *Nombrar, embrujar. Para una historia del sometimiento de la cultura oral en el País Vasco*. Irun: Alberdania.
———. 1998. *La herida patriótica. La cultura del nacionalismo vasco*. Madrid: Taurus.
———. 2000. *Y se limpie aquella tierra. Limpieza étnica y de sangre en el País Vasco (siglos XVI–XVIII)*. Madrid: Taurus.
———. 2001. *Estampas de El Ejido: Un reportaje sobre la integración del inmigrante*. Madrid: Taurus.
———. 2003. *Todos somos nosotros. Etnicidad y multiculturalismo*. Madrid: Taurus.
Butler, Judith, Ernesto Laclau, and Slavoj Zizek. 2000. *Contingency, Hegemony, Universality: Contemporary Dialogues on the Left*. London: Verso.
Efe News Services. 2002. "Más de 60 antropólogos firman manifiesto contra Mikel Azurmendi." 5 August. Accessed through Lexis-Nexis database, 22 January 2004.
———. 2003. "Azurmendi reitera multiculturalismo es gangrena sociedad." 23 January. Accessed through Lexis-Nexis database, 22 January 2004.
Fernández de Pinedo, Emiliano. 1974. *Crecimiento económico y transformaciones sociales del País Vasco 1100/1850*. Madrid: Siglo XXI.
Freud, Sigmund. 1953–74. "On Narcissism: An Introduction." *The Standard Edition of the Complete Psychological Works of Sigmund Freud*, vol. 14. London: Hogarth Press, 67–76.
———. "The Uncanny." *The Standard Edition of the Complete Psychological Works of Sigmund Freud*, vol. 17, 219–259.
Fukuyama, Francis. 1992. *The End of History and the Last Man*. New York: Maxwell Macmillan International.
Gabilondo, Joseba. 2002. "State Melancholia: Spanish Nationalism, Specularity and Performance. Notes on Antonio Muñoz Molina." In Silvia Bermúdez, Antonio Cortijo Ocaña, and Timothy McGovern, eds, *From Stateless Nations to Postnational Spain / De naciones sin estado a la España postnacional*. Boulder, CO: Society of Spanish and Spanish-American Studies, 237–271.
———. 2003. "Savater and State Melancholia: On Spanish History and its Postnational State in Globalization." *Revista de estudios hispánicos* 37, 357–381.
Gibson, Ian. 2002. "Desagravio Pendiente." *El País*. December 17. Accessed through Lexis-Nexis database, 22 January 2004.
Goytisolo, Juan. 2003. *España y sus Ejidos*. Madrid: Hijos de Muley Rubio.
Habermas, Jürgen. 2001. *The Inclusion of the Other: Studies in Political Theory*. Cambridge, MA: The MIT Press.
Hardt, Michael and Antonio Negri. 2000. *Empire*. Cambridge, MA: Harvard University Press.
Kristeva, Julia. 1982. *Powers of Horror: An Essay on Abjection*. New York: Columbia University Press.
Ortega Pérez, Nieves. 2004. "Spain: Forging an Immigration Policy." <http://www.migrationinformation.com/Profiles/display.cfm>. Accessed on 1 January.
Pérez Garzón, Juan Sisinio, et al. 2000. *La gestión de la memoria. La historia de España al servicio del poder*. Barcelona: Crítica.
Riquer, Borja de. 1993. "Reflexions entorn de la dèbil nacionalització espanyola del segle XIX," *L'Avenç* 170, 8–15.
Said, Edward. 1979. *Orientalism*. New York: Vintage.

Sartori, Giovanni. 2000. *Pluralismo, multiculturalismo e estranei. Saggio sulla società multietnica.* Milano: Rizzoli. (Trans. into Spanish as *La sociedad multiétnica. Pluralismo, multiculturalismo y extranjeros.* Madrid: Taurus, 2001).

Ugarte, Michael. 2006. "'Soy tú. Soy él': African Immigration and Otherness in the Spanish Collective Conscience." *Studies in 20th- and 21st-Century Literature* 30, 170–89.

Woodworth, Paddy. 2001. *Dirty War, Clean Hands: ETA, the GAL and Spanish Democracy.* Cork, Ireland; Cork University Press.

Zizek, Slavoj. 2001. *Repeating Lenin.* Zagreb, Croatia: Arkzin.

Chapter 4

Constructing *Convivencia*:
Miquel Barceló, José Luis Guerín, and Spanish-African Solidarity

Susan Martin-Márquez

In Spanish bookstores, on movie screens, and in art galleries, a surprising number of cultural texts now focus on the human interactions that result from journeys between Africa and Spain. Many enumerate the pressing economic, political, and social problems that may motivate some Africans to leave their homes in an attempt to better their situation in Europe, only to trace the tragic fate that awaits those immigrants who fail to survive passage across the Straits of Gibraltar, or who arrive at the borders of a Spain that is represented as violently opposed to signs of difference. But it is possible to identify another tendency, evident in texts that prefer to emphasize the symbiotic relationship between life and death, mobilizing metaphors of construction as well as destruction in their portrayal of exchanges between Africans and Spaniards. Here, I will focus on the work of two visual artists who take on that project: the Mallorcan painter Miquel Barceló, and the Catalan filmmaker José Luis Guerín. While in his "creative documentary," *En construcción* (*Under Construction*/Work in Progress, 2001), Guerín engages in the more familiar task of representing African immigrants to Spain—specifically, Moroccans residing in Barcelona, filmed over a period of several years—Barceló reverses the usual South-North flow, setting up a studio in a tiny Dogon village near Sangha, Mali, where he spends the winter months painting and writing of his experiences. Although both artists depict the harsh realities of human existence, and are clearly aware of the depredations of racism, they avoid presenting Africans as sempiternal victims within a globally stratified geography of oppression. Rather, they present suffering as a more universal phenomenon, tied principally to material concerns: the material deprivation found in all societies subject to capitalism, and the fundamental materiality of human life itself, with its inevitable dénouement in death. Through the formal manipulation of the materiality of their artistic media as well, both Barceló and Guerín engage in what Paul Gilroy has unabashedly termed "planetary humanism" (2000, 2, 17), revealing that "[t]he recurrence of pain, disease, humiliation and loss of dignity, grief, and care for those one loves can all contribute to an abstract sense of a human similarity powerful enough to make solidarities based on cultural particularity appear suddenly trivial" (2000, 17).

Miquel Barceló has confessed that by the time he undertook his first journey to Africa in late 1987, he felt saturated with images. Although he had achieved a remarkable critical and commercial success—his work had been exhibited alongside that of Basquiat and Haring, and the Leo Castelli Gallery in New York had recently sold one of his pieces for $100,000 (Smith 2003, 76)—he felt the need to erase everything, to flee from excess, and turned to producing paintings that were increasingly white, increasingly "blank" (*Miquel Barceló: 1987–1997*, 1998, 18). Crossing the Sahara desert, en route to Mali, however, led him to a different appreciation of materiality; experiencing the hypersensibility characteristic of life in the desert, where the slightest movement or sound produces a tremendous impact, enabled him to comprehend the significant presence of the ostensibly intangible imprints left behind by beings and objects. In his gouache studies of the play of light in the desert, for example, the camels that are viewed from an elevated angle become indistinct clumps bleached out by the sun, but the elongated shadows they cast reveal their true substance (as in "Un chameau" 1988; "Caravanne" 1988); the same occurs with a woman who carries water on her head, for the jug and the female form, both symbols of life and fecundity, may only be perceived through their shadows ("Femme transport de l'eau" 1988). These are paintings that might evoke the cliché of the desert mirage, with one crucial difference: here the phantasmic images are inseparable from a lived reality; they do not substitute for or displace, but rather affirm, that reality.

A similar ecology of presence and absence is also evident in the work stemming from Barceló's travels along the Niger river in Mali. In the early months of 1991, while the nation was undergoing the revolution that would depose the dictator Moussa Traoré, Barceló undertook a 1500 kilometer trip from Ségou to Gao in a dugout canoe that African craftsmen had helped him to build; he was accompanied by his friend and collaborator, the Malian sculptor Amahiguéré Dolo. In the large format paintings produced after the trip, Barceló employs some of the techniques developed by the Abstract Expressionists (like Jackson Pollock, with whom he is sometimes compared) in order to pursue goals that move beyond representation. By spilling streams of paint onto the canvas, the Mallorcan pays homage to his artistic ancestors while fashioning a materiality that strives to incarnate, and not simply evoke, the world he portrays (Juncosa 1994, 14). In "Kulu Be Ba Kan" (1991), for example, once again water is a font of life: the fisherpeople of the Niger are vaguely individualized, but as a compact group, they appear to form an unusual aquatic organism (similar, for example, to his earlier "Gamba" 1980, or "Fishbowl" 1987), which absorbs its vital sustenance from the river. But in "Pluja contracorrent II" (1991), the water becomes threatening; here the figures are not distinguishable, and the boat becomes the center of a whirlpool, a black hole. Barceló wounds the skin of the painting, using a chainsaw (Régis 1998, 133) to produce gashes that mimic the driving rain. Despite the foreboding aspect of this work in which death appears imminent, however, the image also recalls Barceló's many different representations of soup, which according to Enrique Juncosa (1994, 12), function as "a metaphor of art and painting as nutritive material." Indeed, the "primordial soup," which is one of Barceló's obsessions, is figured as a dark vortex of fecundity, as the artist suggests in one of his notebooks: "The black cauldron of the world, lukewarm as the placental fluids. Prenatal. Full of bumps and holes: the world as an infinite cauldron where, slowly, this thick, black, lukewarm water adapts, covers caressingly this orography like a huge stomach ..." (*Miquel Barceló 1987–1997,* 1998, 166).

While the painting and sculptures that Barceló has produced in Africa continue to reflect his characteristic fascination with skulls, cadavers, and the processes of decomposition (apparent since his first public show, held at the Museo de Mallorca in 1976, which was entitled "Cadaverina 15"), now his work tends to underline the presence of life in death, something which was perhaps only suggested earlier. This new perspective has emerged out of Barceló's intimate *convivencia* with the Dogon, whose religious beliefs center around rituals of fertility and death (and here I wish to retain the utopian resonance of the Spanish term *convivencia,* associated with the still somewhat polemical idea that different ethnic and religious groups did manage to coexist peacefully throughout much of the Middle Ages in Spain). The artist's relationship with the residents of the village where he settled has also solidified through reciprocal building projects, in which the metaphorical construction of identity and community has been—quite literally—realized. After Barceló erected a small hospital for the village, for example, his neighbors labored together to design a house and studio for him, drawing upon their understanding of the artist's work habits and their own symbolic system. When the older men complained that their traditional social center, the Togu-Na, had deteriorated beyond the point of habitability, Barceló offered to restore the structure and repair the traditional carved pillars. After several consultations, Barceló was taken for the first time to meet the real leader of the village, of whose existence he had previously been unaware. The elderly man informed him that a new Togu-Na could only be constructed if someone died, and that he would offer his own death so that the building might commence; the leader did indeed expire, and the structure went up. It was then that Barceló understood that the villagers had decided to "open up their world to me so that I would stay on" (Coll 2000, 259). Barceló was also drawn into the elaborate funeral and mourning rites in which the Dogon wear their celebrated carved wooden masks and dance. As the artist has noted of the experience, "without a doubt this influences my work a great deal, but not in terms of iconography; I don't think that it has modified my images too much. It is something much more profound, which is even related to the idea of sacrifice, to the idea of cycles: death and growth" (Coll 2000, 261).

In 1992, as plans for the construction of his house in Mali were developing, Barceló began to undertake formal experimentation, incorporating the remains and the handiwork of termites—insects generally associated with the destruction of homes—into his new artistic creations. When Barceló discovered that termites had nibbled away at the sheets of paper left behind after his previous stay, he decided to convert the holes into a structure—into a skeleton—for his art. After using up all of the original sheets, Barceló began to recruit the voracious insects as collaborators, leaving new paper and cardboard inside large termites' nests, much as he had left organic material out to decompose for his earlier "Cadaverina 15" project. Barceló then supplemented his longstanding preoccupation with what he has termed "zeroes, hosts, white O's" (*Miquel Barceló: 1987–1997*, 1998, 114) with a new fascination for volume, initially evident in the portrait he painted of his wife Cécile a day before she gave birth to their daughter Marcel·la in 1992, in which her pregnant belly protrudes from the canvas. Thus, in his termite paintings, the plenitude of presence cohabits with absence, decay feeds life, and life shelters decay. This paradox is evident in his similarly themed "Dona parint" (1994), where a termite has marked out the "hole" of the vagina, from which a baby is about to emerge. In his painting of a market scene ("Sin título VII" 1994)—a recurring image in his work—the termite holes form the openings of sacks of food, the tabletops of merchandise, the jar carried by a shopper, the guts and the genitals of merchants and animals, and the swollen belly of a woman, who may also be with child. A politicized reading of the work would focus on the representation of the great privation that may characterize life in Mali, since a number of the apertures are strategically utilized to perhaps suggest that both stomachs and food receptacles are frequently empty. Yet as with the image of the woman giving birth, it is important to recall the painter's affirmation that only in Africa has he managed to mend the gaps that had characterized his earlier work, covering them over with "flesh" (*Miquel Barceló: Obra sobre papel,* 1999, 287). Here, in fact, out of a raw material signifying destruction, the artist constructs an animated scene; the visual echoes created by the termite holes demonstrate that material necessity motivates the great encounters of the market, the lively circulation of people, and the formation of a community. The imperfections, which expose multicolored layers of cardboard, also serve to prefigure the natural transformations, and perhaps even the destruction, that his work will suffer, an eventuality imagined by the artist himself in his writings of the same time period. Even so, Barceló expresses the desire that something of the fertile creativity of life and art will survive (as he writes in his notebook on April 11, 1994): "When the termites have devoured the museums. When my work has been reduced to dust. If some fragment should survive, be found anew, I beg of the heavens that it be an open papaya or the roundness of a belly ..." (*Miquel Barceló: Obra sobre papel,* 1999, 186. See also "Crône et fruit" 1994; "Papaye et mangue" 1994).

In order to produce objects that appear to have survived the ages, Barceló enlisted the termites' aid to create a false patina on his wood sculptures, an idea inspired in the fake Dogon pieces sold to credulous tourists (*Miquel Barceló: Obra sobre papel,* 1999, 186). Although many of Barceló's works celebrate the traditional markets that bring together people from neighboring communities, a number of the artist's works also allude to the impact on Mali of the global market, from the era of colonialism to the present age of tourism, foreign investment/exploitation (principally in the lucrative gold mining industry, from which few Malians profit), and World Bank development projects. The throwaway culture of capitalism, for example, is referenced in "Crâne du Mali" (1999), made up of a collage of consumer goods cast-offs: colorful but weather-beaten flattened boxes, with labels in English, French, Arabic, and Chinese, for small auto parts, light bulbs, concrete nails, cigarettes, thread ... Thickly painted over the center of the piece is one of Barceló's trademark skulls, casting an elongated shadow. As one of the artist's many variations on the traditional *vanitas* genre, this work signals the futility of consumerism, ironically even as it "immortalizes" the featured products, some of which are designed to stave off illness and death (germicidal soap, mosquito coils, expectorant, and blood pressure medication), or facilitate the achievement of eternal life (a Catholic calendar listing holy and saints' days). Fragments of product wrappers and ads are also incorporated into

"Enfants autour d'un bidon" (1999), where they make up the clothing of the children gathered around an oil barrel, suggesting that young Africans are already subjects of—and subject to—the globalized market. Since the children are using the container as a drum, however, Barceló's collage also underlines their creative appropriation of the detritus of capitalism for self-expression. Admiring the forms of resistance evident in the art of *bricolage* practiced by many Africans (Gaillemin 1994, 68), Barceló too recycles scraps strategically, noting in a 1992 journal entry, "I am writing with really small handwriting, to economize, I guess. Here I keep every little bit of paper, every bit of canvas. From old paint brushes I make small ones" (*Miquel Barceló: 1987–1997*, 1998, 116). The gesture is an inherently political one and is particularly evident in several 1995 pieces in which Barceló incorporates paper bills from the Central Bank of West African States. The previous year, the Communauté Financière Africaine (CFA) franc had been devalued by 50 percent, a measure that was designed to stimulate economic growth through an increase in exports, but which was initially quite painful for the average citizen. That the devaluation did little to improve the conditions of rural life is suggested in a mixed media sketch in which a rumpled 500 cent note with one end folded up represents a donkey cart, crowded with people (*Miquel Barceló: 1987–1997*, 1998, 194–95). More ambiguous is another mixed media study of two women, posed back to back, whose dresses are made up of torn-off lengths of a 5 and a 500 cent bill (*Miquel Barceló: 1987–1997*, 1998, 163). Perhaps the implication is that such notes are worth so little after devaluation, they might as well be worn; even so, Barceló includes a humorous reference to the still significant difference in value between the two notes, for it is the more slender woman who, requiring less material for her dress, wears the segment of the higher denomination bill.

Of course, incorporating bank notes—even devalued ones—into a collage is perhaps the sort of political gesture that only a "Western" artist could afford. Barceló has made a great deal of his refusal to cater to the market—"I hate compliments and money no longer moves me. As you can see, I no longer work for you, gentlemen ... And the sorry spectacle of the flocks of artists grazing in the shadow of the Ministries of Culture. Shame and damnation"—yet his work still enjoys brisk sales, and has also kept counterfeiters busy (*Miquel Barceló: 1987–1997*, 1998). In Spain, Barceló has met with both critical and popular acclaim (Juncosa 1994, 9), and in 2003, he was awarded the Prince of Asturias prize for art. But what of Barceló's work appeals most to a broad national audience? Which of his images do Spaniards literally "buy into"? One item that has fared very well in the bookshop of the Queen Sofía Art Museum in Madrid, which hosted a major Barceló retrospective in the fall of

1999, is a reproduction of "Pirogue bariolée" (1988), an early gouache of a crowded canoe, which is quite different in tone from the 1991 Niger river series discussed above. Here, the boat appears to glide effortlessly through tranquil waters; the harmonious relationship between the passengers and their aquatic surroundings is beautifully symbolized through the limpid reflection of their brightly colored clothing. Perhaps most moving is the outsized extended arm and hand of the traveler who waves joyfully from the back of the boat. Of course, this reassuring image of Malians securely navigating their own waters might be deemed more attractive by Spaniards who prefer to see Africans happily "in their place." However, Barceló's work could also be viewed as offering consolation to a Spanish public traumatized by the daily newspapers and television news broadcasts that depict the less fortunate African immigrants whose lifeless bodies have washed up on the nation's shores.

That many Spaniards may prefer more hopeful representations of Africans in general, as well as of their own relationship to immigrants from the neighboring continent, might also explain the critical and popular success of José Luis Guerín's *En construcción,* which won the International Critics' Prize as well as the Special Jury Prize at the 2001 San Sebastian Film Festival, the 2001 National Film Prize, and the Goya for Best Documentary in 2002. Despite the fact that documentaries tend to do poorly at the box office, so far this film has fared better than any of the fiction films on Africans in Spain produced over the last fifteen years (ranging from the first of the series, *Las cartas de Alou* [1990], to the polemical *Bwana* [1996], and the well-reviewed *Poniente* [2002] ["Base de datos"]), which typically feature violent encounters and failed romantic relationships between Spaniards and immigrants (Flesler 2004). Although Africans are not the sole protagonists in this largely choral work, it might be argued that the Moroccan day laborer Abdel Aziz el Mountassir functions as a sort of authorial spokesperson, for he is the only character explicitly articulating an informed critique of the processes of gentrification that are recorded in the film; moreover, his warm humanism, and the poignant friendship he cultivates with a Galician bricklayer, also make him one of the single most compelling figures of *En construcción.*

In 1998, shortly after a major exposition of the works Barceló produced after his first trip to Africa was mounted in the new MACBA (Museum of Contemporary Art) in the Raval neighborhood in Barcelona, Guerín and his crew arrived in the historic zone to begin recording the impact of urban renewal, initiated with the building of the museum itself. In his introduction to the catalogue for Barceló's show, Pep Subirós (1994, 13) hints that a parallel might be drawn between the artist's African work and the MACBA, describing the center as an important new cultural venue constructed out of a garbage strewn vacant lot. Yet Guerín's film provides a decidedly more nuanced analysis of the Barcelona government's efforts to "clean up" one of the most richly complex urban spaces in Spain. As a nineteenth-century center for industry that quickly became associated with a thriving—and oftentimes remarkably effective—workers' rights movement, the Raval has also been home to the infamous "Barrio Chino," or red light district, which has attracted a wide range of clients, from members of the Catalan bourgeoisie to sailors from the nearby port. Moreover, the area has also been a magnet for generations of immigrants; in earlier decades, newcomers arrived from other regions within Spain, principally Andalusia, Extremadura, and Galicia; more recently, they have been mostly foreign born, with roughly a quarter of the immigrants from Morocco, another quarter from the Philippines, and significant percentages of Indians, Pakistanis, and Dominicans (Sargatal 2001). In an artfully constructed film employing a studied montage of image and sound that works to erode the boundaries between fiction and documentary, Guerín immerses us in the daily life of Raval residents and construction workers (some of whom also live in the area), as numerous old buildings are torn down and a new apartment complex is erected in their place.

Like Barceló's work produced in Mali, Guerín's *En construcción* is created out of a raw material which signifies destruction and death: footage of the discovery of a sixth-century Roman cemetery underneath the site, which temporarily halts work on the project. Early in the film, cacophonous scenes of backhoes and bulldozers knocking down walls and moving earth give way to the hush of a single man wielding small trowels and a soft brush, as the perfectly preserved bones of a child's hand emerge from the dirt. Crowds begin to gather to observe the excavation. At first, they peer through small slits in the green plastic sheeting that covers the fencing around the site. The camera, situated inside the enclosure, captures the shadows that their otherwise hidden bodies cast upon the sheeting; as in Barceló's desert paintings, it is only those shadows which confirm the material presence of the onlookers. A different sort of excavation then ensues as the green plastic disappears, and the camera begins to scrutinize the reactions of different members of the Raval community—women and men, children and the elderly, Muslims and Christians, natives and immigrants from Africa, the Americas and Southeast Asia, speakers of Spanish, Catalan, Arabic, and Urdu—who come to comment on the bodies that have been unearthed. As the camera continues filming, a microphone records the comments of these viewers, who attempt to identify the remains and come to terms with their own relationship to them.

Here, as elsewhere in the film, sound and image tracks are carefully edited to create the impression that this nuanced representation of the negotiation of identity is unreconstructed footage. Miquel Barceló has stated that "everyone ... would recognize themselves in front of a skull' (*Miquel Barceló 1987–1997,* 1998, 165), and indeed, most of the cemetery observers see themselves reflected in the bones; as a mother explains to her young children, "that's what we look like when we die." While one woman prefers to distance herself from the remains—upon hearing that they are Roman, she asserts with obvious relief, "they're not Spaniards, then"—the majority of the other observers appear intent upon determining their own personal connection to the cemetery's bones, drawing upon their cultural knowledge of the diverse groups of people who have come historically to inhabit the Iberian peninsula. Linguistic issues are of particular concern to one man, who asks (in Spanish) if the dead spoke Catalan. Another group of men engages in a lively discussion in Catalan (subtitled in Spanish) concerning the Roman and Visigothic invasions, seeking out supporting architectural evidence in the arches of the surrounding monuments, such as the adjacent church of Sant Pau. Others wonder if the cemetery might be Arabic; shortly thereafter we see two Moroccan women in headscarves survey the excavation, and their (unsubtitled) comments are interspersed with fragments of another conversation in voiceover that includes references to Romans, Christians, and killings. When a young man who earlier in the scene had amused the crowd with his sense of humor exclaims loudly, "an ethnic massacre!" no one laughs at the joke. The Rwanda genocide is still a recent memory, and the war in Yugoslavia is an insistent if subtle presence throughout the film as television and radio programs communicate news from the front; for a number of the onlookers, the unexpected sight of so many dead bodies also enables them to draw parallels with the sometimes violent relations between different religious, ethnic, and political groups throughout Spain's past. Gazing upon the exposed skeletons, one elderly man laments over "the crimes that have taken place in Spain." Several older passersby prefer to focus on the more recent of those historical crimes, recounting stories of the violence during the Civil War, when Barcelona's nearby Paral·lel street was littered with corpses, while some victims disappeared without a trace in unmarked graves. Others, including a Latin American man with a small child in his arms who dialogues with a Spanish woman, speculate over possible connections to the Franco regime.

Indeed, while the specters of ethnic and other forms of violence are invoked throughout this scene, the different groups of people who gather to view the cemetery also manage to connect meaningfully with one another, oftentimes through recognition of the commonality of human suffering and mortality. One of the most interesting exchanges takes place between a talkative Catalan woman in a housedress and the younger of the two Moroccan women seen earlier conversing in Arabic. The first woman persists in drawing the second into conversation, gesturing toward the bones: "[T]here's no point in getting angry or anything because look at what we are, now. Isn't that so? Look at what we are; look at what we are." Her interlocutor, who initially appears lost in thought, is slow to respond, but once she concurs their discussion quickly gains momentum: "[Y]eah, yeah, yeah, yeah, everyone fits in the same hole" / "Everybody" / "Everyone; the rich as well as the poor" / "Well, there are no differences there" / "Well, there's no difference there" / "Good thing, good thing, because that really would be too much." While some of the other onlookers argue over the provenance of the remains and their significance, the structure of the brief dialogue here—in which each woman repeats, affirms, and expands upon the arguments of the other—reflects their ability to enjoy a brief moment of solidarity. These two women clearly find much common ground in their shared experience of class, despite their religious differences, and both seek some comfort in the observation that wealth is ultimately meaningless in the face of death. The Catalan woman concludes, "Isn't that something; look at how you live on top of the dead and don't even know it."

Throughout the remainder of the film, as the new building is erected above the old cemetery, a number of the film's characters meditate on the significance of this practice of living—both literally and metaphorically—on top of the dead, on top of the gaping hole. As in Barceló's experience building the Togu-Na, the gathering place for Dogon men, which was erected out of the death of the group's leader, construction here is conceived of as a rising up over death, as an affirmation or even exaltation of life, in an attempt (futile though it may be) to contravene the destruction of time. In a series of beautifully framed shots of flickering televisions glimpsed through windows, we see that many of those who live near the construction site are watching Howard Hawks's 1955 ancient Egyptian epic *Land of the Pharaohs*. Over the next few days, the film is commented, directly or indirectly, by a number of the characters. Several of the overseers, for example, contrast the grandiosity of the architectural accomplishments of the past—both the Egyptian pyramids featured in the film, as well as the nearby Roman church of Sant Pau visible in the background—with the haste and impermanence of modern construction. Even so, we see that the present day workers are proud of their work, which they undertake conscientiously and with good humor; moreover, as the project advances, they also build strong bonds of fellowship with one another. And indeed, another important reference to Hawks's film highlights the quiet generosity that the Galician bricklayer Santiago Segade has extended to the young Moroccan day laborer, Abdelsalam Madris, who works alongside him. Thanks to Santiago's gruff tutelage, the initially unskilled and somewhat uncoordinated Abdelsalam learns to lay a course of bricks on his own. Another more experienced Moroccan working with Santiago remarks on the younger man's newfound professionalism, joking, "Finally, Abdelsalam has managed to build a pyramid."

It is the moving friendship that develops between Santiago and the older Abdel, however, that is featured over the course of several lengthy scenes in the final third of the film. Santiago fails to live up to the reputation of his famous namesake, the patron saint Santiago Matamoros (the Moor Killer); though he occasionally responds to Abdel with a brusque "*cállate*" (shut up) or "*no me rompas la cabeza*" (get off my case), Abdel's warmly solicitous concern for his workmate's well-being clearly wins him over. As with the Moroccan and the Catalan women at the Roman cemetery, their conversation tends to revolve around material questions: the class struggle, as well as their more personal struggles with human mortality. In two of the scenes, Abdel begins with a series of Marxist meditations, and here it is evident that, as is oftentimes the case with immigrants, his educational level far exceeds what is required for the job he occupies. When Santiago remarks with resignation, "I'm one of those who says that capitalism existed, exists, and will exist," Abdel seeks to historicize the phenomenon, arguing that capitalism will not last forever; like slavery and feudalism, it too will pass. Although Abdel avoids violating Santiago's comfort zone—the Galician prefers not to talk "politics"—he does weave terms such as "class consciousness" and "alienation" into their conversation; throughout the film, he is the one clear embodiment of the Raval's celebrated tradition of left-wing activism. For his part, Santiago demonstrates an intuitive understanding of religious alienation when he tells Abdel of his frustrating sessions with a priest who was unable to explain to him the mysteries of the Holy Trinity. Although Abdel prefers to champion the religion of the poor—he elicits a smile from Santiago when he describes his daily prayer: "Well I sing the Internationale every morning"—both men acknowledge the temptation to turn to God during moments of weakness. And both acknowledge that the principal source of that weakness is the fear of death. As they work late into the evening, Abdel is disturbed when Santiago recounts that he once worked for the city government in a cemetery, and that he took a midday siesta in one of the niches he built; Abdel confesses that he could never take on such a job, even if he were unemployed. While we hear this exchange in voiceover, we see shots not of the two men themselves, but rather of the inky black shadows they cast onto the facade of the old apartment building in front of the construction site, skimming across the surface of the walls as the dangling light source rocks back and forth; again reminiscent of Barceló's desert paintings, these beautifully evocative visuals symbolize the ephemeral quality of human life. In another conversation, after Abdel extends his heartfelt condolences to a fellow construction worker on the death of his mother ("we all travel along that road," he notes), the two men recount their nightmares. Santiago has dreamed of being surrounded by heavy stones which then crush him (an obvious reference to his earlier practice of sleeping in a cemetery niche), and he has awakened panting, trembling, and sweating; for his part, Abdel describes the ghost who lurked outside his window in the dream that terrified him every night during his father's prolonged death. These "spectral" conversations, somewhat ironically, are the very substance of the life-affirming bond that develops between Abdel and Santiago.

In another scene in which they are joined by the younger Abdelsalam, the dialogue revolves around loneliness and its discontents. Santiago reveals that he spends many hours by himself in his flat drinking entire bottles of cognac; he is friendly with none of his neighbors, and although he claims to have always managed to hook up with women, he does not seem to have connected with them on a more meaningful level. Abdelsalam offers to take him out for a night on the town, adding that he knows several Galician women. Abdel then explains that because there are few bars in Morocco, men must woo women on the street or in the market (here Barceló's own depictions of lively market exchanges in Mali come to mind), and he teases Santiago that he might have been more poetic had he been born Moroccan. In a more serious moment, however, Abdel observes that "loneliness is crushing," insisting that the only solution is to reach out to others: "you have to learn to live with people." Abdel's use of the word *convivir* within the context of this conversation among two Moroccans and a Galician is highly significant. Indeed, the relationship between these three men might be considered the moral center of a film which advocates for the ongoing construction of community out of diversity. And although it might be argued that for many Spanish viewers, as a rigorously secular Moroccan Abdel is a less "threatening" and thus more palatable spokesperson for *convivencia* than a devout Muslim would be, his humanism is also imbued with a decidedly spiritual quality. In fact, when Abdel describes the thick flakes that have begun to fall as "the snow of salvation," Santiago warns him (in his Galician accent) that he's sounding like "*meio cura*" (half a priest).

Despite this somewhat idealized portrayal of the relationship among the workers and Abdel's optimistic claim that capitalism will not last forever, however, the camera returns on several occasions to frame the large rotating clock with the BBV (Banco Bilbao Vizcaya) logo on the obverse side that dominates a portion of the Barcelona skyline. While in other scenes of the film, the three famous smokestacks of the La Canadiense electric company—site of an effective workers' strike in 1919—seem to preside over the zone, this newer landmark is a recurrent reminder that for many, time *is* money; in the era of globalization, money does indeed "make the world go 'round." By the end of *En construcción,* as the building is being completed the "gentrifiers" arrive, and the workers and their concerns begin to fade into the background. As real estate agents usher prospective residents through apartments, we catch glimpses of Abdel, Abdelsalam, and various other laborers, but we will never again be privy to their more "private" conversations. Instead, we learn of the mundane details concerning the housing preferences of the relatively prosperous couples, some of retirement age, most younger, and several with children, who comment in Spanish and Catalan on the building's appointments. One of the agents is intent upon highlighting the "cultural capital" of the site: the historic Roman tombs beneath, the views of the beautiful Sant Pau church to the side. But not all the clients are charmed by the location: one middle-aged man complains of the noise from the nearby school; several object to the battered old façades of the buildings across the street, which one woman describes in Catalan as "ugly; ugly"; one couple expresses distaste at the sight of laundry hanging outside windows (the agent tries to reassure them that it's prohibited by law); and another ventures to criticize the appearance of the Raval residents themselves. (These last two comments are heard as the camera focuses on several children with soulful gazes perched on laundry-laden balconies). In her analysis of the Raval regeneration project, Monica Degen (2003, 872–873) observes that "metaphors of colonization permeate the official discourses": her interviews with governmental proponents and her analyses of the official documents concerning the project expose the underlying assumption that those who move into the neighborhood will "civilize the existing population with their new practices and values." Certainly, throughout this segment of the film, many of the prospective residents' comments would support this characterization of the Raval rehabilitation as a form of "internal colonization." It is telling, however, that Guerín chooses to end this montage by focusing on a well-dressed young couple with an endearing little daughter in tow who, unlike the others, does make a concerted effort to establish friendly contact with the "natives." Although the father is preoccupied that his daughter not get too close to the open railing, the mother encourages her to wave and say hello to one of the several elderly people who stand out on their balconies in the building across the street; when he fails to wave back, she explains to the girl in a disappointed tone that he has not seen her. This scene—near the end of the film—concludes in a touching way when the girl does finally capture the man's attention, and he smiles and waves back. This moment exemplifies the way in which Guerín's film continues to advocate for *convivencia,* even as it exposes the formidable barriers to the construction of community.

In her study, Degen ultimately prefers to focus on the residents' creative resistance to the renewal project. In Guerín's film, too, many of the characters' survival strategies might recall Miquel Barceló's depiction of the Malian practice of *bricolage,* as a more or less explicitly political gesture. Those who live in the Raval are constantly recuperating cast-offs and practicing personal forms of recycling: pictures discarded from demolished homes are rescued out of dumpsters for reuse elsewhere; an ex-sailor who is forced out onto the street over the course of the film takes great pleasure in his treasure trove of mass-produced trinkets, such as a hot pink snorkeling mask; another wizened homeless man borrows Abdel's makeshift lunch stove to heat up a meal out of a tin. And everywhere the energy of protest explodes in colorful graffiti across the walls of the neighborhood: the camera constantly pauses to frame the great variety of urban art, from the most direct of messages (a blood-red "E$PECULACIÓ" scrawled on a wall above the remnants of demolition), to the wistful images of suburban homes with flowers drawn in chalk by neighborhood children, to more dramatically original works, such as the spray painting of an enormous white rat with a building dangling from its mouth, and the omnipresent icon of the "OKUPA" (squatters) movement.

Degen (2003, 878) notes that residents of the Raval have indeed engaged in their own pointed forms of occupation, particularly of the open spaces adjoining the new contemporary art museum, concluding that "the gentrification and regeneration of the Raval is not as straightforward as we might expect ... In an active demonstration of appropriation, locals have renamed the square in front of the MACBA as the 'square of the nations,' reflecting the reality that the area has remained a port for immigration and not a middle-class enclave." That Miquel Barceló's African-produced art was selected for a major exhibition, however, suggests that even the MACBA's curators recognize that the space they now occupy— the Raval, Barcelona, or even Spain itself—has indeed become the "square of the nations." And it is in this space of intersection between the work of Barceló and Guerín that I have sought to identify an alternative perspective on Spain's relationship to the larger global network, and particularly to the African connection that resonates so strongly with the Iberian nation's own "multicultural" past. These two artists envision a new practice of *convivencia*, acknowledging that although suffering has all too often resulted from encounters between diverse groups of people, it may also form the very cement that bonds individuals together as they attempt to build a community based on the fundamental pain—as well as the joys—that all humans share. Like Paul Gilroy's study (2000, 27), their work contests the current emphasis on the incompatibility of the different racial, ethnic, cultural or religious affiliations that traditionally have been mobilized to define "humanity"; instead, both Barceló and Guerín have chosen to scrutinize the terms of our common material existence, in order to participate in the more utopian project of constructing a "planetary humanism."

Bibliography

"Base de datos de películas." <http://www.cultura.mecd.es/cine>.
Coll, Tónia. 2000. *Miquel Barceló: Insularitat i creació*. Barcelona: Assaig.
Degen, Monica. 2003. "Fighting for the Global Catwalk: Formalizing Public Life in Castlefield (Manchester) and Diluting Public Life in el Raval (Barcelona)." *International Journal of Urban and Regional Research* 27, no. 4, 867–880.
Flesler, Daniela. 2004. "New Racism, Intercultural Romance, and the Immigration Question in Contemporary Spanish Cinema." *Studies in Hispanic Cinemas* 1, no. 2, 103–118.
Gaillemin, Jean-Louis. 1994. "Les mirages de Barceló." *Connaissance des Arts* 510 (October), 63–69.
Gilroy, Paul. 2000. *Against Race: Imagining Political Culture Beyond the Color Line*. Cambridge: Harvard University Press.
Juncosa, Enrique. 1994. "De rerum natura." In *Miquel Barceló: 1984–1994*. London: Whitechapel Art Gallery, 9–16.
Miquel Barceló: 1987–1997. 1998. Barcelona: Museu d'Art Contemporani de Barcelona. [Translations of Barceló's notebook entries in French are drawn from the English version of this catalogue.]
Miquel Barceló: Obra sobre papel 1979–1999. 1999. Madrid: Museo Nacional Centro de Arte Reina Sofía.
Régis, Luc (1998). "Skulls and Tomatoes." In *Miquel Barceló: Il Cristo della Vucciria*. Milano: Charta, 123–159.
Sargatal, María Alba. 2001. "Gentrificación e inmigración en los centros históricos: El caso del Barrio del Raval en Barcelona." *Scripta Nova: Revista Electrónica de Geografía y Ciencias Sociales* 94 (August). Accessed electronically 31 May 2004 <http://www.ub.es/geocrit/sn-94-66.htm>.
Smith, Paul Julian. 2003. "Pure Painting? The Miquel Barceló Sketch Book." *Contemporary Spanish Culture: TV, Fashion, Art and Film*. Cambridge: Polity. 61–86.
Subirós, Pep. 1994. "Miquel Barceló: Return from Africa." In *Miquel Barceló: 1984–1994*. London: Whitechapel Art Gallery, 11–29.

Chapter 5

Galicia Beyond Galicia:
"A man dos países" and the Ends of Territoriality

Cristina Moreiras-Menor

> For it is by living on the borderline of History and language, on the limits of race and gender, that we are in a position to translate the differences between them into a kind of solidarity.
> *Homi Bhabha*

> To the question 'What is a border?' ... it is not possible to give a simple answer. Why should this be? Basically, because we cannot attribute to the border an essence which would be valid in all places and at all times, for all physical scales and time periods, and which would be included in the same way in all individual and collective experience.
> *Etienne Balibar*

The words of Bhabha and Balibar encourage reflection on the space "in between," and on frontier space, the limit of contact and separation, as a locus of decentered origins, constantly in the making and unmaking, from which we can approach the difficult theme of national cultures on the periphery. Such cultures, on the margins of the nation-state, have been obliged to establish a tense and traumatic relationship with the culture that exerts hegemony and reserves all possibilities of identity for itself. I am referring to those *other* national cultures that are required to engage in constant negotiation with discourses proposed and imposed as the only vehicles of national character and "essence" by the nation-state. It is this type of hegemonic national culture that establishes fixed frontiers from which clear narratives of identity are established, expressing and containing the defining features of what constitutes the "being" of the national subject, as well as the latter's specific location within the national territory. For such hegemonic national cultures, the line that emphatically demarcates the inside and outside of nationhood presents no conceptual ruptures: responding to a geographical frontier (which becomes mythic in its discourse), it is constructed upon a transparent definition of identity and difference. Conversely, *other* national cultures, those that are necessarily constructed not from presuppositions of sameness—like "Spanish" culture—but from presuppositions of difference (Catalan, Galician, Basque), assume only with difficulty this notion of a frontier as a fixed, univocal space of demarcation imposed without ruptures or leakage. Precisely because they are situated in the experience of the frontier, they question, resist, and transgress their relationship with a national culture that erases or expels their national difference to make it enter the hegemonic national narrative.

In addition to these tensions and conflicts between national states and stateless nations which different cultures encompass in their self-representations, a further tension derives from those repressive globalizing and transnational tendencies whose natural effect is to erase local differences through a constant circulation of those who cross, move, and modify frontiers (Balibar 2002). The rapid and unstoppable circulation of people, goods, and money has radically transformed notions of frontier, national culture, national subjects, and even identity and difference. This situation is intensely problematic not just for the nation-state but also, and perhaps more radically, for stateless nations in that the loss of borders tends to erase more emphatically local and regional difference. Nevertheless, while subjects cross, transgress, and modify frontiers, with a profound impact on the human geography of nations, nationalist discourses retain a clear position in regard to the limits these frontiers demarcate; for them, frontiers continue to be the checkpoints of a closed and well demarcated space.

It is in this context of cultural destabilization and, in my view, confusion, that I would like to reflect on contemporary Galician literature and the way in which it radically challenges the ideas of national frontier, national subject, and national identity. Galicia is a country that has long needed to negotiate its relationship to Spain—a negotiation in which writers from Rosalía de Castro, Vicente Rico, and Alfonso R. Castelao to Manuel Rivas, Suso de Toro, and X.L. Méndez Ferrín have fully engaged. At the same time, emigration has also made it necessary for Galicia to negotiate with itself and with those other nations to which Galicians have migrated: England, Switzerland, Argentina, Brazil, Venezuela, and the United States, to name only some of the most common destinations. This situation places Galician culture in an especially valuable position as a space of reflection on the idea of frontier and nation. On the basis of an analysis of a narrative by Manuel Rivas, "A man dos paiños," translated into *castellano* as "La mano del emigrante" [The Emigrant's Hand], this essay examines how contemporary Galician literature articulates the frontier. It explores approaches to difference and "national" culture through the recovery of displaced memories of a transcultural subject, the emigrant.[1] The emigrant's displacements—geographical, historical, mythical—reveal the fundamental tensions beneath the experience of the "national" and the European, the local and the global, at a historical moment characterized by (to use Balibar's term) the "vacillation" of frontiers, as national identity is placed into question.

The arrival of Catalan, Galician, and Basque literatures on the Spanish literary scene, particularly from the transition to democracy after 1975 and the entrance of Spain into the European Community, has meant a transformation in the discipline of literary studies, in terms of aesthetics, philology, and cultural politics. Spanish literary studies are experiencing an important reevaluation, in an epistemological sense (What is the object of study? Do we include "peripheral" literatures whose language is not Castilian?) and in terms of its scope (Should the discipline address literature exclusively, or culture more generally, encompassing film, popular culture, history, etc.?). This reevaluation is closely associated with rethinking the relationship between literature and the intellectual history of national traditions: not merely in regards to traditional Spanish cultural nationalism, but equally in regards to the national cultural histories of the peninsular periphery. Similarly, the literary traditions of the peninsula are establishing profound interconnections with the cultural histories associated with the diasporas of European and transatlantic Spain. Among these is the Basque diaspora to the United States, Galician emigration to Europe and America, and recent forms of mass immigration from North and Western Africa and Latin America. Peninsular culture has come to encompass writing by or about these new immigrants, for instance literary production by writers from Equatorial Guinea working within Spain. All of this is radically transforming peninsular cultural geographies, infusing tension and instability in a homogenous narrative of Spanishness (Moreiras-Menor 2003).

Many contemporary Catalan, Galician, and Basque writers address national and regional identity, indeed the question of Spain and Europe, not from a stable position founded on the homogenizing logic of the nation or supra-nation, but from the instability of frontier writing and the ruptured, ghostly, space of the border. Their writing responds to present experience and to cultural memory from the perspective of a subject (dis)located between spaces, a subject whose ontological potential lies not so much in a univocal essence of identity as in migration between identities and bounded geographic, historical, and cultural spaces.[2] These writers and decentered narratives are committed to the radical redefinition of cultural memory on the periphery as a means of establishing intellectual agendas reflecting on the present and the subject from positions *other* than those structured exclusively on the basis of the domination of nationalities, the nation, or Europe. This process of critical redefinition interrogates the very concept of "Spanish" and "Galician" on the basis of cultural representations differing significantly from the more canonical constructions of a unified Spanish or Galician national culture. The authors mentioned reflect on nationalism and the national subject from the conviction that culture as it is currently experienced, in the context of its globalizing and transnational contacts, is associated closely with a crisis of national ideologies. For this reason, one of the greatest anxieties in these writers' narratives is derived from the personal and collective experience that "home is no longer one place. It is locations." It is, rather, "that place which enables and promotes varied and everchanging perspectives, a place where one discovers new ways of seeing reality, frontiers of difference"(Massey 1992,15).

If anything characterizes Galicia, it is precisely its innumerable variety of displaced locations and "homes." Hence the experience or emotional condition of *morriña,* the sentimental cousin of Portuguese *saudade,* an untranslatable form of nostalgia for the lost homeland which every emigrant carries with them when they depart. *Morriña* has become the representation *par excellence* of the transculturated Galician emigrant in any corner of the globe. Galicia, in this form, can be found in the Basque Country, in Switzerland, England, and Germany, in Buenos Aires, Caracas or Rio de Janeiro, in New Jersey, New York—where Castelao writes, *amorriñado,* his *Sempre en Galiza*—or Castile, where Rosalia's Galicians were treated "like Negroes." Galicia is the land of emigration, and by virtue of this, it can be found anywhere. As John Dos Passos remarked, "Go to the ends of the earth and you'll find a Galician" (Rivas 1994). Galicia is an unstable land; the mist distorts and phantasmagorically alters its contours. Meanwhile, the clouds of *morriña* hide and erase its human geographies.[3] The main features of the landscape that can still be discerned are, for Rivas, attachment and loss. *Morriña,* nostalgia, and *saudade* derive fundamentally from the experience of a country which lives in and from the frontier, absolutely unable to demarcate boundaries which separate it from, or join it to, other traditions, nations, and experiences. The frontiers, the limits of Galicia, are not so much lines of separation or union as they are zones of contact, constantly marked and unmarked as and when subjects are displaced and relocated. Manuel Rivas expresses this frontier Galicia in the following way:

The Galician heads out into the world and takes on the color of the earth wherever he goes as a biological defence mechanism, like an octopus or a chameleon. To compensate, like a spiritual ginseng root, there grows within him the absolute certainty that the promised land is precisely the one that he left. And this happens to the Galician even when he travels as a tourist. (Rivas 1999, 262; all translations here are original)

Writers from Galicia, taking this sentiment and this "national" experience as a mark of their Galician identity, engage from the nineteenth century onward with the problem of the nation, national culture, and national difference. Manuel Rivas echoes this constant concern, associated fundamentally with the mark of difference from which a marginal identity, transgressive in relation to the nation-state, "should" be forged:

> It would not be excessive to include Galicia, a realm with a long history, a nationality recognized in the Spanish constitution, among those communities where the discourse of difference is almost an obsession. You turn on the radio and hear endless debates about whether or not there is a Galician school of painting, if the fashion industry in Verín is or is not Galician, if Christopher Columbus was Venetian or if he came from a parish in Pontevedra. Galicia is a fine topic of conversation for Galicians. (Rivas 1994, 38)

In a humorous but nonetheless serious tone, Rivas addresses a fissure that constitutes one of the most pressing problems of a nation, Galicia, formally recognized as such only in the constitution of 1978, and compelled to experience constant migration within and beyond its borders for economic, cultural, and political reasons. This fissure is not, of course, exclusive to Galician identity, but rather is characteristic of all migrant communities. As Angelika Bammer writes, referring to the works of the anthropologist Roger Rouse on Mexican emigration and his proposal for a new cartography based on the daily life of such people:

> To the Mexican migrants, in whose creative forms of resistance and transformations Rouse finds a model of such remapping, 'home' is no longer just the rural Mexican township that they leave to find work across the border in Silicon Valley, it has become the place of community that they create in the multiple and constantly changing links between there and here. 'Home,' for these migrants, has become a moveable concept, plurilocal—'a single community spread across a variety of sites.' (Bammer 1992, ix)

A similar process occurs both for those Galician communities remaining in their homeland (troubled by the rupture of family space) and for those who must leave, taking with them a part of their land (finding expression in the sentiment of *morriña*) and their memories. These memories, in order to be remembered, must be dislocated, displaced, contaminated, in the constant need to find a space that may be called "home." Those Manuel Rivas' characters who stay share in the *morriña* of those who depart: "When we said goodbye, of course we all cried. But remember, who were the ones who cried most? Those who had to stay on land. They were the ones who really had *morriña*, because they could not leave" (Rivas 2000, 15).

In the context of the need to reflect on a permanently and intrinsically displaced, transcultural nation, contemporary intellectuals and writers engage with cultural tradition and memory—as their nineteenth and early twentieth century predecessors did—to integrate it into a present still haunted by the specters of the past. Following in the footsteps of Rosalía de Castro or Castelao, these authors depict an experience of the nation in a way that echoes their predecessors. They portray a country without frontiers, without a closed geography, its territorial boundaries vacillating with its inhabitants' incessant movement, making it impossible to demarcate frontiers, be they external borders with Portugal, Spain, Latin America or the United States, or the internal borders erased with the presence of travelers from elsewhere. The point of departure for these writers then, is the continual motion of people on a constantly fluid frontier. For Xosé Luis Méndez Ferrín, for instance, this is a land whose people endlessly transgress the imaginary borderline between Galicia and Portugal (Moreiras-Menor 2003). The narratives of both Rivas and Ferrín (and the poems of Celso Emilio Ferreiro, Castelao, etc.) are linked by the idea that frontiers are spaces of transgression and resistance, continuously being dislocated and relocated. Both writers, and many other Galician authors reflecting on emigration, *morriña,* loss and return, transgress the idea of a boundary that simultaneously divides and unifies multiple geographical spaces, multiple critical regions, separating and uniting one culture from others. Ultimately, they resist the idea of the frontier as a fixed and immovable space, and create hybrid characters crossing them with every step, not merely in a spatial sense but also historically, mythically, and culturally.

The idea of an unstable geography permeating Galician cultural history becomes especially clear in the literary resurgence (*rexurdimento*) of the 1980s and 1990s. This resurgence seems to repeat, albeit with one fundamental difference, the equivalent movement of the last two decades of the nineteenth century led by Rosalía de Castro, a movement from which the anxieties of many Galician writers of the period after the Civil War also seem to derive. (Among the postwar writers who explore these themes are Neira Vilas, Carlos Casares, Camilo Gonsar, and Méndez Ferrín). Now, global market forces propel Galician writers toward translation and integration, always unstable, into a literary and cultural canon in the process of reformulation.[4] This means integrating the stories of the transculturated Galicians, of the inhabitants of a border zone that ceases to be purely territorial to become a broad space of conflictive encounters and dis-encounters, lost and recovered memories, pointing from their deep wounds to the emergence of spectral presences. These specters give shape, not always through words but through traumatized texts, to a present experience colored by loss and attachment. Their stories bespeak a cultural geography inhabited by the ghosts of hunger, emigration, loneliness, and civil war, in which the present is reconstructed not from a regional critique (nostalgic nursery of foundation myths, where Galicia is the perfect "home"), but rather from a critical regionalism. Here, what is at stake is not so much the origin of a sentiment or story, but rather the encounter between that phantom origin with the sediments accumulated over time that make it possible to envision multiple places and specificity and difference. These sediments are contained in a space of fusion, between residues left behind by tales of loss and an encounter and present experienced through alienation and a sense of not belonging. Regional criticism of this kind is able to "mediate the impact of universal civilization with elements derived *indirectly* from the peculiarities of a particular place ... Critical Regionalism depends upon maintaining a high level of critical self-consciousness" (Frampton 1983, 26).

Morriña, the sentiment that steeps the Galician in melancholy and returns him to a phantom, mythic origin, is handled by contemporary Galician writers as a form of discursive currency that signals simultaneously to past loss and present experience. Charged with ambiguity and multiplicity of meaning, it points both inward—to hearth and homeland—and outward to the space of disconnection, loneliness, and individual histories. It provides a space in which the possibility of return, and encounter with the lost object of affection, confronts its own impossibility: the frontiers between inside and out have been dissolved. *Morriña,* in other words, now deconstructs the notion of identity as a fixed space (Galicia as "home"), making room for the experience of outside as a substantial part of the mark of identity, always in transformation.

> This is in contrast to many readings of place as home, where there is imagined to be the security of a (false...) stability and an apparently reassuring boundedness. Such understandings of the identity of places require them to be enclosures, to have boundaries and—therefore and most importantly—to establish their identity through negative counterposition with the Other beyond the boundaries. (Massey 1992, 13)

In their narratives, Manuel Rivas, X.L. Méndez Ferrín, Suso de Toro, Susana Fortes, and others create geographies under constant construction and deconstruction, seeking to excavate the residual layers left in silence by histories of loss and encounter, emigration and return. They bring to the surface the identity of a culture that feeds precisely from the experience of disconnection and loss and from the encounter with the outside. The origin, the phantom home, toward which they feel a constant impulse to return, gradually reveals its ambiguity, and the nostalgia of which it is the object is gradually transformed from purely affective reason to critical reason.

"A man dos paíños" is a narrative, representative of this form of thought, which seeks to recover the sediments accumulated throughout a long experience of loss—unspeakable in the paralysis of *morriña*—in order to integrate in the present a nation which collectively forms itself from a permanently dislocated frontier. It is a story centered on the trauma of the civil war, a violent geography, emigration, and their effects on the Galician subject. Rivas constructs here a frontier space, in which the protagonist's memory draws upon his hybrid condition, containing his own memories and others, his own body and another's, fused and becoming one and the same. The narrative revolves around the relationship between two emigrants, the narrator and Castro. Like the narrator, Castro lives in London, works as a stretcher-bearer in a hospital, gets together with his Galician friends in a pub, and talks about both Galicia (land of origin and loss) and England (land of work and life). The narrator is irrationally fascinated by a tattoo on Castro's hand showing three small marine birds (*paíños*), a species which "lives on the open sea" (epigraph) and is "the sailor's last companion" (Rivas 2000, 14). The story of Castro and his Galician friends, who have lived and worked in London since the 1960s, is focused on their gatherings in an English pub to drink beer, talk about politics, and reminisce nostalgically about the Galicia they left behind. But Castro has a tense relationship with his place of origin, a relationship which, without being verbally articulated, leads him to be less critical than his friends toward England and to feel that the land to which he has emigrated, and which has accepted him, is also his own.

> You know what? I love my mother, who's all I've got left there, I love my ancestors, I love the house with the fig tree, which doesn't exist any more, I love the Bay of Orzán, I love memories, good or bad, but don't ask me to love my country. My country's the place where I work and they treat me well. (Rivas 2000, 16)

During the Christmas holidays, Castro and his best friend, the narrator, get ready to return to Galicia to visit their remaining family members and the places of their childhood, already transformed. During the journey to Heathrow airport, in a taxi driven by a Kashmiri immigrant (another displaced subject situated in a border zone infused with colonial and postcolonial memories) they listen on the tape deck to "some music from his country, a woman's voice, a melancholy coming and going which seemed connected, in an obsessive dance, to the windscreen wiper" (Rivas 2000, 25). In this moment of contact between subjects wounded by their memories of disconnection and loss, the narrator causes a fatal accident on the motorway by asking the driver, in a spirit of empathy and nostalgic memory, if he is happy in London. But as if suddenly rushed, the taxi driver's facial features tense up, and he begins to accelerate. The result, caused by the impossibility of answering a seemingly trivial question that in fact calls out to the depths of the emigrant condition, is the death of both Castro and the taxi driver. The narrator loses his hand and thus the accident also provokes a physical deformation that will give rise to a hybrid body: onto the narrator's arm is grafted a new hand on which he will tattoo Castro's *paiños*. The rest of the story unfolds in two spaces: the hospital where the narrator, under anesthesia after the accident, recovers from the loss of his hand and the transplant of another, and fantasizes that it is Castro's; and Galicia, where the community of Galician emigrants sends him with Castro's ashes to be buried by his mother and tossed into the sea. In Galicia, the narrator discovers and absorbs Castro's story, and acquires his friend's memory, as he gradually gets used to his new hand, alien and dead until now. The hand awakens with the story told by Chelo, Castro's mother, as she relates her son's childhood in minute detail one evening. She tells of the double loss of his father (first in a faked emigration, later in a faked death), the loss of his sister, dragged into the familiar but violent ocean while she was clutching his hand, and finally his going to sea. The tale is shot through with the cruelty of the sea; and with war, the reason for the loss of the father, who hides for years in a cave while his son believes him to be in Argentina, where an uncle—passing himself off as the father—writes him letters. Both the ocean and the war lead Castro to emigrate.

Castro's story, then, is told by a narrator who, like him, is a Galician emigrant in London. The temporal and spatial dimensions of the narrative appear fractured in a sort of coming and going between present and past, London and Galicia. It is interrupted by the brief, unelaborated memories of the friends from the pub, by fleeting, inconsistent references by Castro to the past, by the dreams and desires of the narrator himself in his anesthetic limbo, and by the mother's tale of a distant past (the war) which is also very present as the basis for the current trauma (Castro's story). This kind of temporal and spatial fracturing unfolds two stories that eventually converge in the emigrant's hand, which without being Castro's original hand perpetuates its memory in the tattoo of the *paiños*, becoming intermixed with the memory of the narrator himself. The first story is that of Castro, whose presence in the Galician community in London is admired and respected by his fellow emigrants. Castro makes a "home" of his hand, and indeed makes it the familiar space of the patients he carries on the hospital stretchers:

When the stretcher-bearer carries a patient down the waxed corridors, the sea birds caw with the wheels. They flutter around the patient's eyes when the silent stretcher-bearer replaces the IV tube or folds the top of the sheet back over his chest, a last gesture of support. In the first moments of anaesthesia, the *paiños* ride the rippled crest of the wave of sleep and settle on his eyelashes ... Sleep is deep, but not fathomless. In the immense clinic, when he comes out of the operating theatre and comes around, the patient begins to reconstruct his life with the stretcher-bearer's tattoo. (Rivas 2000, 18–19)

The second story in the narrative is the one that relates, from a displaced time (the present) and place (Galicia), becoming displaced throughout the narrative, the apprenticeship of the narrator. He learns to recognize himself, firstly, as a transculturated subject, a Galician who must learn to make dislocation the place of his home (as Castro and the *paiños* taught him). Secondly, he comes to see himself as a hybrid subject, bearer of *other* memories than his own, a subject whose origins (already forever transformed by the mix of different elements in his own body and experience), become consciously phantasmagoric, making his body and memory the place of conciliatory nostalgia.

This is therefore a narrative that combines a retroactive gaze of recovery—Castro's life—with a present gaze designed to make sense of a transformation in body and memory (becoming a *collective* memory through its encounter with the memory of Castro and his mother) originating in another time, story, and body. The return to Galicia, accompanied by Castro's remains and with a transplanted hand refusing to become his own, remaining in no man's land, exposes the narrator to a historic universe previously unknown to him. When he arrives in his native land, he carries with him Castro's ashes to return them to his mother and toss them into the Bay of Orzán. Far from content, he goes to Galicia as if asleep, seemingly without desires, with an alien hand that does not belong to him. His anesthetic dream in which he possesses Castro's hand, and his disillusionment when he wakes up, prevent the hand from being accepted. "That hand was simply plain. During the interminable days lying prostrate, the image of the bad-weather *paiños* in the refuge of the hand had helped me to overcome my restlessness. Now, there was nothing to see" (Rivas 2000, 38).

However, the return of both emigrants opens the horizon of memory, a memory produced only in the moment of return, without nostalgia, to a landscape disquietingly both familiar and alien, to a land both native and foreign. This return is virtually residual: one returns as ashes, the other as a body mutilated as the result of an encounter with melancholy (that of the Kashmiri emigrant), the return of which is an attempt to recover the sense of home that Castro's hand had provided. The story proposes this residual return—the ghost, emerging only in inarticulate memory—as precisely the kind producing the possibility of an encounter with a memory not previously narrativized or historicized. The narrator's gaze on Castro reveals the ghostly traces of inarticulated memory formed of silhouettes and fragments, light traces that amass in his words and his body, in the hand where eventually the Galician locates his "home." Through the mother's story, the narrator gradually perceives that Castro's own view of the world was permeated by memory, by past events and emotions, but that these were forgotten, although retained in fragments in the image of the *paiños*, moving with the rhythm of his hand. Memory becomes spectral through gestures that the narrator can now invest with meaning. When Chelo finishes recounting the episode of the death of Castro's sister, torn from her brother's hand by the sea, he says:

> But the memories came after us, sniffing our trail, lying in wait for years, prowling around at night, climbing up the ivy and the pipes, like weevils in the drains, snaking like jellyfish through the greasy guts of the city. You could hear them panting bronchially in the old walled-up chimneys of the rented rooms, in the dank corners of housing projects with Edenic names. They pursued us in the commuter trains, in the lair of the Underground, or in bus shelters in the small hours, until they found us again. Memories always came upon us. And they ordered us: come with us, step up into the carriage. Horses, horses! The horses of memory, galloping, galloping down Ladbroke Grove, with their plumes of ostrich feathers. (Rivas 2000, 52)

The present time of the first part of the story, focused on Castro and his hand, his wanderings through the city, and his conversations in the pub, finds echo in memories glimpsed between words, on the emigrant's hand and in his gestures, without being articulated in language. When Castro dies, the narrator, wishing to give sense to these unspoken memories, returns to Galicia. He does not want merely to carry his friend's ashes to his native land, but also to pursue the moment when Castro made his hand his "home," the home of all those who perambulate through the frontier spaces between life and death, past and present, homeland and abroad. This is a search guided at the same time by a sense of loss and a sense of attachment. In Galicia, the narrator will learn that when Castro had entered the museums of London to see their collections and take shelter from the cold, he had been driven by the need to see the painting of a storm (to connect with his past as a sailor). He had been driven, too, by the memory of his stepfather's words when he was a child, in an attempt to convince his mother to migrate to Germany: "There's heating, Cheliño, and it's free" (Rivas 2000, 65). In the same way, the narrator learns the significance of the times when Castro had stroked the dogs in the English parks, calling all of them Karenina, discovering that this was the name of the dog who had accompanied him when he was a child. Karenina had reached Castro by sea (he was a shipwrecked dog), and had gone away with him when his mother threw the dog out so that he would not reveal the husband's hiding place in the cave. Gestures (stroking the dogs, looking at the painting) and actions (buying chestnuts or cherries, calling all the dogs Karenina), not language, form unspeakable memory. *Morriña* is inscribed on the emigrant's hand, where memory is given a familiar space. Memory in turn is narrativized and made present when the narrator returns to Galicia with the ashes and listens to Chelo's story. As her story emerges, impelled by the narrator's question "Do you remember when he tattooed his hand?" (Rivas 2000, 43), the hand awakens, "stung by the truth" (Rivas 2000, 55), and the irrational fascination with the hand becomes a story, a form of knowledge, and a common memory. The senselessness of the present takes on retrospective significance and the emigrant's hand awakens from its death. Castro's own explanation of the reasons for his tattoo, empty of meaning when the words were spoken, now becomes part of the narrator's own memory and home. At the beginning of the text, the narrator recounts that:

> I marvelled at his hand. A hand that navigated the air, shimmering in the cross light, as if every finger were a reel still joined to the dart by a thread of nerve. Then it pulls back. It closes into a powerful fist. It spins slowly around at the wrist. And then it unfolds again, the fingers drumming in the air. The hand is a living being. It is the place where Castro is now, his viscera pulsating, his eyes lying in wait, his mouth gasping. (Rivas 2000, 13)

By the very end of the story, once the narrator has undertaken his return to Galicia, he has encountered Castro's memory and made it his own, his unknowing fascination transformed into the possibility of life. This life is patterned on the presence of the emigrant's hand, and its inscribed memory, the only form of memory capable of giving the narrator a full existence as frontier subject located in no man's land, a hybrid subject whose hand is his fellow emigrant's.

> No one was surprised in the Old Crow when I showed up with the picture of the birds on my hand. I had the tattoo done in Saints, on Portobello Road, next to the Salvation Army, where there's a poster with a bottle that says Eternity. Good liquor, yes, sir.
>
> When I was playing darts, and missed, which was every time, I drank a little bitter and murmured into the palm of my hand, between my thumb and index finger: Don't worry about it, Castro, don't worry. We can't win every time! (Rivas 2000, 58–59)

"A man dos paíños" is interwoven from multiple dislocations, and its narration gradually reveals the residues that these dislocations have left. The place of origin, Galicia, becomes increasingly a place that has disappeared, with its constant transformations and the fundamental loss of home and memory. This loss, and the narrative recuperation of this loss, is gradually modified, however, as the result of the encounter and hybrid superimposition of two bodies and two memories. The misplacement of Galicia as home, and its recuperation, is amplified by the reencounter with a history of violence and the geography of uprooting, a broken history and geography spectrally present in the sentiment of *morriña*. The loss of land, of familiar geography, the experience of these as expulsion, now gives way—through the narrativization of a story only possible in the return of a subject opened to hybridity—to the recuperation of collective cultural memory. This memory is partly that of the civil war, but also that of a land cruel to its own inhabitants, its national subjects, impelling them to unmake the geographical and cultural frontiers which contained them, and to construct, and deconstruct, the frontiers of what they had called home. *Morriña,* nostalgia, has made way—through its transformation from affective experience to critical reason—to the possibility of an encounter with a place of shifting frontiers now called home.

The narrator, with his emigrant's hand now grafted on by the recuperation of memory in the tale, unmakes the discourse of nostalgia by confronting it with the Spanish Civil War, and with death. Repeating the gesture of his friend, both absent and present, "I let [my hand] adorn my solitary speech from time to time" (Rivas 2000, 58). The narrator has finally been able to heal the wound that separated his arm from his new hand, which, before hearing Chelo's narrative, had no life: "everything was perfect ... from the first moment the blood started to circulate. It was alive, though with the life of a limpet" (Rivas 2000, 39). The other man's hand is now his own, forming an integral part of his body, and with it he reencounters his memory, that of an emigrant living on the frontiers, simultaneously his own and that of the other. This memory puts an end to the myth of territoriality (native land as the location of "home"), confronting the native land with its own violence and dislocation.

"A man dos paíños" opens up new spaces for reflection on local, regional, and national historical experience. Both in this story and in other novels and essays, Manuel Rivas deconstructs marks of national identity (in this case, *morriña*), giving habitation to its ghosts (its absences), and revealing the instabilities of the nation. He returns to the national past in order to narrativize the history of the absent *émigrés* who transport the frontiers of the land in their silent stories. Galicia is no longer the area bordering Portugal, Spain, and the Atlantic. Rather, it is formed through a mixture of those Galicians who depart and those who remain, all of them living with *morriña* and with multiple loss. The distinctive mark of difference that unites them is the convergence between that which is one's own and that which is another's, between reality and ghosts, history and its forgotten, nation and beyond. In this sense, Rivas's narratives tend to remain outside those historically constituted national narratives, dominated by homogenizing tendencies and ideas of essence. He proposes new reflective spaces that articulate a form of nationalist thought, open to what lies beyond, radically different from those constructed within closed and fixed frontiers. Emigration and return, loss and attachment, become the pillars of a new form of rethinking the "home," and that which is one's own, at a time when globalization—like folkloric Francoism before it—threatens to silence a regional cultural memory immersed in ambiguity and contradictions. This is the gift of the hand grafted onto the emigrant: heterogenizing difference, incorporating otherness, constructing reality from the frontier, from the crossroads that (un)form the border, and thus re-encountering familiar space. The frontier of the nation, of national subjects and cultures, ceases to be a line of demarcation and instead becomes a zone of contact, constantly mobile and open to otherness. Rivas leads us to rethink an outside that turns out to be the inside of the nation, toward the phantoms of violence which transgress its borders—geographical, historical, cultural, mythical—in their eternal migration, and the magical wandering of its inhabitants as they crisscross the territories of memory. Balibar affirms that the difficulty of defining the frontier derives from the fact that to do so is to delimit it, and therefore to demarcate new frontiers. The historical and cultural reality of Galicia, however, reveals how it exists simultaneously within and beyond itself. The uncanny, that frontier space between oneself and the other, whose fusion generates unease and anxiety, constitutes the very space from which Manuel Rivas rethinks Galicia from its migratory displacements and the vacillation of its frontiers.

Trans. Simon R. Doubleday, Hofstra University

Notes

1. This narrative is included in an eponymous volume that contains two other texts, "O álbum furtivo"—a collection of photographs of places associated with "A man dos paiños"—and "Os náufragos."
2. Consider, for instance, *Obabakoak* or *El hijo del acordeonista*, by Bernardo Atxaga, *El último azul* by Carme Riera, or Méndez Ferrín (1991, 1994).
3. Amongst contemporary writers, the works of Suso de Toro, María Xosé Queizán, X.L. Méndez Ferrín, Carlos Casares, and Manuel Rivas are especially notable texts in their deconstruction of a unitary Galician essence. Violence and cruelty in the landscape, history, politics, and economy allow these authors to reflect on the contradictions, ambiguities, and complexities of Galicia.
4. For an exhaustive and important study of the emergence of Galician literature in transition and its relationship to market politics, see González Millán (1996).

Bibliography

Balibar, Etienne. 2002. "The Borders of Europe." In *Politics and the Other Scene*. London: Verso, 87–103.
Bammer, Angelika. 1992. "Editorial." *The Question of 'Home'*, New Formations 17 (Summer), vii–xi.
Bhabha, Homi. 1994. *The Location of Culture*. London and New York: Routledge.
Frampton, Kenneth. 1983. "Toward a Critical Regionalism: Six Points for an Architecture of Resistance." In Hal Foster, ed, *The Anti-Aesthetic. Essays on Postmodern Culture*. Washington: Bay Press, 16–30.
González-Millán, Xoán. 1996. *A narrativa galega actual (1975–1984). Unha historia social*. Vigo: Edicións Xerais de Galicia.
Massey, Doreen. 1992. "A Place Called Home?" *New Formations* 17 (summer), 3–15.
Méndez Ferrín, Xosé Luis. 1991. *Arraianos*. Vigo: Edicións Xerais de Galicia.
———. *Arraianos*. 1994. Barcelona: Ediciones Ronsel.
Moreiras-Menor, Cristina. 2003. "Regionalismo crítico y la reevaluación de la tradición en la España contemporánea." *Arizona Journal of Hispanic Cultural Studies* 7, 196–209.
Rivas, Manuel. 1994. *Galicia, bonsái atlántico. Descripción del antiguo reino del oeste*. Madrid: El País Aguilar.
———. 1999. *Galicia, Galicia. Antoloxía dunha década de periodismo crítico (1989–1999)*. Vigo: Edicións Xerais de Galicia.
———. 2000. *A man dos paiños*. Vigo: Edicions Xerais de Galicia.
———. 2001. *La mano del emigrante*. Madrid: Alfaguara.

Chapter 6

Foreignness and Vengeance:
On Rizal's El Filibusterismo

Vicente L. Rafael

> The question of the self: "who am I?" not in the sense of "who am I" but who is this "I" that can say "who"? What is the "I" and what becomes of responsibility once the identity of the "I" trembles in secret?
>
> Jacques Derrida

I

In nearly all towns in the Philippines today, one finds monuments to the country's national hero, José Rizal (1861–1896). Most of these are smaller variations of the main monument, located in Manila. Erected in 1912 under the United States colonial regime, this monument contains the hero's remains and stands close to the site where he was executed in 1896 by the Spaniards for the crime of fomenting revolution. What is worth noting about the monument is its foreignness. It was designed and built by the Swiss sculptor Richard Kissling, who had won an international competition sponsored by a committee of American colonial officials and Filipino nationalists including Rizal's older brother.[1] Shipped in pieces from Europe and assembled in the Philippines, the monument depicts Rizal in a winter coat, holding a copy of each of his two novels, *Noli me tangere* (1887), and its sequel, *El Filibusterismo* (1891), both written in Castilian. The monument has since become the focus of official commemorations of Rizal's birth and death, as well as the shrine for various civic and religious groups dedicated to preserving his memory.

Yet the figure of Rizal, in this and other monuments, remains peculiar (Ocampo 1991). Attired in nineteenth century European clothing suitable for winter climates unimaginable in the tropics, he cradles two novels in a language that less than 1 percent of the population can read, much less write.[2] Even during his lifetime, Rizal was regarded as unusual, if not out of place, in the Philippines. Colonial authorities suspected him of being a German spy, because of his fluency in German and his praise for German schooling. Common folk who had heard of him or seen him perform medical treatments (he was a doctor) regarded him as a miracle worker, while others saw him, especially after his death, as a Filipino Christ.[3] The revolutionary organization, the Katipunan, took him as their guiding spirit (even though he himself had disavowed the movement) and used his name as their secret password. It was as if his appearance and name provoked everyone in the colony to see in him a range of references he did not originally intend. He had a seemingly remarkable ability to cross geographical borders (by virtue of his frequent travels in and out of the colony) and linguistic differences. Aside from Tagalog, his mother tongue, he spoke and wrote Spanish fluently and was adept enough in German, French, English, and Italian to translate works in these languages into Spanish and Tagalog. He also knew Greek and Latin, and dabbled in Japanese and Arabic. In this sense, he could be thought of as a figure of translation. Linking disparate linguistic regions and social groups both inside and outside the archipelago, Rizal's image was deemed capable of transmitting messages from outside to those inside the colony, and vice versa. The image of Rizal—its reference to external origins and foreign languages—lends it the character of a *lingua franca*. As with Castilian, the language common to *ilustrado* (enlightened) nationalists who spoke a variety of local languages, Rizal's image seems capable of permeating the entire social hierarchy. Both Castilian and Rizal's image seemed common to all because they are native to none.

We might think of his monuments, spread out across the archipelago, as traces that evoke the foreign origins of the nation. However, that foreignness has largely been domesticated. His monumentalization seems to suggest that he now belongs to "us": that "we"—Filipinos, not Spaniards—claim him as our own. "We" heard his message, which was meant only for "us," and we responded by rendering to him the recognition denied by Spanish authorities. His memory is now "our" property. One can, then, think of Rizal's monuments as a means of acknowledging his foreignness while simultaneously setting it aside. As with all national monuments, that of Rizal's marks his death, bringing "we" who recognize him into a relation with his absence. Yet his death, which is another dimension of his foreignness, need no longer exercise pressure on the nation's self-conception. If Rizal's strangeness is still palpable in the Philippines today, there is a generalized sense that it has nonetheless been contained, buried, as it were, in the popular assumption that he is the "father" of the nation, the "first Filipino."

In a similar vein, it is rare today for Filipinos to read his novels in their original form. These have long been translated into English and other local vernaculars. In 1965, as part of the so-called Rizal Law, over the objections of the Catholic Church, Congress required the reading of the novels among college students in English (the linguistic medium of instruction in schools), which further dampened interest in the originals. In more recent years, film, operatic, and comic book versions of the novels have tended to displace the novels themselves altogether. The monumentalization of his novels has effected the flattening out of their heterogeneous language and the stereotyping by Filipino readers of the novels' characters as stand-ins for the various political positions opposed or held by its author. In the same vein, the literary nature of his books has been summarily cast as being "realist," or "derivative" of Spanish and French models, as social documents for the late nineteenth century, or as gospel sources of nationalist wisdom.

As with Rizal's image, the novels have foreign origins. The *Noli* and the *Fili,* as they are popularly known, were written while Rizal traveled through Europe. The first was composed mostly in Paris and published in Berlin in 1886; the second was begun in London, continued in Biarritz, Paris, Brussels, and finally published in Ghent in 1891. While monetary considerations forced Rizal to find the cheapest publisher, there is nonetheless the sense here of nationalist writings emanating from the unlikeliest places beyond the empire, paralleling the primary nationalist newspaper, *La Solidaridad,* (published in Barcelona and Madrid from 1889–1895). Both novels were declared subversive by Spanish authorities, and their transport and possession was criminalized. Rizal and his friends had to arrange for their clandestine delivery to the Philippines. They were smuggled in, usually from Hong Kong, and bribes were routinely paid to customs officials to allow for their entry (Schumacher 1973, 82, 235).

The conditions under which the novels were composed and circulated further underlines their strangeness. They were written outside colonial society, addressed to an audience absent from the author's immediate milieu. Their clandestine circulation required the corruption of officials while their possession, declared a crime, resulted in imprisonment, and their author was himself exiled in the southern Philippines for four years and eventually executed. Thus were the alien origins of the *Noli* and the *Fili* conjoined to the putative criminality of their effects. Indeed, it is this connection of foreignness with criminality that is thematized most persistently in the second novel. In this essay, I turn to *El Filibusterismo* in order to inquire about this link. It is, as we shall see, a novel about messages to which responses, detained by the dead, have long been overdue.[4]

II

Along with a few other nationalists, Rizal entertained from an early stage the possibility of Philippine separation from Spain as an alternative to the political assimilation favored by most of the other *ilustrados*. As early as 1888, he was complaining in several letters that Spain was simply "unwilling to listen."[5] Within months of finishing his second novel in 1891, he left Europe for Hong Kong and then moved on to the Philippines, convinced that the struggle should be waged there. He would follow the train of his words, returning as it were to the scene of the crime.

We might ask: what was the manner of this return and the nature of the crime? We get a sense of both in Rizal's dedication of the *Fili:* "To the Memory of the priests Don Mariano Gómez, Don José Burgos, and Don Jacinto Zamora," it begins, referring to the three Filipino (i.e., non-peninsular Spaniard) secular priests who were falsely implicated in a local uprising in 1872 and unjustly executed by Spanish authorities.[6] Having earlier criticized the Spanish friars' monopoly over the colony's wealthiest parishes in the 1860s, these three secular priests had also challenged Spanish assumptions about the inferiority of natives and *mestizos* and the inability of non-Spanish secular priests to run their own parishes. Thus, they were regarded by *ilustrado* nationalists as their precursors. Representing proto-nationalist instances of resistance to rule by the friars, regarded as the most repressive aspect of colonial rule, the fate of Fathers Gómez, Burgos, and Zamora also signified assimilationist aspirations gone wrong.

In recalling their deaths, Rizal commemorates their innocence. He "in no way acknowledges [their] guilt;" instead he holds Spain "culpable for your deaths." "Let these pages serve as a belated wreath upon your unknown graves; and may all who … attack your memory find their hands soiled with your blood!" Like a gravestone, the book's dedication marks the death of Filipino fathers. Their execution had made a lasting impression on Rizal when he was a young student in Manila. He wrote to friends later on that had it not been for Gómez, Burgos, and Zamora, he would have been a Jesuit (Schumacher 1973, 29). In their deaths, Rizal hears a message and is compelled to respond. Mourning their deaths leads him not only to mark their "unknown graves." It also leads him to utter a threat: that those who attack your memory will be soiled in your blood. They, too, should be made to suffer your fate. The deaths of the Filipino priests instill in Rizal a desire for vindication. The dedication thus brings together mourning and revenge as two parts of the same reply that he directs to the fathers: those who are dead and those who are guilty. Writing becomes a practice of gathering and giving back what one has received. In the *Fili,* returning a message means remembering what was said and responding in kind.

But again we might ask: who determines the nature of the message and decides the forms of its return? There is, of course, the author himself, Rizal. Yet in the *Fili,* the author is shadowed by another agent who returns the call of death: the figure of the *filibustero.* In the book's epigraph—what we might think of as its other dedication—Rizal quotes his Austrian friend and nationalist sympathizer Ferdinand Blumentritt, who writes:

> It is easy to suppose that a *filibustero* has bewitched (*hechizado*) in secret the league of friars and reactionaries, so that unconsciously following his inspirations, they favor and foment that politics which has only one end: to extend the ideas of *filibusterismo* all over the country and convince every last Filipino that there exists no other salvation outside of that of the separation from the Motherland. (Rizal 1891, unpaginated; all translations from Rizal are my own)

One of the definitions of a *filibustero* is that of a pirate, hence a thief. But as one who, we might say in English, "filibusters," he is also one who interrupts parliamentary proceedings, smuggling his own discourse into those of others. In either case, we can think of the *filibustero* as an intruder, breaking and entering into where he does not properly belong, and doing so by surprise and often in disguise. Small wonder then that by the latter nineteenth century, *filibustero* was also glossed as "subversive," connoting a disruptive presence, a figure who—by word or deed—suddenly and surreptitiously undercuts the social order. Thus nationalists were referred to by Spanish authorities as *filibusteros.* Their wish to speak and disseminate Castilian as a route to economic and social reform challenged the friar sanctioned practice of dissuading the majority of natives from learning the language. The friars, from the beginnings of colonization in the sixteenth century, had administered God's Word in the numerous local vernaculars. They also translated native languages into Castilian for the benefit of the colonial state and their clerical orders. Thus they had long enjoyed the role of privileged mediators between the metropolis and the colony. For Filipino nationalists to seek to spread Castilian to the populace would in effect undercut the mediating authority of the friars. In their desire to communicate in Castilian, *ilustrado* nationalists were asking to be recognized as other than what colonial authorities regarded them to be: the equal of Spaniards. Instead, Spanish authorities, prodded by the friars, saw nationalists to be speaking out of place. Speaking in a language that did not belong to them, they appeared alien to and disruptive of the colonial order.[7]

The political implications that grow out of linguistic disruptions take on a particular inflection in Rizal's citation of Blumentritt. The *filibustero* here is put forth as a kind of sorcerer, a malevolent medium. Later on, in his preface, Rizal will refer to the *filibustero* as a "phantom" (*fantasma*) who roams about, "haunting" (*amedrentado*) the populace. Its presence is thus a secret, so that one may be in contact with a *filibustero* without being aware of it. The power of the *filibustero* lies in his ability to make you think what he wants you to without your knowledge. Possessed by the thoughts of an other you cannot even recognize, you begin to act in ways you did not intend. Thus, the malevolence of the *filibustero* consists of separating you from your own thoughts. And in a colonial context, such a separation can bring you to cut yourself off from the mother country, that is, to mistake separation from Spain for independence.

While the *filibustero* is thought to subvert one's control over one's thoughts and that of the mother country over her sons and daughters, it also insinuates its way to the top of the colonial hierarchy, inserting itself where it does not belong and causing authority to act in ways that go against its interests. The *filibustero* then is a kind of foreign presence who exercises an alienating effect on all those it comes in contact with. Being out of place, it can travel all over the place, promoting the misrecognition of motives and words. For this reason, we can think of the *filibustero*'s foreignness as the force of a transmission that troubles social hierarchy. It is the power of translation that the *filibustero* possesses— the capacity to cross boundaries and put diverse groups in contact with one another—but translation in the service of something outside of colonial society.

What is the "outside" that the *filibustero* works for? Independence, perhaps? Rizal himself remained uncertain. Until the end of his life, he never explicitly favored a final break with Spain even though he considered political assimilation to be doomed. We can think of the *Fili* as the site within which he rehearsed this founding ambivalence of nationalist sentiment. The novel is a record of hesitations and anxieties raised by the failure of assimilation, giving rise to the specters of separation. The figure of the *filibustero* was its medium for tracking and trafficking in the emergence, spread, and containment of such anxieties. It is this fundamentally unsettling nature of the *filibustero* as both medium and message that infects (as it were) both the author and his characters. I try to trace the spread of this infection below.

III

All commentaries on the *El Filibusterismo* of which I am aware rank it as an "inferior," less polished work compared to Rizal's first novel, *Noli me tangere*. For these commentators the *Fili* lacks the narrative coherence and cheerful humor of its predecessor and has polemic pronouncements and sarcastic laughter in its place (Guerrero 1963, 271–285; Schumacher 1973, 235–243; Mojares 1983, 137–150). In writings about nationalism and Rizal, the *Fili* is quickly passed over, its complications put to one side.

Such complications begin with the absence of a single narrative line. Instead, the novel is loosely woven around two plots, from which several others emerge. One concerns the attempts, ultimately foiled, of an association of university students to establish a self-supporting academy for the teaching of Castilian in Manila, autonomous from friar control. The other plot deals with the story of Simoun, a mysterious jeweler of unknown origins who, having ingratiated himself with the Governor General, the friars and local officials, uses his wealth to spread corruption in the colony in the hope of intensifying general misery and hastening a popular uprising. An important twist to this story is this: Simoun is actually Crisóstomo Ibarra, the protagonist of the first novel, who was thought to be dead. Persecuted in the earlier novel for his reformist ideals and his love for María Clara, the illegitimate daughter of a Dominican priest and a devout native woman who had been unable to conceive with her feckless Chinese *mestizo* husband, he flees the country. In the *Fili*, Ibarra returns years later disguised as Simoun the wealthy merchant intent on rescuing María Clara from her seclusion in the convent and orchestrating a revolt to wreck revenge on all those he deems responsible for ruining his future.

Both plots end in failure. The students' petition for a Spanish academy is denied. They are subsequently blamed for the mysterious appearance of posters deemed "subversive" at the university. Many are rounded up and imprisoned and although they are all eventually released, they retreat into an embittered cynicism. At least one, Basilio, is drawn to Simoun's plot. However, Simoun's plans also unravel. He discovers that María Clara has died and his plans for instigating an uprising are discovered by colonial authorities. He flees to the rural retreat of Padre Florentino, an older Filipino priest from the generation of Gómez, Burgos, and Zamora. In the end, nothing is resolved. Simoun dies of his wounds and disappointment and Rizal, speaking through Padre Florentino, launches on what by then was a familiar polemic about the necessity of education, virtue, and sacrifice in confronting oppression and injustice. The novel is remarkably inconclusive. Its plots do not add up to a political program—in fact such a program is studiously avoided. Rather, disillusionment takes on almost baroque proportions. What remains in the end is the author's voice speaking through Padre Florentino asking the "youth" to come forth and sacrifice themselves for the nation. And after hurling them to the ocean, he addresses the jewels of Simoun, which the latter used for corrupting officials and buying weapons for his uprising, commending them to the care of "Nature" for use in more noble purposes in the future.

What interests me are the ways by which this open-endedness and negativity produce a space for the emergence of an authorial voice addressing an absent audience. In between the twisting and twinning of these plots, Rizal constructs a series of scenes around particular characters. Many of these have only the most tenuous connections to the narratives. Instead, they bear out another kind of emplotment. In these scenes, Rizal obsessively details the recurrence and effects of the foreign detached from its origins in hierarchy. What emerges in these foreign encounters is a certain politics, one colored by anticipation, shame, and resentment, one that envisions a response through translation. It is my contention that the receipt of the foreign, its recognition and its return, is precisely what marks the domestication of nationalism as specifically "Filipino." Additionally, the failure of recognition and the deferral of the return are built into such a politics, one whose translation requires a voice whose appearance seems new. Such would be the voice of the author.

One place to see the emergence of the foreign and its domestication is in the classroom. Rizal writes at length about education in his political essays. For Rizal, education is the key to reformulating social relations. It places youth in the position of receiving and realizing a future. Through education, the future comes across as a promise; hence, a kind of performative utterance directed at the youth. But, as we saw, the friars who controlled the educational institutions in the colony are the force that blocks this speech from reaching its destination. In a chapter entitled "La Clase de Fisica" (The Physics Class, 98–108), the novel shows how this blockage is produced. Rizal describes the conditions at a Dominican university in the following way:

> No one went to class in order to learn, but only to avoid getting marked absent. The class is reduced to reciting lessons from memory, reading the book and once in a while, answering one or other trivial, abstract, profound, cunning, enigmatic questions. True, there was no shortage of little sermons (*sermonitas*)—they were always the same—about humility, submission, respect for the religious ... (1891, 89).

In class, then, one's main concern was to avoid being marked absent, yet one's presence amounted to little since it entailed the mechanical recitation of texts and the occasional answer to questions as trivial as they were abstract. Education was a matter of hearing what one has already heard before, such as the *sermonitas* on submission and humility, just as it required the repetition of formulaic answers to predictable demands. Nothing truly new was allowed to emerge, and in this sense, the classroom was an extension of the church. Hence, for example, the scientific instruments in the physics laboratory were never used by the students and were taken out only on rare occasions to impress important visitors, "like the Holy Sacrament to the prostrated faithful: look at me but do not touch" (Rizal 1891, 90). In a similar vein, to memorize and repeat the words of a textbook is to turn oneself into a vessel for the passage of the words of authority. One is not expected to make these words one's own, but rather to submit to their force and bear them back to their source as the friar stood by and measured one's fidelity. Schooling did not lead to a future but to the perpetuation of familiar forms of servility. It was meant to maintain students in their stupidity.

Yet, what made the classroom different from the church was that students were required to recite individually. They could not receive a grade and pass the course, Rizal writes, until they had been recognized (*ser conocido*) and called upon by the professor. By recognizing the student, it is as if the professor sees in him a capacity to speak up. At the same time, that capacity constitutes a potential for disruption. In speaking up, the student might also talk back; in repeating the textbook, he might make a mistake and thus utter something uncalled for and unexpected. Such possibilities make the classroom a volatile arena for the reiteration of authority, a place for the potential exposure of authority's limits.

In the physics class, Rizal describes the professor, Padre Millon, as one who "was not of the common run." He knew his physics, but the demands of colonial education required that he assume his role in the ritual of the classroom. Having called the roll, he begins calling on students to recite the day's lesson "word for word." Rizal describes their response: "The phonographs (*los fonógrafos*) played, some well, others bad; others stuttered and were prompted. He who recited without a mistake earned a good mark while he who committed more than three mistakes a bad one" (Rizal 1891, 92).

Used as a medium of instruction, Castilian here has a curious role. In speaking like "phonographs," students mechanically reproduce the lesson. They respond in a language that is wholly exterior to them. Castilian thus comes across not as a means of self-expression but of self-evacuation. One who recites Castilian phonographically demonstrates, among other things, that this language has no place in one's mind. One speaks it without knowing what one is saying, so that it seems to be merely passing through one's body. Drained of intelligibility and detached from intentionality, Castilian thus becomes truly foreign to the students. In speaking it, they become mediums for the reproduction of its foreignness. One's capacity to reproduce Castilian earns one a mark. One's presence is noted down and one is left alone by the friar as he moves on to call another student. Their grade signifies their submission to the demand for repetition. However, repetition signifies not only their acknowledgement of the professor's authority; it also conveys their distance from his language. For speaking Castilian in this context requires its separation from the rest of one's thoughts. That is, it entails the recognition of the foreign as foreign, as that which belongs to someone else and over which one does not have a proper claim. In speaking up to authority, one acknowledges the sheer passage of the latter's language through oneself. One thus confronts Castilian as that which cannot be appropriated: the materialization of an alien presence that periodically assails one and which one periodically is required to fend off. When called to recite, one speaks Castilian in order to put it out of mind in the hope of sending it back where it came from.

However, these recitations are never smooth. Both students and professors find themselves in the midst of other signs that can at times interrupt the circulation of the language of authority. Rizal's interest lies precisely in recording the static against which these signals take place. Amid the tedium of recitations, the friar-professor scans the faces of his students looking to catch someone unprepared, "wanting to startle him" (*quiso asustarle*). He spies on a "fat boy with a sleepy face and hair stiff and hard like the bristles of brush, yawning almost to the point of dislocating his jaw, stretching himself, extending his arms as if he were on his bed." The professor zeroes in on the unsuspecting student:

> *Oy!* you (*tú*), sleepy head, *aba!* What! And lazy, too! Maybe (*seguro*) you don't know the lesson, *ja?!* Padre Million not only addressed all the students informally (*tuteaba*) like a good friar, but also spoke to them in the language of the marketplace (*lengua de tienda*) ... The interpellation, instead of offending the class, amused them and many laughed: this was something that happened routinely. Nevertheless, the sleepy head did not laugh; he rose up with a jump, rubbed his eyes, and like a steam engine gyrating a phonograph, began to recite ... (Rizal 1891, 92)

The boredom of one student triggers the interest of the professor. The latter sees in the former an opportunity to break the monotony of the class. It works. He surprises the student much to the delight and laughter of his classmates. What is worth noting here is the mode of the friar's speech. He not only speaks down to the students, addressing them individually as *tú* rather than with the more respectful *usted*. More significant, he speaks to the class in *lengua de tienda,* the language of the marketplace, or what has also been referred to as *español de la cocina,* kitchen Spanish.[8] Consisting of an unstable mix of Castilian and Tagalog, it is a language spoken to and at the lower end of the social hierarchy. In addressing his students in this language, the friar momentarily disrupts the ritual of recitation and turns the classroom into another place, closer to that of the market than the church.

Hearing this linguistic disruption, one which was a matter of daily routine, the other students laugh. In their laughter, they find themselves occupying a different position. No longer are they anxious and expectant targets. Rather, they become spectators to a comical encounter. Thus they are momentarily released from the grip of Castilian. They come to share as audiences in another language that belongs neither to them nor to the friar: the *lengua de tienda*.

Their identification with one another, however, finds its locus in the body of the fat boy. Interrupted from his reverie, he bursts out in a convulsive repetition of the lessons like a "steam engine gyrating a phonograph." Startled, he takes shelter in repeating what he does not understand. As if wielding an amulet, he repeats the lesson hoping to protect himself from further intrusions. But rather than fend off authority, his response sets him up for another ambush. "'*Para, para, para!*' the professor interrupted. 'Good lord! What a racket!'" The professor then proceeds to ask the student a question about the day's lesson on the nature of mirrors that is not mentioned in the textbook. Uncomprehending, the student tries once again to recite the text. And again he finds himself interrupted by the friar, "inserting *cosas* and *abas* at every moment," while mocking his appearance. Rather than receive a mark for his submission, the student is marked as the object of derision in the language of the market and the laughter of the other students.

Throughout this exchange, the professor's authority comes less from speaking Castilian as from interrupting its flow. He dominates the production of surprise, thereby controlling not only the circulation of Castilian, but its possible deviations. Herein lies the importance of "market Spanish." Through *lengua de tienda,* he alerts students to the fact that he is able to hear in Castilian the outbreak of another form of speech. He knows what they are aware of but cannot say: that Castilian can be spoken in ways that evade linguistic authority. He thus communicates the miscommunication intrinsic to colonial sociality and thereby shows himself capable of anticipating the semantic crisis built into the economy of colonial communication. The students in their laughter also come to recognize their professor's authority. However, it is not in this instance an authority that derives from the language of God or the state, but one that comes from the ability to overhear and transmit the intermittent and interruptive language from below. They see in their professor one who can draw from other sources the means with which to communicate in ways that evade the language of the textbook. Mixing linguistic registers, he appears to mimic those at the periphery of the linguistic hierarchy. Thanks to the friar, Castilian appears to give way, becoming another language that makes possible a momentary joining of his interests with those of his students.

That joining of interests, however, is as evanescent as it is transitory. More significant, it relies on the targeting of an other who can barely speak and cannot laugh. Such is the fate of the fat boy who is finally reduced to saying, in response to a longwinded question that ends with, "What do you say?" "Me? Nothing!" When he does speak in a Castilian other than that of the textbook, it is to say that "I" am "nothing." The boy speaks Castilian and finds himself unrecognizable even to himself. Compelled to answer in a foreign language, he finds himself converted into one who is utterly foreign. The professor and his students are thoroughly complicitous in the interruption of Castilian by sharing a language from below. But the result is not the end of hierarchy; only its reconfiguration at the expense of a designated alien. Interrupting the possibility of interruptions, the friar and his students are led to discover and domesticate the foreign residing in their midst, including both the Castilian of the lesson and the embodiment of its failure to be correctly returned in the fat boy.

Rizal, however, raises a third possibility. Rather than repeat the language of authority or disrupt its demand in order to reformulate hierarchy, one can say "no" to both. In such a case, conflict would replace subservience. Rather than scapegoating, there would be confrontation; in place of laughter, revenge. This third possibility is played out when Padre Millon calls on another student, the felicitously named Plácido Penitente (Rizal 1891, 95–99). Plácido is caught by the friar trying to prompt another student who is being grilled. Seeing the native student's embarrassment (*vergüenza,* shame, also connoting the private parts of an individual), the professor relishes the thought of further humiliating him. He attacks Plácido with a barrage of tendentious questions meant to confuse him to the usual amusement of others. Indiscriminately mixing registers, the priest punctuates his questions with Latinisms and *lengua de tienda,* repeatedly punning on Plácido's name and forcing him to stutter and commit several errors while reciting. Throughout, the student finds himself the recipient of the professor's assaults and the laughter of the class.

However, something unexpected happens. Turning to his record book to grade the student, the friar discovers that Plácido had been marked absent for the day. He had come in late just after his name had been called on the roll. Officially, he was not there. Yet, not only was he being given a grade, he is also told by the friar that he has fifteen absences and is one short of failing the class. Plácido takes exception, for he knows that he's only been absent three times and tells the friar so in impeccable Castilian. The priest replies once again in Spanish pidgin, "Jusito, jusito, señolia! ... si te descuidas una más, sulung! Apuera de la fuerta!" ("Enough, enough, *señorito* ... any more discussions and you're out of here, out of the door!")—this time with a Chinese accent that gives a sharper edge to his mockery of the student's protestations.[9] He tells him that he multiplies each absence by five to make up for all the times he does not call the roll. Hearing this, Plácido is outraged. He is doubly misrecognized, taken as a mere *indio* incapable of speaking Castilian even when he does, and as a fool incapable of telling the difference between his absence and his presence. It is at this point that Plácido's embarrassment is converted into anger. Cutting off the friar at mid-sentence, he says,

> 'Enough, father, enough! Your Reverence can mark me for mistakes as much as he wants, but he does not have the right to insult me. Your Reverence can stay with the class, but I cannot stand it any longer.' And without taking leave, he left ... The class was shocked (*aterrada*). Similar acts of indignity were almost never seen. Who would have thought that Plácido Penitente ... ? The professor, surprised, bit his lips and watched him leave, moving his head with a menacing motion. With a trembling voice, he then began a sermon on the usual themes, though with much more forcefulness ... about the increasing arrogance, the innate ingratitude, the vanity, the excessive pride which the demon of darkness had infused in the youth, the little education, the lack of courtesy, etc., etc., etc. (Rizal 1891, 98)

Rizal imagines a moment when the *indio* speaks up not in order to confirm authority in its place but to reject it altogether. Plácido tells the Spanish father "enough!" in the latter's language. Addressing the friar as "your reverence" (*V.R.*), he discovers in Castilian a place from which to separate his interests from those on top. Castilian allows him to fashion an "I" that can say "I can't stand it anymore," an "I" that can get across to and more importantly surpass hierarchy. Through Castilian, the "I" appears as one who, in saying "no" to the father, can begin to imagine taking the latter's place. Plácido in Castilian interrupts the friar, until then the master of interruption, thereby ceasing to reproduce the latter's interests. Instead, he converts Castilian into his own language, seeming to possess and contain its alien force.

It is the sudden appearance of this mastery that shocks (*aterrar*) the rest of the students. They hear Plácido and understand what he says. Yet, they can no longer recognize him. "Who would have thought that Plácido Penitente ... ?" It is as if the students sense in Plácido a communicative force that, in responding directly to authority, overtakes its demands. He thus comes across as someone other than who he was supposed to be. Refusing the father, he also separates himself from the rest of the class. He manages to return the surprises of the friar with a surprise of his own:

he leaves. But in leaving, he takes on the risk of failure and shows that risk to be an element of his speech.

Where the other students speak Castilian in order to put it out of mind, Plácido turns Castilian into a language for staking his own. In this way, he becomes a new kind of figure, one who is "rarely seen." Like the *ilustrado* nationalists, Plácido's newness appears strange to those who see it. The friar can only respond with stunned silence, then with a mechanical sermon, the usual harangue whose tediousness Rizal signals with "etc., etc., etc." The friar finds himself in the place of the fat student, retreating behind the repetition of words that everyone has already heard. It is as if he finds himself confronted with a different kind of foreignness, one that is not available to the usual modes of domestication. While it speaks in the language of authority, it exceeds hierarchy as if it were addressing another location.

What is this other location? How else might one come to discover it? What sort of recognition flows out of this other locus of address? In the case of Plácido Penitente, the discovery of this address begins with a sense of embarrassment that is converted into anger through the misappropriation of Castilian, both on the friar's and his own part. But what of those who cannot speak Castilian, or at least cannot do so in the ways that might skirt around or past hierarchy? How are they to be recognized? And by whom? To address these questions, I want to turn to one of the chapters in the *Fili* concerning the story of Juli, a young native woman whose entire family had suffered in the hands of the colonial authorities (Rizal 1891, 227–235). Her father, Cabesang Tales, is a farmer whose lands are unjustly taken away by the friars and their native lackeys. He is subsequently kidnapped by local bandits, forcing Juli to place herself in the domestic service of an older wealthy woman in town in order to pay his ransom. Her fiancé is the student Basilio who is arrested by Spanish authorities on charges of putting up subversive posters at the university. She is compelled to seek the aid of the parish priest, Padre Camorra, popularly known in town as *si cabayo,* or horse, for his "frolicsome" ways with women. Juli is terrified at the prospect of having to submit to his advances even as she is desperate to seek his intercession to free Basilio from jail. She is thus overwhelmed by guilt. She would be guilty of giving up her honor should she submit to the friar; and guilty if she does not since it would mean abandoning any hope of helping Basilio. Either she sacrifice her beloved to keep her virtue, or sacrifice her virtue to save her beloved.

Her predicament unfolds through a series of dreams, "now mournful, now bloody ..." In these dreams, "complaints and laments would pierce her ears."

> She imagined hearing shots, seeing her father, her father who had done so much for her ... hunted like an animal because she had hesitated to save him. And her father's figure was transformed and she recognized Basilio, dying and looking at her reproachfully ... blood issuing forth from his mouth and she would hear Basilio say to her: "Save me! Save me! You alone can save me!" Then a burst of laughter would resound, she would turn her eyes and would see her father looking at her with eyes full of reproach. And Juli would awaken and sit up on her mat, would draw her hand over her forehead and pull back her hair; cold sweat, like the sweat of death, would dampen her. (Rizal 1891, 232–233)

In her dreams, Juli is assailed by voices and stares from her father and her fiancé, each meshing into the other. In their absence, their dream images occupy Juli's mind, insisting to be heard and attended to. She has no control over their return and cannot find the means to meet their demands. Here, guilt is associated with the sense of being filled with voices and images from beyond one's waking life. Such presences convey a single message: "Save me!" Unable to keep from hearing it, Juli is nonetheless unable to reply. Guilt arises from this failure to stop listening and the inability to fashion an answer. Instead, one is burdened with a sense of obligations unmet and losses unmourned. In Juli's case, it is this failure to return what has been given to her that keeps returning, lodging itself inside, like an alien presence that she cannot get rid of. She is held hostage to the recurring presence of absent fathers. The only other alternative—consorting with the Spanish father—is really no alternative at all since it amounts to incurring further guilt. It is as if to undo one crime, she must commit another.

What might have saved her from this spiralling guilt would have been the intervention of a third term coming between her and her ghostly fathers. It would have been a figure who might have spoken on her behalf, fending off the fathers' demands and effectively absolving her of her debts. Without this third term, debts can only pile up, pushing one to do what one should not, triggering more guilt, and so on around the circle. In Juli's story, the only resolution turns out to be suicide. Entering the priest's quarters, she is "filled with terror ... she saw death before her" (Rizal 1891, 235). Before the priest could advance on her, she plunges to her death out of the convent's window. Unable to domesticate the spectral presences of her fathers and unable to speak past the expectant friar, Juli kills herself. Hearing of her death, the people of the town can do no more than murmur their dismay, "dar[ing] not to mention names." They, too, it would seem are unable to respond adequately to her death. For this reason, they become complicitous in her demise and become infected with her guilt.

In hearing the story of Juli, everyone seems implicated. Her guilt may have been absolved by her death, but it is nonetheless passed on to those who hear of her fate. Rizal in retelling this tale takes on her guilt and distributes it to his readers. Just as Juli was overcome by the insistence of a message she could not return, so we (the readers) are placed by Rizal amid a loss we cannot account for. In the midst of this guilt, there are at least two possibilities. One might, as in Juli's case, feel blocked and be driven to suicide, symbolic or otherwise. But one might also take a different route: that of repaying debts by way of revenge. By doing so, one would constitute oneself as an agent of recognition: as one who receives and registers messages of distress by virtue of one's proximity to another address: that of death. It is this route of revenge that others take that I now want to take up in the following section.

IV

As we saw in the dedication of the *Fili,* the question of revenge is linked to the imperative to mourn the dead. The author styles himself as the agent of this double duty. In writing, he pays tribute to the memory of dead fathers and sends a message to those he deems responsible for putting them to death. He faces two ways. In doing so, he also finds himself speaking from two places. As an author, he stands outside of his text, marking the threshold of its fictional reach. But he also exists as a voice who, in addressing his readers and characters, exists inside the text. His identity as the singular author from whom the novel originates is contingent on the dispersal of his presence and the dissemination of his voice throughout other voices and figures in the book.

We might think of Rizal, then, as a double agent: his role as an author a function of his shifting positions in the stories he tells. We can see this doubleness refracted in the language of the novel itself. Though written in Castilian, the *Fili* is remarkably heteroglossic, full of regional slang, idiomatic expressions, Latinisms, bits of untranslated French, German, and Tagalog, and broken up by the occasional appearance of *lengua de tienda* and Chinese-inflected Spanish. Just as the author's position is split and unstable, so are the languages he finds himself writing in. Mixing identities and linguistic registers, Rizal as "Rizal" is a figure in the historical emplotment of Filipino nationalism as much as he is a figure whose presence haunts the *Fili;* an author as much as a fictional character—not one or the other but both/and. He thus remains eccentric to any particular identity and removed from any one position. His historical specificity lies in his unspecifiability. In his doubleness, it is tempting to see Rizal approximating the situation of the *filibustero.* For in the novel, the *filibustero* is a figure of corruption as well as critique. It stands astride the tasks of mourning and revenge, translating the demands of one into the force of the other. Yet, as we shall see, the figure of the *filibustero* is precisely what Rizal must conjure up in order to renounce, and in renouncing, clarify his status as the author of this text, a status far from settled in the unsettled conditions of the late nineteenth century.

In the novel, the figure of the *filibustero* looms most ominously in the character of the jeweler Simoun. Central to Simoun's identity is his mysterious appearance. He speaks with a "strange accent, a mixture of English and South American ... dressed in English fashion ... his long hair, completely white in contrast to the black beard ... which indicated a *mestizo* origin." Always he wore "a pair of enormous blue-tinted glasses which completely covered his eyes and part of his cheeks, giving him the appearance of a blind man or one with a defective vision" (Rizal 1891, 5–6). Wherever he appears in the colony, people take notice. His unknown origins are the regular subject of gossip and speculation. Alternately referred to as a "Yankee" because of the time he had spent traveling in North America, as an "American mulatto," an "Anglo-Indian," or a *mestizo,* the mysteriousness of Simoun's origins is compounded by his "strange [Castilian] accent" and his ability to speak Tagalog and English. And because of his reputed access to both the friars and to the Governor General, he acquires such nicknames as the "brown cardinal" and the "black eminence" (44). While Simoun is thought to originate outside of the colonial order, he is nonetheless able to traverse the various levels of colonial society and move up and down the linguistic hierarchy. What enable him to circulate within colonial society are his powerful connections, cultivated by his wealth. Money allows him to cross geographical and social distances without having to be absorbed by any locality or social group. In this sense, money augments his mysteriousness, drawing others to further speculate on what lies beneath his appearance. Such speculations suggest that the figure of Simoun is seen as something more than what he appears to be. He compels others to read him as a sign of and for something else—secret arrangements, unaccountable events, unexpected possibilities, hidden conspiracies—which escape detection.

Simoun's mysteriousness, however, is a disguise. Early on in the novel, the student Basilio while walking through a cemetery, sees Simoun without his glasses and, much to his surprise, realizes that he is in fact Crisóstomo Ibarra, the *ilustrado* protagonist of Rizal's first novel. Ibarra as Simoun has come back to exact vengeance from the colonial authorities he holds responsible for destroying his life. Thanks to the machinations of the friars in particular, Ibarra's father was killed, his body dumped in the river never to be found; his fiancé and the focus of his future happiness, María Clara, taken away from him and sequestered in a convent; and his name ruined by being associated with a revolt of which he did not even know. Hounded as a *filibustero* for seeking to introduce educational reforms, he barely manages to escape from the civil guards who think they have shot and killed him as he went down a river. As Simoun, then, Ibarra returns. Long thought to be dead, he comes back to life, but now as a disguised presence. Whereas Ibarra had in the past sought to use Castilian as a way of securing for himself a place in a reformed order, now as Simoun he seeks to use money to blast that order apart. He explains himself to the stunned Basilio:

> Yes, I am he who [was here] thirteen years ago ... Victim of a vicious system, I have wandered throughout the world, working night and day in order to amass a fortune and carry out my plan. Today I have returned in order to destroy this system, precipitate its corruption, hurl it into the abyss ... even if I have to spill torrents of tears and blood ... Summoned by the vices of those who govern, I have returned to these islands and under the cloak of a merchant, I have traversed the towns. With my gold I have opened the way ... and since corruption sets in gradually, I have incited greed, I have favored it, the injustices and abuses have multiplied; I have fomented crime, and acts of cruelty in order to accustom people to the prospect of death ... I have instigated ambitions to impoverish the treasury; and this being insufficient to lead to a popular uprising, I have wounded the people in their most sensitive fibres ... (Rizal 1891, 46–47)

Revealing his secret to Basilio, Ibarra implies that underneath his disguise he has not changed. The "I" that announces its return in order to mourn its losses is the same "I" that has wandered the world and now brings with it a plot of revenge. "Simoun" is a fiction, a ruse that allows Ibarra to circulate in the colony. As such, it is a second, malleable identity within which to conceal an unchanging one. The strangeness of "Simoun" is thus recognizable to Basilio and the reader as that which refers to Ibarra, carrying out the latter's plans, acting on his behalf, serving to collect what is owed to him. Here, disguise seems to conceal one's identity only in order to consolidate one's claims on the world and one's certainty about oneself.

Money plays a crucial role in "Simoun's" plans. Through money, he—or they, that is, Ibarra and Simoun—is able to incite greed and spread corruption. Simoun is thus not really a merchant, since his interests do not lie in the conversion of money to capital and the accumulation of surplus value. Instead, he seeks to harness money into an instrument of his will. It is as if at the end of each transaction, he does not expect to receive more money, but rather, produce more misery. Contrary to Marx's capitalist who sweats money from every pore, Rizal's fake merchant exudes money in order to sow crime and incite popular uprisings. Like disguise, then, money is an object whose foreignness here is readily transparent and whose disruptive effects are meant to be calculable and knowable in advance, at least from the point of view of Ibarra. Money and disguise encapsulate a set of prior wishes and are made to serve the self-same identity. Behind "Simoun" stands Ibarra; behind money, Ibarra's plan. Thus Ibarra can imagine himself the author of his plot, the one who holds its secret and determines its unfolding.

Thinking of himself at the origin of his appearances and his plot, Ibarra speaking through Simoun depicts his return as a response to a summons issued by "the vices of those who govern." Arriving at the scene of the crime, he sees that neither the victim nor the perpetrator can be helped. Both are so corrupt and so weakened that only through more corruption can they be saved. What might seem like a paradoxical notion takes on a certain force when Simoun declares to Basilio, "I am the Judge (*Yo soy el Juez*) come to punish a system by availing myself of its own crimes ..." (Rizal 1891, 49). Ibarra as Simoun thus sets himself up as a third term that intervenes and adjudicates matters between colonizer and colonized. He speaks beyond the law and thereby becomes a law unto himself. As judge, he regards himself as the locus of all address and the source of recognition. Such is possible insofar as he is also the author of a plot whose elements take him as their privileged referent. As judge and author, Ibarra surpasses and subordinates all others in colonial society.

Revenge here entails a particular kind of fantasy. It gives rise to a particular scenario about one's place in relation to others. It entails the idealization of the self as one who was once misrecognized and made to suffer for it, but now returns in control of its appearances. It is a self capable of distinguishing and disentangling itself from the misperceptions of others. Hence, though one may look and sound foreign, underneath one is in control of one's identity. In effect, taking vengeance is simultaneous with putting the foreign in its "proper" place: outside of oneself, a mere disguise and thus an instrument with which to carry out one's will.

We see this fantasy at work in Simoun's emphatic dismissal of assimilationist politics. Addressing Basilio in proper Castilian, he mocks the students' efforts to encourage the learning of the language. For Simoun, such a project is doomed. The friars and the government will never allow it; the people will never take to it since it is a foreign language incapable of expressing their native sentiments. At most, Castilian will become the language of a privileged few, thereby aggravating one's separation from the people. Indeed, the students' advocacy of Castilian amounts to the betrayal of their mother tongue (Rizal 1891, 47–48), while their wish for hispanization is like the desire of "the slave who asks only for a little rag with which to wrap his chains so these would make less noise and not bruise the skin ..." (Rizal 1891, 53). Instead of "slavish thoughts," he urges them to think "independently," which means that "neither in rights, nor customs, nor language should the Spaniard be considered here as being in his own home or thought of by people as a fellow citizen, but always as an invader, a foreigner, and sooner or later, you will be free" (Rizal 1891, 49).

For Simoun then, freedom does not lie in identifying with the colonizer as equals, but in separating oneself from the colonizer. One needs to forget about Castilian and remember only that Spain is a foreign presence that belongs elsewhere. In this way, one need no longer look toward Spain for reforms. Rather, one can in one's own language constitute oneself as an agent of change and recognition. We can think of revenge as a relationship of reciprocity whereby one returns what one has received wrongfully back to where one imagines it came from (Siegel 1997, 169–170). To take vengeance is to communicate something about Castilian: that it came as a result of an invasion; that it does not belong here; and that it should therefore be returned to its original owners. Only then can "we" regain our proper place at "home." This separatist logic assumes that the domestication of the self occurs simultaneously with the containment of the foreign, its relocation as that which is external and distant. One who speaks Castilian in this case no longer need feel burdened by the stirrings of that which it cannot possess. The economy of revenge allows one to think of assuming the place of the other as the privileged agency of translation and recognition. Rid of this foreignness, "I" can be free from the need to seek the other's recognition even as "I" continue to speak in its language. In this way, revenge entertains scenarios of authorship as the basis of authority, exclusion as the basis of freedom. Dissolving one kind of hierarchy, it promotes the desire for another to take its place.

In Simoun's scenario, revenge is associated with a violent uprising coming as the culmination of widespread misery and indiscriminate deaths. Basilio, for example, would eventually come to join his plot when he learns of Juli's death. Vengeance takes a violent form, because it entails responding to a prior violence. It is as if one who takes vengeance speaks in the place of the dead, as the dead's representative. And given the semiotic logic of revenge, to represent the dead is not only a matter of speaking in its place, but speaking as if one came from the dead. This intimacy with the dead is, of course, the position of Simoun, who speaks for Ibarra come back to life; and Ibarra who, like Rizal, speaks for his dead father. Thus one can see revenge as a form of mourning in that the dead are given a proper place in the world just as the foreign is returned to where it came from. The flow of blood is the image of violence that links the two, serving as a kind of *lingua franca* enabling one to commemorate the absence of the dead while absenting the foreigner from one's midst. In this way, the phantasm of revenge seeks to domesticate nationalism as that which refers back "here," to the "Filipinos" in the Philippines, where the genealogies of the living can be traced to the unmourned dead, rather than something which translates and transmits Filipino demands for reform to the rest of the world.

In the *Fili,* however, revenge ultimately fails to deliver on its promise. All of Simoun's plans unravel. He is betrayed by Basilio, who cannot reconcile himself to the use of violence. But even before Basilio, Simoun is detained by Rizal himself. Alone in his room on the eve of the uprising, Simoun's reveries about the revolt he has planned is "suddenly interrupted":

> A voice was asking in the interior of his conscience if he, Simoun, was not also part of the garbage of the cursed city, perhaps its most malignant ferment. And like the dead who are to rise at the sound of the oracular trumpet, a thousand bloody phantoms, desperate shadows of murdered men, violated women, fathers wrenched from their families ... now arose to echo the mysterious question. For the first time in his criminal career since starting in Havana ... something rebelled inside of him and protested against his actions. Simoun closed his eyes ... he refused to look into his conscience and became afraid ... "No, I cannot turn back," he exclaimed, wiping away the sweat from his forehead. "The work has gone far and its success will justify me ... If I had behaved like you (*vosotros*), I would have succumbed ... Fire and steel to the cancer, chastisement to vice, and if the instrument be bad then destroy it afterwards! ... The end justifies the means ... And with his brain swirling he went to bed and tried to go to sleep. (Rizal 1891, 145–147)

Revenge holds out the promise of domesticating the alien in both its forms: as the dead whose ghostly returns intrude on the living, and as the colonizer whose language assails one into shame, guilt, and submission. But what domesticates revenge? If vengeance is the exchange of violence for violence, does it not, like guilt, risk spiraling out of control? Can the language of blood call into existence a response other than more of the same? If not, can revenge do any more than increase the frequency of ghostly returns? Rather than lead to domestication of nationalism, revenge in this case would lead to keeping the foreign in circulation, forcing one to dwell amid its incessant returns.

Perhaps seeing this possibility, Rizal intervenes. He addresses Simoun by way of the latter's conscience. Breaking and entering into his thoughts along with a chorus of ghostly voices, this interior voice mimics the sound of God at the Last Judgement. One might say that the author appears in disguise. His is a voice that emanates from within his character's head, yet confronts him like the sound of voices from the edge of the grave. Speaking from a posthumous perspective, the author situates himself as a foreigner residing within his characters. He periodically interrupts their speech to confront them as a fearsome presence emanating from beyond the colonial order, yet understandable only within its linguistic confines. Thus, the author's voice is like that of a second language. Its sudden emergence from within one's own language compels one to reframe one's thoughts. Simoun is asked by this second voice: are you not also guilty? That is, it forces him to reformulate his thoughts in response to this demand. The second holds the first accountable and so contains the latter's speech in both senses of the term. Under the cover of a fictional voice, the author subordinates all other fictional voices, framing all other plots. The foreign returns in its most intimate yet most impersonal form.

In searching for revenge, Simoun, disguised as a foreigner, has sought to exceed and thereby take the place of the law. But Rizal, as the second voice, seeks to surpass revenge and put it back in its place: as a criminal act answerable to a higher law. Simoun tries to talk back to the author, seeking to separate himself from his characterization. Refusing Rizal's intervention, he imagines himself at the origin of hierarchy, not subject to it: a source of terror, not its recipient. But he falters, his "brain swirling." His plans already doomed, he finds himself in the grip of authorship's interruptive arrival.

What did it mean to be an author in Rizal's time? In the absence of any scholarship on the sociology of authorship in nineteenth century Philippine colonial society, we can only speculate. (In the same token, literary critics tend to regard Rizal's novels as "realist" without explaining what counts as "real" in his time: Guerrero 1963; Schumacher 1973; Mojares 1983). We might start with the question of Rizal's name. According to his own accounting, his was a name that did not originally belong to him nor did it come down from his father. His father's name was Francisco Mercado and his mother's Teodoro Alonso. "Rizal" was added by a provincial governor, "a friend of the family," as a second surname in order to distinguish them from the other Mercados in the country to whom they bore no relation (Guerrero 1963, 18–19). It is possible, though difficult to ascertain, that this addition may have followed from the 1848 decree of Governor General Claveria requiring all colonial subjects to take on Spanish surnames in the interest of regularizing the collection of taxes. Hence, even those who already had Spanish surnames, like Rizal's family, were given another name so as to distinguish them from others with similar names, rendering them more visible to the state. It should not come as a surprise that the family of Rizal continued to refer to themselves in the father's original name, Mercado, and the mother in her father's name, Alonso, thinking that they owed neither allegiance to, nor affiliation with, the second name, Rizal. "Rizal" was then a supplementary formation, something that came from outside the family rather than one that was handed down from the father's or mother's line. Not until 1872, the year of the Cavite revolt resulting in the execution of the three Filipino secular priests, Gómez, Burgos, and Zamora, did the name "Rizal" take on a new significance. In a letter to his Austrian friend, Blumentritt, Rizal recalls how his older brother Paciano enrolled him at the Jesuit run secondary school, the Ateneo in Manila, under this second name. Paciano had been associated with one of the martyred priests, José Burgos, and it was out of a desire to protect José that he had him enrolled under another name. "My family never paid much attention [to our second surname]," Rizal writes more than a decade later, "but now I had to use it, thus giving me the appearance of an illegitimate child!" (Guerrero 1963, 38). Rizal sees in the history of his name the convergence of a set of contingencies—the act of a colonial official following a state decree, the shadowy but no less tragic events of 1872, the predicament of his older brother—all of which gives him the appearance of something other than who he was supposed to be. His surname functions not as a way of linking him to his father and family, but precisely as a way of obscuring such a link. "Rizal" offered José a disguise. The second name concealed the first and thus allowed him to pass through the suspicious gaze of colonial and clerical authority.

The secondary name, however, comes to take on a primary importance out of proportion to its intended function. José as "Rizal" soon distinguishes himself in poetry writing contests, impressing his professors with his facility with Castilian and other foreign languages. In Europe, he signs his name to a series of political essays critical of the colonial order and challenging Spanish historical accounts of pre-colonial Philippine societies. Though he occasionally uses pseudonyms, everyone, *ilustrados* and Spanish authorities alike, knew exactly who these names referred to. And his two novels not only bear this name, but also the phrase "Es propiedad del Autor," the property of the author. Indeed, by 1891, the year he finished the *Fili,* this second name had become so well known that, as he writes to another friend, "All my family now carry the name Rizal instead of Mercado because the name Rizal means persecution! Good! I too want to join them and be worthy of this family name ..." His mother had previously been harassed and arrested by the colonial police because, among other things, "she did not identify herself as Realonda de Rizal but simply as Teodoro Alonso! But she has always and always called herself Teodora Alonso!" (Guerrero 1963, 297–298).

His name thus came to signal a certain notoriety, and his family, having been forced to take it on, were subjected to persecution. Originally meant to conceal his identity, his second name became that through which he was widely known. For this reason, what was meant to save him from suffering now became the means with which to harm and ruin others. As his foremost biographer, Leon María Guerrero wrote, "He must have felt utterly alone, surrounded though he was by his family, for he alone must bear the responsibility for their ruin; because of him they had been driven from their homes in his name" (Guerrero 1963, 299). Racked by guilt, Rizal returns to the Philippines. His return is a response to the distress caused by his name, one that he used to authorize a series of texts. Authorship in this instance brings to Rizal recognition that leads to ruination. He feels himself responsible for his family's fate. The "illegitimate child" now assumes the focal point of the family's identity, at least from the point of view of colonial authorities. His name takes on a patronymic significance, as the means whereby his family comes to have a public identity and is made a target of colonial pressure. His name reverses the family genealogy. It is now through the youngest son that the family comes to be known. In taking responsibility, Rizal stands as the author of this reversal, one whose effects are linked to criminal acts of subverting authority and reversing hierarchy.

The colonial state thus invested the name "Rizal" with a certain communicative power, seeing in it the medium through which passed challenges to its authority. They recognized in his name far more than Rizal himself had ever intended. In his trial, colonial prosecutors claimed that his name had been used as a "rallying cry" by the revolutionary organization, the Katipunan, to enlist the support of Filipinos and *indios,* of the wealthy and the poor alike (Costa 1973, 106). Indeed, what Guerrero refers to as the "magical power" of Rizal's name was used by the members of the Katipunan as a secret password (Rizal 1891, 382). "Rizal" in this sense worked like a second language, crossing the line between the upper and lower levels of colonial hierarchy, while bringing the disparate groups in each level in touch with one another. It was a watchword through which one came into contact with something new and unexpected.

During his trial, Rizal repeatedly objected to the state's accusations and lamented the rampant misappropriation of his name. "I gave no permission for the use of my name," he writes in response to the charges that it has served to instigate the revolution, "and the wrong done to me is beyond description" (Guerrero 1963, 421). It was as if Rizal found himself confused with Simoun as the author of a separatist conspiracy, caught within a phantasm of revenge he had sought to control. He condemns the revolution as a "ridiculous and barbarous uprising, plotted behind my back ... I abominate the crimes for which it is responsible and I will have no part to do with it" (Costa 1973, 103). Unlike the ruination of his family, he could not be held responsible for the catastrophe he thought was about to befall the colony. "How am I to blame for the use of my name by others when I neither knew of it nor could stop it?" (Guerrero 1963, 425). Against the misreading of his name by those above and those below,

Rizal claimed innocence. "I am not guilty either of organizing a revolutionary society, or taking part in such societies, or of participating in the rebellion" (Costa 1973, 134).

In claiming innocence, Rizal disavows responsibility for the uses to which his name had been put outside the domestic circle of his family. The state sought to attribute the upheavals of 1896 to a singular author. Rizal, for his part, could not (or refused to) recognize these events as anything but "barbaric" and "criminal." Revolution appeared as the failure to sublimate revenge. For him, it involved the emergence of a kind of speech from below that was not properly traceable to his thoughts and which eluded his ability to translate. For as in the *Fili,* authorship was about the rehearsal and subsequent containment of shame, guilt, and revenge. In his God-like interventions within his characters' speech, he had sought to transform such affects of identification into a discourse of responsibility constituted by "education," "virtue," and "sacrifice." Nationalist authorship, "properly conceived," was a matter of identifying with and domesticating the force of translation, thereby displacing the hegemony of the Spanish friar. As the various scenes of the *Fili* show, the corruption of authority is imagined by Rizal to give rise to an interruptive voice that re-forms relations of inequality. Translation thus brings with it the desire for hierarchy, not its elimination. Insofar as nationalist authorship concerns the designation of the foreign as an ominous but potentially domesticated element of oneself, which one can recognize and so control, it mirrors the logic of Christian conversion in its colonizing context. In both, there exists the wish for communicative transparency: that all messages, whether intended or not, have the same address, and that figures such as the missionary or the author serve as indispensable relays for their transmission.

However, Rizal's life, especially his trial, reveals something of the unexpected and unaccountable consequences of this wish for authorship. Just as evangelization resulted in conversions and translations beyond the reach and outside the expectations of Spanish missionaries—resulting, for example in the emergence of "folk Catholicism," or figures such as the *filibustero* or even "Rizal"—so nationalist authorship sparked readings that it could not anticipate, much less control. For rather than lead to the domestication of desires and languages out of place, nationalist authorship tended in fact to spur them into uncharted directions.

In all cases, Castilian played a key role, keeping a sense of the foreign—that is, that which escaped assimilation either into the colonial or the national—in circulation, available for all kinds of use and misuse. The history of conversion made Castilian into a medium for transmitting a fantasy about direct communication and unlimited transmissions across socio-geographical divides. Similarly, the name "Rizal" retained the sense of the foreign that even he himself could not recognize and account for at the point when Castilian was denied to the rest of the colony's subjects. Proclaiming, "I am innocent" meant that "I" did not intend to commit a crime that nevertheless bears his signature. His innocence then implies his guilt, the culpability he incurred in ignoring the effects that a second, foreign name would have on those who felt its force.

Notes

1. Kissling was actually the runner up. First place went to the Italian sculptor Carlos Nicoli, but for a number of reasons he was unable to build the monument. The commission then went to second placer Kissling who also won P100,000 (Baliza 1996).
2. It is interesting to note that the first known monument built to commemorate Rizal, erected shortly after the first anniversary of his death while the revolution against Spain was still being fought, did not have his figure. It was instead a simple obelisk with "Masonic-tinged abstractions on which only the titles of his two electrifying novels were inscribed—as if to say, Read Them! Then Fight For Your Country's Liberty!" (Cited in Anderson 1993, 5). The statue on the official monument is modelled after the last known studio photograph Rizal posed for in Madrid around 1891. The seriality of Rizal's monuments is thus based not on an original but on a photographic reproduction, just as his books were also mechanically reproduced. They are then copies for which there are, properly speaking, no originals. See Rafael (1990).
3. Guerrero (1963) is the standard and most lucidly written biography of Rizal. See also Retana, (1905); Craig (1913); Foronda (1961); and Ileto (1982).
4. I defer a reading of the *Noli* here; cf. Rafael (1984).
5. Quoted in Schumacher (1973, 227, 243). Rizal's frustration with Spain grew from a number of other factors: Spanish intransigence combined with the politically volatile situation in the Spanish parliament where control shifted rapidly between liberals and conservatives between the 1860s and 1890s, and a series of family tragedies: the imprisonment of his mother and sister under false charges, the exile of his brother-in-law, father, and brother, and the loss of the family's lands in Calamba, Laguna to the Dominicans. Both novels teem with allusions to these events.
6. For details concerning the life and death of Gómez, Burgos, and Zamora, see Schumacher (1981).
7. For a more detailed discussion of the linguistic hierarchy informing colonial rule and the challenges to it by Filipino nationalists, see Rafael (1999); and for a history of translation in the conversion of the native populace, see Rafael (1993).
8. Blumentritt. Other kinds of pidgin Spanish existed in the Philippines at this time, including Chavacano, which is still widely spoken among residents of the town of Ternate in Cavite near where the Spanish shipyards used to be and in parts of Zamboanga province on the western coast of Mindanao. The contemporary descendent of *lengua de tienda* is of course Taglish.

9. The friar here not only parodies Chinese pronunciations of Spanish, he also mimics the Tagalog tendency to confuse "f" for "p" as when he tendentiously mispronounces "afuera" as "apuera" and "puerta" as "fuerta."

Bibliography

Anderson, Benedict. 1993. "Republica, Aura, and Late Nationalist Imaginings," *Qui Parle* 7, no. 1, 1–21.
Baliza, R. J.C. 1996. "The Monument in Our Midst." *Starweek,* 29 December, 10–12.
Costa, H. de la, ed. 1973. *The Trial of Rizal: W.E. Retana's Transcription of the Official Spanish Documents.* Quezon City: Ateneo de Manila University Press.
Craig, Austin. 1913. *Life, Lineage, and Labors of José Rizal, Philippine Patriot.* Manila: Philippine Education Company.
Foronda, Marcelino. 1961. *Cults Honoring Rizal.* Manila: RP Garcia.
Guerrero, Leon Ma. 1963. *The First Filipino: A Biography of José Rizal.* Manila: National Historical Commission.
Ileto, Reynaldo. 1982. "Rizal and the Underside of Philippine History." In David Wyatt and Alexander Woodside, eds, *Moral Order and the Question of Change: Essays on Southeast Asian Thought.* New Haven: Yale Southeast Asian Program Series, 274–337.
Mojares, Resil. 1983. *Origins and Rise of the Filipino Novel: A Generic Study of the Novel until 1940.* Manila: University of the Philippines Press.
Ocampo, Ambeth. 1991. *Rizal Without the Overcoat.* Pasig City: Anvil Publishing.
Rafael, Vicente L. 1984. "Language, Gender and Authority in Rizal's *Noli*." *RIMA* (Review of Malaysian and Indonesian Affairs) 18, Winter, 110–140.
———. 1990. "Nationalism, Imagery and Filipino Intelligentsia in the Nineteenth Century." In *Critical Inquiry* 16, no. 3, Spring, 591–611.
———. 1993. *Contracting Colonialism: Translation and Christian Conversion in Tagalog Society Under Early Spanish Rule.* Durham: Duke University Press, 1993.
———. 1999. "Translation and Revenge: Castilian and the Origins of Nationalism in the Philippines." In Doris Somer, ed, *The Places of History: Regionalism Revisited in Latin America.* Durham: Duke University Press, 214–235.
Retana, W.E. 1905. *Vidas y Escritos del Dr. José Rizal.* Madrid:Victoriano Suarez.
Rizal, José. 1891. *El Filibusterismo.* Reprint ed. (1961). Manila: Comisión Nacional del Centenario de José Rizal.
Schumacher, John. 1973. *The Propaganda Movement, 1880–1895.* Manila: Solidaridad Publishing House.
———. 1981. *Revolutionary Clergy: The Filipino Clergy and the Nationalist Movement, 1850–1903.* Quezon City: Ateneo de Manila University Press, 1–47.
Siegel, James T. 1997. *Fetish, Recognition, Revolution.* Princeton: Princeton University Press.

Chapter 7

Through the Eyes of Strangers:
Building Nation and Political Legitimacy in Eighteenth-Century Spain

Alberto Medina

Spain enjoyed a very particular kind of exemplarity in eighteenth-century Europe. It was the model against which any modern idea or development needed to define itself. For the new "enlightened" Europe, Spain was the radical outside, its last frontier, an anachronistic space—untouched by modernity—whose superstition, ignorance, religious fanaticism, disdain for labor and lack of scientific research made it necessary to isolate it in preventive otherness to avoid contagion. This cultural quarantine should be understood in the context of growing political isolation. Philip V (ruled 1700–1746), the first Bourbon king of Spain, would never quite resign himself to the international order that followed the War of the Spanish Succession (1701–1714).[1] The Treaty of Utrecht (1713) drew up a new European landscape in which England, Holland, and France conceived a political balance, preventing the hegemony of any particular country or dynasty. The possibility of Bourbon predominance in Europe was thus curtailed. However, Spain, although a secondary power, did not cease to be a threat to that balance. Philip V never forgot his dream of succeeding to the French crown or of recovering former Spanish possessions in Italy so that each of his sons would receive an honorable, albeit small, crown. This attitude and the consequently aggressive (and usually disastrous) adventures of the Spanish armies made political isolation a priority for other European governments. And if, in political terms, Spain would take long to reconcile itself to the new Europe, in cultural terms it would be portrayed as an exterior space, beyond the reach of the new cultural trend, the Enlightenment.

This hostile European attitude toward Spain throughout the eighteenth century had perhaps its two most important points of reference in 1721 and 1783: Baron de Montesquieu's seventy-eighth "Persian Letter" and Nicolas Masson de Morvilliers's entry on Spain in the *Encyclopédie Méthodique ou par ordre de matières*.[2] Both authors repeated arguments that were ubiquitous in European intellectual circles. What distinguished these arguments was their unusual repercussion in Spain: paradoxically, these were the most dangerous and harmful critiques precisely because they came from respected and admired sources. Montesquieu was, for example, one of the *philosophes* most revered by the author who would write not one but two books defending Spain from the baron's attacks: José Cadalso (1741–1782). Equally, the *Encyclopédie Méthodique*, less ideological and polemical than the *Encyclopédie* edited by Denis Diderot and Jean D'Alembert (published 1751–1775), was the perfect vehicle for the introduction of a moderate version of the Enlightenment in Spain. Hence its success there, and the considerable number of subscriptions that it generated, until the appearance of Masson's infamous entry on Spain. The pivotal question in Masson's article is a perfect formulation of that will to "expel" Spain from European modernity: "After two centuries, after four or ten, what does Europe owe to Spain?" *Que doit l'Europe á l'Espagne?* Why, implicitly, should one consider Spain a part of Europe at all? Masson identifies the status of Spain with that of a colony:

> Nowadays, Spain resembles one of those weak and unfortunate colonies that constantly need the protecting arm of the metropolis ... [I]t resembles one of those desperate sick people who, unable to feel even their own pain, refuse the arm that comes to return them to life. (Cited in Roura i Aulinas 2002, 219)

Spain is located in a colonial exteriority in relation to Europe, implying the need for a cultural "conquest" that would civilize and modernize that backwardness. The colonial history of Spain is ironically inverted: the old metropolis is now the space of otherness. One of the main rhetorical strategies of the Black Legend, the identification of the conqueror with the savagery that he ostensibly intended to suppress, is taken one step farther. The eighteenth century marks the beginning of an "orientalization" of Spain that would continue throughout the next century. Spain becomes a "familiar" other: not so distant as to radically defy comprehension, but distant enough to offer a convenient counterpoint for European progress. However, the political and intellectual will to position Spain outside of Europe, to "expel" it to the other side of the frontiers of modernity, overlooked a far more complicated reality, in which the fluidity and instability of political and cultural frontiers was the norm.[3] This went far beyond the fact that Philip V was French, that Charles III had been king of Naples and Sicily before succeeding to the Spanish throne, or that their most important ministers included Italians like Giulio Alberoni, the Marquis de Grimaldi, and the Marquis de Esquilache. (When they moved to Spain, both Philip V and Charles III brought with them a good number of advisors and ministers from France and Italy). The constant fluidity of political elites was paralleled in the cultural sphere. Between the reigns of Philip V and Charles IV (ruled 1788–1808), the Bourbon court in Madrid systematically employed musicians such as Domenico Scarlatti, Luigi Boccherini, and the singer Carlo Broschi, "Farinelli"; painters like Anton Raphael Mengs and Giovanni Battista Tiepolo; and architects such as Filippo Juvarra and Francisco Sabatini. Like any other European court, then, it was part of a fluid cultural market parallel to the circulation of royal families, bureaucracies, and political infrastructures.[4]

As we will see in the following pages, the very identity of modern Spain may be considered, in part, the work of these foreign elites. They would be responsible for both political and symbolic changes, but we will focus on the contradictory symbolic strategies developed by foreign artists—specifically on Tiepolo and Mengs—as a means of designing a new image of Spain closer to contemporary European ideals associated with the new enlightened paradigm. This symbolic attempt to return Spain to Europe and modernity is simultaneous with, and inseparable from, an attempt to gain legitimacy for a new dynasty bringing with it a new conception of monarchy and power management. This legitimacy was to be generated through an identification of the monarchy with a new concept of the nation: one that attempted, at the same time, to erase the "difference" of an infamous past and to develop a new project that would allow a new kind of citizenship.

The international circumstances and the change of dynasty at the beginning of the eighteenth century have traditionally been identified as the point of departure of "Spain" as it is conceived in the modern context. According to Antonio Domínguez Ortiz, "the loss of the European territories outside the peninsula can be said to constitute Spain as a well-defined political entity" (cited in León Sanz 2002, 58; my translation). At the same time, the suppression of the *fueros* (regional privileges) and changes in local administration forced Spaniards to conceive of themselves primarily as such: as part of that national unity called "Spain." The political project of the Bourbons, parallel to similar processes of centralization throughout Europe, required a new kind of citizenship, one whereby citizens might participate actively in the new model of state. Again as in other parts of Europe, the monarchy needed to develop an alternative form of legitimacy that served, at the same time, as a stimulus to the political and economic participation of the people. The relationship between monarchy and people as conceived by the Habsburgs would be totally reconfigured. Before the arrival of the Bourbons, the rules of the political game were founded on a certain degree of independence and mutual trust. A system of regional privileges and a form of local administration focused on the institution of the *villa* had worked through an extreme "proliferation of jurisdictions": that is, through the dissemination of power. Loyalty to the king was founded on legal independence:

> The Habsburg monarchs in Castile fragmented local administration, creating hundreds of newly autonomous towns. Yet, ironically, the long term benefit to the monarch was the same [as with centralization], for newly chartered towns were intensely loyal to the monarchy that had liberated them from the control of cities and older towns. (Nader 1990, 1)

The relationship with the monarch had previously consisted, then, not so much in direct obedience as in a certain degree of freedom and independence from central power. This would radically change with the new Bourbon schema. All administrative changes under the Bourbons would be directed toward centralization and the attempt to limit local and regional powers. To take just one example, the nationwide censuses conceived under Ferdinand VI (ruled 1746–1759) and completed under Charles III certainly had a disciplinary function—every citizen and his economic position was to be accounted for—and marked a decisive step toward the *única contribución,* the unification and centralization of taxes. Yet they also worked as an instrument for building and mapping the national community as such. If the *catastro* and *planimetrías* were supposed to map rural and urban space,[5] offering to the king's eyes (and those of his tax collectors) the exact components of his kingdom, they also communicated effectively to the people that they belonged—at least administratively— to a clearly defined political unity called "Spain." These initiatives were accompanied by modernization of internal markets and industrial infrastructures: new roads, channels, and inns were built in an attempt to improve communication in the peninsula.

The nation, as administrative unity, would no longer be complicated by local or regional centers of power that might be perceived as counterpoints.[6] The new Spaniard would start to feel closer to his monarch by means of a new kind of bureaucracy that simplified payments (without alleviating them) and functioned simultaneously as a network of power distribution. Relative independence under the Habsburgs would be substituted by absolute obedience in a context of centralization. The relationship with the king would no longer be founded on the limited freedom of its subjects, or on a logic of relative invisibility from the eyes of royal authority. For the people, to be a patriot would now mean to obey; for the king, to rule. In Juan Pablo Forner's words:

Newton said that attraction is the fundamental law upon which rests the permanence and order of the universe. From the hidden tendency or virtue which inclines all beings to seek each other out and unify in a common center comes the admirable unity which may be observed in that great system of stars and planets which inhabit the immensity of space, whose limits are known only by the Almighty. This, which is a hypothesis of Physics, is a law necessary for the conservation of political states. The tendency of all individuals toward the center, that is to say the propensity to promote public happiness, not only maintains order precisely as does the attraction of each planet in its orbit, but forms that indestructible link and indissoluble unity that every machine requires in order to carry out those effects for which it is destined ... (Forner 1795, 20–21)

Public wellbeing is thus strictly linked to the concept of unity and attraction to a common center. But what might that center be? Not just the monarch but also the nation. Indeed, it could be said that both work as mutual icons of unity.[7] One stands for the other. In that sense, the birth of the modern concept of nation in eighteenth-century Spain is strictly tied to the new political system and its code of political subjection. The medieval conception of "the King's two bodies" is now secularized through the concept of nation.[8] "Patriotism" is the new religion that mediates the loyalty between the people and the monarch, and the strategy for involving the will of the people more actively in the political order. In the words of Eric Hobsbawm, "states required a civic religion (patriotism) all the more because they increasingly required more than passivity from their citizens" (1990, 85). The political and administrative process of unification and centralization needed a symbolic and cultural parallel. If the administrative relationship between the king and the people was to change, a reinterpretation of their symbolic relationship was necessary. In symbolic terms, the political project of the Bourbons was supported by a radical overhaul of the cultural world: from urbanism to theater, from new uses of the press to the creation of a nationwide cultural net through the *sociedades de amigos del país*. Here, however, I will focus on the configuration of the new "center" of the country, the monarchy itself. As in the rest of Europe, a favored means of creating legitimacy and civic participation would be the creation of a national consciousness at the same time as the systematic identification of the monarch as its symbolic center.

If the new legitimacy of the king came from his identification with the country, and if it was impossible to separate political subjection from national identity, the symbolic configuration of Monarchy/Spain was an essential component of the new imagined community. However, the king did not merely wish to identify himself with Spain, but rather, more specifically, with a *new* Spain, one cleansed of its anachronistic Habsburg attributes, closer to European Enlightenment, and far removed from the Spain described by Montesquieu or Masson. The new Spain needed to return to Europe, to erase its difference. And here lies the foundational paradox of the cultural project undertaken by the Bourbons. The new imagined community had to define itself against itself. It had to create a certain image of "difference" with which Spaniards might identify in order to participate in the new political project, but at the same time, it had to erase that form of difference unanimously proclaimed in Europe as a means of marginalization.

One valuable way in which to study this paradoxical process is to consider the symbolic self-representation of the monarchy. In this self-representation, a foreign cultural elite frequently assumed a prominent role; the new Spain cannot be conceived apart from Europe, as French or Italian intellectuals might have wished, but rather as one of the battlefields of those intellectuals and artists. These foreigners bore heavy responsibility for the new "imagined community." Among the very first symbolic projects of Philip V was the construction of a new royal palace in Madrid, after the old *alcázar* burned down in 1734. This huge project would take the rest of the century to be completed, costing the crown an enormous sum of around two hundred million *reales,* and it would employ dozens of the best architects, painters, and decorators in Europe. The decorations of the palace would be conceived as variations on a single theme, the "Glory of the Spanish Catholic Monarchy." The palace would be built with two "implied observers" in mind. From the outside, it would be the most visible image of the monarchy, its favorite stage for public appearances and spectacular displays. From the inside, its frescoes, sculptures, and innumerable paintings would be a self-reflective script for new forms of power. What monarchs and political elites would see when gazing upon the ceiling frescoes of the most important rooms in the palace—such as the "Throne Room"—would be an ideal script, a map for future action, the image of a Spanish Enlightened monarchy as it should be put into effect. The semantic logic of the palace would be more performative than representational. It had to reflect a new Spanish Monarchy led by the Bourbons, free from the anachronistic burden of the Habsburgs, more focused on the present and the future than on the questionable glories of the past.

A certain analogy can be perceived, in other words, between the building of the palace and that of the new political structure of Spain. Philip V draws the exterior image of the new country; he signs the treaties that will outline the geographical limits of modern Spain; he cancels the regional privileges through the *Decretos de Nueva Planta* and starts building the administrative infrastructure of a new centralized state. And in a parallel way, it will be under his command that the facades and the architectural structures of the palace will be built. Nevertheless, it is significant that due both to the unfinished state of the royal palace and to the king's absolute aversion to public ceremony, Philip would always prefer his summer place at La Granja, in the foothills of the Sierra de Guadarrama, to the west of Madrid. The symbolic project of integrating Spain into modernity, thereby returning it to Europe, after all, confronted a problem of genealogy. The Bourbons were a new dynasty, their genealogy that of strangers. Philip would never really inhabit the symbolic center of the Spanish monarchy, uncomfortable in that space and that role. The relative marginality of La Granja, a place withdrawn from the public gaze and designed to appeal to the taste of his wife, Elisabeta Farnese (1692–1766), could be read as a kind of "inner exile."[9] The country palace, built as a kind of small replica of Versailles was a mixture of Italian and French tastes. The main architects for the palace were Italian, and the gardens were created by a Frenchman. La Granja was a reproduction of the Italian or French splendor that Elisabeta and Philip had known in earlier days, a nostalgic escape from a present in which they felt like strangers. Relative stability and prosperity allowed Ferdinand VI to consolidate the new monarchy, and internal reform. Paralleling these changes, Ferdinand transformed the royal palace into the center of an extensive cultural program, directed by the Italian singer and businessman Farinelli. Yet cultural activity remained focused on the entertainment of the court itself, removed from the eyes of the people.

The massive use of propaganda, awareness of the existence of "public opinion," and more broadly a systematic strategy to give Spain a new symbolic identity, would therefore await the reign of Charles III (ruled 1759–1788). Regulating everything from the personal attire of his subjects to the new lightning of the streets, Charles would politicize bodies and appearances, the way in which citizens used urban space, and even the ways in which they perceived reality (and were in turn perceived by the gaze of power). He made extensive use of propaganda and cultural spectacle, simultaneously restricting rebellious forms of public opinion such as oppositional newspapers like *El censor*. Charles thus repeated a strategy of legitimization that he had earlier used as King of the Two Sicilies (1735–1759). There, his arrival had been celebrated as the foundational moment of a new country, independent at last of international powers.[10] Indeed, the new king had to create a country in a more explicit way than later in Spain, an old empire and a "closed" nation created three centuries before. As King of the Two Sicilies, Charles was the main promoter of archaeological excavations in Pompeii and Herculaneum (Pelzel 1968, 128): a buried civilization was the perfect tool to promote national identity. Under the new king, the glory of the past was to return. In the case of Spain, that antecedent was used in a different way. The distant period of classical culture was a means of recovering not a sense of independent identity but rather a new, enlightened, and ahistorical one. Spain was to become a modern country by appealing to universal principles, breaking with its own historical isolation (Roura i Aulinas 2002, 170–71). One of Charles' first renovations of the royal palace in Madrid is illuminating on this point. The original plan for the façades included sculptures of all ninety-four kings and queens who had ruled in Spain; among these, the four Spanish-born Roman emperors were given special prominence on the main façade, supporting the central balcony. In 1760, shortly after Charles' accession, it was decided that all sculptures other than those of the four Roman emperors should be removed (Jones 1985, 221). The identification between the Spanish monarchy and the Roman past had already been used by the Habsburgs, but the crucial difference in Charles III's gesture was his will to erase history. The present and the classical past were juxtaposed, forming a particular complicity against local history. After these small but significant changes in the exterior of the royal palace—to which he moved in 1764—the king would concentrate on the interior. Here, too, the iconography has a mythological or Roman content. Historical figures and events are conspicuously absent unless they belong to the Roman past of the peninsula, as in the "Apotheosis of Trajan" of the German painter Anton Mengs (1728–1779).

The political and symbolic project of the king was in certain ways parallel to the artistic renovation defended by one of the most influential aesthetic thinkers of the century, Johann Joachim Winckelmann (1717–1768), to whose admiration Mengs owes most of his fame. For Winckelmann, the real center of European art, and the only place where it made sense to go and learn, was Rome, where he moved in 1754, and where he would spend the rest of his life researching Greek and Roman antiquity. In the opening pages of his most influential text, Winckelmann states, "There is but one way for the moderns to become great, and perhaps unequalled; I mean, by imitating the ancients" (Winckelmann 1972, 61). For him, Greek art was not interested in the accurate representation of nature but rather in the search of an ideal that could only be found fragmented and scattered in that nature. The role of the artist was to create unity and harmony from that fragmented space, avoiding violence and contrast, shadows and ugliness. The artist should be suspicious of all "particular expression" and create through induction from individual cases an ideal that could be grasped by reason rather than just the senses. Clarity and beauty were more related to the intellect than to feeling or perception: painting had to go beyond the senses. Winckelmann's furiously anti-Baroque program used antiquity and, paradoxically, art history to erase not only historical time but also the present. The absolute primacy of the ancients, and the aesthetic values that they stood for, meant that only a nostalgic discipline of restoration through which the modern artist might negate the postclassical history of art as a deviation or degeneration, provided the right path to beauty.

At the core of Winckelmann's theory, a series of connections is established: the negation of history as a process of degeneration is linked to the cult of unity and reason. "Difference," heterogeneity, fragmentation, and the expression of particular feelings and passion were merely obstacles to be overcome. The analogies with the political program of the Bourbons and particularly that of the "individual" discipline implemented by Charles III are obvious. The process of political subjection coincides with the reduction of the particular to the general. "Unity" is the constructive principle of the new monarchy in which heterogeneity and difference were to be suppressed for the common interest. The construction of that "unity" is also an exercise in amnesia and restoration: the ideal time of the ancients allows the erasure of an inconvenient history, and the invention of a new genealogy and tradition. The positioning of a classical ideal as a political or aesthetic model was a convenient remedy against the "orientalization" of Spain. It was no longer extravagant anachronism that should characterize Spain: rather, the reincarnation of the very core of European culture, its classical past. At the same time, that re-Europeanization of Spain was parallel to the implementation of a new political culture founded on the cult of unity. Both in politics and in culture, the "difference" of the new Spain would be characterized by the extinction of differences and particularities. The negative exemplarity of Spain as an exception to modernity was going to be inverted, and a new, positive kind of exemplarity had to be achieved, following a resurrected classical script.

To an even greater extent than the previous stages in the building of the royal palace, the artistic production of foreign artists would be instrumental in the self-representation of the Spanish monarchy. Painters such as Anton Mengs and Giovanni Battista Tiepolo (1696–1770), the two most highly paid artists at the royal court, were entrusted with the design of the most important frescoes of the palace. Although the stylistic complexity of their work continuously challenged their public image, these two painters represented two radically different trends in European art. Tiepolo was already considered the last great artist within the Baroque mode; he was a nostalgic, extravagant, and theatrical painter who articulated in images the agonic apotheosis of an old idea of politics. Mengs, on the other hand, was perceived as the quintessential, avant-garde neoclassicist, a pioneer of a promising future of radical change that would be at once aesthetic and political. The ambiguous, even contradictory, choice of these two artists perfectly suited the paradoxical self-imaging of the new monarchy. Radical renovation and negotiation with the past were simultaneously necessary. A total programmatic break would alienate political subjects and compromise long-term modernization. The artistic contradictions confronting a viewer of Mengs and Tiepolo in the royal palace paralleled those facing the political subject. Even if the paintings were far removed from the gaze of the common people, the king became a first citizen interpolated by the new image of monarchy. He and the other members of the political elite would be the first to experience the contradictions of their own plan of reform, designed to achieve the "Glory of the Spanish Monarchy."

No artist could be more convenient in this program than Winckelmann's favorite painter, Anton Mengs. He had arrived in Madrid from Rome in 1761. He was already one of the best known painters in Europe and Charles III had been his patron in Naples between 1758 and 1759. He was to paint four frescoes and numerous smaller paintings in the royal palace, located in both private and public spaces. "The Apotheosis of Trajan" and "The Apotheosis of Hercules," his two most important works, were to decorate the vaults of the *Antecamara* and the *Saleta* respectively. The latter was the space where the king dined publicly and held his *audiencias ordinarias,* one of the most visible and frequented rooms of the palace (Sancho 1997, 515). In Mengs' frescoes, designed to allegorize the "Glory of the Catholic Spanish Monarchy," the figures of Trajan and Hercules are used as antecedents of the current king, Charles III, and his role in the renovation of Spain. He was also to work in the drawing room of the Queen Mother, where he painted an Aurora, and in the King's oratory, on the main altar of which he painted a Nativity. The rest of his smaller works consisted largely of portraits and religious canvasses to be displayed in the King's private rooms.

Despite his prestigious and extremely well paid position, Mengs would never feel entirely comfortable in Spain. Both the taste of the monarch and the requirements of the commissioned works forced Mengs to a partial return to Baroque modes; his style in this period has been analyzed as a "deviation" from his previous, more "neoclassical" work (Pelzel 1968, 127–30). Yet the painter's ideas remain as purist as ever, as is made clear in his "Letter to [Antonio] Ponz," and public perceptions of his work continued to read him as neoclassical. In 1776, Ponz refers to his works in the Royal Place as "the fruit of Mengs' continued studies and observations of the works of the ancient Greeks" (Pelzel 1968, 141). Unlike Tiepolo, Mengs follows Winckelmann's principles of allegory: clarity, simplicity, and grace, and has no intent to amaze through difficult intellectual exegesis. The chosen motifs and their relationship with the historical circumstances of the present are crystal clear.[11] "Part of its modernity resides in its eschewal of complex and over-elaborate allegory, so that the composition alludes by a direct pictorial metaphor to the modern hero" (Sancho 1997, 517). In Mengs, reason is a useful tool of decipherment, not an untrustworthy one as in the Baroque paradigm represented by Tiepolo. Reason establishes a direct and unambiguous link between classical antiquity and the political present. Charles reenacts the actions of Trojan or Hercules, opening the doors for a new stage in Spanish history that is a return to ideal antiquity, pre-Hispanic in the sense that Spain did not yet exist. Reason is again used to suppress time and history in the name of a cultural-political ideal reincarnated in Charles III. The models to follow are found in an intersection between the local and the universal. If Trojan and Hercules had some relationship with the geographical space that later was to become Spain, they were also, and perhaps primarily, universal figures, a Roman emperor and a mythological character.

The same didacticism and clarity that structures the use of allegory in Mengs can be perceived in more technical aspects of the paintings. Both the use of light and the composition follow a "radial logic" in which a central motif (and source of light) is the "origin" and absolute center of the whole painting.[12] Again following Winckelmann's teachings, Mengs avoids the "irrational" and theatrical light effects of the Baroque style to implement a graduation of light, more brilliant where its source is to be found in the center of the composition, and gradually dimmer when our eyes get farther from that source.[13] At the same time, the interaction of gazes and physical movement of all the figures in the composition are uniformly directed toward the center of the painting. It does not matter where the spectator focuses; the composition will always take his eyes to the central motif. At the same time, no individual expression in any of the secondary figures attracts our attention; they are mainly onlookers, unimpassioned witnesses, contemplating and making us contemplate without disturbing or troubling us with strong individual feelings that might distract us from the harmonious unity of the whole. In Winckelmann's words:

> The beauty of composition consists in wisdom, that is, it should resemble a collection of civilized and wise people, not of wild and angry spirits, like those of Lafage. The second characteristic is thoroughness: that is, nothing in it should be unused and empty, nothing set, as verses for the sake of the rhyme, so that the subordinate figures do not look like grafted twigs but like branches from the main trunk. (Winckelmann 1972, 100)[14]

For Mengs, the object of the spectator's gaze is always the whole, the composition as unity. No details should distract him, no emotions should come between him and distanced rational contemplation. All components matter only as long as they contribute to the clarity of the unity. Another key theorist of neoclassical aesthetics, Diderot, expresses the same idea making use of an illuminating political rhetoric: "The principal idea must exercise its despotism over all the others. It is the driving force of the machine, which, like the force that maintains the celestial bodies in their orbits ... acts in inverse ratio to distance" (cited in Fried 1980, 85). If the different figures of the frescoes are devoid of individuality in the name of totality, the role of the spectator follows the same logic: he is required to place himself in a pre-established spot to take part in that unity. The composition of the painting asks for a spectator with no freedom of perception or movement. It could be said that Mengs' frescoes imply an ideally quiet and serene spectator, one that does not need to walk around the room to discover marginal motifs hidden behind shadows, one who will not become disturbed or intrigued by the dramatic expression of any of the figures. He is in command of his reason and uses it to consider the painting and integrate himself in that hierarchical logic. Individual identity has to be temporarily suspended to gain access to a universe of reason. The spatial logic in which the spectator is immersed works in a parallel way. It really does not matter where he is; what matters is rather the distance between his location and the center of the composition. His goal is to get as close as possible, both in a perceptual and conceptual way. His position is precisely analogous to the one designed by Jean-Jacques Rousseau for the citizen in his relationship with the social contract: in Ernst Cassirer's words, "Any clause inserted into the social contract to the advantage of any individual rights would destroy its real meaning and content. Real unity can only prevail if the individual not merely gives himself up to the whole, but submits himself to it entirely" (1951, 263). Individual difference must be suspended for the sake of unity.

That process of interpellation in which the individual is made to consist in his relationship with a center and a model, in which "difference" is merely an obstacle to be overcome in the path toward unity, is the basis of a radical paradox when applied to our particular historical context. What the "implied beholder" of Mengs' paintings in the Spanish royal palace confronts is a new Spanish identity, a new script of citizenship that coincides with a classical, universal model, that is totally con-fused in a center with no eyes for the particular (be it either historical or geographical). That new Spanish identity coincides with the extinction of its own difference, with its becoming a model of rational, universal order.

Tiepolo's fresco in the throne room, the most important space of the palace, can be read simultaneously both as another variation on that "becoming model" of the Spanish monarchy and as its meticulous undermining and deconstruction. Most critics of this fresco consider it a relative failure, especially when compared with Tiepolo's masterpiece, the

Treppenhaus at Würzburg. The work at the royal palace often repeats the imagery of the latter. It lacks originality and the conditions of space and light in the throne room were so bad that they made Tiepolo's project almost an impossible task. The scarcity of light (despite numerous mirrors placed in the room) and the dimensions of the room, with its relatively low ceiling, make it impossible for a spectator to appreciate Tiepolo's work as anything other than a series of partial details among shadows. The whole painting can never be perceived as such. If there is any possibility of conceiving it as a unity, it necessarily implies a conceptual exercise reconstructing partial visual perceptions in the mind of the beholder. Nevertheless, it might be argued that the precarious spatial and lightning conditions of the Throne Room fit Tiepolo's style perfectly, precisely because they continuously disturb the viewer, forcing him to establish a dynamic and difficult relationship with the painting.

Tiepolo's work can be read as the exact opposite of Mengs'. In conceptual terms, his use of allegory is extraordinarily cryptic and difficult. It has much more to do with the baroque pleasures of the *concetto,* or the twisted exegesis of Gongorist aesthetics than with the didactic clarity advised by Winckelmann and implemented by Mengs. It was Tiepolo's work in the palace, along with the work of other late Baroque painters such as Corrado Giaquinto (1758–1823), that lay behind Ponz's criticism of allegory and his admiration for Mengs:

> If paintings are books for idiots, how are they to be taught by those enigmatic books that leave the most learned subjects, after having examined them, in large part or entirely none the wiser as to their contents? It would be good, given the practice of representing themes by means of fantastical figures, if there were to be some explanation on the walls and ceilings where they are located, in which one might easily ascertain the painter's intentions or those of the patron who employed him. Let this be said in order that it be understood that in regard to such paintings one will speak in merely general terms, without attempting to divine the significance of each figure, which would be a useless, and more than a little tiresome, undertaking for readers. (Ponz in Sancho 1997, 517)

The difficulties of exegesis are increased by the fragmented composition in which different groups of figures are involved in partial events without paying much attention to what could be happening in the rest of the painting.[15] The lack of a clear center in the composition and the accumulation of figures in the margins, leaving large empty spaces at the center, add to the disorientation of the viewer and his ever frustrated search for unitary meanings. These can only be local, fragmentary. In a parallel way, the use of dramatic contrasts in light and the extreme expressivity of the faces turn the surface of the fresco into a juxtaposition of different theatrical stages. The viewer moves from one to the other, attending different scenes of a total narrative that escapes him.

The "implied viewer" in Tiepolo's fresco is, then, the opposite of Mengs': rather than quiet, he has to be an "eye with legs" in constant movement (Alpers and Baxandall 1994, 8), always forced to become conscious of himself and his unstable position. "By liberating us from control, Tiepolo makes us self aware of our movements and our proclivity to make sense. He lacks the habit of command" (Alpers and Baxandall 1994, 10). Our ability to make sense of the painting implies the need to establish an individual and open exercise of exegesis in which "reason" lacks any clear set of instructions to follow or even a clear object to focus on. The viewer is constantly fascinated by an extraordinary display of theatricality and emotion that makes impossible any attempt to gain analytical distance. Tiepolo's is a "universal world of distraction" (Alpers and Baxandall 1994, 42) in which the beholder is an orphan, condemned to open his own paths with no clear light in front of him.

The content of the fresco gives a geographical dimension to this disorientation. Following a schema that had already been used at Würzburg, Tiepolo places the Spanish monarchy as the center of the admiration and reverence of the four continents for which it is supposedly a guide and a model. Yet far from a clear central figure, what those continents find is quite an empty and ambiguous space. The model and center is absent, the continents are indeed left alone with their differences, underlined by Tiepolo's imagery of exotic animals and costumes, endlessly distracted by their local interests, unable to fit harmonically in a well ordered universe under the command of the Spanish Monarchy. Indeed, the viewer finds himself almost exclusively focused on the appreciation of the margins of the painting where most of the figures are placed and disregarding the empty center.

The implied beholder of this painting has little to do with the new model of citizenship that the Bourbons wished to implement. Indeed, it has more than one feature in common with the model they wished to erase. As in the Habsburg's administrative model, the dissemination of networks of power, the importance of the local and its relative independence are essential components of the whole. Difference is ubiquitous, and to find that difference is to be able to belong to a de-centered totality. Tiepolo's conception of Spanish exemplarity and difference is quite different from that implied by Mengs. While the latter, following the modernizing attempt of the Bourbons against the European marginalization of Spain, conceives Spain as the perfect incarnation of a universal model; Tiepolo annihilates the possibility of such a role. He displays an uncomfortable script of the Spanish monarchy that has much more to do with a Habsburg utopia of the past. Here, the empire is precariously held together through the recognition of its own weakness. Its inability to subject all its citizens to a unitary discipline makes it necessary to delegate power to individuals and local entities.

The Bourbons' attempt to build a new symbolic image of Spain, one that would bring it closer to Europe, becomes a radically contradictory enterprise. Tiepolo and Mengs reproduce to perfection in symbolic terms the political battle that had to be confronted, the distance between a new enlightened utopia and a baroque utopia inherited from the past. Both have to deal with the impossible, sharing the same space, either a palace or a nation. Every time Charles III entered the throne room he was confronted with a utopia that was not his. The past had invaded the very core of the empire, had managed to infiltrate its symbolic center, the throne room where Charles III could not be but a stranger.

Two years after the ceiling of the throne room was completed, the Esquilache Revolt would take that contradiction to the streets, endangering the survival of the reforms and radically challenging the path taken by Charles III. The xenophobic rhetoric of the revolt and the role played by the so-called "Partido Español" would make it very clear that there was another idea of the nation that resisted the enlightened utopia, one still tied to the disseminated political schema of the Habsburgs and, as such, able to identify itself with the "Spanish" tradition. This nation wanted to define itself, not within Europe, but as opposed to it. The political opposition to the reforms was able to appeal to the hearts of the people, to their passions. Charles III was too busy with reason. The main political problem that he had to confront after the revolt was not fundamentally different from what was happening elsewhere in Europe. The popular disenchantment with, and detachment from, enlightened reforms could only be overcome by establishing a link between the "reason" of state and the passion of its subjects. That dilemma will mark the birth of modern nationalism in Europe: a means of identity construction that would fill the void left by universal reason, a way of finding a "difference" for which it would be worthwhile participating in the political process.

Notes

1. See for example Bethencourt (1998), and León Sanz (2002, 42–62).
2. The eighteenth-century anti-Spanish attitude is not new, but rather a continuation of the "Black Legend" already visible in the sixteenth century and later reinforced by the political uses of Las Casas' writings throughout Europe. Essential studies are those by Juderías (1974) and Maltby (1971).
3. Outside the peninsula, every single international confrontation and subsequent treaty meant a change of frontiers in America and the European vestiges of the

empire. Even its very "center" was not safe: Gibraltar was lost to the British in Utrecht and it remains British territory to the present day.
4. Anderson (1983) gives "pilgrim bureaucracies" a crucial role, providing the framework of new national consciousness. He is referring mainly to colonial contexts, but the administrative structure of an overextended empire like Spain make it possible to observe the same mechanism working within Europe, where the same government employees could work in Italy, Spain or the Low Countries. Here, the circulation of "national" ideas parallel to administrative structures works in a disseminated way throughout Europe. This "proto-nationalism" is then, at the same time, a form of internationalism.
5. The *catastro* was an attempt to account for all the properties in rural Spain so that they could be properly taxed. The *planimetrías* had a similar objective in the urban space. And they would be an essential tool in the urban reforms implemented by Sabatini in Madrid under Charles III. See Pro Ruíz (1992), Reguera Rodriguez (1993), Equipo Madrid (1988).
6. The relationship between administrative and national unities has been pointed out by Anderson: "To see how administrative unities could, over time, come to be conceived as fatherlands, not merely in the Americas but in other parts of the world, one has to look at the ways in which administrative organizations create meaning" (1983, 53). Anderson's observations are not only valid for postcolonial situations such as those to which he is referring in America, Asia and Africa. They may be extended to the processes of creation of "imagined communities" in eighteenth-century Europe. If Spain and other countries had been conceived as fully established political entities, the way in which this conception changes may be illuminated by the same factors that Anderson finds in postcolonial "new" imagined communities.
7. In this sense, Eric Hobsbawm's reading implies a reciprocal dimension: "The most satisfactory icons from a proto-national point of view are obviously those specifically associated with a state, i.e., in the pre-national phase, with a divine or divinely imbued king or emperor whose realm happens to coincide with the future nation" (1990, 72).
8. Kantorowicz (1957) studies how much the medieval division between the king's body natural (mortal) and body political (immortal) owe to such theological conceptions as the king's *character angelicus:* "the body politic of kingship appears as a likeness of the 'holy sprites and angels,' because it represents, like the angels, the Immutable within Time. It has been raised to angelical heights ..." (8–9). Another theological counterpart would be the analogies between the conception of the church and that of the monarchy. What is clear is that the distinctions between political loyalty and religious devotion in medieval times were systematically blurred.
9. The Habsburgs had been no less prone to "inner exile" than the Bourbons, Philip II's withdrawal to El Escorial being the most famous example. Nevertheless, the underlying reasons had been very different. In the Habsburg context, there was no nostalgia for a lost past, no geographical dislocation, but rather a religious contempt for the vanity of court and urban life that had a lot to do with a contemporary attitude illustrated by a ubiquitous *topos* of Renaissance and Golden Age Literature, *menosprecio de corte*.
10. In November 1748, a treaty signed in Aix-la-Chapelle among the great European powers "ushered in half a century of peace by establishing Italy as a separate state system, insulated from the rivalries of the great powers. The Italian branches of

the Habsburgs and Bourbons dynasties were severed from their parent houses" (Marino 2002, 118).
11. The didactic analogies are analyzed by Pelzel (1968, 139) and Sancho (1997, 518).
12. Both Winckelmann's ideas and the imagery of French absolutism that the Spanish Bourbons had assimilated owed a substantial debt to Neoplatonism, which is secularized and politicized at the same time.
13. "Few Works of Caravaggio and Ribera can be beautiful with regard to light and shade: for they go against the nature of light. The basis for their dark shadows is the principle: contrasting objects are more effective if placed together, as is the case with white skin next to a dark dress. But nature does not work according to this principle; it proceeds gradually in light, shadow and darkness, and before the day comes the flush of dawn, before the night comes the dusk" (Winckelmann 1972, 101).
14. The preference for "wisdom" versus passion, applying not only to figures within the painting, but also to the ideal viewer (whose particular interest should be displaced by objective reason), is reflected in changes in aesthetic theory in the eighteenth century such as those introduced by Kant: "Everyone must admit that a judgment about beauty, in which the least interest mingles, is very partial and is not a pure judgment of taste. We must not be in the least prejudiced in favor of the existence of things, but be quite indifferent in this respect, in order to play the judgment in things of taste" (Simon 1995, 162).
15. "The figures do not react to each other as we expect in a pictorial group. They are all performing at once. It resembles what, speaking of young children, is called parallel play ... the figures are combined, not subordinated" (Alpers and Baxandall 1994, 16–17).

Bibliography

Alpers, Svetlana and Michael Baxandall. 1994. *Tiepolo and the Pictorial Intelligence.* New Haven: Yale University Press.
Alvarez Junco, José. 2001. *Mater Dolorosa: La idea de España en el siglo XIX.* Madrid: Taurus.
Anderson, Benedict. 1983. *Imagined Communities: Reflections on the Origin and Spread of Nationalism.* New York: Verso.
Bethencourt, A. de. 1998. *Relaciones de España bajo Felipe V.* Las Palmas.
Cassirer, Ernst. 1951. *The Philosophy of the Enlightenment.* Princeton: Princeton University Press.
Equipo Madrid. 1988. *Carlos III, Madrid y la Ilustración.* Madrid: Siglo XXI.
Forner, Juan Pablo. 1795. *Amor de la Patria.* Sevilla: Real Sociedad Económica de Sevilla.
Fried, Michael. 1980. *Absorption and Theatricality: Painting and Beholder in the Age of Diderot.* Chicago: The University of Chicago Press.
García Cárcel, Ricardo, ed. 2002. *Historia de España Siglo XVIII. La España de los Borbones.* Madrid: Cátedra.
Gellner, Ernst. 1983. *Nations and Nationalism.* Ithaca: Cornell University Press.
Hatfield, Henry Caraway. 1943. *Winckelmann and His German Critics.* New York: King's Crown Press.

Hobsbawn, Eric J. 1990. *Nations and Nationalism since 1780: Programme, Myth, Reality.* Cambridge: Cambridge University Press.

Jones, Leslie. 1985. "Peace, Prosperity and Politics in Tiepolo's *Glory of the Spanish Monarchy.*" *Apollo* 121, 220–27.

Juderías, Julián. 1974. *La leyenda negra: estudios acerca del concepto de España en el extranjero.* Madrid: Editora Nacional.

Kantorowicz, Ernst H. 1957. *The King's Two Bodies: A Study in Medieval Political Theology.* Princeton: Princeton University Press.

León Sanz, Virginia. 2002. "La llegada de los Borbones al trono." In Ricardo García Cárcel, ed., *Historia de España, siglo XVIII.* Madrid: Cátedra, 41–111.

Maltby, William S. 1971. *The Black Legend in England: The Development of the Anti-Spanish Sentiment 1558–1660.* Durham: Duke University Press.

Marino, John A., ed. 2002. *Early Modern Italy 1550–1796.* New York: Oxford University Press.

Nader, Helen. 1990. *Liberty in Absolutist Spain: The Habsburg Sale of Towns, 1516–1700.* Baltimore: The Johns Hopkins University Press.

Pelzel, Thomas Orbelin. 1968. *Anton Raphael Mengs and Neoclasicism: His Art, His Influence, His Reputation.* Ph.D. diss., Princeton University.

Pro Ruiz, J. 1992. *Estado, geometría y propiedad. Los orígenes del catastro en España (1715–1941).* Madrid: Ministerio de Economía y Hacienda.

Reguera Rodríguez, A.T. 1993. *Territorio ordenado, territorio dominado. Espacios, políticas y conflicto en la España de la ilustración.* León: Universidad de León.

Roura i Aulinas, Lluis. 2002. "Expectativas y frustración bajo el reformismo borbónico." In Ricardo García Cárcel, ed, *Historia de España, siglo XVIII.* Madrid: Cátedra, 167–221.

Sancho, Jose Luis. 1997. "Mengs at the Palacio Real, Madrid." *Burlington Magazine* 139, 515–28.

Simon, Julia. 1995. *Mass Enlightenment: Critical Studies in Rousseau and Diderot.* Albany: SUNY Press.

Whistler, Catherine. 1986. "G.B. Tiepolo at the Court of Charles III." *Burlington Magazine* 128 199–203.

Winckelmann, Johann Joachim. 1972. *Writings on Art.* London: Phaidon.

Chapter 8

On Imperial Archives and the Insular Vanishing Point:
The Canary Islands in Viera y Clavijo's Noticias[1]

Francisco-J. Hernández Adrián

en medio del profundo silencio de la patria[2]

In recent critical accounts of "the Atlantic world," there is often a puzzling absence of any serious reflection on how islands are configured as a specific category in the vast field of Atlantic studies. The emergence of a critical discourse on insularity is precisely what occupies me in this piece on an eighteenth-century historian from the Canary Islands named Joseph (or José) de Viera y Clavijo, born in 1731 in El Realejo Alto, not far from the then important Puerto de La Orotava, on the island of Tenerife. Viera studied at the convent of Santo Domingo in La Orotava. As a young man, he was locally renowned as a fine poet, and applied himself to the study of the European languages. It was, however, through the works of the Spanish Benedictine Benito Jerónimo Feijoo, and, later, the works of Voltaire, that Viera began developing his own critical attitude beyond the strictures of eighteenth-century Spanish scholasticism. As a preacher, Viera imitated French models, and he became well known for his preaching in the years before 1770. He moved to La Laguna in 1757, where he joined the famous *tertulia* (enlightened circle) of the Marquis of Villanueva del Prado and had access to the latter's important library. The "patron saint" of this group of *afrancesados* was Voltaire. It is in this circle that the project of writing a general history of the Canary Islands began to take shape. This is also a period when Viera actively engaged in journalism. His wealthy friends from the *tertulia* in La Laguna helped him go to Madrid to start publishing his *Noticias* in 1770. Viera soon found a job as instructor for the son of the marquis of Santa Cruz de Mudela, a member of the influential Silva family. The marquis was close to Charles III and figured as a prominent member of the *ilustrado* intelligentsia in Madrid. Viera remained a friend and *protégé* of the marquis for the next fourteen years. In 1774, after the publication of the second volume of *Noticias,* he was accepted to the Academia de la Historia. From 1784 until his death in 1813, he lived and worked on various writings and natural science experiments in the Canary Islands (Joaquín Blanco Montesdeoca, "Biografía," in Viera y Clavijo 1950, xi–xliii; Millares Carlo 1932, 515–569).

My argument in what follows is that Viera, in his four-volume *Noticias de la historia general de las Islas de Canaria* (1772–1783), established an unprecedented critique of Spanish imperialism and colonial dependence in the Canary Islands.[3] I am arguing that Viera's *Noticias* is undoubtedly *critical* history in something like a Kantian, enlightened sense. Clearly, Viera's work expresses a radical transformation in intellectual attitude with regard to his predecessors in the Canary Islands and in Spain; a certain "coming of age," perhaps, as we shall see, which re-locates an insular discourse within Spanish and Atlantic mappings of the late (enlightened) eighteenth century. But there is something else to Viera's project, an aspect of his work which can not be assimilated to the specifics of Kant's formulation of *Kritik,* or which may be called *critique* only insofar as we can start imagining a pre-Nietzschean and pre-Foucauldian engagement with the (un)truth about origins, which the islands of the Atlantic effectively embody in their interface of over six centuries with Western subjugation and governmentalization. Viera's unique critical intervention is itself a form of engagement with the epistemic geographies of his time, and this form is, as I argue below, the articulation of an *insular perspective* which contains both critical and theoretical ramifications. (Throughout this chapter, I will use the words "insular" and "insularity" in their senses of "remote" and "islandness," rather than in the senses of "inward-looking" or "narrow-mindedness"). Viera was highly conscious of Enlightenment notions of space and territory, and his *Noticias* recognizes spatial categories as quintessentially historical and primordially critical.[4] It was precisely at the juncture of territorial history and the imperial present that Viera launched a critique of the limits of imperial sovereignty from an insular perspective.

Islands

Let us start by looking at the text's authorial, institutional, and historical locations. Viera's institutional location must figure at the heart of any reading of his work as a historian and critic. As a member of the enlightened clergy, he maneuvered privileges and leaves from ecclesiastical duty, and as an extremely well-connected and charismatic individual, he did not cease to gain access to social, literary, scientific, and academic circles.[5] From his days as a local figure in the city of La Laguna in Tenerife to his ascendancy as a member of the Academia de la Historia in Madrid, Viera remained a uniquely adventurous eccentric among Spanish *afrancesados*. Without his close relations in these various circles, it would be unthinkable that the *Noticias* could have been the work of one author, or that it would have appeared at the end of the eighteenth century at all. Cosmopolitan in spirit and intent, Viera's *Noticias* is written in what we may call the author's (somewhat belated) exploration years. The first volume was published in Madrid in 1772; the last one appeared in 1783.[6] Since his arrival in the capital of the Spanish Bourbon empire, Viera had been busy teaching his pupil, the young marquis del Viso, translating, studying, and writing poetry. More importantly, he had been traveling and uncovering the historical lacunae that he had identified in local archives and private collections where he worked, on the Islands and on the Spanish mainland. He wrote a famous diary on the occasion of a trip through La Mancha in 1774, and he made journals of his subsequent journeys in Europe.[7]

The *Noticias* was shaped by the creation of new institutional spaces, predicated, no doubt, on an unprecedented *largesse d'esprit* under Charles III of Spain. Yet it would be inaccurate to subsume this work into the mainstream of eighteenth-century Spanish historiography, where bibliographical oddities are not lacking. What I find most intriguing in Viera's work is his insistent performance of an eccentric cultural and geographical location, where at least three centuries of imperial politics in the Atlantic interface with the peculiar locative status of the Canary Islands (that first transatlantic territory of old Castilian imperialism). The various moments when this text exhibits its critical intention are not to be located within the specific contexts of historiography alone, but in the *longue durée* of an articulation of imperial territoriality and persistent political crisis (Kamen 2003, esp. 439–485). Thus, Viera's scholarly intervention establishes a critical reading of the imperial eighteenth century as seen from one of the margins of the Bourbon Atlantic empire. Ever since the inception of the new dynasty in 1700, the politics of Bourbon imperialism were mired in what we may call the dialectics of inter-imperial violence and the rearrangements of geopolitical and geoeconomic definitions of European imperialisms. My reading of the function of Viera's *Noticias* in this "landscape" focuses on the text's construction of the Canary Islands as primordially *insular* spaces, and so it is important at this point to recall, even in a very cursory manner, some of the insular scenarios in which any invocation of insularity at the end of the eighteenth century must fit. Concurrent with the inter-imperial shockwaves incessantly destabilizing pre-eighteenth century territorialities, the islands and coasts of the Atlantic (but also of the Mediterranean and the Pacific Ocean) were subject to multiple invasions, repeated devastation, and demographic and economic violation. In the manner of boats whose crews and cargoes were violently replaced or simply annihilated, islands were vulnerable, unstable sites: one flag defining them today, another, or none at all the next day or month.[8] Think, for example, of the French attacks on Santo Domingo (the Spanish side of the island of Hispaniola) at the end of the seventeenth century; then Spanish and British retaliations against Cap Français (in Saint-Domingue, on the French side of Hispaniola); French retaliation against Jamaica, etc. (Moya Pons 1998, 68–72). Only a few years into the new century, in 1704, the English took Gibraltar from Spain, and in 1709, the Spanish island of Minorca. In 1713, upon signing the crucial Treaty of Utrecht, Spain ceded the island of Sicily to Savoy.[9] Take, also, the seizure of Havana by the English in August 1762 (Stein and Stein 2003, 51); and their invasion of Manila in October 1762, when "a small and ramshackle force improvised from the resources available in the Bay of Bengal sufficed (with a good measure of luck and daring) to take one of the largest and richest Spanish cities in the world" (Rodger 1998, 178). While the Canary Islands, unlike many of the lesser and even larger Antilles, no longer contained large sugar mills or slaves to provision warring empires, their unique geostrategic location made them highly desirable, and increasingly vulnerable to localized attacks (especially on its main port cities) and, potentially, to permanent invasions, physical destruction, and economic and cultural transformation.[10] This is, to put it simply, how crisis was the ongoing predicament for insular spaces across inter-imperial territories under the geopolitics of eighteenth-century imperialisms.

Thresholds

The first volume of the *Noticias* is preceded by a "Dedicatoria," "Al Rey Nuestro Señor Don Carlos III," and by a "Prólogo." Didactic and laudatory, this "Dedicatoria" is no mere flattery of the monarch. There is a somewhat peculiar locative anxiety in this initial threshold to the ambitious text: the author writes "From the heart of the Atlantic Ocean" and inscribes, in one first, sweeping sentence, a string of meaningful locations. The vassal's "trembling hand" writes from "those happy Islands which serve as first meridian and as a kind of communicating bridge between the two worlds subject to the glorious *imperium* of the best of Kings ..." (Viera 1950, 3). A long, articulate reverence follows, Viera obviously knowing how to flatter well, but the complex gesture also involves a self-reflexive scene. Indeed, Viera states, "whosoever says Spanish vassal, and a vassal from the Canary Islands, has already stated all that there is of most loyal and submissive in the whole universe ..." (Viera 1950, 4). He goes as far as to imagine the "spectacle" of this gesture of offering the fruits of his research to the king of Spain, and of the king's reception of the humble gift. But one gesture leads to the next, and so Viera proceeds to educate His Majesty. He reminds Charles III of how, at the end of the fifteenth century, his predecessors had acquired the Canary Islands "as one of the most precious and interesting possessions of the Spanish Monarchy" (Viera 1950, 4); that the Islands were added to the Crown of Castile, which they served, and that they were crucial in "the astonishing discovery of the West Indies" (Viera 1950, 4). As if to counterpoint the unavoidably Castilian nature of it all, Viera mentions the protracted colonizing efforts by "rare men, originating in the most illustrious houses of the Spanish, French and Italian nobility" (Viera 1950, 4). He is perhaps implying (and this will be supported by various genealogical passages throughout the *Noticias*) that this is no *natural* region of the Spanish empire, but one which has been a cosmopolitan site in the changing maps of expanding Southern European trade and imperialisms articulated as a historical community of regions. He revisits the exploits of Canarians in the New World, no doubt exaggerating for the occasion their role in the conquest and colonization of the *Indias Occidentales*.[11] The islanders are depicted here as a conquering and civilizing force, but also as a working and military one. He concludes his list of virtuous exploits through a return to the theme of allegiance to the Crown. Ever the good enlightened subject, he explains how the Islands have remained faithful to Philip V.[12] In the face of an always impending monarchical crisis, Viera construes the Islands as faithful, forward-looking subjects of the Bourbon succession—Spain is to remain a Bourbon state or cease to exist as an enlightened project. Viera's flattery has the specific purpose of highlighting, once again, the Islanders' unconditional faithfulness to the cause of Bourbon enlightened despotism; and those other, wealthier, yet vacillating provinces are Catalonia and Valencia.[13] These regions had indeed sided with the Habsburgs in the Spanish War of succession, which finally secured Philip V of Anjou (the first Spanish Bourbon) the crown of Spain. Viera illustrates insular zeal with an irrefutable example: had not the Islands resisted bravely and effectively, "even in the midst of all the penury engulfing them" and "without any succour from Europe" (Viera 1950, 5) when the English attempted to conquer them in 1706? Viera chooses this example among others because the year coincides with the middle of the long War of Succession (1701–1714), under Philip V. The event supports Viera's construction of Canarian military heroism, unflinching attachment to the House of Bourbon, and resistance to the old Habsburg dynasty and its British allies. Yet surely this is no ultimate guarantee of perpetual allegiance, and so Viera ends his paragraph in a pointed remark: the English had indeed propositioned the Islands at a time of great uncertainty—England "tempted their constancy with propositions as splendid as they were flattering" (Viera 1950, 5). In this imperial context, and in a century where Atlantic cartographies had often been traumatically renamed, Viera's sinuous interpellation of the (enlightened) royal ear served as a way of underlining imperial crisis. The problem of sovereignty being, from Viera's insular perspective, embedded in a logistics of voluntary allegiance and geopolitical location, this text enunciates for Charles III of Spain the *critical* necessity of heeding territorial pleas for military and economic attention, lest even the Canary Islands (that most faithful, most servile of colonies) be lost to a foreign empire, and to the British in particular.

Anthony Pagden (1995, 160) has argued persuasively that eighteenth-century "[European monarchies] provided their *subjects*—persons by definition excluded from active political life—with protection rather than welfare." This may sound like too broad a generalization if applied to the Canary Islands; empires "act" under multifarious guises at different points. Pagden's book expounds on such differences, yet his claim, far from being too far-reaching, falls short, perhaps, of adequately representing the situation in the Canary Islands. What did "public welfare" (Pagden 1995, 157) mean in this insular context? Viera's text implies that the Spanish empire had provided *neither* protection *nor* welfare. In his accounts of the recent historical past, it is precisely a reversal of imperial paternalism that we are made to witness. Not only has Europe (the Spanish empire, or its Bourbon allies) not come to the rescue of small island armies perpetually cut off from the continent, but the Islands have provided the Crown repeatedly with soldiers, money, and various resources in exchange for little protection and an endlessly postponed expectation of welfare.[14] When, in the previously quoted passage from his "Dedicatoria" to Charles III, Viera mentions England's *proposiciones tan brillantes como halagüeñas,* he is referring to the commercial, and perhaps other, benefits which the Islands might have accrued had they performed a militarily imposed imperial crossing. This becomes clear from his comments later on in the *Noticias,* when he refers to Admiral Jennings' failed attempt at an invasion of Santa Cruz de Tenerife.[15] Indeed, the gradual collapse of the wine trade between the Canaries and Britain had dire consequences for local economies on the archipelago.[16] The Canary Islands had benefited from the rare privilege of legal trade with Britain since the seventeenth century. They figured, as contemporary historians still put it, among "the Wine Islands of Madeira and the Canaries" (Price 1998, 89).[17] Once again, the islanders' commercial interests had been sacrificed for the sake of something that Viera can only represent here as humble allegiance to the Bourbon monarch, and such selfless (one can also think colonial), heroic conduct is the proof of obedience he willingly offers Charles III. But is this narrative not also proof of a deep-seated ambivalence with regard to an unconditional, almost slavish, attachment to the Spanish empire? Perhaps what Viera understood—in any case what his text enacts with great audacity—was the crucial import of imperial territorial politics in an increasingly tense, fragmented Atlantic space.

Clearly, the Islands were not in a position to demand an autonomous space of power. Empowerment, in Viera's view, had to come in the form of reclaiming a space of visibility, an elocutionary space, which would respond to the arbitrariness of conquest, the foundational brutality of violent annexation and slavery, and the specious "origin" of mythical virginity and availability. Power, in other words, is negotiated in Viera's text as a vast presentation—and interpellation—of historical reason, yet this is not Kantian or Hegelian reason (*Verkunft*), a universal a priori which does not need and does not hear the historical record of colonial violence and dispossession. This is, rather, the kind of understanding (*Verstand*) that entails rigorous investigation and exhibits archival truth. The very enterprise of decentered history-making is at stake here. Half a century before Hegel infamously declared vast regions of the world history-less in his *Lectures on the Philosophy of History,* Viera might have seen the danger already at the door, and he confronted it by signaling the threat to his readers—and to His Majesty.[18] Having stated his argument that the history of the Islands had not yet been properly written (that is to say, not written at all), Viera extends his explanation of the reasons for writing his *Noticias* into the *critical* domain.[19] And this domain is contingent, open to transformation and expansion, the *Noticias* merely providing, in Viera's own words, "essays, studies, or groundwork to write [the true history of the Canaries] well" (Viera 1950, 7). In Viera's view, previous attempts at deciphering insular archives had proved insufficient because they had not been enlightened enough, their authors lacking the scholarship or the talent—the *critique,* the *style*—and, in one word, because they were lacking in *reason.*[20] Viera's own motives for this grand undertaking seem modest at first sight: to inform and educate his fellow "vassals" and to publicize the glorious deeds of these islanders. But why monumentalize such good intentions in the form of critical history, of enlightened discourse? What is at work here is perhaps a form of power, an enlightened ethics of power, which can only be comprehended from the perspective of the relatively powerless. As "faithful vassals," subjects from the Canary Islands had long lived in a precarious position in relation to the Imperial Crown, and this is perhaps an unprecedented opportunity to open up a space for critical transformation. After all, Viera's words to the king might not have been just a deployment of customary obeisance, but the eloquent signs of a genuinely thoughtful will to inscribe a radically different historical viewpoint in one imperial-Atlantic context. This is what I mean by "insular perspective."

De una sola ojeada

In the first paragraph of his "Prólogo," among his principal motives for writing the *Noticias,* Viera mentions "above all the utility or, let us say, the necessity of some books which, containing the description, nature, character, and the series of the most noteworthy events of the Canary Islands, may unite *as in a vanishing point* the exact idea of all their best things" (Viera 1950, 7, my emphasis). He seeks to accomplish this ambitious unifying project by projecting onto a long, articulate text, the metaphor of *un punto de perspectiva.* The visual trope is certainly not devoid of critical and political implications. What I have called, following Viera, an "insular perspective," is realized in this text as an act of performative identification with the specificities of geohistorical location. This invocation of a local viewpoint intervenes in the totalizing domain of imperial geopolitics by naming, and expounding on, one location in the space-time of imperial sovereignty.

While history-making is the means by which Viera chooses to represent the "idea cabal" on all things pertaining to this location, the logistics of performing a meaningful intervention must also respond to other ideas, prevailing "truths" on the trans-historical and locative position of the Islands. We find one example of what modern anthropology and critical theory would describe as *resistance* to an exoticizing, objectifying gaze in Viera's response to a history of the Canary Islands unearthed locally and publicized internationally in a Northern European town. In 1764, a Scottish author by the name of George Glas published an English version of Fray Juan de Abreu Galindo's *Historia de la conquista de las siete islas de Gran Canaria* (1632).[21] Viera's concern at the untimely publication of this text (one of his primary sources for the *Noticias*) in a foreign language is quite telling: he refers to Glas as "a foreigner," "a man who does not trust the land" and "an adventurer from Scotland." Viera imagines a messenger from the future telling Abreu Galindo that his work would never be published in the Spanish original, but "en Londres y en inglés" (!). Such horrifying news elicit this verbal (and performative) reaction in the dismayed Spanish chronicler: "a monstruous dream" (Viera 1950, 11).[22] Viera responded, then, by collocating the enlightened notion of understanding (*Verstand*) with the production of "unas relaciones siniestras," which Canary Islanders can not recognize as representative of their lived experience or their own (local) knowledge. Whether simply an attack on Glas's book, or just a pretext for responding to possible competitors in an imagined race for accurate representations of exotic lands, Viera addresses the ever-present phenomenon of ethnographic and geographical objectification/subjectification traversing imperial geographies and modernities. Clearly, Viera's stakes are also political, in view of the old enmity between England and Spain, and of the alarming contents of Glas's book.

In *The History of the Discovery and Conquest of the Canary Islands*, George Glas leaves no doubt as to his feelings for the Islands: "Although these islands are little esteemed by the Spanish government, yet in fact they are of the utmost value; for if they were once subdued by another nation, Palma and Tenerife would fall of course, because they are supplied with corn from Lancerota and Fuertaventura [*sic*]" (1764, 222).[23] The Islands imagined by Glas are desirable assets, ready for easy management. Curiously, he transposes local urban geographies onto an expanding cartography of wealthy Northern European towns: "A person who has been in Holland, and compares St. Christobal de La Laguna with Santa Cruz, will naturally think of the difference between the appearance of Delft and Amsterdam" (Glas 1764, 248). Is this not, Viera may have thought, a blunt display by Habsburg allies of their intentions for the Canary Islands? In effect, Glas's book contains careful descriptions of ports, towns, and castles; it charts (from an English viewpoint) commercial, military, agricultural, and institutional arrangements on all the islands.[24] The dream of possessing them one day comes across as a calculated project, not just a fantasy. In a *captatio benevolentiae* at the end of his Introduction, Glas writes, symptomatically, "[t]he candid reader is requested to censure this performance on account of the inelegance of the style: the editor preferring faithfulness in translation, and *accuracy in description*"; "and though he may sometimes dwell on *circumstances which may appear trifling* to many readers, yet he flatters himself that *they will be found useful and interesting to those whose business or curiosity require a more particular knowledge of these islands*" (Glas 1764, viii, my emphasis).[25] In his "accurate description" of islanders, he takes the upper hand, deploying the fine eye and opinionated command of authoritative European ethnography (how can we not be reminded of Columbus' first *Voyage*?).[26] At the end of Book XV, Glas refers to "the Baron of Montesquieu," who "has been very particular in telling us what effect the air and climate has upon the temper and genius of the inhabitants of different countries" (Glas 1764, 287). However, "although no attentive traveller can ever be persuaded to agree with him in his notions of these things," he goes on to reinscribe Montesquieu's ideas with a different twist. It is a matter now of the attractiveness and curious intelligence ("sense, penetration, and quickness of apprehension") of "the natives of the temperate climates" based on their geographical location. The confused dislocation of his discourse in the same passage is perhaps proof of the lack of an established discursive apparatus among British imperialists at this point in the eighteenth century, "for, to whatever cause it may be owing," writes Glas, "it is certain that the northern nations, Blacks and Indians, are a heavy, phlegmatic, and stupid people, when compared with the Libyans, Arabs, Spaniards, and Canarians: but this difference cannot be so well observed as in such of these people as have not had the advantages of education, but are left entirely to nature" (Glas 1764, 287). The useful and adaptable native, particularly the one "left entirely to nature" appears as if split into corroborating images; images, perhaps, related to deep-seated ideas of the "civilized" or converted subject against her "natural," savage, or undiscovered ancestor.[27] The figures of eastern—"Oriental"—stereotyping appear here as a contaminating factor prevailing in a miscegenated population. Geographical location (which islands lie closest to Africa?) produces a dividing border in Glas's insular mappings, where the imperialist imagination draws stereotypical "knowledge" from *cultural* prejudice and fear of "the (Barbary Coast) barbarian."[28] As if the catalogue were not sufficiently precise, he adds: "They neither speak nor understand any other language than the Castilian, and this they pronounce *most barbarously*" (Glas 1764, 201, my emphasis).

Viera was surely aware of the multiple ways in which the Islands had been imagined by Europeans as mythical, wondrous, and monstrous sites for centuries (Martínez 1998; Lecoq 2002; Gannier 2002; Mittman 2003; Salih 2003). He addressed mythical matter of various kinds in several sections of Book I of the *Noticias*.[29] He saw how myths organized the general view of that part of the world where the Canary Islands had *appeared* as part of the broadening map of late medieval Europe. With regard to the prestigious legend of Saint Brandon, he established, in one of the longest chapters of the entire *Noticias* (Viera 1950, 82–106) a historical genealogy of the modern myth, starting in the sixteenth century. His deployment of the local archive in this chapter includes a record of four fruitless expeditions and attempts at discovering and conquering the island; various witness accounts of sightings and even landings on the island itself; and what he calls three systems of approaching the *problem* of the island of Saint Brandon (Viera 1950, 90). He ascribes each system to a different social realm: the "superstitious plebeians" or the lowest classes (Viera 1950, 90); those who insist on the existence of the island and manipulate or minimize evidence to the contrary; and finally, "the [system] of critics and philosophers, who deny categorically that such an island may exist outside our eyes or our imagination" (Viera 1950, 90). Precisely because Viera wants to represent the Islands as *real* with regard to imperialist uses of myth and territorial hierarchies, he resists, in my opinion, any reinscription within his own text of these myths as anchors of insular origin or identity. Something like insular originality, or essence, which we have learned to presuppose in practically any work on islands, is definitely not present in Viera's examinations of mythical accounts. The fact that Viera did not silence these discursive "traces," but rather chose to consider them as *faits de discours* signals for us an important aspect of his critical practice (Foucault 2003, 708). If Viera's project does express, as I am arguing here, a desire to intervene critically in the *longue durée* of Spanish imperial and territorial self-images, it is only logical that he would have used his text to redress a central *fait de discours* contained in iconographic and textual accounts of the Islands, repeated not only in Spain and Portugal but also by a myriad of European travelers over several centuries (Pico and Corbella 2000, ix–lxii). By engaging the possible sources, misunderstandings, and historical transfigurations of insular myths, Viera was enacting the very purpose of enlightened histories and encyclopedic practices: to dispel certain superstitions, to reveal the shining surfaces of *real* nature, and to stage a new concept of scientific representation even in those places where reality had always (dis)-appeared at its most precarious. By recording insular myths, the historian was also responding to, and attempting to dispel, longstanding imaginations of the Islands as less-than-real, sub-historical sites. Since Viera seeks to demystify and recodify insular spaces as *real*, the process of resymbolization (the text) must establish an intelligible locus for discourse production, for, and from the non-fixated loci of insular (in)visibility and historical *minority*.[30]

Imagination in the *Noticias* is neither visual nor mythical, but textual. Textual imagination here consists in deploying a textuality which, through critical questioning of established iconographic imagings of the Islands, seeks to inform *rational* (enlightened) judgement, to substitute the iconographic foundation of an Atlantic rhetoric of wonders and monstrosities with a new rhetoric of rational and scientific questioning and archival truth. Rather than exciting the exoticist desires of his readers, Viera sought to educate them, and to appeal to their rational imagination. Partly out of necessity and partly out of the inertia of his own intellectual referents, the *Noticias* do not seek to reproduce images, but to alter a pre-existent imagination by superimposing enlightened discourse—a self-conscious discourse of reason—on the old representational regimes. It is perhaps through the paradoxical force of this invisible visibility that nonvisual insular representations "exhibit" the maximum tension of island-imperial attachments. The expectation and, no doubt, the desire for images of these subtropical sites is interrupted in this text, and substituted with long, articulate series of narrative parts. The text includes few visual images, and no elaborate maps; instead, it contains endless references to islands imagined out of archival proof and critical questioning.

These Islands, located on the fringes of European self-imagings, risked (and this is always at stake throughout Viera's text) not only new territorial trespasses, but erasure from European history as well. Whereas inclusion in European historical genealogies is clearly important for Viera, his text also intervenes as a reinscription of imperial, colonial memory and archival truth in a different direction. To established patterns of enlightened history-making, he responds by locating history in an Atlantic location. In this way, his construction of an insular perspective opens up a new dimension in Atlantic history-making. Viera's inscriptions of a new textuality for the Canary Islands, his presentation of enlightened knowledge—of a new discourse on archival truth—and his affirmation of a different past, is everywhere in this text addressing countless errors in previous historical work. His overall project was to relocate insular imaginaries in their double dimension of self-representation (he speaks as an islander, and *for* other islanders) and interpellation: he is also writing for the king, and for the multitude of his fellow imperial subjects. If Viera's project was, as I am arguing here, to reimagine a specific case in insular coloniality, his texts also undeniably succeeded in altering longstanding images of the Islands. As a critical performance, this text established new theoretical premises—"ensayos, memorias o aparato"—adequate for a fresh consideration of regional or local history in an imperial context. This ambitious critical work would have been considered a failure from the standpoint of its own enlightened premises had the text not been able to perform a forceful act of *visibility*. Just as Viera's image of obeisance before Charles III of Spain evokes the *spectacle* of a courtly scene, so does his discourse constantly erase maps, portulans, engravings, and chronicles by challenging their knowledge with a new discourse born out of trans-local, cosmopolitan archives. The very power of self-images consists in the secrecy of their intersticiality, and in the possibility of communal sharing, not exhibition.

Cosmopolitan Archives

Noticias was not only planned as a careful reassessment of local knowledge, or as enlightened reaction to the seemingly monolithic authority of imperial *savoirs*. The text grew and changed as Viera travelled and met with many scholars of the new sciences in several European cities. As I explained earlier, his institutional location granted him access to the (multiple) cosmopolitan archive: his critical perspective relied on both insular and metropolitan archival sites. Island textuality is here decentered, and insular archives are only (but crucially) the first indices of a kind of historiographic and territorial instability. In the course of his researches, then, Viera had to follow the traces of insular textuality in several imperial collections. In order to gain the necessary proximity to the objects he was both reflecting on and constructing (broken continuities, insular pasts, *lacunae*), the archivist must have been compelled to imagine the immensity of empire, the fragility of insular reality, and the Islands' quasi-miraculous location as part of the larger territoriality for almost three hundred years. The process of organizing archival knowledge, of founding a new insular perspective out of scattered pieces, was also the process of imagining a critical archive.

Contemporary reflections on archival work insist on configuring the material archive as a critical site. Derrida's questions in his *Mal d'Archive* veer in this direction, in dialogue with Freudian psychoanalysis (Derrida 1995, 55–57). Viera's text (unlike Freud's) responds to Derrida's anxious questioning by stating that the archive splits into *archives* and necessitates geographical mobility, not univocal and temporal immanence. To put it in different terms, the "ipseic" originality of the word "archive" (Derrida 1995, 11) names not an origin but a series of mnemonic repositories, sites, and, potentially, places of historical recovery and empowerment for the subhistorical "native." What is at stake in Viera's archival practices, in other words, is not *the subject,* but the critical scene itself. This scene, inscribed in every page of the work, functions as the only *archè:* a place of encounter with past voices. The commandment to speak turns here into an ethical and, inevitably, legal scene: texts found at the archives (which the researcher visits out of critical responsibility) *speak* before the finished work—an enactment of the archive—accomplishes its task. I can find no better way of responding to this deployment of the insular archive than to imagine it as a provocation to think in performative (and not purely visual) terms. The *Noticias,* then, can be read as a staging where (imperialist) subjectification of (colonial) subjects is told. And how could this spectacle remain untold, but through meaningful silences, archival lacunae, historical un-truth? I take my "spectacular" cues from Feijoo (his *Teatro crítico*), but also from Arlette Farge, who in her extraordinary book *Le goût de l'archive,* presents this notion differently by stating that "the archive plays at once with truth and with the real" (1989, 37). She reminds us that, "the archive does not perhaps say the truth, but it says *truth,* in the sense in which Michel Foucault understood it, that is, in this unique way it has of exposing another's *Speaking,* caught between power relations and himself, relations which he not only suffers but actualizes by reporting them" (1989, 40).[31] Farge "reads" the archive in terms of its "ambiguous position where, by unveiling a drama, actors stand caught in the net, where transcribed words harbour perhaps more intensity than truth" (1989, 37). Indeed, suggests Farge, intensity and life are more important categories than truth—or, we may add, than psychoanalytic knowledge and patriarchal complicity, as Derrida also reminds us (Derrida 1995, 143–148). But *the real,* and not necessarily the true (or truth) must be acknowledged in its appearance, side by side with intensity and life: "This ebb and flow, the archive, which carries so much (of the) real despite its possible lies, stirs up reflection" (Farge 1989, 37). The *drama* of conquest and colonial violence was unveiled for Viera in very specific ways in the course of his researches in Madrid, Paris, Rome and Vienna. Which truth, we must ask, did Viera seek to address when he was faced with "the real" as it was inscribed, open to critical reflection, in the documents he consulted? How did he transform "intensity" and distress ("la détresse" (Farge 1989, 37)—others' and his own) into critical discourse? Elsewhere in her book, Farge speaks about those voices whose traces persist beyond oblivion in the archive as "unfinished discourses" (Farge 1989, 40).[32] Perhaps no translation is needed in order to re-locate the somewhat general, decontextualized quotation in an insular, Atlantic context: I imagine these "unfinished" discourses which apply to the *peuple menu* of eighteenth-century Paris (the context of most of Farge's archival research) as another way of naming the subhistorical discourses reverberating at power's doors in an eighteenth-century insular location. By recovering them, Viera showed how these discursive traces had been suppressed within those colonial societies that refused to recognize them as *real* history. Ethical responsibility and political intervention are dynamically articulated here as a *response* to the question of historical erasure. This response is enacted in Viera's text as the production of *critical* history.[33] The "scattered words" of Farge's text resonate powerfully and meaningfully with Viera's efforts at gathering the missing fragments, lacunae, of an imagined, cosmopolitan insular archive. His journeys to the dislocated archipelago, his critical labor in metropolitan archives, reconstituted, however imprecisely, a space of coherence for words and traces of *distress* in insular history—thus, in the *Noticias,* the production of *reality* in an Atlantic site.

Viera's investigations enabled him to ground his experience of encyclopaedism on the material reality of the Islands: his work refers to monuments—and not only to archival documents—and thus qualifies as what Michel Foucault called *archéologie*.[34] Foucault's ideas on the archive and archives were long in the making; their articulation was sporadic and spasmodic, and point—like the related concepts of archaeology, genealogy, and history—at the development of new methods for approaching analytically the materials of critical and historical practice. In Foucault's view, the archive is not only the *legal,* organizing and ruling principle structuring a given system of statements, the archive is also a regulating principle permitting appearance and preventing disappearance (Foucault 1969, 170). Material archives contain the archive for a certain culture, for a certain historical field. Without the perusal or desecration of their silence, archivists or *archéologues* may not be able to ground their own discourse (their own intervention in the cultural archive), or *see* the traces of another's voice, to recover their words. In order to gain a sense of distance, Viera needed to swim deep into these disperse archives; only then could he speak, forcefully, from a certain insular perspective, from "scattered words" and on their "appearing." There is no search for origins, no ontological *"archè"* in the *Noticias*.[35] The only ground Viera delineates here is *critical:* archival, archaeological, institutional, and material. The Canary Islands emerging in this text are places imagined as material and real, their marvelously rich landscapes resisting conflation with flattened or idealized representations of "the (mapped, cartographic) island." Undoubtedly, Viera's "fever" (his *mal d'archive*) owes much to a contemporary obsession with precision and classification (he was active in fostering such practices in Madrid, Paris, and in the Islands). Yet his insistence on cataloguing and demonstrating the undeniable reality of insular specificity can hardly be ascribed to a thirst for origins, primeval meaning, or immanent *Grund*—such obsessions belong elsewhere, they are not common to all encyclopedic culture, or to all colonial or European intellectual quests. Viera's archival investigations took him from local archives in the city of San Cristóbal de La Laguna to metropolitan archives elsewhere, where the lacunae could be "brought back," or effectively recovered, for the project of constructing a critical, insular perspective.

Spaces of Crisis

As I have tried to show through my close readings of several passages in the *Noticias*, Viera's text, whatever the multiple motivations—intellectual, sentimental, ideological—inspiring its many parts, expresses itself as a reaction to geopolitical and territorial crisis. The Canary Islands imagined from this discursive articulation of the present are constructed as new theoretical grounds for the revelation (for the inscription) of imperial crisis. Critical insularity, then, or insular theorization, Viera's work asks some of the crucial questions that critics who locate their work within the emerging field of Atlantic studies still have to consider today. Seen or imagined from this insular perspective, Eurocentric versions of Atlantic modernities intertwine in a protracted collapse, and fail to convince us that the effectiveness of any totalizing discourse is sufficient grounds for the recovery of insular and Atlantic locations. As we learn from Viera, exploitation can be judged, slavery can be critiqued, economic and military abuse may be recorded and repulsed. This "vision" of an "Atlantic world" seen from an insular perspective ought to lead us in the direction of a more critical understanding of Atlantic historical constructions. Imperialist uses of the archive organized the discursive production of *worlds* precisely at a time when several generations of European intellectuals were busy constructing a Europe different from its classical and medieval imaginations. And this "other space" around the European world (*where* is Europe located, but in relation, in collocation with its many exteriors?) simply does not hold as *real space;* it is a vague, loosely constructed domain made of mirages, heterotopic sites and sights: exoteric, mysterious, luxurious, and monstrous "space." These other spaces constituted a world devoid of unity, or not really a world, but a constellation of fragments—an *extension* across the coastal and insular fragments of oceanic vastness (Foucault 1986). Viera's insular account intervenes here, it speaks for the irreducible complexity and *rarity* of an intercontinental experience, an experience always other and always on the edge of accepted, hegemonic reality. This history of the Canary Islands is not only an example of cultural codification in an Atlantic context, and of symbolization in the linguistic and political sense. It is also an important precedent in the theorization of a critical site, a multiple insular site where reality (administered by Europe, that "ipseic" "master discourse") is reclaimed as local imagination and used to respond to the inhumanity of imperial sovereignty and the perpetual, perhaps constitutive crisis of territorial identification. Undoubtedly, other works of insular historiography (other insular archives, other critiques) in Atlantic contexts enact a similar ambition. And other such works (if we will read them today, as researchers and archaeologists of the imperial archipelago) perform similar declarations of critical responsibility. In this work, in any case, islands, as textual reproductions of multiple exchanges and territorializations, are uniquely enunciated in the form of *Noticias* written on the edges of archival consciousness, of "real" history and imperial sovereignty.

Notes

1. I am grateful to Marc Schachter, Gabriela Basterra, and Roberto Dainotto for helpful comments on an earlier version of this chapter. My heartfelt thanks also to Helen Solterer, for mentioning *Le goût de l'archive,* and to Elizabeth Dunn, of the Duke Special Collections Library, for her expert help and contagious enthusiasm.
2. "How many times, in the midst of the deep silence of the *patria*, for a short piece of news, for a single date, it has been necessary to sacrifice time, inclination and even expense!" (Viera y Clavijo 1952, 14–15).
3. Quotations and references to the *Noticias* are from the 1950–1952 edition, published in three volumes. I have also consulted, but not quoted, the 1978 edition, published in two volumes. All translations from *Noticias* are my own.
4. Not unlike Kant in his *Physical geography,* Viera thinks in terms of land, of territorial continuities and transformations, before establishing any critical judgment on politics, human geography, archival history, local cultures or myth. See Michèle Cohen-Halimi and Max Marcuzzi's introduction to the French edition of Kant's *Physische Geographie,* in Kant (1999, 7-55).
5. Viera had been appointed by Charles III *arcediano* (archdeacon) of Fuerteventura at the cathedral of Canarias, on the island of Gran Canaria, in 1782 (Blanco Montesdeoca 1950, xxxiv). He did not start his new office until 1784, upon his return to the Islands. In his last years, Viera lived in Gran Canaria, joined the local Real Sociedad Económica and also the one in Tenerife, run by his old friends from the *tertulia* in La Laguna. Firmly an ecclesiastical authority, Viera continued his work as a scientist and historian (he finished his *Diccionario de Historia Natural de las Islas Canarias* in 1799). If Viera's reading of the works of Feijoo and Voltaire as a young man marked his progression from being a typically decadent baroque figure, his 'coming of age' relatively late in life distinguished him as a progressive Spanish *ilustrado.* See Lopez (1994a and 1994b).
6. The original edition of the *Noticias* appeared in Madrid out of the presses of Blas Román, in four volumes, encompassing a total of nineteen *libros* or parts, in 1772, 1773, 1776, and 1783. A new edition came out in 1858 and at least four more followed during the twentieth century. Each volume had a new prologue.
7. In the summer of 1776, Viera traveled with his young pupil and sick wife to Southern France and Paris. In Paris, he visited the libraries, museums, and academies—including the Académie Française. He worked with the astronomer Mesier, with Sigaud de la Fond in his laboratory, and met Voltaire at the Académie des Sciences. In the summer of 1779, just before his return to Madrid, the marquis of Condorcet honored Viera by asking him for a copy of the *Noticias* for the library at the Académie des Sciences. In 1781, after the death of his pupil, Viera traveled again with the marquis of Santa Cruz to Italy, Vienna, Germany, and Paris. In Rome, the Pope granted him permission to see forbidden Spanish and Portuguese

documents in the Vatican collections. In Vienna, Viera met other scholars, once again gaining access to precious documents pertaining to the Islands under the Habsburg emperors (Blanco Montesdeoca 1950, xxiv–xxxvi). See Viera y Clavijo (1976). An account of Viera's *Viaje a la Mancha* appeared in Morel-Fatio (1906, 387–413). Alejandro Cioranescu (1976, 12–13), pointed out that Viera's other *récits de voyage* (a *Diario de mi Viaje desde Madrid a Italia y Alemania* and a journal of his Parisian stage) may have been suggested, or commanded, by his employer and benefactor, the marquis of Santa Cruz, in the course of several trips through Europe. Millares Carlo (1932, 529, 532) mentions the *Apuntes del Diario é itinerario de mi viage a Francia y Flandes* for the years 1777–1778, published in Santa Cruz de Tenerife in 1849, and *Estracto de los apuntes del Diario de mi viaje desde Madrid a Italia y Alemania*, 1780–1781, published in Santa Cruz de Tenerife in 1848.
8. For an account of seventeenth-century Dutch, English, and French expansionism in the Hispanic Caribbean, see Moya Pons (1998, 51–72). For the critical period between the War of the League of Augsburg (1689–1697) and the Treaty of Utrecht (1713), see Sheridan (1998, esp. 397–398).
9. As part of this Treaty, "[t]he English retained Gibraltar and Minorca and secured the *Asiento,* a contract allowing them to import into the Spanish colonies 4000 Negroes [sic] a year and to keep one ship stationed at Porto Bello" (Langer 1960, 450; cf. Lenman 1998, 156). "[A]s early as 1713, the Treaty of Utrecht confirmed the emergence of Britain as the leading naval and military power in Europe and as a mercantile and industrializing economy on its way toward dominance in supplying services, shipping, credit, insurance, and distribution, as well as manufactured commodities to global markets" (O'Brien 1998, 65).
10. For a long study of the endless attacks and raids on the Canary Islands by English, Dutch, French, and North African armies and corsairs in the seventeenth and eighteenth centuries, see Rumeu de Armas (1950).
11. Cf., for example, "Ventajas que halló en las Canarias la navegación a la América" (Viera 1951, 234–235); "Salen de Tenerife algunos conquistadores del Río de la Plata" (Viera 1951, 258); and "Proezas del segundo adelantado y demás canarios en la América" (Viera 1951, 259–261).
12. "Lastly, they are those same Islands, which were staunchly faithful to Your Majesty's glorious Father and to the indisputable rights of His Royal House, and which, while other, wealthier provinces of the Monarchy grumbled in their hesitant fidelity, offered the example and true testimony of their loyalty before the whole world ..." (Viera 1950, 5).
13. On the crown of Aragon's support of the Habsburg candidate in the course of the Spanish War of Succession, see León Sanz (2002, 47–56).
14. To these grievances we must add Viera's complaints about depopulation, "the spectre which haunted much eighteenth-century social theory" in the words of Pagden (1995, 172). Thus, for example, "Ventajas que halló en Canarias la navegación de América" (Viera 1951, 234–235): "Thus continued the Canary Islands to offer their very best services to the American continent, and to give up their people with the desire of making their fortune" (Viera 1951, 235). See also "Salen de Tenerife algunos conquistadores del Río de la Plata" (Viera 1951, 258–259; cf. 259–265). And in "Leva forzada para el ejército de Flandes" (Viera 1951, 571–572):
    The *cabildo* of Tenerife, whom (don Luis de Góngora) communicated the king's [Philip IV's] resolution, had to respectfully explain to him the deplorable ab-

sence of people which one could start noticing in the islands, more threatened then than ever by the crown's enemies; but, since the long and bloody war against France and Holland persisted with such force ... it seemed indispensable to rise at least up to one thousand Canarians, and to take them away from defending their homes so that they may go and acquire honour in the army.

15. In "Invade la escuadra del almirante Genings el puerto de Santa Cruz de Tenerife. Valor y lealtad con que es rechazada":
    When the English general noticed such a firm response, considering the damages his squadron had suffered from the fire coming from the town and realizing, through the warm acclamations with which the islanders hailed Philip V, that it would be impossible to make even the slightest progress in their sworn fidelity, he tried to withdraw, as if out of spite, at 7 in the evening. And with the English withdrew as well the commerce in our wines, so flourishing up until that time, and which ever since then has neither been restored nor risen from its low fortunes. (Viera 1951, 668)
    On the English admiral sir John Jennings, see Rumeu de Armas (1950, 225–233).

16. The history of the Canary Island wine trade is long and complex. Although Viera suggests that the events of 1706 were the cause for the wine crisis, other causes have been put forward by contemporary historians of the period. There is a consensus that the Spanish War of Succession marked the onset of the crisis for the decline of wine exports from the Canary Islands to England. As Guimerá Ravina explains, ever since the creation of the Laws of Navigation (1651–1673), England began imposing increasingly high taxes on all imports into the English American colonies. The English protected the less expensive Portuguese wines from Madeira, the Azores, and Cape Verde, and these began gaining ground as the preferred "wine islands." Through the Treaty of Methuen (1703), signed during the Spanish War of Succession, England committed to privileging Portuguese wines in exchange for a kind of monopoly of Portugal's wine export market. This treaty, and not Jennings' attempt at invading Tenerife, would therefore signal the turning point in the story. See Guimerá Ravina (1985, 317–348).

17. Ever since their "re-discovery" by Southern European navigators in the late fourteenth century, the Canary Islands had been a kind of experimental zone for a number of Atlantic trades: slavery (of Canary Islanders and black Africans), sugar *ingenios,* and wine. Before being known as part of the "wine islands," the Canaries had figured among the very first 'sugar islands' of the Atlantic. See Fernández Armesto (1982, 151–176); and Blackburn (1997, 100, 108–112, 134–135).

18. For Hegel's famous 1822, 1828, and 1830 lectures, see Hegel (1965). Toward the end of his "Prólogo," Viera writes:
    Let the Canarians' ears become used to hearing, without false flattery or satire, the events and facts of which the Islands have been the theatre or the mobile; and, leaving to the barbarian peoples of Scythia or of America the fierce privilege of being lacking in history and of knowing only through tradition that there were other men before them in their lands, let us learn in the school of our familiar examples to esteem those actions worthy of some glory and to flee those which can only bring about confusion. (Viera 1950, 12)

19. Indeed, Viera writes ("Prólogo" to volume I), "because, although I shall not deny that the Canaries had their historians, I dare to affirm, however, that their true history is still to be shaped and that attempts, in this work at hand, will only serve as essays, studies, or groundwork to write it well" (Viera 1950, 7; cf. 11–12).

20. Viera is referring here to his most distinguished predecessor among historians of the Islands, Don Juan Núñez de la Peña, who "unfortunately was one of those men lacking in sufficient instruction, without style, nor critique, nor any of the other skills needed to fulfill the chronicler's difficult mission"(Viera 1950, 7). Núñez de la Peña's work is his *Conquista, y Antigüedades de las Islas de la Gran Canaria, y su descripción* (Madrid, 1676). See Millares Carlo (1932, 379–384).
21. Viera 1950, 11, n. 2. The 1632 manuscript by the Franciscan priest Juan de Abreu Galindo was probably based on a previous manuscript source. A second edition of Glas's book (Dublin, 1767, 2 vols.) contains a biographical account of the author, including a narrative of his death. I will be quoting from, and describing, the 1764, London edition, book and page numbers.
22. Thus, Viera replies to the reinvention and internationalization of historical accounts of the Islands with a caustic, aggressive remark: "In effect, Mr. Glas errs, like the greatest part of that cloud of travellers of hasty judgement who, thinking that they have understood from one single look the character, uses, customs, nobility, procedure, laws and inner economy of our towns, only succeed in spreading through the world some sinister accounts, which we Canarians are hard-pressed to recognize whenever they appear before our eyes" (Viera 1950, 11).
23. As one can tell from the long title, Glas's book is composed of several parts. After an introduction by Glas, and the three books corresponding to Abreu Galindo's text, there are three more works, also by Glas: *An Enquiry concerning the Origin of the Natives of the Canary Islands; A Collection of all the Words extant in the Languages of the Ancient Inhabitants of the Canary Islands, gathered from the History of the Discovery and Conquest, together with the Words of the same meaning in the Shillha or Libyan Tongue that resemble them;* finally, *A Description of the Canary Islands, &c.,* in twenty chapters.
24. See, for example, his observations on Tenerife wines, in Glas (1764, 262).
25. But Glas's descriptions are not accurate on all accounts. He misrepresents the climate bluntly when he states that "[f]or eight months of the year the summits of all the Canary Islands, Lancerota and Fuertaventura [sic] excepted, are generally covered with snow" (Glas 1764, 269).
26. [I]n my opinion there are as many handsome people to be found here (in proportion to the number of inhabitants) as in England. For the English, though excelling all the people I have seen in fineness and freshness of complexion, yet their countenances in general are dull and unmeaning, when compared with those of the natives of the Canary Islands: yet, upon the whole, it must be owned that the old people here look more like demons than the human kind. (Glas 1764, 218)
27. Of the "natives" of the western islands he writes that they are "extremely quick and flexible"; and that "[t]he women are remarkable for their vivacity and sprightly conversation, which far exceeds that of the French, English, or other northern nations" (Glas 1764, 287). On the eastern islands of "Lancerota and Fuertaventura" (i.e. Lanzarote and Fuerteventura), he begins: "Although the natives of these islands pass for Spaniards, yet they are sprung from a mixture of the ancient inhabitants, the Normans, and other Europeans who subdued them, and from some Moorish captives ..." (Glas 1764, 200). He goes on to describe them more closely: "They are, in general, of a large size, robust, strong, and of a very dark complexion ... [B]y what I have had occasion to observe of them, they seem to be avaricious, rustic, and ignorant, especially those of Lancerota" (Glas 1764, 200–201).

28. On the verso of the last folio in the table of contents, readers will find the following editorial announcement: "Speedily will be Published, / By the same Author. / A History and Description of that Part of AFRICA which is bounded on the West by the Atlantic Ocean, on the East by Nubia and Abyssinia, on the North by the southern Frontiers of the Kingdoms of Morocco, Algiers, Tunis, and Tripoly, and on the South by the Rivers Timbuctu and Senegal: with an Account of the Blacks inhabiting the Banks of those Rivers."
29. See "Por qué fueron reputadas por Campos Elíseos y se llamaron islas Afortunadas" (Viera 1950, 25–9). In "Descripción que hace Plutarco de ellas" (Viera 1950, 29–33), he invokes Erasmus to respond to Petrarch's identification of the Canaries as marvelous and monstrous islands: "In sum, it is evident that these or other famous monstrosities, after which, guided by their imagination or their enthusiasm, the ancient poets let themselves go, are not found in the Canaries" (Viera 1950, 33; see also 34–42 and 45–46).
30. *Unmündigkeit* ('minority' or 'immaturity'). See Kant (1983, 41).
31. Translations from Farge's book are my own.
32. "These unfinished discourses, forced by power to explain themselves, are one of the elements of society, one of the aspects that characterize it" (Farge 1989, 40).
33. "What is visible here, in these scattered words, are those elements of reality which, through their appearing in a given historical time, produce meaning. One must work on their appearing, here is where one must attempt to decipher" (Farge 1989, 40–41).
34. I shall call an *archive,* not the totality of texts that have been preserved by a civilization or the set of traces that could be salvaged from its downfall, but the series of rules which determine in a culture the appearance and disappearance of statements, their retention and their destruction, their paradoxical existence as *events* and *things.* To analyze the facts of discourse in the general element of the archive is to consider them, not at all as *documents* (of a concealed significance or a rule of construction), but as *monuments;* it is—leaving aside every geological metaphor, without assigning any origin, without the least gesture toward the beginnings of an *archè*—to do what the rules of the etymological game allow us to call something like an *archaeology.*" (Foucault 2003, 402–403)
35. See, for example, Viera's critical response to mythical narratives on the origins of the primitive islanders: "Origen fabuloso que los historiadores atribuyen a los primitivos habitantes de las Canarias" (Viera 1951, 109–117, esp. 110; cf. 117–118).

Bibliography

Blackburn, Robin. 1997. *The Making of World Slavery. From the Baroque to the Modern, 1492–1800.* London: Verso.

Blanco Montesdeoca, Joaquín. 1950. "Biografía." In "Introducción," José de Viera y Clavijo, *Noticias de la Historia general de las Islas Canarias.* Ed. Elías Serra Ràfols. Santa Cruz de Tenerife: Goya-Ediciones, 1: xi–xliii.

Cioranescu, Alejandro. 1976. "Introducción." In José Viera Clavijo [sic], Tomás de Iriarte, *Dos viajes por España.* Ed. Alejandro Cioranescu. Santa Cruz de Tenerife: Aula de Cultura de Tenerife, 9–22.

Derrida, Jacques. 1995. *Mal d'Archive. Une impression freudienne.* Paris: Galilée.
Farge, Arlette. 1989. *Le goût de l'archive.* Paris: Seuil.
Fernández Armesto, Felipe. 1982. *The Canary Islands after the Conquest. The Making of a Colonial Society in the Early Sixteenth Century.* Oxford: Clarendon Press.
Foucault, Michel. 1969. *L'archéologie du savoir.* Paris: Gallimard.
———. 1986 [1984]. "Of Other Spaces." Trans. Jay Miskowiec. *Diacritics* 16:1, 22–27.
———. 2003. "On the Archaeology of the Sciences: Response to the Epistemology Circle." In Paul Rabinow and Nikolas Rose, eds, *The Essential Foucault. Selections from Essential Works of Foucault, 1954–1984.* New York: The New Press, 392–422. [Trans. of "Sur l'archéologie des sciences. Réponse au Cercle d'épistémologie." *Cahiers pour l'analyse*, no. 9, summer (1968), 9–40].
Gannier, Odile. 2002. "Le voyageur de la Renaissance et son bagage: l'esprit du Moyen Âge à l'épreuve des Caraïbes." In Monique Pelletier, ed, *Les îles, du mythe à la réalité.* Paris: Éditions du CTHS, 53–65.
García Cárcel, Ricardo, ed. 2002. *Historia de España. Siglo XVIII. La España de los Borbones.* Madrid: Cátedra.
Glas, George. 1764. *The History of the Discovery and Conquest of the Canary Islands: Translated from a Spanish manuscript, lately found in the Island of Palma. With an Enquiry into the Origin of the Ancient Inhabitants. To which is added, A Description of the Canary Islands, including The Modern History of the Inhabitants, and an Account of their Manners, Customs, Trade, &c.* London: R. and J. Dodsley.
Guimerá Ravina, Agustín. 1985. *Burguesía extranjera y comercio atlántico: La empresa colonial irlandesa en Canarias (1703–1771).* Santa Cruz de Tenerife and Madrid: Gobierno de Canarias/C.S.I.C.
Hegel, G.W.F. 1965. *La raison dans l'Histoire. Introduction à la Philosophie de l'Histoire.* Trans. Kostas Papaioannou. Paris: Plon.
Kamen, Henry. 2003. *Empire. How Spain Became a World Power, 1492–1763.* New York: HarperCollins.
Kant, Immanuel. 1983. "An Answer to the Question: What is Enlightenment? (1784)." In *Perpetual Peace and Other Essays.* Trans. Ted Humphrey. Indianapolis: Hackett Publishing, 41–48.
———. 1999. *Géographie. Physische Geographie.* Trans. Michèle Cohen-Halimi, Max Marcuzzi and Valérie Seroussi. Paris: Aubier.
Langer, William L. ed. 1960. *An Encyclopedia of World History*, rev edn. Cambridge, MA: The Riverside Press.
Lecoq, Danielle. 2002. "Îles du dedans, îles du dehors. Les îles médiévales entre le réel et l'imaginaire (VIIe–XIIIe siècle)." In Monique Pelletier, ed, *Les îles, du mythe à la réalité.* Paris: Éditions du CTHS, 17–51.
Lenman, Bruce P. 1998. "Colonial Wars and Imperial Instability, 1688–1793." In P. J. Marshall, ed, *The Oxford History of the British Empire.* Oxford: Oxford University Press, 2: 151–168.
León Sanz, Virginia. 2002. "La llegada de los Borbones al trono." In Ricardo García Cárcel, ed, *Historia de España. Siglo XVIII. La España de los Borbones.* Madrid: Cátedra, 41–111.
Lopez, François. 1994a. "Une mutation tardive." In Jean Canavaggio et al., eds, *Histoire de la littérature espagnole.* Paris: Fayard, 2: 13–32.
———. 1994b. "Renaissance de l'ésprit critique," in Jean Canavaggio et al., eds, *Histoire de la littérature espagnole.* Paris: Fayard, 2: 33–50.

Martínez, Marcos. 1998. "Islas flotantes." In Nilo Palenzuela, ed, *Las islas extrañas. Espacios de la imagen.* Las Palmas de Gran Canaria: Centro Atlántico de Arte Moderno/Cabildo de Gran Canaria, 47–67.
Millares Carlo, Agustín. 1932. *Ensayo de una bio-bibliografía de escritores naturales de las Islas Canarias (siglos XVI, XVII y XVIII).* Madrid: Biblioteca Nacional.
Mittman, Asa Simon. 2003. "The Other Close at Hand: Gerald of Wales and the Marvels of the West." In Bettina Bildhauer and Robert Mills, eds, *The Monstrous Middle Ages.* Toronto and Buffalo: University of Toronto Press, 97–112.
Morel-Fatio, Albert. 1906. *Études sur l'Espagne. Deuxième série.* Paris: Honoré Champion, 2nd ed.
Moya Pons, Frank. 1998. *The Dominican Republic. A National History.* Princeton, NJ: Markus Wiener Publishers.
Nuez Caballero, Sebastián de la, ed. 1981. *Noticias de la historia de Canarias*, vol. 3, *Historia de Canarias siglos XIX–XX.* Madrid: Cupsa Editorial/Editorial Planeta.
O'Brien, Patrick K. 1998. "Inseparable Connections: Trade, Economy, Fiscal State, and the Expansion of Empire, 1668–1815." In P. J. Marshall, ed, *The Oxford History of the British Empire.* Oxford: Oxford University Press, 2: 53–77.
Pagden, Anthony. 1995. *Lords of all the World. Ideologies of Empire in Spain, Britain and France c. 1500—c. 1800.* New Haven: Yale University Press.
Papaioannou, Kostas. 1965. "Hegel et la Philosophie de l'Histoire." In G.W.F. Hegel, *La raison dans l'Histoire. Introduction à la Philosophie de l'Histoire.* Trans. Kostas Papaioannou. Paris: Plon, 5–19.
Pico, Berta, and Dolores Corbella, coords. 2000. *Viajeros franceses a las Islas Canarias.* La Laguna, Tenerife: Instituto de Estudios Canarios.
Price, Jacob M. 1998. "The Imperial Economy, 1700–1776." In P. J. Marshall, ed, *The Oxford History of the British Empire.* Oxford: Oxford University Press, 2: 78–104.
Rodger, N.A.M. 1998. "Sea-Power and Empire, 1688–1793." In P. J. Marshall, ed, *The Oxford History of the British Empire.* Oxford: Oxford University Press, 2: 169–183.
Rumeu de Armas, Antonio. 1950. *Piraterías y ataques navales contra las Islas Canarias*, vol. 3. Madrid: CSIC/Instituto Jerónimo Zurita.
Salih, Sarah. 2003. "Idols and Simulacra: Paganity, Hybridity and Representation in *Mandeville's Travels.*" In Bettina Bildhauer and Robert Mills, eds, *The Monstrous Middle Ages.* Toronto and Buffalo: University of Toronto Press, 113–133.
Sheridan, Richard B. 1998. "The Formation of Caribbean Plantation Society, 1689–1748," In P. J. Marshall, ed, *The Oxford History of the British Empire.* Oxford: Oxford University Press, 2: 394–414.
Stein, Stanley J., and Barbara H. Stein. 2003. *Apogee of Empire. Spain and New Spain in the Age of Charles III, 1759–1789.* Baltimore: The Johns Hopkins University Press.
Viera y Clavijo, José de. 1950 (vol. 1), 1951 (vol. 2), 1952 (vol. 3). *Noticias de la Historia general de las Islas Canarias.* Ed. Elías Serra Ràfols. Santa Cruz de Tenerife: Goya-Ediciones.
———. 1976. "Viaje a La Mancha." In José Viera Clavijo [sic], Tomás de Iriarte, *Dos viajes por España.* Ed. Alejandro Cioranescu. Santa Cruz de Tenerife: Aula de Cultura de Tenerife, 29–69.
———. 1978. *Noticias de la historia de Canarias,* 2 vols. Ed. Alejandro Cioranescu, Madrid: Cupsa Editorial.

Chapter 9

Manso de Contreras' *Relación* of the Tehuantepec Rebellion (1660–1661):
Violence, Counter-Insurgency Prose, and the Frontiers of Colonial Justice

David Rojinsky

It is around noon on Easter Monday, 22 March 1660: there is mayhem in the town of Guadalcázar, Tehuantepec Province, in the diocese of Antequera, New Spain. A mob has surrounded the *Casas Reales* of the town; the nearby stables are going up in flames and black smoke is billowing up high into the air. The desperate neighing of the animals trapped inside is only just audible amidst the cries of the rioters and the thunderous clatter of rocks and stones of all shapes and sizes that are being showered upon the buildings. Suddenly, the apparently impregnable doors of the *Casas Reales* swing open: three figures, armed with short swords and small shields, make a run for it, hopefully to the sanctuary of the nearby church, bowing their heads and raising their arms as if they could somehow save themselves from that deadly hail which greets their appearance in the light of day. One of the figures is the *Alcalde Mayor*, Juan de Avellán, reviled for his ruthless imposition of a crippling *repartimiento* system upon the local Zapotec community. He is the first of the three to fall, a rock catching him solidly just above his left ear and embedding itself firmly in his cracked skull. Even though he is almost certainly already dead, the insurgents are upon him, opening up his ribcage with his own sword and pummeling him with sticks and clubs until he is left face down in the dirt. Virtually naked, covered only by his underwear and the bloodstained rag that was once a shirt, his lifeless body lies there, filthy with blood and dust. Sure of his death, the crowd disperses. But while her companions converge upon the now vulnerable *Casas Reales,* a Zapotec woman, Magdalena María, la Minera, refusing to let her own personal rage be left frustrated, straddles Avellán's lifeless body, battering the despised tyrant repeatedly with the sharpest rock she can find. (She will be reminded of the verbal abuse that she unleashes upon her former tormentor a year later when she is sentenced for her part in the riot. On that very spot where Magdalena María now sits upon the corpse of the fallen official of the Crown, a gallows will be erected. Magdalena herself will not be sentenced to death, but to a humiliating shaving of her head, one hundred lashes to be delivered whilst being shoved along the public thoroughfares and then finally, to having a hand cut off and nailed to the gallows' post). Meanwhile, however, crowds of people are now emerging triumphantly from the *Casas Reales* and approaching the spot where Magdalena María remains seated. They have captured one of the *Alcalde Mayor*'s servants—Miguel de los Buenos Créditos, a Spaniard who was hiding inside and whose fate is surely to be that of the other two (the cacique of Quiechapa, Don Jerónimo de Celi, though Zapotec, still regarded as little more than a "collaborator" and benefactor of the *repartimiento* system and a black servant of the *Alcalde Mayor* whose name is unknown) now lying pathetically alongside their master. The wretch, his hands bound behind his back, is forced to his knees before the jeering, seething crowd. He begs hysterically for the opportunity to confess his sins before the final moment comes. Managing to mouth several words of the "Credo," his wish appears to have been granted until, too late— his words come to an abrupt end when his head is split clean down the middle by a merciless, two-handed machete blow.

This summary of the initial events which took place in Tehuantepec on that day 348 years ago is true to the aesthetic of violence characterizing the official accounts of the uprising which were drawn up in its aftermath. Since the aim of these official accounts was to legitimize the material suppression of the rebellion and the brutal punishment of its leaders, special emphasis was placed on the apparent contrast between indigenous violence and the supposed leniency of the colonial law enforcement that followed. This dichotomy, in its turn, was intended to reassert the "legitimacy" of (legal) state-sanctioned use of force (law enforcement) against the "criminality" of illegitimate violence (rebellion).[1] In effect, the underscoring of the "frontiers" between "legal" force and "illegal" rebellion and between law enforcers (vice-regal officials) and rebels (indigenous criminals) served as a rhetorical strategy for rewriting the territorial frontiers of empire which had supposedly been challenged by the uprising. Such accounts, therefore, besides representing a reconstituted territorial body metaphorically, also represented the reconstituted regal and legal bodies (on which that same territorial body depended for its governance), which, in the minds of vice-regal officials, had been violated and dismembered by the uprising.

My intention in imitating this official aesthetic of violence at the outset is to stress that such accounts of rebellion present us with a rather interesting parallel between the *material* violence being depicted and the *discursive* violence used to produce the scriptural objects contained in the narrative. Prose of this kind is itself *violent* in the sense that it *reduces* the complexity of colonial reality into a series of clearly demarcated oppositions (law/violence; (just) Spaniard/(rebellious) Indian; legitimate use of force/rebellion) and into a corresponding series of impermeable metaphorical bodies (ethnic, legal, regal, and territorial) whose "contours" had to be defended and rewritten if they were to continue providing the ideological buttressing necessary for maintaining the political status quo. Nevertheless, my intention is also to stress that accounts like these can be reappropriated so that rather than serving to condemn indigenous violence and to celebrate the triumph of the colonial order, they can serve to challenge the apparent "frontier" between colonial law and violence. For, by stressing that discursive violence is inherent to the prose that reports this particular example of material violence and its corresponding law enforcement (and also, as I shall explain, to the rituals devised to perform it), we are encouraged to denaturalize the opposition between colonial "justice" and colonial violence, especially, moreover, when we also consider the fact, as we shall see, that this particular instance of indigenous violence was unequivocally law *preserving*. In short, the writing up of the Tehuantepec rebellion need not necessarily be accepted as the triumphant reaffirmation of a series of dichotomies. Instead, we might regard such prose as a commemoration of the fact that the dividing lines between these dichotomies were more often than not sites of contention where a struggle took place over which kinds of violence were to be regarded as legitimate and which subjects might "be violent" with impunity.

The account of the rebellion I focus on here is the version of events recounted by the alderman (*regidor*) of Oaxaca of the time, Cristóbal Manso de Contreras, in 1661 after the rebel leaders had been captured and punished (Manso de Contreras 1974, 311–367). I have chosen to examine this account of the rebellion in particular since—apart from the miscellany of assorted documents which are extant, including Juan de Torres de Castillo's account of the parallel uprisings that affected the Oaxacan provinces of Nejapa, Ixtepeji, and Villa Alta during the same period— Manso de Contreras' account is the most extensive, comprehensive, and, more importantly, in my opinion, most stylistically striking document that has come down to us with respect to the uprising in Tehuantepec. Manso de Contreras, not surprisingly, as a crown official, stood to gain substantially for his efforts (both in the field and on paper) to "pacify" the region. His intention was clearly to use the opportunity for wider political purposes, not least of all, as Israel (1975) has pointed out, to reaffirm the administrative powers of vice-regal functionaries like himself over indigenous communities. More specifically, however, the account was designed to claim credit for the pacification of the rebellion for the administration of the new viceroyalty of the Marqués de Leiva y de Ladrada, Conde de Baños (1660–1664), while, in the process, reproaching the former Viceroy Albuquerque and the contemporaneous Bishop Cuevas Dávalos of Oaxaca for their apparent failure to deal with the rebels appropriately (Israel 1975, 262).[2]

My reading of this *relación* is therefore, first and foremost, a critique of what Guha (1988) has termed the "prose of counter-insurgency" or a discourse designed to reinstate the legitimacy of colonial rule and its linear history by transforming rebellion into an opportunity for the ideological reaffirmation of empire. The similarities between Guha's definition of what he labels the "primary discourse" of "counter-insurgency prose" and the writing up of the Tehuantepec insurrection by Manso de Contreras are immediately apparent. In the first place, he is essentially an administrator taking up the pen of a historian to present an official record of events. Secondly, what is essentially a regional uprising against widespread corruption among vice-regal officials is presented in grandiose terms which equate the rebellion with attempted revolution against the whole colonial system. Finally, Manso de Contreras claims to prove the veracity of his account by supporting his own contribution with a series of letters written by the principal protagonists of the whole affair and transcriptions of the public *autos* and *ordinanzas* which put an emphatic seal on the rebellion:

> And because it only remains for me to provide evidence for the truth I profess in this account, exposed to popular censure, I will provide hard evidence in the form of a letter that the townspeople wrote to his Excellency the Viceroy, who ruled at that time, along with other letters written by the Bishop of Oaxaca and the Viceroy himself. Each one of these letters—leaving aside others of lesser importance—gives much to consider and sufficient material when placed alongside the rest of the account. I have also made use of formal legal documents from the case although the original publication of this case should be proof enough. (Manso de Contreras 1974, 323; all translations are my own)

It is as if by juxtaposing the different documents produced by those involved in the rebellion and its suppression, he might create the semblance of a fair and well-balanced "dialogue" rather than a text biased toward the interests of the Conde de Baños' administration. In practice of course, the dialogic nature of the account simply offers Manso de Contreras the opportunity to critique what he perceived as the inaction of the former Viceroy, the Duke of Albuquerque, as manifested in the official missives issued from his office in the immediate aftermath of the rebellion; the opportunity to reject the Bishop of Oaxaca's calls for leniency for the rebels as expressed in his correspondence with the vice-regal office; and finally, to refute the rebels' claims as outlined in their own brief correspondence with the Crown bureaucracy that their actions had not been treasonous. In effect, the writing up of the rebellion could hardly be considered a politically neutral and transparent documentation of "the facts." Instead, it might be better regarded as an illustration of an official desire to document the textual restitution of the colonial order under the new Viceroy and to provide the final, *authoritative* word on the matter. Indeed, in the Viceroy's *auto general,* which brings the compilation of documents to a close and serves to proclaim a general pardon for the majority of the insurgent population, the Viceroy affirms that "I declare perpetual silence on absolutely all that has resulted and may result with respect to the aforementioned uprising, deaths and other related incidents so that nothing more is either written or said about the incident, as if it had never happened" (Manso de Contreras 1974, 363). In this way, the Crown had intended to apply ideological closure and a *punto final* to what has been described by some as the most significant uprising of the seventeenth century in New Spain (Sermo 1981; Beas 2000; Mecott Francisco 2002).

After the riot and the murder of Avellán, the rebels had remained in charge of the Province's affairs and the stability of the region was uncertain until 1661, when the new Viceroy, the Conde de Baños, commissioned Juan Francisco de Montemayor de Cuenca to act as the Crown's Prosecutor in the case and to see that "justice was done" and order returned to the insurgent region.[3] Montemayor de Cuenca used a combination of subterfuge, deception, and terror tactics to arrest and punish the rebel ringleaders in the towns that had risen up. In particular, the *Oidor* was able to exploit the insurgents' insistence on their loyalty to colonial law and to assure them that there would be no armed attack organized against the rebels nor any generalized punishment against the inhabitants of the region and that the matter could be resolved through diplomatic uses of the justice system. The *Oidor* proceeded to arrest 53 of the ringleaders in the initial uprising, rejecting their avowals of loyalty and deeming them guilty of treason by equating the rebellion to a revolt against the King.[4]

The sentences brought down upon the ringleaders were of the spectacular nature typical of a period in which the power of the sovereign and the incontrovertibility of the law might be manifested publicly on the bodies of those found guilty of such transgressions to public order. The gruesome punishments ranged from death by drawing and quartering to bodily mutilations, amputations, whippings that left the victim virtually dead, and periods of forced labor combined with forced exile, which were also little short of death sentences. These exemplary punishments were intended to terrorize the rest of the largely illiterate population into submission with a corporal "writing" that everyone could read and understand. At the same time, fearing that such severe reprisals might rekindle the flame of rebellion, the authorities had a desire to demonstrate the merciful leniency of the legal system and they issued a general pardon to the rest of the population. While condemning the behavior of the abusive *Alcalde Mayor*, the authorities also issued public *autos* to reaffirm the laws that had been designed to protect the indigenous populations from such mistreatment as if they were *new* laws that had been introduced in response to the indigenous plight of late, and as if to stress that, henceforth, the laws would be upheld by Crown officials as long as the local community desisted from taking the law into their own hands.[5]

In his account, Manso de Contreras sought to embellish the "clean-up" operation by reinscribing the boundaries of colonial identities—both subaltern and hegemonic—which depended on the integrity and force of the law for their construction and preservation. Especially relevant here is the fact that Manso de Contreras' rhetoric involves the mobilization of an orientalist discourse to dehumanize the insurgents and, despite evidence to the contrary, to present the rebellion as a *guerra de castas* between Spaniard and Indian, and, by extension, an anti-colonial war of epic proportions.[6] The important point here, needless to say, is that the rebellion was *not* strictly an ethnic conflict between Zapotec and Spaniard: in fact, one of the main aims of the rebels had been to replace those indigenous functionaries who favored and facilitated the abusive and excessive *repartimiento* system, to the detriment of the local population, with leaders from their own ranks and of their own choosing.

The account of the rebellion, however, tells the story of how the "wild" and violently "out-of-control" indigenous bodies responsible for bringing colonial order to the verge of chaos were "reined in" materially (by law enforcement) and then textually (by the writing of the account itself). In effect, the rebels undergo a transformation as the compilation of texts making up the account reaches its climax: the vision of the rebels as they are described during the actual rebellion and murder of Crown officials as savage, inhuman, frenzied, and wild, irrational maniacs, yields, in the transcribed *autos* and laws which follow, into the diametrically opposed vision of obedient, law-abiding vassals whose natural proclivity for drunkenness and idleness must be combated with discipline. Compare the following two extracts for example:

> Without allowing anyone to help the Mayor, because all at once they took to the streets, occupied the squares, surrounded the houses of his residence and reached the hilltops. For each action there were more than enough Indians, both men and women. The women were the worst, most stubborn, daring and bravest stone-throwers, while the men, finding no resistance, acted like brutes and fought desperately, wounding and killing, threatening and beating anyone who opposed them; such was the terrible fear of these rebels that the most determined men had retreated. (Manso de Contreras 1974, 318)

> Upholding obedience, peace and order as they should, the Indians should also respect and obey their superiors, and refrain from conspiracies, fights, riots, political factions and drinking binges, busying themselves instead with work, as is just, and they must do so to avoid the idleness which usually provokes them to the aforementioned vices. (*Auto general del Oidor,* 358)

The fact remains, nevertheless, that the uprising was hardly a short-lived, spontaneous outburst of violence lacking in any formal planning and organization. Not only was the uprising planned, but, as we have noted, involved the replacement of Crown officials (both Spanish and indigenous) with rebel leaders and hence the assumption of the bureaucratic structure established by the colonial authorities. This is a fact that does not go unnoticed by the Bishop of Oaxaca, who, in the letter sent pleading for merciful treatment for the rebels and demonstrating sympathy for their cause, given the excesses of the late *Alcalde mayor,* stresses the political sense behind the actions of the rebels. "Great attention should be paid to the calmness and sense with which this mob carried on in the heat of the moment and in all the chaos, as is shown by the fact that they obliged the most highly-regarded Indians to take up the staffs of legal office in all the towns of this province" (Manso de Contreras 1974, 328). Unfortunately, the Bishop then becomes entangled in the contradictions of his own attempt to defend the native population: for while stressing this political "sense," the Bishop also appeals to the early colonial notion that the indigenous peoples were naïve, defenseless, childlike innocents who could not be condemned for such serious actions. For even though they apparently suffer from a weak nature which has caused them to act so atrociously, the Bishop pleads with the Viceroy and King to show pity to creatures so "pobres, míseros e indefensos" (Manso de Contreras 1974, 330). Manso de Contreras, meanwhile, rejects this plea outright. He counters the Bishop's arguments, first by inverting the notion of "good sense" and transforming the rebel actions into evidence of a natural inclination for deviousness that complemented their barbarous violence and simply served as further evidence of their intention to challenge colonial rule through such treasonous behavior:

In a period of more or less five hours, they succeeded with deed, action and disposition in achieving what appears impossible! The infernal fire, which they had set and which burned the whole time, could be seen as proof of their superhuman powers and just how belligerent they were! The way they blocked military posts and cut off paths and passes showed how well organized they were! They killed, wounded and defended with great bravery! In making off with an abundance of treasures and jewels from the *Casas reales,* how industrious they were! In stealing muskets and banner from the armoury, how daring they were! They then armed themselves and formed a company of guards as if they were lords of their own manor! They elected a governor, mayors, aldermen and other officials as if they had the political power to do so! Then, in sending out messages to other towns and plotting against the whole land, how ambitious they were! In urging others on by their own example and with letters from jurisdictions far and wide, how clever they were! To then go and destroy the sanctity of a place of worship, how sacrilegious they were! Tossing corpses into the open field or into the fire, how tyrannical they were! Forming councils and conspiracies to kill the Spanish and to force them from the church, how extraordinary they were! Acclaiming their own King, how treasonous and disloyal they were! (Manso de Contreras 1974, 322)

Manso de Contreras therefore dismisses any appeal to the innocent, mindless, and docile natures of the indigenous rebels as irrational creatures without any *real* political or ethical sense, and hence incapable of any genuine attempt to harness political authority for themselves. But he appears nonetheless to be the victim of the ambivalence inherent to the orientalist discourse he is championing. His portrayal of the insurgents simply as rioting thugs bent on overthrowing the whole viceroyalty or then, subsequently, as docile vassals beaten into submission, can hardly be reconciled with the fact that they had undertaken a premeditated, concerted, and synchronized plan of action.

This paradox is further illustrated by the fact that while he is clearly incensed by the nerve of the insurgents to attempt to perform—to "mimic" in the Bhabhian sense—the functions of government by appointing officials from their own ranks, he cannot help but affirm their unquestionable success in doing so. In the immediate aftermath of the storming of the *Casas Reales,* for instance, Manso de Contreras describes in horror, but also amazement, how the insurgents armed themselves with muskets, raised the royal standard, and formed a drum-beating, pipe-playing procession to proclaim their assumption of power and their intention to fill the vacant political offices with members of the rebel leadership:

The insolent insurgents (as if there were a single one amongst them who was not) were found to be so skilful, cautious and informed that all at once, as if their designs had been well planned for each individual action, they sacked the armoury. Making their way to the municipal buildings of the town, they carried forty muskets and the royal standard along with them in a drum-beating, flute-playing procession as if to make a public declaration of their victory. They then formed a company of guards with five hundred Indians, sending many more through the streets and the main square while, with arrogance and false political authority, they named a governor, mayors and aldermen and other officials. (Manso de Contreras 1974, 321)

This allusion to their cunning, their daring, and their arrogance, but also to their skill and their preparedness, cannot help but dispel any doubts about the mobilization and organizational skills of these insurgents, intent on defending their legal status as protected vassals of the Crown from *within* the colonial system. Here it is worth quoting the letter by the rebels themselves, which is included in Manso de Contreras' documentary compilation. "We united and formed a council and elected a governor in the name of your Majesty so as to let no-one interpret our actions as rebellious or as actions which refuse obedience to our King and Lord; on the contrary, we are at your Majesty's command as loyal vassals" (Manso de Contreras 1974, 326). The rebels thus make it clear that they are not in fact "rebels," but loyal vassals of the king who have been forced to take the law into their own hands and to act accordingly. Their appropriation of the victory march and the political election of their own officials is symbolic of this assumption of a colonial judicial system which had failed them.

While struggling to reduce the complexity of the insurgents' actions and identities, and to reassert the frontier between "law-abiding Spaniard" and "violent Indian," Manso de Contreras also takes great pains to present the rebels as having made an attack on the sanctity of the legal institution itself and, by the same token, to present the Crown authorities as having responded with the unequivocal serving of justice. In effect, an isomorphic relationship between Law and Justice is affirmed, while the rebels and their cause are located within the realm of the "outlaw" and the "unjust." The force inherent to the Law and its use as an instrument of state-sanctioned violence might thereby be concealed beneath the veil of ethical behavior associated with "Justice" as a transcendental ideal. Needless to say, in Manso de Contreras' estimation, the enforcement of the Law and serving justice *do* preclude violence, and, since the *Oidor*'s tactics did not involve a full scale slaughter of the indigenous population of the Isthmus, but only the threat of such a slaughter, the Prosecutor's actions should be hailed as a triumph for the force of law rather than |the force of arms. Indeed, Manso de Contreras's reproduction of Montemayor de Cuenca's *auto general* in the account reaffirms this opposition between the irrational violence of insurrection and the serving of justice:

> The Divine Majesty has been served by the fact that without an uproar, without force of arms, without scandal or any breach of public order, but through the use of certain prudent preventive legal measures which were gradually taken and executed, the desired peace, order and calm has been achieved. In this way, justice has been satisfied and done without losing sight of the compassion and mercy which was shown to the principal leaders in the uprising and rebellion of this province. (Manso de Contreras 1974, 356)

Nevertheless, more importantly, both Manso de Contreras and Montemayor de Cuenca deny or ignore the possibility that the violence of the

Law lies not solely in its permitting the use of force for legal ends, but also in the symbolic violence perpetrated by the enforcement of law through ritual. The public reading of Montemayor de Cuenca's *auto general* in Tehuantepec itself was followed by a solemn Mass in which the indigenous population were exhorted to acknowledge the clemency of Crown justice and to pledge their allegiance to the King; on leaving the church, another ceremony took place in which a portrait of the King was put on public display in the *Casas Reales* and before which the population of the town were expected to swear an oath of allegiance and pay their respects by walking past and bowing. Finally, it was decreed that the ceremony should become institutionalized and repeated each year:

> And, so that in future times the memory of his Majesty's mercy and clemency shall endure, every year this day will be celebrated on the same day as the feast of the aforementioned glorious St. Isabel. In saying her Mass as well as a commemoration of Our Lady, St. Michael and St. Dominic, attention will be paid to the fact that this holy queen was an ancestor of his Majesty and that she had a special gift from Our Lord God for dispensing peace and for setting the calm spirit of princes against the violent fury of war. (Manso de Contreras 1974, 357)

The implicit threat here is against any future reemergence of rioting and rebellion. The call for a yearly ritualized celebration of obedience and subjection to the Crown is tantamount to an act of symbolic violence demanding subjection from the indigenous population: they must agree to give up their right to violence for *natural* ends for the sake of the viceroyalty's monopoly of violence for *legal* ends.[7] Swearing this oath and participating in a ritual of this kind is a physical act of contrition, which serves as a spectacular manifestation of the power of the law in the same way that it manifests the subject population's lack of access to "legal" force. In effect, the ritualized ceremony is analogous to forms of punishment that involved bodily mutilation and amputation: both ritual and public punishment represented law preservation through the inscription of the law upon the king's subjects. The writing up of this ritual in the *relación* serves Manso de Contreras in his attempt to create a space in which transcendental symbols of justice might confront, defeat, and then inscribe themselves upon those responsible for a material violence which, ultimately, must cede any power it might have briefly created for the insurgents. In the end, such violence is no match, either for a transcendental law as represented by the portrait of the King, or for Montemayor de Cuenca, the personification of justice.

It is clear that the rebellion was punished and then to be remembered as if it had in fact been an assault on the sanctity of the Law and on the king's symbolic body. The uprising, however, if we accept the pledge of the rebel leaders, amounts to a case of using violence for *law preserva-*

tion rather than an example of violence directed against and challenging the Law itself. In that sense, the rebellion was *not* anti-colonial or treasonous, but perhaps, in the minds of the rebel leaders, a case of justifiable tyrannicide against an abusive usurper of legislative power, and executed in the hope of reasserting the colonial law and order which was meant to guarantee protection from the abuses inherent to the *repartimiento* system. In the minds of the vice-regal officials, of course, any subaltern assumption of violence, even for apparently justifiable ends, constituted a threat to their own monopoly of force for "legal" ends. Indeed, curiously, while berating those who called for mercy for the ringleaders, Manso de Contreras appears, perhaps unwittingly, to actually suggest that the biggest crime committed by the rebellious mob had not been the actual murder of a Crown official and his servants, or even to have provoked a regional uprising, but the fact that this state monopoly on the use of violence had been challenged: "there is absolutely no law which would allow them the use of the violence which by their own hands they executed, thus removing it from the authority of the Superior Courts" ["no hay ley ninguna que les permita la violencia que por su mano ejecutaron, quitándola a los Tribunales Superiores"] (Manso de Contreras 1974, 323). One might argue that the object pronoun "*la*" here, refers to "*ley*." But it seems more likely that it refers to "la violencia" and hence, confirms that the only ones appointed to use violence for legal ends are those same *Tribunales Superiores* and never a private party, however just their cause or however great a loyalty to the king they might claim. The supposed frontier between indigenous violence and the serving of vice-regal justice through law enforcement, apparently so cherished by Manso de Contreras and Montemayor de Cuenca, would appear, in this case, to have been momentarily overlooked.

By way of a conclusion, and as a means for locating the rebellion in a wider history of the Isthmus region, I would like to adopt the terms *dismembering* (deconstructing) and *re-membering* (re-constructing) offered by Etienne Balibar in his own consideration of the relationship between the law, justice, and violence (Balibar 2002, 140); not least of all because several of the ringleaders of the Tehuantepec rebellion were literally (physically) dismembered (in the punishments which followed), *textually* dismembered (that is, transformed from politically motivated insurgents into wild, mindless outlaws), and then re-membered, at least in the *relación,* as having been punished with justice for their attack on the colonial order. We might therefore view Manso de Contreras' writing up of the rebellion as an official remembrance of how a territorial body, a regal body, and a juridical corpus had been dismembered by material violence and then, through the intervention and application of the justice system, reconstituted in their entirety. Nevertheless, rather than perpetuating the notion that the rebellion was yet another instance of how colonial justice triumphed over an ineffectual indigenous violence, I have chosen to read Manso de Contreras' account as a means for problematizing the apparent dichotomy between colonial violence and colonial justice. This document thereby presents us with the opportunity to deconstruct (*dis-member*) an account (a textual *body*) of how "justice" successfully contained "violence" and encourages us to reconstruct (*re-member*) this violent rebellion as an illustration of indigenous political mobilization and collective agency that go beyond the interpellations of seventeenth century colonial ideology.

Having said that, I am of course aware that contemporary historians like Macleod (1998), Spores (1998), and Patch (2000) have warned us that we should not romanticize indigenous rebellions like Tehuantepec by exaggerating their impact since, at the end of the day, colonialism succeeded in impoverishing the indigenous population and keeping them under heel.[8] Yet even though this warning could serve us as a caveat, not least of all because the Tehuantepec insurgents, as we have noted, at no time launched a full scale anti-colonial uprising, the implicit dismissal of the significance of the rebellion should be addressed. For, if, rather than romanticizing or idealizing indigenous rebellions, we regard them as overlooked footnotes to a wider national history, then we might see the historian's task as one of *recuperation* rather than as an attempt to evaluate the immediate success or failure of a given rebellion. By recuperating these rebellions from a colonial historiography that emphasized their triumphant quashing by the viceroyalty, one would hope that a Benjaminian "quotation" from the past might be restored to the collective memory of the present as a reminder that the region's colonial history was fluid rather than static, was marked by constant violence, and hence negotiated in a continual process in which indigenous rebellion played a central role. I am not, of course, thinking of a "quotation" in the sense of a restored element within a historical continuum characterized by the illusion of national "progress," but as an integral element within a constellation of conflictive events in which colonial, national, and postnational identities were and are still being negotiated today.

Needless to say, the recuperation of the Tehuantepec rebellion in such terms is particularly relevant in a region of Mexico that has witnessed more than its fair share of political, socioeconomic, and ethnic violence over the centuries. As the narrowest part of Mexico, stretching some 140 miles between the Pacific port of Salina Cruz, in the state of Oaxaca, and Coatzacoalcos, Veracruz, on the Gulf of Mexico, the Isthmus of Tehuantepec has long been recognized—at least since the period of the early conquest by Cortés—for its strategic location. The geographic importance of the region is underlined by the fact that during the nineteenth century, before Panama was finally seized upon as the route for the canal that connects the Atlantic and Pacific oceans, the Isthmus of Tehuantepec was itself considered a potential canal zone. Nowadays, with the Panama Canal at its absolute capacity for handling inter-ocean traffic, international attention has once again been drawn back to the Isthmus in the shape of the controversial "Plan Puebla Panama" (PPP).[9] And, most significantly, militant organizers of indigenous communities in the Isthmus region who are striving to speak out against the PPP claim that the Tehuantepec rebellion of 1660 still resonates as a key moment in a history of political mobilization by the indigenous communities of the Isthmus:

> In the mega-project for the Isthmus plan, no one takes into account the existence of the Indian peoples who over the last five hundred years have demonstrated that they are experts in resistance. In many different ways, these communities resisted the Spanish invasion, colonialism and now a brutal and exclusive capitalism ... In different moments of our history, the indigenous communities of the isthmus have mobilized themselves to defend their interests and their own survival ... Moreover, when necessary, this resistance became violent. In 1660 one of the most important rebellions in the colonial history of Mexico broke out in the Mexican isthmus. The so-called Tehuantepec Rebellion spread through almost the whole of the State of Oaxaca and was crushed in blood and fire. (Beas 2000, 21)

The 1660 Tehuantepec rebellion, then, perhaps peripheral to a wider national history, has lost none of its political significance for local leaders hoping to raise the historical and political consciousness of the communities most threatened by the PPP.[10] Ultimately, rather than being considered a record of how another indigenous rebellion was crushed by the vice-regal forces of law and order, Manso de Contreras' narrative from 1661 reminds us that the colonial "frontier" between "justice" and "violence" (both material and discursive) is today still a site of contention, rather than a natural barrier.

Notes

1. Those familiar with Benjamin's classic "Critique of Violence" essay from 1927 and more recent readings of the essay by Derrida (1992), Agamben (1998), and Balibar (2002) will recognize some of the theoretical considerations he raises in my reading of this account of the Tehuantepec rebellion. Derrida, Agamben, and Balibar point out that in the English title of Benjamin's "Critique of Violence," the translation of the original German *Gewalt* as "violence" fails to capture the fact that *Gewalt* also signifies "authority," "public force," and the notion of a state-sanctioned use of violence, thus ignoring a clear allusion to a case in which

violence is legitimated by law. Benjamin's essay is also particularly useful for understanding violence in terms of 'means' and 'ends,' in the sense that if violence is justified as a necessary *means* to reach just *ends,* its use by the state no longer constitutes violence but an instance of the enactment of force *to make* law. Echoing both Machiavelli and Hobbes, Benjamin argues that, despite the fact that the commonwealth might respect the right of the individual to use violence for 'natural' ends, that same right must, by law, be given up so as to protect the integrity of the commonwealth and to allow a state monopolization of the use of force for legal ends. Hence, any use of violence by individuals is potentially a threat to the foundations of the Law itself rather than the enactment of a natural right for, for example, self–protection. Meanwhile, the *subordination* of individuals to the state's monopoly over violence constitutes an act of "law-preservation." In the specific case of the Tehuantepec uprising, we are presented with a rebellion deemed *illegal,* though it aims to be clearly *law preserving* rather than law destroying, while the application of the law in the form of severe punishments serves to exemplify how "doing justice" cannot be but a violent process. Derrida's usefulness also hinges on the fact that he convincingly denaturalizes the foundational conception of the Law as a transcendental institution and emphatically prizes the concept of *justice* free from its automatic identification with the Law. Derrida underscores the fact that both the application of the Law and the foundation of origin of any social taboo cannot be divorced from an inaugurating act of force, since it obviously depends on the threat of force for its authority (Derrida 1992, 13).
2. Of course, it is not within the scope of this study to make any more than the briefest of allusions to an understanding of the Tehuantepec rebellion in terms of the power struggle between the different factions of the colonial elite or, by extension, of the economic crisis affecting New Spain between 1620 and 1670. For a detailed analysis of economic conditions in New Spain during the sixteenth century, Israel (1975) is particularly illuminating. The classic essay by Borah (1951) is indispensable, while Blanco and Romero Sotelo (1999) provide a contemporary assessment of Borah's original hypothesis. On the direct relationship between this rebellion and the economic crisis facing Spain both in Europe and in the Americas, see the relevant contributions in Díaz-Polanco and Sánchez (1992).
3. On the relationship between the uprising and the crisis that shook the Conde de Baños' brief period in office (1660–1664), see Basilio Rojas (1964, esp. 227–248).
4. Modern studies of the causes, trajectory, and aftermath of the rebellion include González Obregón (1951), Rojas (1964), Casarrubias (1975), Israel (1975), Covarrubias (1980), Semo (1981), Díaz-Polanco and Sánchez (1992), Spores (1998), Hamnett (1999), Mecott Francisco (2002).
5. Almost predictably, a document issued by the Bishop of Oaxaca some time following these events confirmed that, rather than guaranteeing protection for the local indigenous communities from the illegalities inherent to the *repartimiento* system, the *Oidor*'s actions, *in practice,* had in fact simply strengthened the position of the vice-regal bureaucracy by reasserting the legitimacy of a system which had been responsible for provoking the uprising in the first place. See Münch (1982, 390).
6. On the role played by indigenous leaders chosen by the vice-regal bureaucracy as instruments for facilitating the exploitation of the indigenous communities dur-

ing this period, see Israel (1975), Carmagnani (1992), and Díaz-Polanco and Sánchez (1992).
7. On the use of violence for "legal" and/or "natural" ends, see note 1 above on Benjamin's use of the terms in "Critique of Violence."
8. On the other hand, historians have also argued against the equally damaging myth of the inconsequentiality of indigenous rebellion. See Casarrubias (1975).
9. Following the precedent set by the 1996 "Megaproyecto del Istmo," the Plan Puebla Panamá has, since 2001, involved the integration of markets within Southern Mexico and Central America, increased exploitation of the abundance of natural resources possessed by the region, and stimulated huge investment in creating improved rail and road communications across the Isthmus between the Atlantic and Pacific oceans. What concerns the local population is that this expansion means increased privatization and fewer concerns with the wishes of the local population as to what benefits they themselves will reap from the plan. See Vera Herrera (2001), and Beas (2000).
10. Beas and other members of the Grupo de Trabajo Colectivo del Istmo and Unión de Comunidades Indígenas de la Zona Norte del Istmo have also produced a collection of essays designed specifically for informing the local communities of their history and the threat posed by neoliberal policies like the PPP to their livelihoods: *Ante el Plan Puebla Panamá Mesoamérica resiste* (2002).

Bibliography

Agamben, G. 1998. *Homo Sacer: Sovereign Power and Bare Life.* Stanford: Stanford University Press.
Balibar, E. 2002. *Politics and the Other Scene.* New York: Verso.
Beas Torres, Carlos. 2000. *Megaproyecto de istmo: La invasion global.* Available at <http://www.mesoamericaresiste.org>.
Benjamin, Walter. 1978. "Critique of Violence." In *Reflections.* New York: Schocken Books, 277–300.
———. 1985 [1968]. "Theses on the Philosophy of History." In Hannah Arendt, ed, *Illuminations. Essays and Reflections.* New York: Schocken Books, 253–264.
Blanco, Mónica and María Eugenia Romero Sotelo. 2000. *Tres siglos de economía novohispana, 1521–1821.* México: Universidad Nacional Autónoma de México.
Borah, W. 1951. *New Spain's Century of Depression.* Berkeley and Los Angeles: University of California Press.
Carmagnani, M. 1992. "Un movimiento político indio: La 'rebelión' de Tehuantepec, 1660–1661." In Héctor Díaz-Polanco, coordinador. *El fuego de la inobediencia: Autonomía y rebelión india en el Obispado de Oaxaca.* México: CIESAS, 81–101.
Casarrubias, Victor. 1975. *Rebeliones indígenas en la Nueva España.* México: Metropolitana.
Covarrubias, Miguel. 1980. *El sur de México.* México: Instituto Nacional Indigenista.
Derrida, Jacques. 1992. "Force of Law: The 'Mystical Foundation of Authority.'" In Drucilla Cornell, Michel Rosenfeld and David Gray Carlson, eds, *Deconstruction and the Possibility of Justice.* New York: Routledge, 3–67.
Díaz–Polanco, Héctor and Consuelo Sánchez. 1992. "El vigor de la espada restauradora. La represión de las rebeliones indias en Oaxaca (1660–1661)." In Héctor Díaz-Polanco, Coordinador, *El fuego de la inobediencia: Autonomía y rebelión India en el Obispado de Oaxaca.* México: CIESAS, 53–79.

Gónzalez Obregón, Luis. 1951 [1906]. *Rebeliones Indígenas y Precursores de la Independencia Mexicana (en los siglos XVI, XVII y XVIII)*. México: Ediciones Fuente Cultural.

Grupo de Trabajo Colectivo del Istmo y Unión de Comunidades Indígenas de la Zona Norte del Istmo. 2002. *Ante el Plan Puebla Panamá, Mesoamérica Resiste*. Fundación Solidago: Matías Romero, Oaxaca.

Guha, R. 1988. "The Prose of Counter-Insurgency." In Ranajit Guha and Gayatri Chakravorty Spivak, eds, *Selected Subaltern Studies*. New York: Oxford University Press, 45–86.

Hamnett, B. 1999. *A Concise History of Mexico*. Cambridge: Cambridge University Press.

Israel, J.I. 1975. *Race, Class and Politics in Colonial Mexico, 1610–1670*. Oxford: Oxford University Press.

Macleod, Murdo J. 1998. "Some Thoughts on the Pax Colonial, Colonial Violence, and Perceptions of Both." In Susan Schroeder, ed, *Native Resistance and the Pax Colonial in New Spain*. Lincoln: University of Nebraska Press, 129–142.

Manso de Contreras, Cristóbal. 1974. "Relación cierta y verdadera de lo que sucedió y ha sucedido en esta villa de Guadalcázar, provincia de Tehuantepec, desde los 22 de marzo de 1660 hasta los 4 de Julio de 1661, cerca de que los naturales indios de estas provincias, tumultados y amotinados, mataron a don Juan de Avellán, su Alcalde Mayor y Teniente de Capitán General, y a tres criados suyos, procediendo a otros gravísimos delitos, hasta aclamar rey de su naturaleza." In *Documentos inéditos o muy raros para la historia de México*. Publicados por Genaro García. México: Porrúa, 311–367.

Mecott Francisco, Mario. 2002. *Tehuantepec insurgente*. Oaxaca: Carteles Editores PGO.

Münch, G. "La rebelión de Tehuantepec en 1660." *Tlalocan*. México, 9: 385–395.

Patch, Robert W. 2000. "Indian Resistance to Colonialism." In Michael C. Meyer and William H. Beezley, eds, *The Oxford History of Mexico*. Oxford: Oxford University Press, 2000, 183–212.

Rojas, Basilio. 1964. *La rebelión de Tehuantepec*. México: Sociedad Mexicana de Geografía y Estadística.

Semo, E., coord. 1981. *México: un pueblo en la historia*, Vol. 1. México: Editorial nueva imagen y la Universidad Autónoma de Puebla.

Spores, R. 1998. "Differential Response to Colonial Control among the Mixtecs and Zapotecs of Oaxaca." In Susan Schroeder, ed., *Native Resistance and the Pax Colonial in New Spain*. Lincoln: University of Nebraska Press, 30–46.

Vera Herrera, Ramón. 2001. "'El Istmo de Tehuantepec no se vende': Marcos." *La Jornada,* 26 February.

Chapter 10

(The) *Patria* Besieged:
Border-Crossing Paradoxes of National Identity in Cervantes's Numancia

Michael Armstrong-Roche

Cervantes's *La destruición de Numancia* (ca. 1581–1585)[1] is a play about a heroic last stand waged by the Celtiberian Numantines against Rome. Numancia—capital of the *arevaci,* near today's Soria in northern Castile—was indeed destroyed by Scipio Aemilianus in 133 B.C. but won an enduring reputation for courage.[2] Only a few years before Cervantes wrote *Numancia,* Philip II's chronicler Ambrosio de Morales celebrated this Celtiberian legacy as a decisive moment in Spanish history (in the *Corónica general de España,* 1574), although ancient Numancia and Habsburg Spain shared little more than the accident of geography and a reputation for warrior audacity and prowess, preoccupation with honor, pride, and, above all, courage.[3] Because *Numancia* dramatizes an historical event that had begun to acquire the status of an origin story for sixteenth-century Habsburg Spain, the play lends itself to an exploration of the conceptual shortcuts needed for imperial and national myth-making. The role of violent conflict, selective memory, and nostalgic idealization in the fashioning of a narrative that draws on a past thought exemplary for the present, is starkly highlighted in this siege of Celtiberians identified as ancient Spaniards. In part, this is because the event itself pits two ancestral peoples taken to be foundational for modern Spain against one another, the Celtiberians and the Romans locked in a bitter fight to the death. But the play also prompts questions about the use of history to define national identity (Which past is ours? The Celtiberian or the Roman?), the value of literature—in this case, public theater—for imagining the past and restoring nuances omitted in official histories, and the dramatic possibilities of that contested past as a mirror for the contemporary Habsburg adventure of world-straddling dominion.

A question that remains alive is whether Cervantes participates unabashedly in the myth-making use of Numancia to celebrate sixteenth-century Habsburg Spain or whether the play is to be read as a cautionary tale about the wages of empire. Readings that regard *Numancia* as an untroubled celebration of Spanish heroism, and Cervantes himself as a patriot for whom Numancia's destruction heralds Spanish imperial glory, are authorized explicitly in prophecies voiced by the Duero river in Act 1, War (*Guerra*) in Act 4, and Fame (*Fama*) as she brings the curtain down (Vivar 2000). These personifications appear on the stage to immortalize the heroic valor of the Numantines seen as a precursor people for Habsburg Spain and to promise future renown and the humiliation of Rome by a long series of invasions capped by the Sack of 1527 and the defeat of the Franco-Papal alliance in 1557. The destruction of Numancia is taken by these prophetic voices for a providential death, necessary sacrifice, and historical tragedy resurrected, redeemed, and avenged by the rise of sixteenth-century Spain. Numancia's body politic dies like Christ on the cross only to live again in the spirit associated insistently with courage, the renown for valor won by the Spanish sword from Ferdinand of Aragon (vv. 1997–1999).[4] Its Second Coming is cast, among other ways, as the fulfillment of the old dream of peninsular union with Philip II's inheritance of the Portuguese crown in 1581.[5] No longer prevalent in Cervantes scholarship, this line of interpretation remains a theme in accounts of Spanish history that draw on "the national author" as a resounding voice for *patria* (fatherland), who sooner reinforces than questions symbols and myths of patriotic fervor (Alcalá de Zamora Queipo de Llano 2000, 104–105). Although such readings are grounded in the providential accounts of history voiced by Duero, War, and Fame, their drawback is that they claim these voices for the play's or Cervantes's last word.

Other readers have ventured to interpret the play allegorically, not as a fundamentally antiquarian exercise whose connection to the author's present is limited by what Duero, War, and Fame "foretell," but also as in some sense about the actual rather than the anticipated world of Philip II's Habsburg Spain. Avalle-Arce (1975), for example, identifies the Roman consul Scipio and his army with Philip II and his forces, relies on the Duero river's and Fame's expression of faith in imperial ideals, and suggests that the Romans newly disciplined under Scipio will make themselves worthy of empire, to be revitalized with even greater glory by sixteenth-century Spaniards. This argument reminds us that Cervantes's contemporaries were liable to recognize themselves in both Numancia and Rome. Because of the sheer extent of his dominions and the resources at his command, Philip II—though shorn of the imperial title, which passed to his uncle Ferdinand of Austria in 1556—was among the few sovereigns since Charlemagne who could plausibly aspire to revive Augustus's *pax romana* in the new guise of a united Christendom, an imperial ambition routinely underlined by Habsburg royal iconography.[6]

Now dominant in political readings of *Numancia* is the appeal to historical allegory that presses the identification between Scipio and Philip II (and therefore between Rome and Spain), but acknowledges features of the play that cast doubt on the imperial ideal. Taking a cue from its prophetic thrust, the invitation to look ahead and to conjure "future" audiences (especially Spanish legatees of Numancia) and to make them implied characters in the larger historical drama being lived under Philip II, this tendency finds powerful textual support in Plague's (*Enfermedad*'s) and Famine's (*Hambre*'s) Act 4 descriptions of Numancia in flames like a new Troy (vv. 2020, 2024–2025, 2050–2055). The Trojan resonances evoke the epic discourse of *translatio imperii,* the transfer of political and cultural authority in a movement that was said, by convention, to follow the sun (Johnson 1980, 80–81). Virgil's *Aeneid* locates the legendary and heroic origins of Roman imperial glory in the destruction of the Trojans by the Greeks, much as the Duero's prophetic speech in Cervantes's play traces the origins of the Spanish empire to Numancia's defeat. We are thus invited to step both backward and forward in time beyond the limits of the play's action, when history takes over and providentialism leaves off.

If Troy's destruction is to the Roman Empire as Numancia's is to Spain's, and if Rome is heir to and subjugates Greece as Spain is heir to and subjugates Rome, the play's deep sense of history as a set of (political and cultural) translations invites us to wonder what Habsburg Spain's contemporary Numancias might be. It should come as no surprise to us that, in the late 1970s—a period marked especially in the US by ubiquitous images of the horrors of Vietnam, renewed questions about established authority, and concerns about "imperial quagmire" and the threat to republican ideals—*Numancia* should have drawn seminal scholarly readings more disposed to recognize evidence of royal arrogance, injustice, and imperial overreach than had been the case in earlier scholarship. For Alfredo Hermenegildo, the play's siege recalled the bloody suppression of the morisco revolt that took place in the mountains of Granada in 1568–1570, led by Philip II's half-brother Don John of Austria (Hermenegildo 1976, 47–74). Willard King suggested that the play could well have served its early Madrid *corral* audiences as a painful reminder of the notoriously brutal, interminable, and costly war in Flanders, especially the Duke of Alba's failed campaign of terror between 1567 and 1573 (King 1979, 202, 214–217). Because of the play's borrowings from Alonso de

Ercilla's New World epic, *La Araucana,* King also wondered whether Scipio's siege of Numancia could not have evoked Habsburg operations against the *Araucos* of southern Chile led by García Hurtado de Mendoza. Carroll Johnson developed the parallel with the Revolt in Flanders in compelling detail, drawing on the soldier-chronicler don Bernardino de Mendoza's account of the Duke of Alba's campaign (Johnson 1981). In both cases—Numancia and Flanders—a vastly superior military force is projected abroad to a remote province far from central authority, where the customs are different, and where recent imperial representatives are regarded as tyrannical. Other analogies with contemporary Flanders include the practice of siege warfare on walled cities situated on wide rivers, a commander (Alba) more interested in winning than in personal display of courage or shedding of his own troops' blood, terrible famines, and a mutiny.

Although the voices of Duero and Fame make Rome the evil oppressor and Numancia—identified with Spain (*España*) and Spaniards (*españoles*)—the courageous yet woefully outmanned resistors, these kinds of historical readings remind us that the prophetic mode in the play, neo-Roman dynastic propaganda promoting the Habsburg House as imperial Rome's rightful successor, and the realities of Spanish power in the 1580s all conspire to declare that the tables have been turned and Numancia is now Rome. And if Rome once played enemy to Numancia (and therefore to Spain), the irony of history has now cast sixteenth-century Habsburg Spain as a new Rome to contemporary Numancias, such as Flanders, the *moriscos,* and the *Araucos*. In the light of this historical role reversal, the apparently triumphant tale of Numancia's historical defeat, but spiritual victory (and Rome's military victory but Scipio's personal defeat), becomes a cautionary tale for Habsburg Spain. Spain is not only the glorious reincarnation of Ancient Numancia, but also now the New Rome; not only Numancia avenged, but also now the tyrannical oppressor. And Rome's fate in the sixteenth century—crushed twice under the Habsburg boot—could be Spain's tomorrow.

Since the 1970s, some scholars (e.g. Simerka 2003, 77–128) have pursued one or another of the historical allegories outlined (Numancia as Flanders, the *moriscos,* or the *Araucos* among other New World peoples). By and large, however, *Numancia* scholarship has retreated from or subordinated the play's politics to genre criticism, asking whether it should be categorized with classical tragedy, historical tragedy, secular tragedy, tragicomedy, comedy, history or epic (Bergmann 1984; Lewis-Smith 1987; Tar 1990; Rey Hazas 1991; Martín 1996; Karageorgou Bastea 1997; Armas 1998; and Maestro 2004).[7] In the pages that follow, I return to the possibilities raised in those earlier readings of *Numancia*'s politics by exploring how the text makes visible the later historical role reversal that would put Numancia (Spain) in Rome's place. The play's chief strategy is, as I will argue, its paradoxical handling of identity. I mean paradox in its root sense here, as a proposition contrary to received opinion. And rather than defend a triumphalist patriotic or anti-imperial critical reading of the play as has already been done very well, I am interested in drawing attention to the way the text plays those implications off one another in the light of Numancia's sixteenth-century consolidation as a proto-national myth for Spain.

By emphasizing the complexity of the play's approach to history and national identity, I am proposing that it engages in a kind of debate with historical and royal discourses keen to advance national or dynastic interests by appeal to an idealized version of the past, whether Numancia's or Rome's. And its chief contribution to this debate is, as I see it, to answer the moral certainties and pieties of patriotic discourse about Numancia and Rome by highlighting not only the continuities, but also the discontinuities between precursor and current communities imagined as making up a *patria*. It will become apparent that *Numancia* defeats any single-minded effort to identify Habsburg Spain with Numancia (promoted by such contemporary historians as Morales) or Rome (promoted by Habsburg royal iconography), because both are presented as morally suspect. Nevertheless, since the triumphalist view of Numancia (and Spain) is supported explicitly by key speeches, my emphasis is on countervailing voices, actions, and characterizations that convey a reiterated impulse to muddy what seems on the face of it to be clear. The play's profiles in courage unsettle facile appropriations, undercutting the easy identification between either Numancia or Rome and early Spanish audiences, the homogeneity within what passes for Numantine and Roman "culture" (as we might call it), and the clean-cut polarization of Numancia and Rome.

What does Cervantes make of this emergent national myth of Spanish courage and liberty? And how does the play explain the link between ancient Numancia and sixteenth-century Spain, the developing sense of a *patria* or national identity continuous in time? The play's several references to *patria* are to the city-state of Numancia (vv. 717, 2369, 2399) and it finds many occasions to identify that Numantine *patria* explicitly with Spaniards (*españoles*) and Spain (*España*) set over against Romans and Rome. The Roman consul Scipio speaks of Numantines as "Spaniards" (españoles; v.115), "this puny hispanic people" (*este pequeño pueblo hispano;* v. 126), and "these rebellious, barbaric Hispanics" (*estos rebeldes, bárbaros hispanos;* v. 164). He also declares that by crushing Numantine pride, all of Spain will submit to the Roman senate (vv. 350–351). For this reason, when the boy Bariato denies Scipio his official triumph by killing himself—one Numantine survivor is needed to prove victory at home—Scipio predicts that his courage will bring glory not only to Numancia, but also to the whole of Spain (vv. 2403–2404).

The Numantines themselves participate in this identification of themselves and their *patria* with Spaniards, Spain, and the Hispanic: the warrior Caravino declares his faith in the "courage of the Spanish arm" (*valor de la española mano;* v. 565) to lift the siege despite overwhelming Roman superiority in numbers. The personification of War speaks of Numantines as "Hispanics" (*hispanos;* v. 1989) and anticipates the day—from the reign of Ferdinand of Aragon (v. 1999)—when Numancia's "hispanic courage" (*valor hispano*) will be known to all the world. Cervantes here follows the lead of the humanist historian Ambrosio de Morales, whose *Corónica general de España* (1574) calls the Numantines "Spaniards" (*españoles*) just as both Romans and Numantines do in the play.[8] This usage suggests that, well before Cervantes, the destruction of the Celtiberian city had come to be regarded as an episode of Spanish national history, a milestone in the history of what John Armstrong has called *Nations before Nationalism* (Armstrong 1982; Johnson 1980, 76).

Numancia's conception of that Numantine *patria* identified with sixteenth-century "Spain" and "Spaniards" is as varied (or confused) as was the range of contemporary reflection on a collective reality still very much in ferment and far from consolidation (Barton 1993; Thompson 1995; Rodríguez Salgado 1996 and 1998). One measure of the play's model of *patria,* and of a patriotism directed to it, is the personification of Spain (*España*). At the end of Act 1, Spain speaks out for Numancia and against perfidious Rome, addressing her lament of Numancia's lost cause to the heavens and to posterity. The stage direction—which describes her as "crowned with several towers, bearing a castle in one hand, representing Spain" (Cervantes 1994, 72)—clearly identifies Spain with the iconography of its leading peninsular kingdom, Castile. This reflex is imitated by the personified Duero river, the besieged Numancia's only lifeline to the wider world and hope for relief. Duero looks ahead to that moment when the "Lusitanian tatter"—once ripped from "the garments of illustrious Castile"—will be restored to her "old self" (*antiguo ser; Numancia* vv. 517–520), Duero's vivid sartorial image for Philip II's annexation of Portugal in 1581. Spain in her lamentation speech (vv. 361–392), and especially Duero in her consolation speech (vv. 473–480), offer yet another vision of what constitutes the *patria* near the end of Act 1, a broadly territorial *ius solis* that embraces the variety of peoples settled and kingdoms established within what is today known as the Iberian peninsula. Such a conception of Spain remained something of an abstraction even in 1581, given the comparative lack—by later standards—of institutional, legal, monetary, and linguistic unity of the chief peninsular kingdoms (Castile, Aragon, and Portugal) that owed the Habsburg Philip II fealty.

Addressing and consoling the personified Spain, the Duero river ends Act 1 by delivering the most elaborate reflection on the historical relation between ancient Numancia and sixteenth-century Spain. Although Duero predicts that Spain's leading champion will be the Habsburg Philip II following the annexation of Portugal and its seaborne empire, it enumerates key themes in the formation of an emerging sense of a "Spanish" community defined by more than loyalty to house and home or even fealty to monarch or dynasty. For instance, it announces the coming of Christianity and insists on associating the key attribute of "courage" (*valor*) with the "Hispanic name" (*nombre hispano*). Indeed, other than geography, the principal link between ancient Numancia and Habsburg Spain is a transhistorical ethopoeia that includes a shared reputation for warrior audacity (vv. 572, 644, 2382, 2384), preoccupation with honor (vv. 592, 593, 605, 1295, 1298, 2143, 2147, 2183), military prowess (v. 2252), and arrogance and pride (vv. 114, 352, 1115, 2201, 2230, 2246). The salient virtue of Numancia is, of course, courage (vv. 1753, 1761, 2376, 2431, 2434, 2440, 2445), a *topos* in sixteenth-century descriptions of Habsburg Spain and Spaniards for those writers who took the warrior code of the nobility for a national virtue.[9]

The character Spain also gives voice to a more troubling attribute destined to a long life as one of the enduring myths of modern Spain: the house eternally divided against itself. She blames internecine strife and even simple discord for the "tyranny" of earlier successive waves of barbarian invaders (she names the Phoenicians and the Greeks in her review of "Spanish" history; vv. 361–384), a Spain divided having made herself easy prey to others only too prepared to enslave her inhabitants. Alone in Spain, Numancia has traded her blood for "liberty" (v. 388). And yet Spaniards too will prove traitors to Numancia. The Numantine chief Theogenes laments the "Spaniards" allied with Rome and prepared to slit Numancia's throat (vv. 545–548), referring to turncoat Celtiberian tribes as if to confirm Spain's and Duero's diagnosis of the *patria*'s historical ill: treachery of Spaniard against Spaniard, disunity of Peninsular kingdoms and peoples. It is in this light that we may understand the providential hopes Duero attaches to the union of Portugal to Castile (and Aragon) in 1581, cast as a fulfillment of the promise of liberty from foreign invasion with the apparently definitive achievement of internal peace.

What national identity is *not* characterized by is equally interesting, because it breaks with attributes that have come to define nationalism. Ethnicity, religion, the law, and key political institutions are neither decisive for marking peoples held essentially to be antagonists for all time (Numancia and Rome), nor certainly a guarantee of unity or peace. Only in the Duero speech does the play identify historical Spaniards ethnically, and it waffles: in part, it looks back to the Visigoths and the heroic deeds with which they will breathe new life into Spain following their invasion (vv. 477–480). It also links Spanish royalty (from Ferdinand and Isabella) with the Visigoths (vv. 503–504), in consonance with dynastic propaganda that promoted identification of the ruling families of Spain with a kind of Visigothic prelapsarian golden age, a nostalgic vision of peace, unity, and Christian orthodoxy shattered by the Muslim invasion.[10] Spain is otherwise associated with the various peoples, especially but not only the Celtiberian Numantines (v. 459), who inhabited the peninsula—many of them, as we noted, traitors to Numancia. Duero envisions "peoples" (*gentes*; vv. 473–476) arriving from "remote nations" (*remotas naciones*) to inhabit Spain's "sweet bosom" (*dulce seno*), peoples joined chiefly by their opposition to Rome (vv. 475–476).

The mere coincidence between Numancia and Rome of crucial "cultural" and political features such as religion, the law, and the senate thematizes the complexities and limits of Spanish historical identification with a Numancia pitted against Rome in the nationalist rhetoric voiced especially by Duero and Fame. Although Cervantes here sometimes follows historical sources, such evidence that Numancia and Rome are more like each other than not fits into a larger pattern peculiar to this play (as we shall see) that knocks the wind out of this myth-making reliance on anti-Roman diatribe. The play's ethnography does indeed Romanize Numancia. Romans and Numantines pray and offer oblations to and sacrifice for the same gods, including Jupiter (vv. 561, 634, 670, 773, 782, 810, 829, 1231, 1936, 2211), Diana (v. 2105), Pluto (vv. 864, 962), Ceres (v. 868), and Charon (v. 971). The debate whether love undermines or steels martial valor, translated into the mythological terms of Mars (vv. 89, 154, 713) and Venus (vv. 89, 123), is first engaged in the Roman Act 1 only to be echoed by the Numantine Act 2. The parallels remind us of what these sworn enemies have in common, and there is no little poignancy in the repeated Numantine invocation of Roman deities called on to defeat the Romans. To be sure, a shared pantheon of non-Christian deities could convey a generic paganism and this may have been sufficient historical accuracy for Cervantes's purposes. Yet the potential dramatic and thematic effect of such a choice is to blur the boundary dividing apparently irreconcilable foes.

Much the same can be said for the handling of the law. The Numantines are political tributaries to Rome, who sue for peace alleging the tyranny of previous consuls. The ambassadors want justice, not independence, citing the avarice, lust, and otherwise unlawful rule of earlier consuls to legitimize their rebellion. In the final scenes of the play, the Numantine Bariato will throw an accusation of broken "treaties and agreements" in Scipio's face (v. 2363). The play here agrees with Roman and Spanish historical sources, including Guevara's account in Letter 5 of the *Epístolas familiares* (1545), which portray an unjust war initiated when the Roman senate authorized Scipio to break a truce and renew hostilities (Guevara 1950, 1, 46–47). The link between the two peoples is reinforced by a shared political institution: the senate was originally Roman, not Numantine, of course, and yet, like Rome (v. 2), the play's Numancia is governed by its own senate (v. 1739). A senate in Golden Age theater often simply meant the audience, addressed through the fourth wall, the sense glossed by Berganza's drummer in Cervantes's own *Coloquio de los perros* (Cervantes [1613] 1989, 2: 335). More pointedly, Alonso de Ercilla calls the governing assembly of the *Araucos* of southern Chile a senate in his epic poem *La Araucana* (1569–1589), about the Habsburg war against this confederation of Amerindian peoples, endowing the governing council of indigenous "others" with a Roman name much as Cervantes does with his Numantine "barbarians" (*bárbaros*).[11] What might otherwise pass for a stylistic convention acquires a potentially charged meaning in a context where the boundary between peoples has been drawn so deep. In both camps, moreover, the senate is associated with an injustice. As the Roman senate authorizes an unjust war, so in the final Act we learn that the Numantine senate is responsible for the decree that orders all women, children, and elderly killed (vv. 1680–1681, 1944–1945). Ostensibly a glorious collective suicide, it will meet with internal resistance and will more than once be given the name of homicide.

Despite evidence that Rome and Numancia have more in common than their deep enmity would suggest, so far we have confirmed there is no lack of grist for the patriotic mill in Cervantes's version of the legend of Numancia. Act 1 plunges the spectator and reader into the Roman camp as Scipio prepares a renewed siege of the city, speeches on both sides tell us that ancient Numantines are Spaniards whose common enemy is Rome, and personifications of Spain and Duero end the act by praising Numancia's courage and love of liberty and by foretelling its death and resurrection in sixteenth-century Habsburg Spain. For good reason the play, like the legend, has been invoked as a resoundingly patriotic defence of Spanish heroism, as an effort to promote the consolidation and celebration of this emergent national myth. Act 2, however, situates us squarely in the Numantine camp, where the exalted views floated in Act 1 are put to severe tests. Up close from Act 2, *Numancia* begins to dwell on typical actions, attributes, and characterizations that undermine the heroic identification of contemporary Spaniards with Numancia. It does so by presenting features of Numancia that could only distance most Spaniards of around 1581, thereby heading off a too facile complacency about a selectively idealized version of past "selves."

First, there is the characteristic Numantine mode of warfare. The Numantine warrior Caravino, chafing at being enclosed "like women" (v. 570), proposes the stand-off between Numancia and Rome be resolved through single combat (v. 574). The motion is seconded by an anonymous Numantine soldier (vv. 613–616) and in Act 3, Caravino puts it to Scipio directly (vv. 1152–1160). The offer of single combat is in part a desperate measure meant to move the war to a terrain on which the outnumbered Numantines might have a chance. Early Spanish audiences may well also have responded to an idealized, mythic image of themselves as swashbuckling heroes determined to die honorably rather than waste away miserably from hunger. As is well-known, long after the mounted, armor-bearing knight had ceased to be an effective military force, the major courts of Europe were swept by a taste for knightly accoutrements, rituals, and rhetoric copied from the late flowering of chivalric literature, especially Garci Rodríguez de Montalvo's *Amadís de Gaula* (1508) and Ariosto's *Orlando furioso* (1516) (Checa Cremades 1987, 187–232). Rivals Francis I and Charles V were not immune to the fashion and, in 1528, made a ceremonial gesture of agreeing to settle the war between them through single combat (Tomás y Valiente 1992, 58–61). In 1596, the extravagant English Earl of Essex stood before the walls of Lisbon during its siege and challenged his counterpart to single combat, asserting the justice of his lord's cause and the greater beauty of his mistress (Meron 1998, 125; Braudy 2003, 150–157).

But such theatrical gestures and bravado were far removed from the realities of military combat as it was actually waged. We might reasonably wonder whether the archaic touch of single combat was not designed to achieve historical plausibility about an ancient people. Indeed Cervantes reveals his concern about, and perhaps also a general disregard in directors and audiences for, elementary verisimilitude when a stage direction in Act 1 requests that the Roman host gathered before Scipio dress "as in Antiquity, without harquebuses" (Cervantes 1994, 60). And yet, the Numantines are cast as throwbacks by contrast not only to late sixteenth-century warfare, but also to classical Roman standards. Roman strategy in the play involves large-scale troop movements and engineering for siege warfare. Scipio not only renews his insistence on unconditional surrender, he scoffs at the challenge to single combat as if it were a joke and a fool's errand (vv. 1179–1184). Indeed Roman strategy would have struck a resonantly "modern" note to contemporary audiences, since fortress-building and siege warfare (especially in the Netherlands) had come into their own by the end of the sixteenth century, much as cannon in the late fifteenth century had lent the advantage to offensive war (Keegan 1994, 325–328). In this same vein, Spaniards in 1581 were renowned for an infantry formation—the *tercio*—that had been regarded as the most effective land force on European battlefields for a century (Elliott 1990, 134). Certainly on that historical score, early Spanish audiences and readers would have seen themselves sooner in Scipio and Rome than in Caravino and the Numantines.

More problematic still for the impulse to embrace Numancia as an idealized *patria* projected into the past is the representation of Numantine religious rituals and beliefs in Act 2. They conspicuously draw attention to the fact that second-century B.C. Celtiberian Numancia and sixteenth-century Habsburg Spain were divided by religion. Two ceremonies are performed in succession and the sequence mimes the contrapuntal relationship between a Roman Act 1 that explicitly emphasizes Numantine Spanishness and a Numantine Act 2 that implicitly emphasizes Numancia's difference from sixteenth-century Spain. The first ceremony, officiated by "priests" (*sacerdotes*), involving water, wine, incense, and a live ram to be sacrificed, strongly suggests a primitive version of the Catholic mass and the Eucharistic sacrament as verisimilar "antique" touch, anticipation, or parody (Cervantes 1994, 89). It clearly departs from them when the priests perform a series of divinatory rites on a sacred fire, read avian and celestial augurs and portents (imperial eagles fighting overhead, thunder, and lightning), and invoke Pluto and the forces of hell in an attempt to divine and then alter Numancia's fate. The attempted propitiatory sacrifice of a ram is thwarted by a demon (vv. 885–886) who emerges from the ground to sieze the ram and scatter the fire and offerings. The second ceremony is officiated by the diviner Marquino and his acolyte Milvio. Marquino's black hair, vials of black water, and black staff, and the reference to "the evil spirits" with which he communes (Pluto, Ceres, Cerberus, and other denizens of the Underworld) sensationally evoke sorcery or black magic. This effect culminates in an act of necromancy, the ritual revival of a corpse to elicit a prophecy that foretells Numancia's fated death by near and dear. The Numantine Leonicio becomes a kind of spokesman for late sixteenth-century Catholic orthodoxy when he dismisses the whole spectacle as "diabolical inventions," "illusions," and "chimeras and fantasies / omens and sorcery" (vv. 1097–1100), at odds with his conception of knowledge (*ciencia;* v. 1102) and the power of the will to defeat portents.

Such staged rituals no doubt serve in part the straightforward theatrical function of evoking a diffuse, pre-Christian paganism while providing its audiences a voyeuristic *frisson* of heterodoxy. This is especially the case here since the portrayal of these ostensibly ancient Spanish religious practices recalls decidedly pagan literary models for necromancy in the witch Erichtho of Lucan's *Pharsalia,* the witch who resurrects her son to divine the future in Heliodorus's *Ethiopian History* (newly translated into Spanish in 1554), and Amerindian sorcery in Ercilla's epic *La Araucana* (1569–1589).[12] Yet following an Act 1 so insistent about the "Spanishness" of Numancia and the Numantines, it can also be seen as a means to achieve a thematic distancing from the emerging national myth of Numancia. Many Spaniards around 1581 may have recognized idealized versions of themselves in Numancia's fierce commitment to courage and honor, but at least officially they would have been hard-pressed to see themselves in its religious rituals and beliefs. By drawing attention to such features, the play spotlights a more historically mixed legacy from Numancia than the Spain, Duero, War, and Fame speeches acknowledge. They expose the shortcuts at work when a myth-making narrative whitewashes features of a past that could not be claimed by historical heirs.

The Spanish identification with the Numantine is especially complicated in the portrayal of collective suicide. It must have turned up the moral heat for those early audiences since Church doctrine declared it a mortal sin.[13] Indeed, in this light it might appear at first glance that the Numantines are never more Roman and less Christian than when they choose honorable suicide over death on the battlefield, continued resistance, suffering, or even dishonor. Roman law opposed any moral condemnation of suicide and hence provided no sanctions against it. Christian authority took the opposite position from Roman law and custom, though gradually. The fullest treatment long remained St. Augustine's in *The City of God* (I.16–27), which argues against the standard Roman teaching with the aim of dissuading Christian women, threatened by barbarians, from preferring suicide to rape—much the same situation that leads the women of Numancia to ask their men to remain with them.[14]

And yet, even within the Christian tradition, there developed a defence of self-sacrifice for the *patria*—the *topos* of *pro patria mori*—of heroic acts, including suicide, whose objective was to head off enslavement, religious conversion or death by the enemy. Medieval historians were liable to compare such self-sacrifice for the fatherland to Christ's for the salvation of humanity.[15] Dante himself condemns suicide, but saves Cato. Cato's suicide is interpreted not as a sign of weakness in the face of adversity as Augustine had it, but as a martyrdom. This unlikely pagan hero is held up as the model for a new man because he resists temptation, shuns idolatry, and defends liberty. In Dante's redeeming of the Republican's suicide, Cato's offer of himself as scapegoat to head off the horrors of civil war becomes an expression of this patriotic conception of charity, of a personal offering of self for the good of the nation (Mazzotta 1979, 60–64). There are moments of Numantine self-sacrifice in Act 4 that do, indeed, seem to fit a kind of proto-Christian virtue of self-sacrifice as *caritas*. A starving mother no longer able to breastfeed her child urges her son to take her body and blood, as if she were herself a literal prefiguration of the Eucharistic offering (vv. 1708–1723). Then again, Marandro and his friend Leonicio die in a raid on the Roman camp designed to procure Marandro's beloved Lira some crumbs of bread, once again to stave off starvation. Leonicio never makes it back, and Marandro himself dies handing over the "bitter bread" (*amargo pan*) to "sweet" (*dulce*) Lira (vv. 1804–1827). Marandro's last words to Lira underline the Eucharistic resonances of the offering, bread mixed with his own and his friend's spilled blood (vv. 1844–1847). Nevertheless, what differentiates these acts of self-sacrifice from the medieval tradition of *pro patria mori* is that they are personal (mother to child, friend to friend, lover to beloved), rather than patriotic in motivation.

Sixteenth-century historians were no less divided than the theologians about the legacy of collective suicide in the name of liberty and honor: for Charles V's chronicler Antonio de Guevara, Numantine suicide was simply a "monstrous thing" (*monstruosa cosa*); for the humanist historian and Philip II's chronicler Ambrosio de Morales, it was a glorious expression of liberty-loving courage and patriotism.[16] Since patristic and historical authorities were available both to justify and to condemn collective suicide (or personal suicide for the commonweal), they cannot— disagreeing as they do—settle the valence of suicide for us. Instead, a renewed look at the play's handling of this aspect of Numantine behavior may tell us whether it compromises the status of a Spanish national myth that exalts Numantine self-immolation as a foundational act for sixteenth-century Habsburg Spain.

The apparently noble act of collective suicide understood as patriotism is shadowed by evidence in Act 4 that the decision does not reflect a unanimous, voluntary giving of self. We are shown an enforced participation that has, by no means, won the consent of all Numantines. Moreover, the play's most insistent response to Numancia's bid for liberation through suicide is to call it "homicide," a reality of escalating horror not argued rhetorically, but named explicitly and displayed graphically. The first instance of this sober evaluation is voiced by the soldier the Numantine diviner Marquino revives in Act 2. His baleful prediction is that there will be no peace, neither Romans nor Numantines will triumph, and that Numantines will perish at the hands of near and dear: "A friendly dagger will prove Numancia's murderer [*homicida*]" (vv. 1079–1080).

The revived corpse then hurls himself into the grave, and Marquino follows suit, preferring to take his own life than bear witness to such a prospect. Marquino's personal suicide anticipates Numancia's collective suicide much as Bariato's recapitulates it at the end. It may be questionable in the light of Church doctrine, because it cannot be excused even as a patriotic act—unlike Bariato's jump from the tower at the end of the play, by which he denies Scipio his human trophy—but it is not homicide, nor does it enforce consent with a particular idea of collective glory.

We are made to witness a variation of this more troubling facet of collective suicide as two unnamed Numantines look on the spectacle of their valuables going up in holocaust (vv. 1648–1671). What is worse, says one to the other, is that we must die by "cruel" sentence and act as our own "executioners" because the Numantine senate has decreed, now that hunger is stalking the city, "that no woman, child or elder be left with life" (vv. 1680–1681). With that decree, the apparent Numantine commitment to chivalry in Act 2—to the bravery and dexterity in arms of single combat and the protection of children and women—is thrown by the board. Rather than give quarter especially to women, children, and the elderly, the senate singles them out for murder. Famine emphasizes the point that famine, fury, and rage have turned Numantines against themselves, and that they have come to find happiness in death, with one objective only: to deny Romans a victory over living Numantines (vv. 2021–2023).

The play is not content merely to announce or describe the senate's resolution. A particularly poignant display of its implications takes place in Act 4 when a Numantine soldier gives chase to a Numantine woman across the stage, hellbent on killing her in line with "the senate decree that no woman's life be spared" (vv. 1944–1945). Lira, mourning her beloved Marandro and brother, has resolved to take her own life before hunger does. She catches sight of the soldier and begs him to kill her instead: "Let her who prizes life keep her own / And take mine now that it is a burden" (vv. 1942–1943), a plea that highlights the effective breach of consent with which the Numantine senate decree of collective suicide is being put into practice. The Numantine woman who does not want to die is spared, but the soldier's perverse sense of duty is thwarted by the power of Lira's beauty rather than reason or principle (vv. 1946–1951). Bewitched, the soldier refuses to be her "murderer" (v. 1949) and helps Lira bury Marandro and her brother (the Roman Mario again uses "homicide" to describe Numancia's self-immolation at v. 2278). The soldier is prepared to kill a Numantine woman who does not want to die, but is unable to kill a woman who does. There is a neoplatonic hint of a beauty capable of eliciting virtue, of civilizing a barbaric impulse, not unlike the effect of Rosaura on the "barbaric" Segismundo in the mountain tower fastness of Calderón's *La vida es sueño*. And yet this paradoxical moment also illustrates the arbitrariness of Numancia's collective decision to do away with itself before surrendering to Scipio's Rome, the breakdown of moral order in which—as Lira puts it—"mercy" (*piedad*) becomes "rigor" (vv. 1952, 1955).

The taboo-shattering bloodbath, chaos, and confusion that ensue from the Numantine senate's decree—which pits husbands against wives, sons against mothers, and parents against children—are given their most luridly gruesome expression by Famine in that same chilling Act 4 (vv. 2024–2055). Indeed, Famine's speech could be set against the Duero's Act 1 prophecy as a kind of pendant; that is, alongside Duero's unvarnished patriotism, we would have to place Famine's alarmingly clear-eyed, counterpatriotic response. Pairing off those speeches (and Acts 1 and 4), each of which in isolation might be cited to make exactly opposite cases for the play's take on the heroism of Numancia and its possible legacy to sixteenth-century Habsburg Spain, starkly highlights what is lost in moral complexity when we reduce this play's voices to one. It also illustrates the thematic and structural counterpoint through which Cervantes achieves that complexity about an issue—suicide in the name of patriotism—that in his own day divided his contemporaries. Famine's speech is worth quoting in full for the cumulative impact of its searing detail:

> Hark to the wailings terrible and dire / Of beauteous women, who to death go down; / Their tender limbs in flame and ashes lie, / No father, friend, or love to heed their cry! / As timid sheep, upon their careless way, / Whom some ferocious wolf attacks and drives, / Go hurrying hither, thither, all astray, / With panting dread to lose their simple lives; / So, fleeing from the swords upraised to slay, / Do these poor children, and these tender wives, / Run on from street to street, O fate insane! / To lengthen out their certain death, in vain. / Within the breast of his belovèd bride / The husband sheathes his keen and glittering brand; / Devoid of pity, and of filial pride, / The son against the mother turns his hand; / The father, casting clemency aside, / Against his very offspring takes his stand, / And while with furious thrusts to death they bleed, / He finds a piteous pleasure in the deed! / No square, or street, or mansion can be found, / That is not filled with blood and with the dead; / The sword destroys, the fierce fire blazes round, / And Cruelty with fearsome step doth tread! / Soon will ye see upon the level ground / The strongest and the loftiest turrets spread, / The humble dwellings, and the temples high, / Shall turn to dust and ashes by and by![17] (vv. 2028–2055)

As if to underscore the horror of the Numantine senate's decree, a little later in the same Act, two boys (Bariato and Servio) sneak on stage wondering which way to escape certain death. Their concern is not the fury of the Roman enemy, but their fellow, murderously rampaging countrymen given permission to kill women, children, and the elderly. Bariato plaintively asks Servio: "Sad boy, do you not see we are pursued / By two thousand swords intent on slaying us?" (vv. 2120–2121). To which Servio responds: "There is no escaping / Those who hound us" (vv. 2122–2123). Servio is too hungry to go on, but Bariato decides to take cover in his father's tower. Like the unnamed woman saved by Lira, their desire to flee—both acts of civil disobedience—brings home the diversity of reactions to the Numantine senate's decree, departures from a genuine consent that might lend it a measure of legitimacy.

Famine prepares us for the most grotesque embodiment of all that might be wrong with the apparent glory of collective suicide in the name of liberty and sixteenth-century Spain, reminding us that no square, corner, street or house is spared the spectacle of blood and death. The audience is called on to watch as Theogenes, the Numantine chief, prepares to kill his wife and sons: "Come. You will see Theogenes / Temper and test on the dear necks / Of his tender children and beloved wife / The homicidal bent of his cruel sword" (vv. 2056–2059). Theogenes's understanding of the moral trade-off is that Roman enslavement of his children and rape of his wife are a worse fate than a father and husband's sword striking them down (vv. 2068–2091). But the same speech suggests he is equally motivated by a less honorable impulse of revenge, the desire to deny Rome (and Scipio especially) a triumph at any cost (vv. 2076–2079).

Theogenes and Scipio, leaders of the Numantine and Roman camps, come to incarnate the dark side of Numantine and Roman exemplarity: Theogenes exemplifies what becomes of courage and noble self-sacrifice when they turn homicidal, Scipio exemplifies what becomes of prudence and moderation—his self-professed virtues (vv. 13–24, 81–168, 1748, 2258)—when they turn blindly arrogant and willful.[18] In their characterizations, they illustrate particularly well the paradoxes of identity portrayed in the play and the morally ambiguous reality of its patriotism. At strategic moments, the two leaders are associated with the rhetoric of a kind of border-crossing conversion, and for those moments they become vehicles for the play's otherwise largely implicit recasting of the patriotic certainties of a Duero or Fame. The Numantine chief Theogenes is closely associated with the two most morally suspect decisions undertaken by Numancia during the siege, the two that would cut most deeply against the grain of Spanish self-perception in 1581. It is Theogenes who proposes in Act 2 that the Numantines draw and quarter, share out, and cannibalize their Roman prisoners to stave off hunger. Framed as his "honorable intention," the language suggests a sinister parody of the Last Supper and the Eucharist: "Our cruel, necessary meal / Will some day be celebrated by Spain" (vv. 1431, 1434–1441). Neither ritual human sacrifice nor customary practice, this survival cannibalism nonetheless departs from other less doctrinally questionable solutions such as Marandro's and Leonicio's raid on the Roman camp for bread.

Theogenes also takes credit for the Numantine senate's motion to enact collective suicide. What is more, he proudly claims paternity for it just as he is preparing to murder his wife and children in the name of liberty and honor (vv. 2081, 2085–2087, 2092–2097). This too, like the survival cannibalism, stands alongside less problematic alternatives proposed by other Numantines, such as rushing the Roman lines, hunkering down behind the city's defensive walls, or even allowing famine to take its course. The women of Numancia, notably Lira, time and again become mouthpieces for a cool-headed prudence and pragmatism opposed to Theogenes's rash, bloody-minded bravado (vv. 1370–1401) and even Marandro's futile heroism (vv. 1522–1545). They give voice to the kinds of doubts raised elsewhere in *Numancia* implicitly about the value and virtue of the cult of self-sacrifice that sometimes passes for patriotism and love in the Numantine camp.

Finally, Theogenes consistently associates honor, glory, liberty, and contentment with death (vv. 2165–2167, 2172–2173, 2180–2183). As if to highlight his more questionable impulses, he is brought out onto the stage "with two drawn swords, and blood on his hands" (Cervantes 1994, 145). He has turned his own hand—as he puts it—against himself, to spill blood "with honorable and cruel vigor" (vv. 2140–2143). After killing his wife and children off-stage, he challenges his fellow Numantines to fight him as if he were a Roman, staging his own death with the characteristic language and action of a revenge tragedy: "O valiant Numantines, do as if / I were a perfidious Roman / And avenge your disgrace on my breast / By bloodying sword and hand" (vv. 2148–2151). We cannot be surprised that Theogenes, chief spokesman for the Numantine senate's choice of collective suicide over surrender to Scipio, would ask his compatriots to kill him nor that he would choose so sensational a way to dramatize his death (and himself) for posterity. And yet the rhetorical form it takes—Theogenes not only asks his fellows to dispatch him, but to do so *as if* he were Roman—figuratively models the play's broader impulse to notice the telling ways in which peoples otherwise poles apart come to resemble one another, if often unwittingly.

Indeed, Theogenes's "Roman" moment foreshadows Numancia's historical "translation" into the New Rome of sixteenth-century Habsburg Spain, repeatedly announced by the prophetic voices in the play and here given a sinister turn. In case we miss the point, Plague calls on a comparable simile to underscore the paradox of Numantine ire run amok, turning on itself as if Numantines were the Roman enemy: "Fierce madness and rage, [famine's] attendant brood, / Have taken possession of every [Numantine] breast / Such that, as if they were Roman battle lines, / They thirst for [Numantine] blood" (vv. 2016–2019). Theogenes, appealing to fellow Numantines to sacrifice him, spells out the topsy-turvy ethical implications of his version of patriotic glory: where once there was tenderness toward friends, there is to be rabid rage as if against the foe (vv. 2162–2163).

That the boundary between Roman and Numantine becomes increasingly blurred under the stress of war is brought home when, in the final act of the play, Scipio, Roman consul, experiences his own momentary conversion, appearing—if only rhetorically—to recognize himself in the Numantines. Following the mayhem of Numancia's frenzied self-destruction, a pall of silence descends on the city. The Romans, baffled, scale the walls and find corpses and ashes where the city once flourished. Scipio stands there gazing on the carnage, his hope of winning an official Triumph at Rome by bearing home at least one live Numantine no more than a charred ruin (vv. 2244–2246, 2261–2263, 2282–2284). Having failed to grasp that the Numantines' collective attachment to honor—the difference between conditional and unconditional surrender—is greater even than his own, Scipio has a rare moment of self-examination. Here is Scipio:

> Was my breast perchance filled / With barbaric arrogance and deaths / And devoid of the most just mercy? / Is it so foreign to my condition / To treat the vanquished with benevolence, / As befits the victor who is kind? / Poorly did Numancia know the valour in my breast, / Born to conquer and to forgive! (vv. 2306–2314)

Initially, the speech offers the hope that Scipio may have learned to acknowledge his own moral failure to show mercy and compassion to the vanquished—*piedad* and *benignidad con el rendido*—but the self-recognition is fleeting and finally denied in the last tercet. It is not Scipio, of course, but the play through him that diagnoses the overweening confidence (*bárbara arrogancia*) that led him to underestimate his foe, to badly misread their desperation and pronounced code of honor, and to rebuff their bid for peace in exchange for justice. The last Numantine, Bariato, however, confirms the play's judgment of Scipio expressed in this speech. Scipio's peremptory Act 1 response to the Numantine ambassadors—"Too late do you show repentance!" (v. 267)—is met in Act 4's final scene with Bariato's equally unyielding answer to his entreaties: "Too late, cruel one, do you offer clemency" (v. 2342).

Scipio and Quinto Fabio earlier introduced the discourse of barbarism in speeches that spin yet one more variation on a routine kind of Roman vilification of the Numantines in the play. They express the fear—as it turns out, entirely warranted—that the enemy may have done itself in compelled by its "barbaric fury" (*bárbaro furor;* vv. 2188–2195 and 2238). In Scipio's later rhetorical question—as quoted earlier—the attribute of barbarism undergoes a displacement from the Numantines to the Roman general himself, by which the play links Scipio with his "barbaric" (*bárbaro*) foes. It is a typically ironic strategy of Cervantes's: to have a character say more than he means, as Theogenes does when he asks to be treated like a Roman. This same speech, which manifests Scipio's loss of military control and gives us a glimpse into his own dark side, is marked by a metrical shift from the stately, epic *octava* to the homespun, familiar *redondilla*, associated with popular song, amorous dialogue, and private conversation between (especially in this play, Numantine) friends and lovers.[19] Scipio is thus metrically demoted, stripped of his rhetorically heroic trappings, and by inference, the attributes ("prudence," "reason," "diligence," and "skill") repeatedly associated with his style of leadership. Just as Theogenes is figuratively Romanized through his grotesque charade, Scipio is seen to resemble the play's "barbaric" Numantines more than he knows (there is a further irony in his echo of Theogenes's equally uncomprehending reference to "just mercy," in vv. 2145 and 2308). Salvador de Madariaga famously coined a phrase to express the ways in which Don Quijote and Sancho Panza—seemingly at odds— gradually reshape and become like one another as the novel unfolds: as Madariaga put it, Don Quijote is *Sanchificado* and Sancho *Quijotizado*. One could just as well speak in this play of the Romanization of the Numantines and the Numantization of the Romans. Scipio's arc, cued by explicit statement, characteristic actions, and even meter, is readily imaginable on the stage, with an actor gradually shedding his Roman attire while donning "barbaric" Numantine garb until the transformation is completed in this speech.

It only gradually emerges from the soaring rhetoric of virtue, liberty, and patriotism that Theogenes and Scipio—bitter foes to the end—are bound together by their chief failing: they are joined at the hip of fame. Their primary motivation, it turns out, is the overriding concern with reputation, the hunger for which becomes their defining attribute and leads them to destroy what they most cherish. Theogenes comes to stake everything on the testimony of "history" (vv. 1418–1421) and "fame" (vv. 2291–2296). Scipio puts fame first too, for instance to justify his "cowardly" choice of siege warfare in the name of winning (vv. 1197–1200). Over the course of the play, Scipio reveals himself less interested in securing a peace for Rome than in personal triumph. As we saw, this blinds him to his enemy and leads to the refusal of key virtues—compassion and clemency—that, he himself recognizes at least rhetorically, may have partially saved the day. Scipio suffers the consequences directly in the play's historical time, namely, he fails to achieve his official triumph, which requires that he return to Rome with at least one live Numantine as a trophy. But even Theogenes's ostensible victory in historical memory is overshadowed by the price paid for glory: not only total destruction, but also the combination of cannibalism and homicidal turning of Numantine against Numantine that, in Act 4, passes for Numantine patriotic courage.

The trajectory undergone personally by the Roman Scipio and the Numantine Theogenes—who figuratively trade places—has its collective counterpart, under the species of history, in the process by which second-century B.C. Celtiberian Numancia becomes sixteenth-century New Rome or Habsburg Spain. Even if we fail to recognize how much alike Numancia and Rome already are on the theatrical stage, the larger stage of history—as Fame asserts—will ensure that political roles are reversed and that they do in this sense become one another. It is because of the play's unflinching gaze on these dramatic and historical ironies, on the yawning distance between the patriotic certainties of a Duero or Fame, and the cannibalistic and homicidal horrors of Acts 3 and 4, that we can say there is a *Numancia* resoundingly patriotic, fully engaged in the creation of a national myth of courage and providential mission, and another *Numancia* skeptical about that legacy and, by indirection, critical of Habsburg Spain and imperial adventurism. The first tendency suggests that Numancia's self-sacrifice is in the service of a higher good that redeems it; the second, that Numancia is for many reasons less apt an ancestor than Rome and that even its apparent act of patriotic charity is marred by homicidal degeneration and a dehumanizing quest for fame. In the voices of Duero and Fame, the play most insistently presents that higher good as sixteenth-century Habsburg Spain. But who has the last word on that score? The triumphalist rhetoric of Duero and Fame or Famine's rather less flattering, blood-drenched portrait of homicidal Numantines? The backdrop of smoking ruins and human carnage, or the uncertain promise that the imperial wheel of fortune will come to a grinding halt in 1581?

Alongside full-throated hymns to *patria* and monarch and nation, *Numancia* also makes conspicuous how patriotic sentiment—confused with virtue, and driven by the imperative of fame—can lead to atrocity, to a betrayal of the principles that a *patria* may otherwise hold most dear in its ideal self-conception. For this reason, the play ultimately defeats any single-minded effort to make it speak for Rome or Numancia, for empire or against it. But if we are prepared to recognize its urge to blur boundaries, it offers us something perhaps more compelling. Seen in all its complexity *Numancia* would seem to treat national identity as a question rather than as a foreordained answer, and the question it raises implicitly is whether the *patria* embodies key virtues or betrays them. It especially draws attention to the moral responsibility incumbent on those who would answer the question "who are we?" by invoking remote ancestors. As we have seen, the play discourages facile replies predetermined by ethnicity, religion, the law, or language. Instead, it responds by dramatizing a pair of conditionals: If we are Numantine, then we are courageous, but also primitive, cannibalistic, and homicidal. If Roman, then we are prudent, accomplished, and Lords of all the World, but also proud, tyrannical, and doomed to be trampled underfoot by once and future Numancias.

Notes

1. On the likely dates of composition, see Canavaggio (1977, 20). Hereafter, Cervantes's play is referred to as *Numancia*.
2. On Scipio Aemilianus ('Scipio Africanus the Younger') and Numancia, see Astin (1967, 35–60, 137–160).
3. Ambrosio de Morales's account of the siege of Numancia appears in book 8 of his *Corónica general de España* (1574). I refer to the following edition: Ambrosio de Morales, *Corónica general de España*, vol. 4 (Madrid: 1791).
4. I cite the following edition: Miguel de Cervantes, *La destruición de Numancia*, ed. Alfredo Hermenegildo (Madrid: Clásicos Castalia, 1994). All references to *Numancia* in this chapter are to verse number(s) from this edition. Translations are my own, unless otherwise indicated.
5. I date the Spanish Habsburg annexation of Portugal from the Estatuto de Tomar (April 1581), which settled Philip's claims to the Portuguese throne. See Bouza (1998).
6. On the imperial theme in Habsburg iconography see Checa Cremades (1987, 185–187 and 195–258) and Tanner (1993).
7. Graf proposes a new political reading of Numancia's sacrifice as an allegory for Philip II's persecution of heretics.
8. On Cervantes's historical and legendary sources, including Ambrosio de Morales's *Corónica*, see especially Cervantes (1922, 6: 34–62); Canavaggio (1977, 40–46; and 1979, 3: 647–653).
9. Herrero García (1966, 15–103) reviews sixteenth- and seventeenth-century texts that followed this rhetorical convention, repeated to the point of cliché.
10. A useful overview of medieval and sixteenth-century Spanish discussions of ancestors, including the Celtiberians and the Visigoths, is to be found in Lupher (2003, 195–226).
11. Ercilla (1993, canto 8, oct. 11, verse 2). On Cervantes's possible debts to Ercilla in this play, see King (1979, 200–221).
12. Armas (1998, 136–153) reviews literary models for this episode.
13. On what was known as the "sin of despair," see Murray (2000, 2: 369–395).
14. For an account of patristic views of suicide, see Murray (2000, 2: 98–121).
15. For the *topos* of *pro patria mori*, see Kantorowicz (1957, 232–272).
16. Guevara (1950, 1: 46) and Morales (1791, 4: 21 and 35 etc.).
17. I use Gibson's Victorian translation for this passage (Cervantes 1885, 96-97). Although his version often reads like a parody of Jacobean verse, here, the fustian works.

18. In Armstrong-Roche (2005), I examine *Numancia's* Scipio as a caustic, revisionary turn on his early modern reception as exemplary statesman of the Roman Republic (promoted by Macrobius, Machiavelli, and Juan Luis Vives), who sacrifices the cardinal virtues in the quest for reputation through conquest. I link this portrayal with the political abuse of the humanist rhetoric of virtue by apologists for the Habsburg monarchy.
19. Navarro Tomás (1986, 206–207 and 265).

Bibliography

Alcalá de Zamora Queipo de Llano, José. 2000. "Idea y realidad de España en los siglos XVI y XVII." In *España como nación*. Barcelona: Real Academia de la Historia.
Armas, Frederick A. de Armas. 1998. *Cervantes, Raphael, and the Classics*. Cambridge: Cambridge University Press.
Armstrong, John. 1982. *Nations before Nationalism*. Chapel Hill, NC: University of North Carolina Press.
Armstrong-Roche, Michael. 2005. "Imperial Theater of War: Republican Virtues under Siege in Cervantes's *Numancia*." *Journal of Spanish Cultural Studies* 6, no. 2 (July), 185–203.
Astin, A.E. 1967. *Scipio Aemilianus*. Oxford: Oxford University Press.
Avalle-Arce, Juan Bautista. 1975. "'*La Numancia*': Cervantes y la tradición histórica." In *Nuevos deslindes cervantinos*. Barcelona: Editorial Ariel, 247–275.
Barton, Simon F. 1993. "The Roots of the National Question in Spain." In Mikulás Teich and Roy Porter, eds, *The National Question in Historical Context*. Cambridge: Cambridge University Press, 106–127.
Bergmann, Emilie. 1984. "The Epic Vision of Cervantes' *La Numancia*." *Theatre Journal* 36, 85–96.
Bouza, Fernando. 1998. "De archivos y antiguas escrituras en la pretensión al trono portugués de Felipe II: La unión de coronas ibéricas de un fin de siglo a otro." In *Imagen y Propaganda: Capítulos de historia cultural del reinado de Felipe II*. Madrid: Ediciones Akal, 121–152.
Braudy, Leo. 2003. *From Chivalry to Terrorism: War and the Changing Nature of Masculinity*. New York: Alfred A. Knopf.
Canavaggio, Jean. 1977. *Cervantès dramaturge: Un théâtre à naître*. Paris: Presses Universitaires de France.
———. 1979. "Le dénouement de 'Numance': Jalons d'une tradition." In *Les cultures ibériques en devenir: Essais publiés à la mémoire de Marcel Bataillon (1895–1977)*, vol 3. Paris: Fondation Singer-Polignac, 1979.
Cervantes, Miguel de. 1885. *Numantia: A Tragedy*. Tr. James Gibson. London: Kegan Paul, Trench, & Co.
———. 1922. *Comedias y entremeses*, vol. 6. Eds. Rodolfo Schevill and Adolfo Bonilla. Madrid: n.p.
———. 1989. "El coloquio de los perros," in Harry Sieber, ed, *Novelas ejemplares*, vol. 2. Madrid: Ediciones Cátedra.
———. 1994. *La destruición de Numancia*. Ed. Alfredo Hermenegildo. Madrid: Clásicos Castalia.
Checa Cremades, Fernando. 1987. *Carlos V y la imagen del héroe en el Renacimiento*. Madrid: Taurus Ediciones.

Elliott, J.H. 1990 [1963]. *Imperial Spain: 1469–1716.* London: Penguin Books.
Ercilla, Alonso de. 1993. *La Araucana.* Ed. Isaías Lerner. Madrid: Ediciones Cátedra.
Graf, Eric C. 2003. "Valladolid *delenda est* la política teológica de *La Numancia.*" In Jesús C. Maestro, ed., *Theatralia,* no. 5, *El teatro de Miguel de Cervantes ante el IV Centenario,* 273–282.
Guevara, Fray Antonio de. 1950. *Libro primero de las epístolas familiares.* Ed. José María Cossío, vol. 1. Madrid: Aldus.
Hermenegildo, Alfredo. 1976. *La 'Numancia' de Cervantes.* Madrid: Sociedad General Española de Librería.
Herrero García, Miguel. 1966. *Ideas de los españoles del siglo XVII.* Madrid: Editorial Gredos.
Johnson, Carroll. 1980. "The Structure of Cervantine Ambiguity." *Ideologies and Literature* 3, no. 12 (March–May), 75-94.
———. 1981. "*La Numancia* y la estructura de la ambigüedad cervantina.*"* In Manuel Criado de Val, ed, *Cervantes: Su Obra y Su Mundo (Actas del I Congreso Internacional sobre Cervantes).* Madrid: EDI, 309-316.
Kantorowicz, Ernst H. 1957. *The King's Two Bodies: A Study in Medieval Political Theology.* Princeton: Princeton University Press.
Karageorgou Bastea, Christina. 1997. "El texto especular y sus implicaciones ideológicas en *La Numancia.*" In Aurelio González Pérez, ed, *Texto y representación en el teatro del Siglo de Oro.* México: El Colegio de México, 23–43.
Keegan, John. 1994. *A History of Warfare.* New York: Vintage Books.
King, Willard F. 1979. "Cervantes' *Numancia* and Imperial Spain." *Modern Language Notes* 94, 200–221.
Lewis-Smith, Paul. 1987. "Cervantes' *Numancia* as Tragedy and Tragicomedy." *Bulletin of Hispanic Studies* 64, no. 1 (January), 15–26.
Lupher, David A. 2003. *Romans in a New World: Classical Models in Sixteenth-Century Spanish America.* Ann Arbor, MI: The University of Michigan Press.
Maestro, Jesús G. 2004. *La secularización de la tragedia: Cervantes y 'La Numancia'.* Madrid: Ediciones Clásicas y University of Minnesota.
Martín, Francisco J. 1996. "El desdoblamiento de la *hamartia* en *La Numancia.*" *Bulletin of the Comediantes* 48, no. 1 (summer), 15–24.
Mazzotta, Giuseppe. 1979. *Dante, Poet of the Desert: History and Allegory in the 'Divine Comedy.'* Princeton: Princeton University Press.
Meron, Theodor. 1998. *Bloody Constraint: War and Chivalry in Shakespeare.* Oxford: Oxford University Press.
Morales, Ambrosio de. 1791. *Corónica general de España,* vol. 4. Madrid.
Murray, Alexander. 2000. *Suicide in the Middle Ages,* vol. 2. Oxford: Oxford University Press.
Navarro Tomás, Tomás. 1986. *Métrica española.* Barcelona: Editorial Labor.
Rey Hazas, Antonio. 1991. "Algunas reflexiones sobre el honor como sustituto funcional del destino en la tragicomedia barroca española." In Manuel V. Diago and Teresa Ferrer, eds, *Comedias y comediantes: Estudios sobre el teatro clásico español* València: Departament de Filologia Espanyola, 253–258.
Rodríguez Salgado, María José. 1996. "Patriotismo y política exterior en la España de Carlos V y Felipe II." In Felipe Ruiz Martín, ed, *La proyección europea de la monarquía hispánica.* Madrid: Editorial Complutense, 49–105.
———. 1998. "Christians, Civilised and Spanish: Multiple Identities in Sixteenth-Century Spain." *Transactions of the Royal Historical Society,* sixth series, no. 8, 233–251.

Simerka, Barbara. 2003. *Discourses of Empire: Counter-Epic Literature in Early Modern Spain.* University Park, PA: Pennsylvania State University Press.

Tanner, Marie. 1993. *The Last Descendant of Aeneas: The Habsburgs and the Mythic Image of the Emperor.* New Haven, CT: Yale University Press.

Tar, Jane. 1990. "*Hamartia* in Cervantes' *La Numancia*." *Aleph* 5, 22–28.

Thompson, I.A.A. 1995. "Castile, Spain and the Monarchy: The Political Community from *Patria Natural* to *Patria Nacional.*" In Richard L. Kagan and Geoffrey Parker, eds, *Spain, Europe and the Atlantic World: Essays in honour of John H. Elliott.* Cambridge: Cambridge University Press, 125–159.

Tomás y Valiente, Francisco. 1992 [1969]. *El derecho penal de la monarquía absoluta: siglos XVI, XVII y XVIII.* Reprint ed. Madrid: Editorial Tecnos.

Vivar, Francisco. 2000. "El ideal *pro patria mori* en *La Numancia* de Cervantes." *Cervantes* 20, no. 2, 7–30.

Chapter 11

Border Crossing and Identity Consciousness in the Jews of Medieval Spain

Mariano Gómez Aranda

Border crossing plays a uniquely fundamental role in the historical consciousness of the Jewish people. God's command to Abraham, "Go forth from your native land and from your father's house to the land that I will show you" (Genesis 12:1), signifies the departure of Abraham from Haran to Canaan and in this sense, the beginning of Jewish history. It was after the exodus from Egypt and the crossing of the Red Sea that Moses is said to have received God's revelation, thus marking the inception of the Jewish religion. Equally, it was after having experienced the Babylonian exile, and having crossed several frontiers to return to their homeland, that the Jews became aware of the importance of preserving their religion as their most significant sign of identity. And it was the destruction of the Temple in 70 C.E. that marked the beginning of a new Diaspora in which the Jews felt the necessity of putting the Oral Law into writing in order to preserve the common traditions that would maintain the union of the Jewish people. Border crossing, then, is associated with the most significant events related to the survival of Judaism in the ancient world, and in large part determined the Jewish people's consciousness of their common culture, traditions, and signs of identity. I will not pay attention to these general processes here, however, because they have been widely addressed elsewhere (Fein 1973; Brueggemann 1986 and 1995; Smith 1978; Eisen 1986; Levine 1986; Don-Yehiya 1992; Boyarin and Boyarin 1993; Scott 1997). In this chapter, I will instead examine the cases of a number of Jewish men who, voluntarily or by force of necessity, shared the experience of moving from one territory to another in the course of the Spanish Middle Ages. I will also show how this situation influenced their lives, their outlook, and most importantly, the construction of their own identity. I will analyze firstly the case of Moshe ibn Ezra (c. 1055–1135), a Jewish intellectual raised in the multicultural milieu of al-Andalus, but who decided to flee from Muslim territory, crossing the border to settle in the Christian part of the Iberian Peninsula. Both in his poetry and his literary work on poetics, he reflected how his personal experience changed his life and his appraisal of the world from which he came. Secondly, I will examine the case of Abraham ibn Ezra (1089–1160), who, after living in al-Andalus for fifty years, felt compelled to abandon his homeland in 1140, and wandered throughout Italy, France, and England, where he died. Abraham ibn Ezra made his living by teaching and writing on a number of scientific, philosophical, and religious topics, knowledge of which he had acquired in his native land. Finally, I will focus on Isaac Abravanel (1473–1508), an exceptional witness of one of the most traumatic events in Jewish history: the expulsion of the Jews from Spain in 1492. Abravanel epitomizes the attitude of the expelled Jews who spent the rest of their lives crossing border after border, unable to find a place in which to settle. His commentaries on the Bible, and his theological and philosophical treatises, reflect this personal experience.

Moshe ibn Ezra: Between Muslim and Christian Spain

Before the arrival of the Almoravids in the Iberian peninsula in 1086, the courts of al-Andalus enjoyed a relatively easygoing and tolerant way of life. Jewish intellectuals participated in the rich and fruitful atmosphere of the Muslim courts. Among them was Moshe ibn Ezra, born in Granada in 1055 to one of the most distinguished Jewish families in the city and, like many other Jews, thoroughly educated in both Jewish and Arabic cultures. Moshe ibn Ezra learned Arab grammar, philosophy, and poetry; and while still a young man began to write poems strongly influenced by Arabic literary models in theme and form (Scheindlin 1986; Drory 1992; Schippers 1994). However, the intervention of the Almoravids, whose assistance had initially been requested by Muslim kings desperate to halt the advance of the Christian armies, radically disrupted this kind of cultural symbiosis, as relatively unsophisticated North African Berbers took advantage of the situation to wrest power for themselves. Many Jewish intellectuals, including Moshe ibn Ezra's family and friends, decided to abandon al-Andalus altogether and to escape to Christian territory. As his letters to his friends reveal, Ibn Ezra, who at first remained in the city of

Granada, felt isolated and abandoned. "I remain in Granada, a city of declining bustle and splendor, like a stranger in the land, like a sparrow strayed from its nest, like a bird banished and driven; and among this generation, wayward and corrupt, there is no refuge for me; there remains no one to remember me and inquire after my welfare" (Moshe ibn Ezra 1977, 1: 292; translation in Baer 1992, 1: 61).

Shortly afterwards, impelled by this sense of alienation and abandonment, Moshe ibn Ezra decided to cross the Christian-Muslim border, and initiated a lifelong itinerant experience in Christian territory.[1] From that moment, his poetry becomes increasingly intimate and personal; the topics of Muslim poetry that had characterized his early poetry give way to lyrics reflecting his own circumstances. It is, more specifically, after Moshe ibn Ezra crosses the border, and after his crushing disappointment at what he encounters in Castile and Aragon, that he becomes most keenly aware of the magnificence and splendor of the Jewish-Muslim culture of al-Andalus. It is striking that he makes no apology of Judaism in relation to Christianity and Islam; rather, what he emphasizes is the cultural supremacy and excellence of Andalusian Judaism in contrast to its Castilian counterpart. He felt uneasy and ill at ease in this new world, considering himself to be living among beasts:

> I am weary of roaming about the world,
> measuring its expanse, and I am not yet done.
> . . .
> I walk with the beasts of the forest
> and I hover like a bird of prey over the peaks of mountains.
> My feet run about like lightning to the far ends of the earth,
> and I move from sea to sea.
> Journey follows journey, but I find
> no resting-place, no calm repose
> (Moshe ibn Ezra 1977, 1: 173; translation in Baer 1992, 1: 61–62)

The poem clearly reveals the unsettlement and dislocation of exile; part of Moshe ibn Ezra's identity is necessarily abandoned in the journey. However, at the same time, this very displacement, the absence of his friends, and nostalgia for his homeland, stimulate inspiration and creativity:

> I feel my eyes injured, not my heart,
> And my tears give testimony to those who see it;
> As if my eyes are transformed into water-skins
> Flowing down my cheeks or into clouds,
> For my friends have abandoned me and they are absent,
> Although they are present in my thought.
> . . .
> The days of my life filled with the nectar of love,
> And drunk with the wine of youth,
> I spent them in the most pleasant land

> With dwellers acting according to their desires;
> I abandoned that part of the land
> Where my heart was broken into pieces
> And all my members were cut into rags
> After the death of their people,
> Deprived of them, dwelling places are like dungeons,
> Because human beings give breath to them,
> And in their absence, only ghosts come to stay.
> (Moshe ibn Ezra 1977, 1: 18–19)

In Castile, Moshe ibn Ezra—a man of refined tastes—felt unappreciated and underestimated by a people he described as "ignorant" and "lacking understanding." He found the Jews living in Christian territory wanting in the exquisite culture he had known in al-Andalus, and criticized their forms of speech: "when I listen to the language of their mouths I feel ashamed." He deplored their lack of the sensitivity necessary for an appreciation of his poetic craft, and described those who misunderstood him as "virgins whom no man had known" or "barbarians, famished for lack of the breath of reason." In contrast, he longed for those friends still living in his beloved al-Andalus:

> O doves, that fly like a cloud towards the west,
> I adjure you by the life of love itself
> To carry greetings to my distant friends,
> Whose tent I have pitched in my heart.
> Tell them how in grief for their absence
> My heart is rent, like the rending of a kid.
> (Moshe ibn Ezra 1977; translation in Goldstein 1966, 83)

Unable to settle, desperately seeking an audience with the requisite sensitivity, Moshe ibn Ezra lamented the circumstances of his new cultural conditions:

> I run from town to town and find the tents of foolishness,
> Spread out by their hands.
> They are exhausted trying to find the gates of my intelligence,
> Unclosed for those who struggle to open them.
> They do not perceive the stars of my glory
> shining in the highest sphere of my words.
> My discourse is heavy for them to hear,
> but is able to open the ears of the deaf.
> (Moshe ibn Ezra 1977, 1: 66)

The Jews living in Christian territory are described as "people for whom the light of truth is clouded" and "wild animals in need of a little learning." In another poem, he writes of them that:

> They consider themselves skilful craftsmen,
> But they are only skilled in destruction.

They do evil and mislead innocents.
They think of themselves as wise people, but they are not.
They make predictions, but they do not have vision.
The wind of their love is unable to clean,
Nor even to sweep like pure wind.
(Moshe ibn Ezra 1977, 1: 18–19)

The imagery of wild animals is another repeated motif:

Among wolves that spend the night in a desert in which
the name of 'man' has never been heard;
It is far better to meet a bereaved bear or consort with a lion
Than to meet or encounter them.
They turn light to darkness, how, then, can their eyes
Distinguish a knave from a nobleman?
(Moshe ibn Ezra 1977, 1: 164).

Moshe ibn Ezra reveals here his pride in belonging to an elite and privileged class, and decries the Castilian Jews' inability to admire his art. Once again, he seeks refuge in longing for his homeland and for the culture he had enjoyed there, evoking the friends, intellectuals and wise men surrounding him and appreciating his own qualities. Such men are described as "the light of my eyes," who "awaited like dew the words of my mouth":

I wish to live among wise men
to place my threshold next to their threshold,
but the more I long to turn to them,
the more my feet are bound with the cords of my iniquity
to a people who do not know me.
I do not belong to them, nor are they a part of my people.
When I try to kiss them as a peace offering,
they think I bite them with my teeth.
To testify to those who have departed is now my lot.
Their writings are a balsam for my grief;
sweet is my intimacy with them,
a treasure among the faithful of Israel.
When I swim in the sea of their knowledge,
I gather pearls to adorn my neck.
In them my eyes and my heart take delight,
for them my lips sing joyfully,
they are light to my eyes, music to my ears, honey to my mouth,
like the scent of cinnamon to my nose.
In them I am exalted and praised.
I think of them as my everlasting fountain.
(Moshe ibn Ezra 1977, 1: 149)

Toward the end of his life, Moshe ibn Ezra composed, in Arabic, his famous *Kitab al-Muhadara wal-Mudakara:* a treatise of literary criticism in which he reviewed the biographies of Jewish Andalusian poets who preceded him, and attempted to demonstrate that Hebrew poetry had the same stylistic resources as Arabic poetry. The treatise certainly represents a vindication of Andalusian Judaism from a literary standpoint, but is also proof of his admiration for Arabic culture in general and its literary qualities in particular. Moshe ibn Ezra acknowledged the excellence of Arabic poetry and poetics, affirming that poetry was a natural gift of the Arabs, whereas for others it was something merely acquired. In this sense, he considered the Jews to be simply imitators of Arab creativity (Moshe ibn Ezra 1986, 1: 7, 10). According to his own introduction, his work was requested by one of his students who wished to know why Arab poetry was considered superior. Moshe ibn Ezra was at first unwilling to accept the challenge, precisely because "most people in our time feel an aversion to literature" (Moshe ibn Ezra 1986, 1: 8). However, he says, he had come to realize that some Castilian Jewish intellectuals were also capable of appreciating this kind of literary meditation, further declaring that no one should succumb to the opinions of the common people, and that, instead, they should follow the opinions of the "qualified." He wished to recall and restore the memory of the great Jewish Andalusian poets in order to avoid the possibility that "their lights be extinguished and news of them forgotten." (Moshe ibn Ezra 1986, 1: 10). We witness here the familiar impulse of the collector or anthologist to record past glories, and to immortalize the past.

Moshe ibn Ezra's intention was to demonstrate that Hebrew literature could vie with the excellence of Arabic literature, since each possessed the same literary elements and methods. In order to prove this idea, he dedicated the last part of his work to the analysis of the literary figures used in biblical Hebrew poetry and formal comparison with their equivalents in Arabic poetry. Ultimately, he aimed to show how use of these stylistic methods might stimulate the production of Hebrew literature in Christian lands. Moshe ibn Ezra's praise of Jewish-Andalusian poetry, in contrast to the impoverishment of Jewish-Castilian poetry, was intimately connected to his exaltation of Arabic rhetorical supremacy. In regard to the Arabs, he affirms:

> God has not favored them with wisdom other than the knowledge of rhetoric, nor did He make them by nature suited to occupy themselves with any branch of learning other than rhetoric and fine speech. They have not excelled other nations and tribes except in the superiority of their language and in their various poetic compositions. (Moshe ibn Ezra 1986, 1: 31–32; Katzew 1984, 184–185)

He praised the excellence of the *Qur'an* and even affirmed that, "the inimitable eloquence of the language of the *Qur'an* is a proof of its veracity." These words, coming from a medieval Jew, make sense only if we consider Moshe ibn Ezra's alienation from the world in which he lived and his longing for the Arabic culture with which he identified. As an intellectual, he identified wholly with the Jewish-Muslim cultures of al-Andalus, which he eulogized, and despised the world of the Jews in Christian Spain.

Abraham ibn Ezra and the Spread of Jewish-Muslim Culture

Around the time that Moshe ibn Ezra abandoned al-Andalus, Abraham ibn Ezra (1089–1160) was born in the Navarrese town of Tudela, still in Muslim hands. He spent the larger part of his life in Muslim territories writing both secular and religious poetry, and living from the charity of his patrons, whom he honored with eulogies and panegyrics (Weinberger 1997). He also dedicated part of his time to acquiring knowledge of Arabic sciences including philosophy, astronomy, astrology, medicine, and linguistics, but during his years in Muslim lands, does not appear to have composed a single work on these subjects. However, in 1140, when he had reached the advanced age of fifty-one, he decided to abandon al-Andalus and to travel to Rome, where he settled shortly thereafter. This departure from his homeland is often viewed as a result of the Almohad conquest of Andalusia, and the consequently declining conditions of the Andalusian Jews (Weinberger 1997, 3). In Abraham ibn Ezra's commentary on Qohelet, he says that he left Sefarad "with grievous soul," and in his commentary on Lamentations, he affirms that, "the fury of the oppressor expelled me from Sefarad." However, the Almohad invasion would take place in 1146, six years *after* his departure.[2] It may instead be surmised that he felt distressed by the deterioration of Jewish life in North Africa, where the Almohad caliph 'Abd al-Mu'min had ruled since 1130. He had visited a number of North African Jewish communities in 1140, and may well have personally experienced the oppression of the Jews by Almohad authorities during his stay. It is possible that he foresaw the arrival of the Almohads in the Peninsula and consequently decided to escape. Other personal circumstances may also have influenced his decision to leave his native land. As indicated by Judah al-Harizi (1170–1235), Abraham ibn Ezra's son Isaac converted to Islam and travelled to "the lands of the East" (Weinberger 1997, 3). This event may well have plunged Abraham ibn Ezra into the deep sadness he evinces. Furthermore, during his years in Sefarad, he wrote several poems complaining of his ill fortune and the difficulties of finding wealthy patrons to support him. The necessity of finding new patrons may well have been behind his decision to leave al-Andalus. From Rome, he continued his wandering life in Italian cities including Lucca, Pisa, and Verona; later, he would spend considerable time in France, dividing his time between Narbonne and Beziers in the south, and Rouen in the north. Finally, he decided to cross the Channel to England, where he is believed to have died around the year 1160.

It is precisely following the moment when Abraham ibn Ezra crossed the frontier of al-Andalus, en route to Rome, that he decided to write on the broadest range of disciplines: scriptural commentaries, astronomy, astrology, philosophy, mathematics, and linguistics. Books on medicine are also attributed to him. His more than one hundred books on these subjects have accorded him a unique place in the history of Jewish literature and science. His works were also able to cross linguistic frontiers, being translated into Latin, French, and Catalan, among other languages, and gaining him lasting fame as an scholar of the first rank. As in the case of Moshe ibn Ezra, the border-crossing experience appears to have acted as an incentive and a stimulus. In the Jewish communities of Rome, Pisa, Narbonne or Beziers, Abraham was received by Jewish notables and intellectuals unfamiliar with the multicultural riches of al-Andalus. Abraham ibn Ezra realized that his Jewish colleagues in Italy, France and England were ignorant of the Greek philosophical theories transmitted by the Arabs into al-Andalus; equally, the astronomical and astrological theories developed by the Arabs in al-Andalus were unknown to them. The application of grammatical and linguistic theories to the rational explanation of scripture was common practice among the Jews in al-Andalus, but was not extensive among Jewish intellectuals in other countries. Abraham ibn Ezra, then, recognized that his signs of identity were precisely those of the intellectuals imbued in the multicultural world of al-Andalus, instructed in the different fields of science and culture. It is likely that he had not written any scientific or exegetical work while living in his homeland, being an unexceptional expert in that context.[3] However, in his new circumstances, he found an excellent opportunity for prominence, transmitting his scientific and cultural knowledge to the Jews of Italy, France, and England. (Sela 2000; 2001a; 2001b; 2003).

When Abraham ibn Ezra decided to teach and write on scientific matters, the first question he took under consideration was the following: how would it be possible to make the complex theories of Andalusian science accessible to a Jewish public to whom the scientific world was largely alien? Abraham ibn Ezra adopted a two-sided approach. On the one hand, he appreciated that it was first necessary to explain and teach the basic rules of mathematics and astronomy, and the practical techniques for using scientific tools and instruments, such as the astrolabe and the astronomical tables. On the other hand, he soon became conscious that, through the interpretation of scripture, science could be admitted and accepted as part of the Jewish culture. It was ultimately through his scriptural interpretations that Abraham ibn Ezra was able to introduce scientific concepts into the minds of the Jewish intellectuals of Italy, France, and England.

Abraham ibn Ezra's first scientific work was his *Sefer ha-Mispar* (Book of the Number), an arithmetic textbook that explains the decimal positional system and basic mathematical operations, such as multiplication, division, addition, and subtraction. He then continued by writing a treatise on the fundamentals of the astronomical tables, entitled *Sefer Ta'amei ha-Luhot* (Book of the Reasons behind Astronomical Tables), and a practical manual on the astrolabe, entitled *Sefer Keli ha-Nehoshet* (The Book of the Astrolabe). During his sojourn in the city of Beziers in Provence, he wrote the central corpus of his scientific production, a series of astrological writings that have been properly defined by Shlomo Sela as an "astrological encyclopedia" (Sela 2000, 154–170; Sela 2001a, 115). These include his *magnum opus, Sefer Reshit Hokhma* (Book of the Beginning of Wisdom), a treatise dealing with the astrological characteristics of the stars, the zodiac constellations, the planets, and other general principles of universal astrology. He also wrote *Sefer ha-Te'amim* (Book of Reasons), *Sefer ha-Moladot* (Book of Nativities), *Sefer ha-Mibharim* (Book of Elections), and *Sefer ha-She'elot* (Book of Interrogations), among others. The main characteristic of these astrological treatises is their didactic purpose:

> If a common factor is required, reflecting the most essential aim and most representative aspects of Ibn Ezra's scientific book, a close to true answer may be that Ibn Ezra's scientific book was designed mainly as a *textbook*, planned to provide his disciples with easy access and understanding of terms, concepts and general principles related to astrology, astronomy and mathematics, particularly intended to teach the use of technical-theoretical tools and instruments. (Sela 2001a, 142)

The didactic purpose of his scientific writings is closely connected to his own experience as an itinerant intellectual; one of the reasons that Abraham ibn Ezra wrote his scientific works was to provide himself with a living.

Abraham ibn Ezra's fame arose mainly from his scriptural commentaries. For him, as for most of the Jews, the Bible was of course not a scientific text, but nonetheless one in which one might find references to current scientific theories. The first text he chose to explain was the Book of Ecclesiastes, a text that had raised several problems of interpretation throughout the history of Jewish exegesis; some of its verses seemed to defend a sceptical view of human fate and the uselessness of human actions in this world. In one of the first verses, its author affirmed that *all is vanity* and wondered, *What profit hath a man of all his labour which he taketh under the sun?* (Ecclesiastes 1:3). Ibn Ezra found in this question a reference to the influence of stars on human beings, and explained that all the actions that human beings take in this world have no benefit, because they are determined by astrological influences. He added that there is only one worthwhile activity that produces benefit, namely, the perfection of the human spirit, and justified this claim by explaining that the human spirit originates in the upper world, not *under the sun,* and therefore not under the influence of stars (Gómez Aranda 1994, 9–10, 12–14). His interpretation had a double purpose. Firstly, he intended to prove that the scientific theories he learned in al-Andalus might serve to make sense of the biblical text; secondly, he intended to teach that these theories were perfectly compatible with the holy book, and did not represent a threat to the strictest orthodoxy.

Another example of how Ibn Ezra used astrological theories in biblical exegesis is to be found in his discussion of the Ten Commandments. In accordance with medieval astrology, Ibn Ezra believed in the idea that each nation is ruled or governed by a planet. The Jews were held to be under the influence of Saturn, the highest planet, and the furthest planet from the earth because it is placed in the seventh sphere. Saturn was considered to be the planet having the most negative influences on the earth, especially on human activities, with the result that human actions taken under its influence were presumed to have terrible consequences. In medieval astrology, it was also believed that there were connections between the planets and the days of the week: Monday is the day of the Moon, Saturday is the day of Saturn, etc. What did these ideas have to do with the text of the Bible? How could these ideas be integrated in Jewish religious thought? In his commentary on Exodus 20:13, Ibn Ezra explained the reason for the fourth commandment, which says, "Remember the Sabbath day, and keep it holy." According to Jewish tradition, this meant that the faithful should not do any work whatsoever. How did Ibn Ezra relate the idea of Saturn as a wicked planet and also as the planet influencing the Jewish people and governing the Sabbath?

> The fourth statement (commandment), the statement about the Sabbath, corresponds to the sphere of Saturn. The astrologers tell us that each one of the planets has a certain day in the week in which its power is manifest ... They say that Saturn and Mars are harmful stars. Therefore harm befalls anyone who begins any work or sets out on a journey when one or the other dominates ... It is therefore unfit for one to occupy himself on Saturday with everyday matters. On the contrary, one should devote himself on this day to the fear of God. (Strickman and Silver 1996, 433–434)

Ibn Ezra thus tried to give a "rational" explanation of the prohibition of work on Saturdays by connecting this religious commandment with the medieval idea of the astrological influence of the planets. It is inappropriate to perform any work on Saturdays because Saturn's influence on this day will lead to terrible consequences. This integration of religion and science illustrates the way in which he attempted to convince his readers that even the most profound tenets of Jewish religion have close connections with the current scientific thought.

Abraham ibn Ezra repeatedly wrote more than one version of the same book, in some cases in different languages. For example, there are four different versions—two in Hebrew and the other two in Latin—of his *Sefer Ta'amei ha-Luhot* (Book of the Reasons behind Astronomical Tables). Each of these four versions was written at a different place and time. The first Hebrew version was written in Lucca in 1146, the second in Narbonne around 1148; the first Latin version in Pisa around 1146, and the second in an unspecified location in France in 1154 (Sela 2001a, 97–104). He also wrote two versions of some of his biblical commentaries: for example, on the Pentateuch, on the Song of Songs, on Esther, and on the Minor Prophets, among others. The existence of several versions of Abraham ibn Ezra's scientific and exegetical works was also a consequence of his border-crossing experience: during his wandering life, the only way that Ibn Ezra found to earn his living was to teach and write on those subjects in which he was an expert. When he settled in a new place and found a new audience, new students and readers, he wrote a new version of his books to fulfill their intellectual necessities. The revised version would sometimes repeat the material found in older versions, but would sometimes add new ideas and perspectives to satisfy new questions and demands. Apart from his original writings, Abraham ibn Ezra also translated Arabic scientific treatises into Hebrew, a figurative form of border crossing. His translation of *Ibn al-Muthanna's Commentary on the Astronomical Tables of al-Khwarizmi* was an important step in the transmission of Andalusian science and culture into other European countries, but it also contributed to the creation of a new Hebrew scientific vocabulary. The Hebrew language, and specifically biblical Hebrew, was no longer a language limited to religious content, but was also open to express secular and scientific ideas (Sela 2001b, 65–88).

In sum, we may conclude that, after his border-crossing experience and living in an entirely different culture, Abraham ibn Ezra became conscious of his signs of identity, those of the Jewish intellectuals of al-Andalus formed and educated in the different fields of Arabic science and culture. He soon realized that his knowledge might serve him as a means of subsistence, and decided to teach and write scientific and exegetical works in order to transmit Andalusian science to the Jews of other European countries. In spite of the several similarities between the cases of Moshe ibn Ezra and Abraham ibn Ezra, there are also significant differences. In Abraham ibn Ezra's writings we find no lament, no nostalgia for the world he lost, as was the case of Moshe ibn Ezra; Abraham's attitude is more optimistic. The reasons may lie in their distinct motives for leaving al-Andalus. For Moshe ibn Ezra, the loss of his friends and family members was the motivation for abandoning Muslim lands. For Abraham ibn Ezra, on the other hand, the apprehension toward the coming arrival of the Almohads, or perhaps the pain he felt when his son converted to Islam, or the scarcity of opportunities for intellectual prominence in al-Andalus were sufficient motive to leave his homeland without nostalgia.

The Case of Isaac Abravanel and the Expulsion of the Jews in 1492

The last scholarly figure whose life will be analyzed here is Isaac Abravanel (1437–1508). Statesman, diplomat, courtier, and financier of international renown, he was, at the same time, an encyclopedic scholar, a philosophical thinker, a noted exegete, and a brilliant writer. The epoch in which Isaac Abravanel lived was of course one of the most tragic in the annals of the Jewish people: the expulsion of the Jews from Spain in 1492 put an end to the Golden Age of Jewish history. Isaac Abravanel was there to experience this terrible event; but he also occupies a relevant position in the history of Jewish literature for his commentaries on the Bible and his theological treatises, often preoccupied with the question of redemption, in which personal experience and contemporary events are reflected. Both his choice of material and the evolution of his views are deeply shaped by his experiences of expulsion and exile. The impetus for this body of work lay precisely in the forcible crossing of frontiers; in Abravanel's wanderings from one land to another. In a letter that he sent to his friend Shaul ha-Cohen a few years before his death, Isaac Abravanel observed that he had written all of his biblical commentaries:

> after I left my homeland; for all of the days that I was in the courts and palaces of kings occupied in their service I had no time to study and looked at no book, but squandered my days in vanity and years in futile pursuit so that wealth and honor would be mine; yet the wealth was lost by evil adventure and "honor is departed from Israel" [1 Samuel 4:21]. Only after wandering to and fro over the earth from one kingdom to another ... did I "seek out the book of the Lord" [Isaiah 34:16]. (Lawee 2001, 9)[4]

Abravanel had been born in Lisbon, the place where his forebears had taken refuge, fleeing from the terrible persecutions of the Castilian-Aragonese Jews in 1391. He belonged to a wealthy family, and received a broad education embracing Jewish religious philosophy and tradition, the basic works of classical literature, and the writings of Christian theologians; he was one of the first Jewish scholars to become influenced by the humanism and the Renaissance spirit of the age. Abravanel also occupied the position of treasurer of King Alfonso V of Portugal. But after Alfonso's death in 1481, Abravanel's close contacts with the Portuguese monarchy came to a sudden end, because he was suspected of having participated in the conspiracy of the nobles against the new king, John II. He was forced to escape to Castile in 1483, and only one year later he entered the service of the Catholic Monarchs. King Ferdinand entrusted Abravanel with the financial administration of the country, and maintained his services until the tragic year of 1492. During this time, Abravanel was in charge of providing financial resources for the pursuit of the war against the Nasrid kingdom of Granada. But his valuable services to the Christian court were curtailed in 1492, when all the Jews of Castile and Aragon were expelled from their lands and obliged to leave their native country forever. Isaac Abravanel was fifty-five years old when he left Spain for Italy. At first, he stayed in Naples; he subsequently had to escape to Sicily and later Corfu. He remained for some time at Monopoli, and then travelled to Venice, where he died in 1508 at the age of seventy-one.

While living in Portugal, Isaac Abravanel had enjoyed a great fortune and his business and financial activities had left him little time to write. In the introduction to his work *Ateret Zekenim* (The Crown of the Ancients) he said, "Now I find myself exiled from meditation, moving to and fro throughout the country, sometimes in the city, sometimes out of the city, always dedicated to my business" (Ruiz 1984, xii). During his stay in Portugal, Abravanel planned to write a commentary on the Pentateuch, and began his commentary on Deuteronomy, a biblical book dealing with questions of Jewish legislation, monotheism, and the covenant of God with the people of Israel. In my view, Abravanel's reasons for choosing this book to initiate the task of explaining the Pentateuch were purely theological, and had no connection to the historical and cultural context in which the author lived at that time. In Portugal, he had also written *Ateret Zekenim* (The Crown of the Elders), a philosophical analysis of a passage in Exodus dealing with questions of the revelation of the Law and Jewish tradition (Lawee 2001, 59–82), and *Zurot ha-Yesodot* (Forms of the Elements), a philosophical analysis of the essential qualities of the four elements (earth, water, fire, and air) of which all substances in the sublunary world are composed. It was also in the course of these years that Abravanel began his *Commentary to the Guide of the Perplexed* in which he opposed some of the opinions of the philosopher Maimonides. We may observe that, while living in Portugal, Abravanel's interest focused mainly on questions of theology and philosophy.

After crossing the Portuguese border, however, and having settled in the kingdom of Castile at the age of forty-six, Isaac Abravanel changed his literary interests. He interrupted his commentary on Deuteronomy and focused his attention on the historical books of Joshua, Judges, Samuel, and Kings. Why did he change his interests? We find an answer to this question in the introduction to his commentary on Joshua:

> Although I am a guest in a foreign country, the Lord has provided me with wise and considerate friends, who always pay attention to my voice. I spend all day discussing with them; they listen to me and consult my opinion on the interpretation of some passages of the Early Prophets. For them my word is sweeter than honey. They have insistently asked me to explain the books of Joshua, Judges, Samuel, and Kings, and put my comments into writing. (Ruiz 1984, lxx)

As in the case of Abraham ibn Ezra, it was after crossing the border that Isaac Abravanel found the most propitious atmosphere for meditation and reflection. He found himself surrounded by a group of scholars who admired his intellectual capacities and were anxious to learn his biblical interpretations. But there were also other reasons for which Abravanel turned specifically to the Early Prophets. These biblical books are called "historical books," because they relate significant events in the history of ancient Israel, such as the arrival in the Promised Land, the establishment of the political system of the judges, and the hotly contested emergence of the monarchy in Israel. As B. Netanyahu remarks, these books also present "a gallery of human leaders with faults and weaknesses, failures and successes, crimes, virtues, and acts of heroism" (Netanyahu 1953, 37). Abravanel found a thoroughly suitable opportunity for using his own personal experience as a politician, statesman, and courtier at the service of the kings in Portugal and Spain to clarify many of the historical and political situations related in these books. In his introduction to his commentary on Joshua, referring to the biblical books of Chronicles, he states:

> Just as now in the palaces of the gentile kings, annals are written daily to record all the incidents of the kingdom, and, when relating these events, many historians allow that flattery and antipathy carry them away, in the same way, similar annals were written in Israel—thus the books of Chronicles are called *dibre ha-yamim,* that is, "the events of the days"—and also the same prejudiced points of view are often found in them. (Ruiz 1984, cvii)

Abravanel's critiques of the monarchy and his defence of the republican system are significant in that they reflect his own resentment toward those kings whom he had served. In his comments on 1 Samuel 8:6, he affirmed that, "the king guides his subjects like asses, but they do not have the same power in every kingdom, and, for example, in the crown of Aragon the king's power is limited; however, the best system is not having a king whatsoever" (Ruiz 1984, cxv).

The expulsion of the Jews in 1492, of course, necessitated a further phase of frontier crossing; and Abravanel changed his intellectual interests once again. His engagement with the Bible was more and more evident: "only in those moments of my life when fortune and vanity disappeared and I found myself wandering from kingdom to kingdom, did I turn to the book of the Lord" (Ruiz 1984, xviii). In 1493, he finished his commentary on the historical books and in the introduction to his commentary on Judges, wrote: "it is good to be humiliated, to compel one to the study of the Law" (Ruiz 1984, cxv). In those tragic moments, the Bible served Abravanel as a refuge and consolation in the face of adversity. During his wanderings in Naples, Corfu, Monopoli, and Venice, in the period before his death in 1508, Abravanel's attention focused particularly on the prophetic books of Isaiah, Jeremiah, Ezequiel, and the Minor Prophets, since these contained the references to the coming of the Messiah. It was precisely the hope of a Second Coming that would bring consolation and comfort to all the Jews who felt desperate and disillusioned by the terrible experience of the expulsion. During the years 1496–1498, Abravanel completed the three treatises dedicated to the Messianic hope of the Redemption of Israel and the national restoration of Israel to the Holy Land. These are *Ma'ayanei ha-Yeshu'ah* (Wells of Salvation), *Yeshu'ot Meshiho* (The Salvation of His Anointed), and *Mashmia' Yeshu'ah* (Announcer of Salvation). If, after leaving Portugal, Abravanel focused his attention on politics and history, after the expulsion, he concentrated on the role of divine justice in the fate of Israel. Abravanel was keenly conscious of belonging to the Jewish people, and affirmed the supremacy of Israel, protected by God Himself, over other peoples, who were protected by their corresponding angels. His thoroughgoing defense of Jewish identity led him to reconsider the role of the *conversos* in the divine plan of future Redemption.[5] Abravanel interpreted the prophecy of Ezekiel 20: 32–37 as relating to the *conversos,* their present condition and final fate, and wrote that: "In the future Redemption there will return to God all the criminals of Israel who left the fold and assimilated among the nations, either forcibly, at the point of the sword, or through temptation and in other ways. In the end of days they will regret their deeds and return to the God of their Fathers" (Netanyahu 1966, 190).

Abravanel's critique of Jewish religion had been far more evident before he experienced exile; after the expulsion, he concentrated his efforts upon the defense of the Jewish tradition. The rational and objective attitude found in his commentaries on the historical books was then transformed into a more personal, passionate, and subjective perspective in his commentaries on the prophetic books. The Renaissance mentality of his early years, when he vindicated the classical authors and scientific and rational thought, gave way to the defense of religious concepts that many Renaissance intellectuals rejected: divine revelation, messianic thought, and salvation. During his early years, Abravanel was influenced by Christian exegetes and philosophers, such as Jerome, St. Thomas Aquinas, and Nicholas de Lyra, but after the expulsion he expressed a strong dislike of Christianity and Christian culture.

In addressing the lives of these three Jewish scholars, we have observed how the border-crossing experience served as an impulse and a stimulus to develop Jewish literature, science, and exegesis, and to consciousness of their own signs of identity. There is a notable difference between the two Ibn Ezras and Abravanel. For Moshe ibn Ezra and Abraham ibn Ezra, the decision to cross the border was motivated by individual, personal considerations, although external factors may have influenced them, and they vindicated their sense of belonging to Andalusian Judaism in contrast to the Judaism of Christian Spain and other European countries. They considered themselves as belonging to that class of Jewish intellectuals educated in the multicultural ambience of Muslim Spain. In the case of Isaac Abravanel, conversely, border crossing was dictated by the repressive decisions of the Catholic Monarchs. From that moment on, his identity was completely marked by his consciousness of belonging to the people of Israel, who, in those new and terrible circumstances wished only for divine Redemption.

Notes

Translations of excerpts from Moshe ibn Ezra's poetry are by Simon R. Doubleday unless otherwise noted.

1. On the relations of Moshe ibn Ezra's poetry and his experience of exile, see Brody (1933–1934); Schippers (1982); Katzew (1984); Navarro (1998); Alfonso (2004).
2. Abraham ibn Ezra wrote an elegy on the destruction of Andalusian and North African Jewish communities at the time of the Almohads; see Weinberger (1997, 96–100). After an analysis of this poem, Nahon (1993) concludes that it is replete with literary tropes and that some of the references do not accord with the historical data; for example, Ibn Ezra refers to the destruction of the community of Lucena and its talmudic academy, but the end of this institution took place in 1140, prior to the Almohad invasion, and for different reasons.
3. The circles of Jewish exegetes and biblical scholars in al-Andalus were familiar with the exegetical works of intellectuals like Jonah ibn Janah, Judah ibn Balaam, Isaac ibn Ghayyat, and Moshe ha-Cohen ibn Gikatilla, among others. These works were written in Judeo-Arabic, a language unknown by the Jews of other European countries. The scientific theories of leading scholars like al-Khwarizmi, al-Battani, Ibn Sina, Masha'llah, or Abu Ma'shar were well known in al-Andalus, but since they were written in Arabic, they were not accessible to the Jews of non-speaking Arabic countries. The same may be said of the works written by Andalusian scientists like Ibn al-Muthanna, Maslama or Azarquiel.

4. On the concept of "homeland" in Abravanel's mind, see Lawee (2001, 219 n.1).
5. For a comprehensive analysis of Abravanel's attitude toward the *conversos*, see Netanyahu (1966, 177–203).

Bibliography

Alfonso, E. 2004. "The Uses of Exile in Poetic Discourse: Some Examples from Medieval Hebrew Literature." In R. Brann and A. Sutcliffe, eds, *Renewing the Past, Reconfiguring Jewish Culture: From al-Andalus to the Haskalah*. Philadelphia: University of Pennsylvania Press, 31–49.
Baer, Y. 1992. *A History of the Jews in Christian Spain*. Philadelphia: Jewish Publication Society of America.
Boyarin, D. and J. Boyarin. 1993. "Diaspora: Generation and Ground of Jewish Identity." *Critical Inquiry* 19, 693–725.
Brody, H. 1933–1934. "Moses ibn Ezra: Incidents in His life." *Jewish Quarterly Review*, New Series 24, 309–320.
Brueggemann, W. 1986. *Hopeful Imagination: Prophetic Voices in Exile*. Philadelphia: Fortress Press.
———. 1995. "A Shattered Transcendence? Exile and Restoration." In S. J. Kraftchick, et al., eds, *Biblical Theology: Problems and Perspectives. In Honor of J. Christiaan Beker*. Nashville: Abingdon Press, 169–182.
Don-Yehiya, E. 1992. "The Negation of Galut in Religious Zionism." *Modern Judaism* 12, 129–155.
Drory, R. 1992. "Literary Contacts and Where to Find Them: On Arabic Literary Models in Medieval Jewish Literature." J. Blau and S.C. Reif, eds, *Genizah Research after Ninety Years, the Case of Judeo-Arabic: Papers Read at the Third Congress of the Society for Judaeo-Arabic Studies*. Cambridge: Cambridge University Press, 53–66.
Eisen, A.M. 1986. *Galut: Modern Jewish Reflection on Homelessness and Homecoming*. Bloomington, IN: Indiana University Press.
Fein, L.J. 1973. "Israel or Zion." *Judaism* 22, 7–17.
Goldstein, D., ed. 1966. *Hebrew Poems from Spain*. New York: Schocken Books.
Gómez Aranda, M. 1994. *El comentario de Abraham ibn Ezra al libro del Ecclesiastés. Introducción, traducción y edición crítica*. Madrid: Consejo Superior de Investigaciones Científicas.
Katzew, J.D. 1984. "Moses ibn Ezra and Judah Halevi: Their Philosophies in Response to Exile." *Hebrew Union College Annual* 55, 179–195.
Lawee, E. 2001. *Isaac Abarbanel's Stance Toward Tradition: Defense, Dissent, and Dialogue*. Albany: State University of New York Press.
Levine, E., ed. 1986. *Diaspora: Exile and the Contemporary Jewish Condition*. New York: Steimatzky/Shapolsky.
Moshe ibn Ezra 1977. *Shire ha-Hol*. Ed. H. Brody. Jerusalem.
———. 1986. *Kitab al-Muhadara wal-Mudakara*. Ed. and trans. M. Abumalham Mas. Madrid: Consejo Superior de Investigaciones Científicas.
Nahon, G. 1993. "L'élégie d'Abraham ibn Ezra sur la persécution almohade. Perspectives Nouvelles." In G. Nahon, ed, *Métropoles et périphéries Séfarades d'Occident*. Paris: Cerf, 59–70.

Navarro, A. 1998. "Some Aspects of Moshe ibn Ezra's Poetry in Exile." U. Haxen, et al., eds, *Jewish Studies in a New Europe: Proceedings of the Fifth Congress of Jewish Studies in Copenhagen, 1994, under the Auspices of the European Association for Jewish Studies.* Copenhagen: C.A. Reitzel A/S International Publishers, Det Kongelige Bibliotek, 550–556.

Netanyahu, B. 1953. *Don Isaac Abravanel, Statesman and Philosopher.* Philadelphia: Jewish Publication Society of America.

———. 1966. *The Marranos of Spain from the Late XIVth to the Early XVIth Century According to Contemporary Hebrew Sources.* New York: American Academy for Jewish Research.

Ruiz, G. 1984. *Don Isaac Abrabanel y su comentario al libro de Amos* (Madrid: UPCM).

Scheindlin, R.P. 1986. *Wine, Women, and Death. Medieval Hebrew Poems on the Good Life.* Philadelphia: Jewish Publication Society.

Schippers, A. 1982. "Two Andalusian Poets on Exile: Reflections on the Poetry of Ibn 'Ammar (1031–1086) and Moses ibn Ezra (1055–1138)." In A. El-Sheikh, C. Aart van de Koppel and R. Peters, eds, *The Challenge of the Middle East: Middle Eastern Studies at the University of Amsterdam.* Amsterdam: Institute for Modern Near Eastern Studies, University of Amsterdam, 113–121, 201–204.

———. 1994. *Spanish Hebrew Poetry and the Arabic Literary Tradition. Arabic Themes in Hebrew Andalusian Poetry.* Leiden: Brill.

Scott, J.M., ed. 1997. *Exile: Old Testament, Jewish and Christian Conceptions.* Leiden: Brill.

Sela, S. 2000. "Encyclopedic Aspects of Abraham ibn Ezra's Scientific Corpus." In S. Harvey, ed., *The Medieval Hebrew Encyclopedia of Science and Philosophy.* Dordrecht: Kluwer Academic Publishers, 154–170.

———. 2001a. "Abraham ibn Ezra's Scientific Corpus—Basic Constituents and General Characterization," *Arabic Sciences and Philosophy* 11, 91–149.

———. 2001b. "Abraham ibn Ezra's Special Strategy in the Creation of a Hebrew Scientific Terminology," *Micrologus* 9, 65–88.

———. 2003. *Abraham ibn Ezra and the Rise of Medieval Hebrew Science.* Leiden: Brill.

Smith, J. Z. 1978. *Map Is Not Territory: Studies in the History of Religions.* Leiden: Brill.

Strickman, H.N. and A.M. Silver, trans. 1996. *Ibn Ezra's Commentary on the Pentateuch. Exodus* (Shemot). New York: Menorah Pub. Company.

Weinberger, L.J., ed. 1997. *Twilight of a Golden Age: Selected Poems of Abraham ibn Ezra.* Tuscaloosa: University of Alabama Press.

Chapter 12

Seven Theses against Hispanism

Eduardo Subirats

One

Hispanic, Hispanism, Hispanist: equivocal words. Once upon a time, the term *Hispania* embraced a plurality of peninsular cultures and languages, subject to the linguistic and civilizing influence of imperial Rome. But from the sixteenth century, this *Hispania* has been reduced through a dark history of crusading and ethnic cleansing, first against the Jewish and Muslim communities and then, on the back of that wounded past, in the colonial expansion of the *monarquía hispánica*. The reduction of the Hispanic to its "Spanish" element, the spinal column of the repressive discourse of Hispanic identity, has been accompanied by a series of violent expulsions—linguistic, political, religious, intellectual, and ethnic—whose effects are still palpable today. Hispanists, therefore, must think twice before deciding whether the Islamic mysticism of al-Andalus, the Jewish and *converso* philosophers from Portugal exiled in Amsterdam in the seventeenth and eighteenth centuries, or the tropical vanguard of Salvador de Bahía with its fundamentally African roots, can be considered *Hispanic*.

The segregationist party has traditionally drawn unbreachable imaginary frontiers, artificially reserving the status of Hispanic identity for the "Spanish," implicitly excluding the Portuguese, Basques, and Catalans as the "periphery." It has left to one side the Iberian cultural renaissance of the twelfth and thirteenth centuries as a matter suitable for scholars of Islam and Judaism, and has dismissed the great pre-colonial cultures of the Americas as a proper subject for anthropologists and archaeologists. Certainly, this perspective is strengthened by the blind sanction of an unquestioned and unbearable academic compartmentalization. In addition, its programmatically reductive vision undercuts some of the most notable cultural expressions of the Hispanic world. These forms cannot be properly appreciated without an understanding of the interaction between, for instance, Inca cosmology and Sufi mysticism, or between the Kabbala and Spanish mysticism of the Baroque period. A more inclusive school, conversely, which today has adopted the banner of "hybrid multiculturalism" or "multicultural hybridism," has tended to content itself with the moral principle of tolerance toward cultural differences, provided that these differences are correspondingly neutralized in the name of a methodological posture of academic impassiveness regarding the conflicts which have marked, and continue to mark, the history of these cultures: Christianity against Islam and Judaism and against the cultures of the "Indians" and the "Blacks." The hermeneutic approach to dialogue and conflict between cultures, which might potentially be included within the frame of the "Hispanic," should not be confused with the missionary strategies of colonial *mestizaje,* or with its postmodern recasting under the globalized banner of hybridity.

While Hispanism and the Hispanic continue to be prisoners of their name, Latin Americanists vigorously debate the difficulties of their own territorial demarcation. The word "Ibero-América," anachronistically adopted by linguistic cultures like the German and defended in Spanish officialdom as part of an imperial nostalgia, is too circumscribed by the limits of the historical period known as the Colonial. The alternative category of "Latin America" broadens the array of influences and forms of cultural violence acting on the peoples who live between the Rio Bravo and Tierra del Fuego, to encompass a variety of modern European colonialisms, particularly French colonialism, which coined the term. Although equally inaccurate, this term is undoubtedly more desirable than "Ibero-American." While the latter is associated with the repression that runs through the Portuguese and Spanish cultures of Europe and the Americas from the Counter-Reformation through the Counter-Enlightenment, the phrase "Latin America" is linked—though nobody knows quite how—to the heroic liberation of postcolonial independence. However, to classify the oral traditions of the Yanomami people as "Latin American" literature would be as conceptually feeble as to make them the object of ethnohistory, thereby implying their cultural death and sanctioning the financial and ecological process of its destruction. In a similar vein, the leading modern Brazilian architect Lina Bo has drawn attention to the indigenous and African roots of his conception of space, which places it beyond the margins of the "Latin" and even the Western. The label "Latin American" is conspicuously applied to contemporary Zapotec poetry, and to the poems of João Guimarães Rosa, which in reality are based fundamentally on the Indian and African myths of Brazil.

In place of the labels "Ibero-American" or "Latin American," which are hostage at the end of the day to old, defeated forms of colonialism, new and eye-catching alternatives have emerged. One might explore the full array of these artistic and cultural expressions—from the feather arts of the indigenous peoples of the Amazon to the paradoxes of Jorge Luís Borges, through the super-modern gaze of the satellite cartography of planetary space, in which there are of course no frontiers. From this cosmopolitan or global perspective, Mayan architecture and *Los ríos profundos* of José María Arguedas might be viewed as expressions of a hemispheric culture, appropriately studied under the departmental category of Hemispheric Studies with a division in Studies of the Americas. Such an approach is very politically correct. But to classify the entirety of artistic expression in the Americas, from the Popul Vuh to twenty-first century Andean popular theatre, and from Christopher Columbus to Octavio Paz, under the epistemological jurisdiction of the global village studied in real historical time, would be legitimate on one condition only. There would need to be a clear sense of the new colonialism of the nation that has usurped for itself the name of America, a sense of where it begins and ends. There would need to be a sense, then, of the relationship—in logical and institutionalized consequence—between its political hegemony, on the one hand, and the hermeneutic exclusions and thematic inhibitions of hemispheric and Pan-American studies, on the other hand. The category of American and Hemispheric Studies runs the danger of reiterating, in the end, the same insoluble colonial dilemmas that afflict the label of Hispanism; and we know well what happens with second versions of the same falsifying principle.

The vindication of archaic, and in the end, entirely illusory, indigenous names—Anahuac, or Nepantla—under the aegis of global politics, might seem to offer an elegant way out of all these frontier dilemmas. However, this tactic has never been more than a bad rhetorical exercise. Beneath the promise of subaltern liberation from old Eurocentric universalisms, one can discern a puerile academic complicity in the renewed imperial globalization of the subcontinent formerly known as Ibero-América. Perhaps, to conclude, we might put an end to all these entanglements by delimiting the vast, diverse cultural territories of the Iberian peninsula and those parts of the Americas that the crowns of Spain and Portugal conquered, simply on the basis of their respective dominant languages: "Spanish and Portuguese." This is a pragmatic solution, not a concept.

Two

The unitary construction of Hispanic identity was formulated by Miguel de Unamuno on the basis of bad metaphysics of an essentialist Catholic Spain; and by José Ortega y Gasset, in accordance with the authoritarian sociology of crusades and conquistadors, fashionably refitted for the modern mission of nationalizing élites. It recurs in Ramiro de Maetzu's fascist and National Catholic imagining of Hispanic identity; and in the writings of José Vasconcelos, under the banner of the mythology of a hybrid Hispanic *raza cósmica*. But it is not merely an old-fashioned construction. Rather, it should be considered an unconscious response to three historical traumas, and to processes of displacement, censorship and the repression of linguistic and cultural memory, processes that affected Portugal and Brazil as much as the rest of Latin America.

The first of these traumas was the elimination of the Jews and the "Moors." Mosques and synagogues were destroyed, libraries were burned, languages banned, and whole peoples persecuted and exterminated. On the heels of these events, the national unity of Christian, monarchical and imperial Spain was constructed, grammatically, theologically, and militarily. The second trauma was an extension of the first: it was precisely the destruction of the mosques which led men like Hernán Cortés and Francisco Pizarro, and their modern heirs, to "discover," conquer and remake the Americas. The third may be defined as a ruptured or decapitated modernity, or as a colonized modernity and postmodernity. The same political and ecclesiastical power that underlay the *monarquía hispánica* also uprooted theological, epistemological and political reform movements both within the peninsula and on the American continent, preventing the construction of the philosophical and political meaning of modernity in the historical sense of the term (as opposed to its banal usage in academic and media jargon). The suppression of cultural diversity and the subsequent constitution of the homogenous unity of National Catholic Spain encompass the elimination of humanism and reform in the sixteenth century and the decapitation of the Enlightenment in its scientific, ethical, aesthetic and political dimensions during the eighteenth century. It also includes the liquidation of liberalism in nineteenth-century Spain and Latin America and, last but not least, the combination of authoritarian brutality and messianic Christianity that has been a feature of a succession of fascist regimes in the twentieth, and still exists today.

All of these are very good reasons to reject the intellectual axis imposed by that tradition of myopic intolerance that has gone by the name of *Hispanidad,* and that has taken refuge in nationalist jargon. Postmodern discourses have not questioned this tradition, but avoided it through eclectic rhetoric, hybridism, and various attempts at transcultural and multicultural camouflage, gender pageants, and other pleasurable forms of micropolitics. It is necessary to construct a hermeneutic perspective that is at the same time fuller and more rigorous than these discourses. We are not interested in Lope de Vega's theater of national propaganda, the Christian mysteries of Pedro Calderón de la Barca, or the school of jurists in Salamanca who founded the first global empire. Studying the derivative, clerical Enlightenment of Benito Jerónimo Feijoo is a waste of time. The truncated positivist modernity of Domingo Faustino Sarmiento, the anti-classical concept of tragedy as Christian Calvary articulated by Unamuno, or the corrupt and neo-Baroque intelligentsia of the *movida madrileña* do not remotely warrant the status of great cultural legacies. For similar reasons, we are also not interested in the hybrid spectacles of Tonantzin-Guadalupe under the cover of which Christian colonialism hides the continued destruction of cultural and religious memories. Nor, for that matter, do we care about the corporate version of the colonial sacrament of universal Holy Communion, Coca-Cola and McDonalds's.

What excites us are the poetics of Luís de León, Teresa of Ávila and Juan de la Cruz: behind the conversion to Christianity, the last call of Sufi mysticism and Iberian Kabbala in Spanish language. What interests us are the intellectual perspectives of Bartolomé de las Casas or Luís Vives, Miguel de Cervantes, and the Inca Garcilaso. All expose in one way or another the decadence of Iberian and American cultures, and the birth of a new, modern tradition of intellectual and critical thought that has been relegated to the margins of Hispanism and *Hispanidad,* despite or precisely because of its moral, intellectual and metaphysical centrality. All are expressions of a modern critical conscience that has been equally ignored by European and North American liberals and neoliberals to the present day. What inspires us is the hidden intellectual voices of Blanco White and Simón Rodríguez, witnesses to a reformism laid waste by absolute monarchy and the Church. We are interested in the aesthetic of Duende, and the Inca spirituality that pervades the poetry of José María de Arguedas (Subirats 2003).

Three

The culture and memory of the Iberian and "Latin American" worlds should be revisited and redefined on the basis of their spiritual centers, not their colonial and neocolonial frontiers and epistemologies. One of these spiritual centers—not the least important either historically or from a contemporary point of view—may be articulated in a single phrase, Ahl-Al-Kitab or People of the Book, historically evoking the shared sacred spaces and symbols, the interchange of mystical experiences, and artistic, philosophical and scientific expressions common to Jews, Muslims and Christians in Iberia. The mystical and erotic cosmology of Ibn Arabi, Ramón Llull's pantheistic conception of nature, and the hermeneutic of Maimonides are all intellectual models of an Iberian renaissance, which began in the twelfth century and concludes with such modern works as those of Juan de la Cruz, Vives and Cervantes. To this, we may add two considerations relating to the Americas. The first has to do with its old cosmological conceptions, its astronomical and medical knowledge, its sacred literatures and its gods. These traditions and forms of knowledge are expressed from the codices and artworks of pre-colonial times, up to the oral artistic traditions of the present. Latin America has been the arena for a wholly original development of African religious traditions, the expressions of which extend across the whole spectrum of cults and artistic works. These forms of expression, like the ways of life to which they are inextricably linked, have survived, often in a pure state, despite the civilizing process of destruction to which they have been submitted. This process stretches from the linguistic *mestizaje* imposed by the colonial Franciscans to the semiological hybridism of the postmodern culture industry.

In this vast panorama of religious and philosophical conceptions, artistic expressions and ways of life, it is necessary to highlight one work in particular: the Sefer-Ha-Zohar, or Book of Splendor, one of the zeniths of Jewish mysticism, written by Moisés de León in the thirteenth century. In 1931, Ariel Bension published an extraordinary introduction to this work, entitled *The Zohar* in Muslim and Christian Spain. Bension's book, entirely ignored by Hispanism, may be considered a departure point for a paradigm shift in the theory and history of cultures in the Iberian and "Latin American" worlds. "The perpetual guide for the exiles," he calls the Book of Splendor, a means by which the Jewish community reestablished the lost spiritual unity with the heavens and earth, with its historical roots and its messianic hopes (Bension 1932, 91). He consequently makes no attempt to diminish the specific importance of the book for the diasporic Jewish communities of the Iberian Peninsula. But at the same time, Bension discovered in *The Zohar* the same relation to the divine which had been formulated by Ramón Llull and Ibn Arabi, and which later made its appearance in the mystical treatises and poetry of Teresa de Ávila and Juan de la Cruz. Bension also emphasized that *The Zohar* articulates the same fundamental allegories running through Christian and Muslim mysticism. Correspondingly, the pantheistic vision of the universe, which characterizes this work, is the same as is to be found in the philosophy of Ibn Gabirol or, again, Ramón Llull. "In *The Zohar*," Bension writes, "we find the crystallization of many centuries of life lived in Spain, associated with Christians and Muslims, resulting from cultural, social, economic and political contacts, which the tolerant ideas of the age made possible. There is no doubt that Jewish mysticism, influenced and inspired by the work of the mystics of the other two faiths, influenced and inspired them in turn" (Bension 1931, 44).

The thought of *Don Quijote* is also, for Bension, one last expression of the spirituality that had been expressed in *The Zohar:* or rather, it is through reading *The Zohar* that we begin to understand the most profound philosophical meaning of Cervantes' novel. But these and other analogies that Bension traces in his posthumous essay may, and should, be taken even further. In the first place, it is worth remembering the historical revisiting of Hispanic memory and identity articulated by Américo Castro, which draws extensively on Bension's more literary and hermeneutic legacy, although he is not mentioned by name. But the most recent interpretations of canonical works, such as *La Celestina* and *Lazarillo* also point to the same spiritual center of gravity. Modern works of poetry—particularly Federico García Lorca's *duende* lyricism—also acquire a deeper significance when contemplated through this philosophical and religious perspective. Much the same may be said for our understanding of key works in the cultural history of the Americas. The messianic mysticism of Christopher Columbus and the visions of a New World paradise among authors from Pero Vaz de Caminha to Vicente León Pinelo draw directly or indirectly on the sources of this same Kabbalistic spirituality. Even those forms of literary expression the culture industry has reduced today to the trivial formula of magical realism find in this philosophical and religious tradition its most illuminating elements; the works of Rulfo, Guimarães Rosa, and Arguedas are notable examples in this sense.

The path which Bension pioneered also leads to a better understanding of a philosophical legacy that has been diminished by colonial and postcolonial rhetoric under the banners of *mestizaje* and hybridism and consequently relegated to a merely regional value: the works of the Inca Garcilaso. Many things about this writer have been ignored, not least the philosophical and metaphysical underpinnings of his "chronicles." But too often it has also been forgotten that his restoration of the political and cultural history of the Incas can only be fully appreciated on the basis of the cosmological philosophy of Jehuda Abravanel. It has equally been overlooked that the work of the Sephardic philosopher Abravanel, translated into Castilian precisely by Garcilaso, is a late expression of Kabbalistic mysticism, one in which we can trace the influences of Hispano-Muslim mysticism and philosophy.

All of this allows a broadening of the historical and philosophical spectrum beyond what Bension achieved. Whether we are dealing with the mysticism of Teresa of Ávila or the thought of Columbus, the poetics of Arguedas or the humanism of Cervantes, the challenge is to understand and rescue the internal dialogue among Jewish, Christian and Muslim authors in the Iberian and "Latin American" worlds. This perspective allows the hermeneutic dissolution of the imaginary religious and philosophical frontiers of a Christian west that today is fearsomely barricaded within the epistemological walls of its own immense powers of destruction, both technological and military. The philosophical and cosmological dialogue articulated by Garcilaso draws upon Jewish and Islamic mysticism and at the same time enters into the deepest heart of the scientific and mythological conceptions of precolonial America. It embodies discursive continuity between oriental philosophies, a part of Jewish and Arab European medieval philosophies, shamanic philosophies of tropical cultures, and the cosmological myths of the Incas. This is a symbolic, conceptual and cultural continuity that the very construction of the West (from the Crusades to the age of global war) has progressively shattered. Such a perspective might positively subvert the boundaries of orientalism inherent to modern civilization, along with the strategies of legitimation through multiculturalism that are intrinsic to postcolonial, posthistorical, postmodern and posthuman imperialism.

Four

Discovery and conquest, the conversion and colonization of the Americas, better described by Bartolomé de las Casas as the "Destruction of the Indies," can only be understood on the basis of their original historical configuration. But their military, economic and religious underpinning is the Christian crusade. The crusade against Islam in Spain, euphemistically named Reconquest, constitutes the model on which the strategies for the first European colonial enterprise were developed. One may cite the work of Antonio de Nebrija as intellectual testimony to the lexicographical, grammatical, theological and political expurgation of the Islamic and Jewish cultures of the Iberian Peninsula and the colonial and imperial projection of the Christian monarchy. However, this very historical and methodological perspective has not merely been forgotten, it has been repeatedly denied in the same measure that it reveals the centrality of the theological discourse of Christianity to the colonial process (Subirats 1993). Postmodern academic studies have privileged the euphemisms of "acculturation," "syncretism," "hybridization," or even "modernization" to describe this process of colonial destruction of historic peoples and cultures. The discovery and colonization of America cannot be understood as a civilizing process without recognizing the discursive and institutional continuum which unifies on the one hand the theological myths of the original sin of the indigenous peoples of the Americas, and its redemption through the cross, and on the other hand, the discourse and the violence of a salvation in the name of critical empiricism, positivism, Marxist-Leninism, or neoliberal progress. The substructures of global domination, which support this institutional and discursive continuity between Christian doctrines of colonization as conversion and the secularized colonization of modernization, reveal the nebulous quality of the frontier between the colonial period and a hypothetical postcolonial period. In Hispano-Portuguese-American history, this continuity is laid bare in two fundamental ways. One is the recognition of the failure of the Spanish revolution and Hispano American independence by its most brilliant intellectual leaders: José María Blanco White, Simón Bolívar, and Simón Rodríguez, to name but three. The second is the adoption of a positivist project of modernization free of critical dimensions in its political, social, and philosophical aspects. This project was initiated by Feijoo and Sarmiento and crystallized with the concept of authoritarian modernization articulated by José Ortega y Gasset—and by the bureaucrats of the International Monetary Fund.

As early as the sixteenth century, the exiled Spanish humanist Luis Vives wrote that the construction of great empires means nothing but raising great ruins. From Arabic and Sephardic literature lamenting lost cultural splendor to Garcilaso's testimony of an American continent not discovered but destroyed and the continual pessimism of the most lucid intellects from Luis de León to Francisco de Goya, broken hopes, violence, and an interminable desert of ruins are constant motifs. These same motifs could be found in the apocalyptic dimensions that Jewish mysticism adopted the day after the catastrophe of expulsion, and in the oral literature of the historic peoples of the Americas who survived the postindustrial strategies of financial and ecological genocide. This negative vision of Hispanic history constitutes a central place in the canonical works of "Latin American" literature in the global era: *Todas las Sangres; Pedro Páramo; El Señor Presidente; Yo, el Supremo.*

Five

The latest scholastic contributions on the subject of liquid, solid or gaseous modernities, unfinished, incomplete or insufficient modernizations, border or peripheral modernities, transmodernizations, not to mention their hybrid varieties, have masked the painful fact that in the *Hispanic* world, modernity is first of all a substantial absence and a visible vacuum. The academic prohibition of *grands récits,* which the culture industry has elevated to a globalized banality, has served as the perfect alibi for a traditional Hispanism, traditionally inclined to disguise its truncated reformism (religious, epistemological, political), and its social decadence, and to hide its philosophical and scientific backwardness.

This absence, the truncated reformism of Hispanic societies and intelligentsias, is not a mere coincidence but rather the necessary result of a formative trauma. The conquering crusade, the absolute monarchy, and the Inquisition, after the destroying the spiritual centers of the Iberian Peninsula and the Ibero-American continent, went on to tear out their hearts. Abravanel fled Portugal. The Inquisition exiled Vives and Sánchez. Garcilaso experienced an interior exile under the jealous, watchful eye of the Inquisition. Spinoza was a descendant of families from Sepharad. In the Enlightenment, Jacob de Castro Sarmento was burned in effigy in Lisbon. Olavide was intellectually liquidated by an *auto de fe.* Blanco White is the paradigm of nineteenth-century ecclesiastical persecution, reinforced by National Catholic contempt in the twentieth century. But it was precisely through many of these philosophers, for instance the intellectual exiles of Amsterdam and Antwerp in the seventeenth and eighteenth centuries, that European modernity was crystallized in its epistemological, ethical and political senses. This vision of modernity encompassed the rigor of knowledge, rational moral discipline, and an aspiration toward a more perfect social cosmology. Their voices were a substantial part of a reflective European consciousness—not of a presumed "Hispanic identity."

In the name of pluralism, reduced to the latest academic fashion, Hispanists have attempted to define modernity on the basis of random and partisan concepts with which they have weathered the inquisitorial, absolutist, *casticista* and now nationalist storms of Hispanic-Portuguese-American history. They have found here a space within the strict institutional codes of the global academic world, at the price of placing themselves philosophically in a dead end street. Modernity has to be defined on the basis of its great discourses: its promises of freedom, its visions for the future of humanity. It has to be explained on the basis of Luther and of the European Humanism's ethical reforms. It has to be reconstructed critically on the basis of Copernicus's epistemological and cosmological reform, and Spinoza's kabbalistic humanism, in which he crystallizes an ethical conception of democracy as an expression of human liberty. Modern philosophy likewise encompasses Newton, Goethe, Schiller and Hegel, and the scientific, pedagogical and aesthetic thinkers of the eighteenth century. In political terms modernity includes the revolutionary thought of Paine and Jefferson. But significantly, none of these modern expressions have had even a pale reflection in the history of the Iberian and "Latin American" worlds.

The broken and colonized character of "Hispanic" modernity has been recognized openly by its leading intellectuals, although their critiques have fallen on deaf ears. Bolívar and Sarmiento formulated such critiques early on. Goya's engravings and the final entries in Blanco White's diaries make the limits of the Spanish and Spanish American revolutions of the early nineteenth century desperately clear. The letters of Simón Rodríguez similarly indicate the failure of the educational reform movement in the multiethnic communities of Bolivia, Colombia and Venezuela, and the crumbling hopes of emancipation on this continent. Intellectuals as diverse as Pi i Maragall, Antero de Quental, Darcy Ribeiro and Juan Goytisolo provide further witness to the same frustration, to the same inner limitations, to the intellectual and political failures of the Luso-Hispanic and Latin American. All coincide in indicating the vacuum bequeathed by whole centuries of spiritual oppression and social regression.

Instead of parroting the tale of an unrealized modern emancipation, or crouching like frightened rabbits beneath the insipid sub-departmental labels of gender and subalternity, the new Hispanism should examine its own conceptual limitations and lethargic projects, and in so doing redefine its past and future.

Six

The concept of an avant-garde is ambiguous. It encompasses futurists and constructivists, the doctrines of modernist Machinism and Functionalism, and from the beginning, it has been intimately associated with the industrial, political and financial world, often allying itself explicitly with totalitarian social and cultural projects. Futurism, Neoplasticism, the European architectural Modern Movement of the first half of the twentieth century, and the North American International Style in the second half, were configured both as *avant gardes* and as a form of culture shock with a colonizing political agenda. In the 1950s, this agenda was given expression through the bland social utopias of functionalism, and in the 1990s through the hard strategies of spectacular cultural colonization on a global scale (Subirats 1997).

When we speak of the "avant-garde" in Latin American and Iberian cultures, we are referring to something altogether different. We are not dealing with a transnational codification of modern artistic styles or the commercial trivializing of global industrial culture. Picasso rejected the concept of avant-garde as a falsification of the irreducible value of the work of art, in order to take up the cultural traditions of the Greco-Roman Mediterranean world and the Renaissance. Lorca vindicated a form of mysticism with Sufi roots and an oriental metaphysics, which approaches Hinduism. Arguedas reconstructed the magical concepts of being deriving from the precolonial cultures and peoples of the Americas. Diego Rivera built a museum to the holocaust of the Americas and a monument to its memory. Wilfredo Lam breathes life into the cosmological myths of Africa and the Caribbean. These forms of expression, to which one might add a limitless number of literary, artistic, and social testimonies, are linked to a reform of culture, far from the aesthetic rules of Paris and New York. In Arguedas we encounter a mystical conception of existence; in Guimarães Rosa, ancient mythologies. García Lorca writes a manifesto against the city and industrial civilization. The *Antropofagia* of Oswald and Mário de Andrade invents an artistic, metaphysical and erotic revolution. Rulfo constructs a new anthropology on the basis of the ancient gods of Mexico. O'Gorman redefines the "Latin American" city on the basis of Aztec and Mayan inspiration, interwoven with the spirit of the Mexican revolution. Roberto Burle Marx and Oscar Niemayer synthesize the modern city and the cultures of the tropical forests.

One might label the linguistic and political project that runs through these works and intellectual testimonies as "modernity." But one could do so only on the condition that we release this word from the high security jail in which Léger and Marinetti's Fascism, Mondrian and Malevich's technocratic utopias, Alexander Block's cult of the masses, Le Corbusier's absolutist rationalism, and the international style missionaries' bureaucratic messianism have imprisoned it. Most important, however, is not the label of vanguard, which after all derives from military language, but the concept of the work of art. The concept that defines the artistic projects of García Lorca, Burle Marx and Yanomami oral literature is primarily concerned with the recovery of spiritual centers lost during the colonization of the Americas, from the destruction of Tenochtitlán to today's biological war against the Amazonian rainforest and its inhabitants.

To reconstruct, rethink, and reformulate artistic and literary thought in the Iberian, Ibero-, Latin-, and Indian-American worlds does not mean accentuating differences, placing them on the altars of national, regional or peripheral identities, or in the academic packages of global postmodernity. Still less does it mean neutralizing resistance to the industrial and postindustrial colonization of the Third World in the name of insignificant multicultural metaphors, the rhetorics of "the border" and the propaganda of hybridism. To rethink and reformulate twentieth-century culture means becoming conscious of its formal and social failure in the civilizing project of industrial and postindustrial colonization (Subirats 2004).

Seven

I will call it critical theory: a concept of critical theory that is not limited to a methodological formula and a specific theoretical discourse. In a methodologically flexible and broad thematic sense, twentieth-century critical theory encompasses sociologists like Georg Simmel and Lewis Mumford, with their interpretations of urban alienation and the decadence of modernity. It also includes Robert Jungk and Günther Anders' analysis of the new cosmic situation of human existence generated by the technologies of nuclear holocaust, brushed under the carpet by conservative postmodernism because of its ethical and political implications. Mariátegui and Darcy Ribeiro's critical reconstruction of colonialism, equally silenced by the academic mainstream, constitutes another fundamental moment in the critical theory of industrial and postindustrial civilization.

Critical theory is fed by old and new sources. Nietzsche's analysis of Christian-scientific civilization, the hermeneutics of self-destructive violence derived from Freud, and Max Horkheimer and Theodor Adorno's *Dialectic of Enlightenment* are some of its classic antecedents. The critique of the aesthetic and existential impoverishment that runs through the process of social rationalization—leveled by a whole tradition of intellectuals and artists from Tönnies to Morris, from Poelzig to Benjamin, is one of the elements of this critical theory. Many other names and approaches from oriental, Arab and African traditions should be added to this intellectual horizon.

In the world of the Americas, this critique of the historical present allows a fuller perspective than is permitted by the globally dominant academic jargon of cultural sociologisms, and deconstructivist pastiches. The invariably discarded indigenous voices of the Americas attesting to the emptiness and nihilism of the civilization that continues to destroy them are not the least relevant testimonies in this respect. The importance of intellectuals like Darcy Ribeiro, Arguedas or Roa Bastos in terms of popular culture, linguistic memory and the global history of civilization from a Third World perspective cannot be sufficiently emphasized.

This concept of critical theory is to be an open one, encompassing diverse philosophical and religious traditions, and different instruments of aesthetic, sociological and hermeneutic analysis: in the words of *The Zohar,* "the words of wisdom to illumine the way" (Matt 2004, 35).

Trans. Simon R. Doubleday, Hofstra University

Bibliography

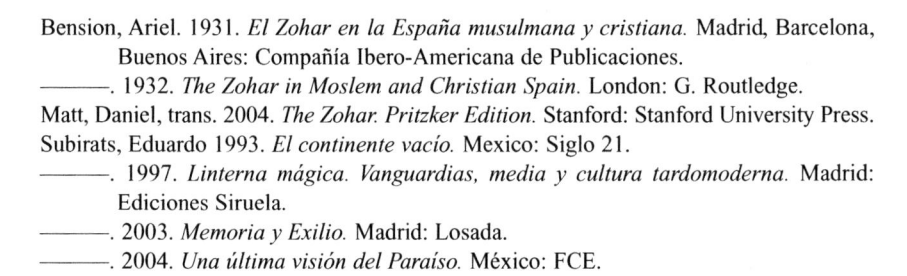

Bension, Ariel. 1931. *El Zohar en la España musulmana y cristiana.* Madrid, Barcelona, Buenos Aires: Compañía Ibero-Americana de Publicaciones.
———. 1932. *The Zohar in Moslem and Christian Spain.* London: G. Routledge.
Matt, Daniel, trans. 2004. *The Zohar. Pritzker Edition.* Stanford: Stanford University Press.
Subirats, Eduardo 1993. *El continente vacío.* Mexico: Siglo 21.
———. 1997. *Linterna mágica. Vanguardias, media y cultura tardomoderna.* Madrid: Ediciones Siruela.
———. 2003. *Memoria y Exilio.* Madrid: Losada.
———. 2004. *Una última visión del Paraíso.* México: FCE.

Notes on Contributors

Michael Armstrong-Roche is an Associate Professor in the Department of Romance Languages and Literatures at Wesleyan University in Connecticut. His book *Cervantes's Epic Novel: Empire, Religion, and the Dream Life of Heroes in 'Persiles'* is forthcoming (in 2008) from the University of Toronto Press. He is now at work on a book that traces voices of dissent in early modern Spain and the New World.

Simon Doubleday (co-editor) is Associate Professor in the Department of History at Hofstra University. His interests include the social and cultural history of medieval Castile; the ethical and political responsibilities of the historian; and the concept of historical "relevance," particularly in the context of medieval studies. He is author of *The Lara Family: Crown and Nobility in Medieval Spain* (Cambridge, MA: Harvard University Press, 2001; published in a revised Spanish edition as *Los Lara: Nobleza y monarquía en la España Medieval* (Madrid: Ediciones Turner, 2004)), co-editor of *In the Light of Medieval Spain. Islam, the West, and the Relevance of History* (Palgrave, forthcoming in 2008), and is currently completing a post-empirical study of a thirteenth-century Castilian courtesan entitled *The Quest for María Pérez*.

Joseba Gabilondo is Assistant Professor at the Department of Spanish and Portuguese at Michigan State University. He has published a number of articles on Hollywood cinema in the context of global culture, Spanish nationalism, postnationalism, masculinity, and queer theory. He has edited a monographic issue for the *Arizona Journal of Hispanic Cultural Studies* on the Hispanic Atlantic (2001), and recently published an essay collection on contemporary Spanish-, American- and French-Basque literature entitled *Nazioaren hondarrak* (Remnants of the Nation; Bilbao: University of the Basque Country Press, 2006). He is currently finishing two book manuscripts, *Before Babel: A Cultural History of Basque Literatures* and *The Barbarian Divide: Neoliberalism and Multiculturalism at the New European Border*.

Mariano Gómez Aranda is a tenured researcher at the Consejo Superior de Investigaciones Científicas (Madrid), and has been Head of the Department of Biblical Philology and Ancient Eastern Studies at the CSIC since 2002. He is member of the Editorial Board of *Sefarad* and of the Advisor Editorial Board of *Miscelánea de Estudios Árabes y Hebreos*. His areas of expertise include the Biblical commentaries of Abraham ibn Ezra (1089–1165) and medieval Jewish science; he is specifically interested in analyzing connections between Jews and Arabs in the context of cultural crossing and interchange. His books include *El Comentario de Abraham ibn Ezra al libro de Job. Edición crítica* (Madrid, 2004), and *Sefarad científica: la visión judía de la ciencia en la Edad Media* (Madrid, 2003).

Francisco-J. Hernández Adrián is Assistant Professor of Romance Studies at Duke University. He teaches courses on modern and contemporary Caribbean texts and visual cultures, and on the historical avant-gardes in Atlantic contexts. His work focuses on theories of insularity and the Atlantic world, and on constructions of islandness in relation to Spanish and European imaginaries. His research interests include visual, gender, and race theories of the Hispanic Caribbean and the modern Atlantic. He has published articles on Cuba, Puerto Rico, the Canary Islands, and the Modern Atlantic. He is currently working on a book manuscript entitled *On Tropical Grounds. Avant-Garde Imaginations of Insularity in the Hispanic Caribbean and the Canary Islands*.

Susan Martin-Márquez is Associate Professor in the Department of Spanish and Portuguese, Director of the Program in Cinema Studies, and a member of the African Studies Program at Rutgers University. She is the author of *Feminist Discourse and Spanish Cinema: Sight Unseen* (Oxford University Press, 1999) and *Disorientations: Spanish Colonialism in Africa and the Performance of Identity* (Yale University Press, 2008). She is also working on a collaborative book project under the direction of Jo Labanyi, *Cinema and the Mediation of Everyday Life: An Oral History of Cinema-Going in 1940s and 1950s Spain* (Berghahn Books, forthcoming).

Alberto Medina is Assistant Professor at Boston University. He is the author of *Exorcismos de la memoria: políticas y poéticas de la melancolía en la transición española* and is finishing a book on the construction of political subjectivities in eighteenth-century Spain. He has published extensively on Spanish and Latin American contemporary literature and cultural studies in periodicals such as *Hispania, Revista de Estudios Hispánicos, Bulletin of Hispanic Studies,* and *Iberoamericana.*

Cristina Moreiras-Menor is Associate Professor of Spanish Literature and Culture and Women's Studies at the University of Michigan (Ann Arbor). She has published extensively on nineteenth- and twentieth-century Spanish literature and film as well as on Spanish Women Writers and Galician literature. She is the author of *Cultura herida: Literatura y cine en la España democrática* (Libertarias, 2002) and the editor of a monographic issue of the *Journal of Spanish Cultural* Studies entitled *Critical interventions on Violence.* She is currently working on a book on the cultural history of Galicia and the notion of (national) borders entitled *Galicia y sus fronteras: Escritores, márgenes y el canon nacional (siglos xix y xx).*

Parvati Nair is Professor of Hispanic Cultural Studies at Queen Mary, University of London. Her research focuses on ethnicity, gender, and migration in the Hispanic world and on cultural representations of these issues in film, music, and photography. She is the author of *Configuring Community: Theories, Narratives and Practices of Community Identities in Contemporary Spain* (MHRA, 2004) and *Rumbo al norte: inmigración y movimientos culturales entre el Magreb y España* (Edicions Bellaterra, 2006) and co-editor of *Gender and Spanish Cinema* (Berg, 2004). At present, she is writing a book on the photography of Sebastião Salgado, entitled *A Different Light* (Duke University Press, forthcoming).

Vicente L. Rafael is Professor of History at the University of Washington in Seattle. He is the author of *Contracting Colonialism* (Duke UP, 1993), *White Love and Other Essays in Filipino History* (Duke UP, 2000), and most recently, *The Promise of the Foreign: Nationalism and the Technics of Translation in the Spanish Philippines* (Duke UP, 2005).

David Rojinsky is Assistant Professor of Hispanic Studies at the University of Toronto. His articles have appeared in *JLACS, BHS, La corónica,* and *Hofstra Hispanic Review.* His book manuscript *Companion to Empire: A Genealogy of the Written Word in Spain and New Spain, c. 550–1550* is forthcoming with Ediciones Rodopi, and addresses the intersection between alphabetic writing and Spain's monolingual pretensions on the one hand, and its instrumentality for the consolidation of imperial expansion, on the other.

Benita Sampedro Vizcaya (co-editor) is Associate Professor of Colonial Studies at Hofstra University. Her research interest focuses on issues of Spanish colonialism in both Africa and Latin America, specifically on processes of decolonization and postcolonial legacies. She has published extensively on empire, exile, colonial discourse and resistance, most recently on topics relating to Equatorial Guinea, the only African state in which Spanish remains the official language. She is currently working on a book manuscript provisionally entitled *Spanish Colonialism, African Decolonizations, and the Politics of Place,* intended to draw the attention of a wide and worldly audience to a country whose political situation, economic inequities and cultural and intellectual activity have largely passed below the radar of academia and media. Her intellectual agenda is geared toward a redefinition of Afro-European relations from a colonial/postcolonial perspective, a reconception of the way we teach, formulate, and generate knowledge and culture from a Romance Languages and Literatures perspective, and a revisiting of links between colonial Africa and colonial Latin America beyond the frame of the different imperial Atlantic networks.

H. Rosi Song is Associate Professor of Spanish at Bryn Mawr College. She is the co-editor of the volume *Traces of Contamination: Unearthing the Francoist Legacy in Contemporary Spain* (Bucknell University Press, 2005) and is currently working on two book projects, one on intellectuals in contemporary Spain and another on the use of Hispanism as a cultural doctrine.

Eduardo Subirats is Professor in the Department of Spanish and Portuguese at New York University. He is a specialist in modern philosophy, cultural theory, avant-garde aesthetics, and criticism of the colonial and imperial legacies. His numerous books and edited volumes include *El continente vacío* (1995); *La linterna mágica* (1997); *Culturas virtuales* (2001); *Intransiciones. Crítica de la cultura española* (2002); *Memoria y exilio* (2003); *América latina y la guerra global* (2004); and *Viaje al fin del paraíso* (2005).

Index

Abraham ibn Ezra, 229, 234–239, 241, 243, 243n2
Abravanel, Isaac, 229, 239–243
Abravanel, Jehuda, 252, 255
Abreu Galindo, Fray Juan de, 172–173, 184n21
'Abd al-Mu'min (Almohad caliph), 234
Adorno, Theodor, 258
Africa: contemporary relationship between Spain and, 1–2, 42, 44, 52, 60n3, 71, 75–76, 78, 90–92, 94–97, 103–104, 107; medieval and early modern relationship between Spain and, 174, 183n17, 229, 234; presence in global 'Hispanic' cultures, 246–248, 251, 257–258. *See also* Leïla, Mali, Morocco
al-Andalus, 228–246
Albacete, Alfonso, *I Love You, Baby*, 47–49, 51, 55–56, 59, 60n9
Alberoni, Giulio, 149
Alba, Fernando Álvarez de Toledo y Pimentel, duke of, 206–207
Albuquerque, Francisco Fernández de la Cueva, duke of, 191–192
Almodóvar, Pedro, 61
Almohads, 234, 243n2
Almoravids, 229
Amadís de Gaula (Montalvo), 213
Andalusia, 71–74, 78–79, 84, 97. *See also* al-Andalus
Anders, Günther, 258
Andrade, Oswald and Mário, 257
Arana, Sabino, 80
Arguedas, José María, 248, 250, 252–253, 257–258
Ariosto, Ludovico, *Orlando Furioso*, 213
Armendáriz, Montxo, *Cartas de Alou*, 43, 96
Atlantic studies, 165–187
Augustine, Saint, *The City of God*, 215
Azurmendi, Mikel, 71–86

Balibar, Étienne, 2, 9, 105–107, 118, 198
Baños, Juan de Leiva de la Cerda, count of, 191–192, 201n3
Barceló, Miquel, 90–104
Basque country and culture, 78–86, 106–108, 246
Benjamin, Walter, 200n1, 258
Bension, Ariel, 251–253
Bhabha, Homi, 3, 16, 19, 21, 39, 45–46, 49–50, 52, 57, 105, 195

Black Legend, 148, 161n2
Block, Alexander, 257
Blumentritt, Ferdinand, 124–125, 141
Bo, Lino, 247
Boccherini, Luigi, 149
Bolívar, Simón, 254, 256
Bolivia, 256
Bollaín, Icíar, 53, 61n14; *Flores de otro mundo*, 47–48, 51–54
Borges, Jorge Luis, 248
Bourbon dynasty, 147–155, 160–161, 167, 169–171. *See also* Charles III (king of Spain); Charles IV (king of Spain); Philip V (king of Spain)
Bourdieu, Pierre, 17
Brazil, 246–249
Broschi, Carlo Maria, "Farinelli", 149
Burle Marx, Roberto, 257
Bwana (Uribe), 43, 96

Cadalso, José, 148
Calderón de la Barca, Pedro, 250
Canary Islands, 165–187
capitalism, influence on contemporary international relations of, 16, 18, 20–21, 25, 32, 36, 38–40, 200; and contemporary cultural/political formations; 65–66, 78, 84; cultural responses to, 91, 95, 100, 102. *See also* globalization
Cartas de Alou (Armendáriz), 43, 96
Casares, Carlos, 110, 118n3
Castelao, Alfonso R., 106, 108, 110
Castro, Rosalía de, 106, 108, 110
Castro, Américo, 6, 12, 65, 252
Castro Sarmento, Jacob de, 255
Catalonia and Catalan culture: 38, 96–103, 106–107, 235, 246
Cervantes, Miguel de, 250–253; *Don Quijote* (Cervantes) 222, 252; *La destruición de Numancia*, 204–227
CETI (Centro de Estancia Temporal de los Inmigrantes, Ceuta), 34–38
Ceuta, 1 2, 5, 15–41, 75
Charles I (king of Spain; Charles V, Holy Roman Emperor), 213, 216
Charles III (king of Spain), 148–150, 153–157, 161, 162n5, 166–167, 169–171, 176, 181n5
Charles IV (king of Spain), 149
Chile, 207
City of God, The (St. Augustine), 215

Colombia, 256
Columbus, Christopher, 248, 252–253
Cortés, Hernán, 249
Cosas que dejé en la Habana (Gutiérrez Aragón), 47–48, 51, 55–58, 60n9
Cuba, 47–48, 52–53, 56, 58, 168
Cuevas Dávalos, Juan Alonso de (bishop of Oaxaca), 191–192, 194, 201n5

D'Alembert, Jean, 148
Dante, 215
Derrida, Jacques, 7–8, 120, 177–178, 201n1
Diderot, Denis, 148
Dogon (ethnic group), 90–94, 99
Dominican Republic, 47, 57, 97. *See also* Santo Domingo
Don Quijote (Cervantes) 222, 252
Dutch Republic, 246, 255. *See also* Flanders; Imperialism, Dutch

El Ejido, 71–73, 75, 78, 80
En construcción (Guerín), 60n6, 97–104
EC (European Community), 73, 107. *See also* EU
England, 112–113, 170, 173, 184n6, 235–236. *See also* imperialism, British; Gibraltar.
Ercilla, Alonso de, 206–207, 212, 215
Esquilache, Leopoldo de Gregorio, marquis of, 149, 161
EU (European Union), 23, 27, 31, 35, 39, 42, 60n1, 86. *See also* EC

Farge, Arlette, 178
Farnese, Elisabeta, 153
Feijoo, Benito Jerónimo, 250, 254
Ferdinand I (archduke of Austria and Holy Roman Emperor), 206
Ferdinand V (king of Castile, and king of Aragón), 205, 209, 211, 243
Ferdinand VI (king of Spain), 150, 153
Ferreiro, Celso Emilio, 110
filibusterismo, El (Rizal), 120–146
Flanders, 206–207. *See also* Dutch Republic
Flores de otro mundo (Bollaín), 47–48, 51–54
Fortes, Susana, 111
Foucault, Michel, 16–17, 19–21, 166, 178–179
France, 45, 80–81, 84, 169, 178, 181n7, 205; eighteenth-century continental power, 147, 149, 183n14; Enlightenment, 147–148, 165, 167 (*see also* D'Alembert, Diderot, Kant, Montesquieu, Morvilliers, Voltaire); medieval, 229, 234–236, 238. *See also* imperialism, French
Francis I (king of France), 213
Franciscans, 87n2, 251

Franco, Francisco, 28–29, 42–43, 49, 54–56, 61n11, 73
Freud, Sigmund, 68–70, 87n4, 258

Galicia, 106–107
García Lorca, Federico, 252, 257
Gibraltar, 15, 25, 29, 162n3, 168, 182n9
Giaquinto, Corrado, 159
Gil, Jesús, 31–32, 34–35
Glas, George, 172–174, 184n21, 184n23
globalization, 3, 18–19, 26, 38, 65–66, 71–72, 77–79, 85–86, 87n2, 94–95, 102, 106, 108, 110, 118, 247–248, 250, 253–258
Goethe, Johann Wolfgang von, 255
Gonsar, Camilo, 110
Goya, Francisco de, 254, 256
Goytisolo, Juan, 12, 30–32, 80, 256
Granada: 229–230, 240. *See also* Andalusia
Grimaldi, Jerónimo (marquis of Grimaldi), 149
Guerín, José Luis, *En construcción,* 60n6, 97–104
Guevara, Antonio de, 212, 216
Guha, Ranajit, 191
Guimarães Rosa, João, 248, 252, 257
Gutiérrez, Chus, *Poniente,* 96
Gutiérrez Aragón, Manuel, 56; *Cosas que dejé en la Habana,* 47–48, 51, 55–58, 60n9

Habsburg dynasty, 150–154, 160–161, 162n9, 169–170, 173, 182, 204–227. *See also* Charles I, Philip II
Hegel, Georg Wilhelm Friedrich, 171, 255
Hispanic identity, 246–247, 249, 255
Horkheimer, Max, 258

I Love You, Baby (Albacete and Menkes), 47–49, 51, 55–56, 59, 60n9
Ibn Arabi, 251
Ibn Gabirol, 252
IMF (International Monetary Fund), 254
imperialism: British, 112, 170, 174, 182n8–10, 183n16 (*see also* Gibraltar); colonial attitudes in academia, 247–248; contemporary global imperialism, 247–250, 254; contemporary Spanish and European, 44–47, 49–50, 57, 67, 87n5, 102, 256; Dutch, 182n8, 182n10; early modern Spanish, 8–12, 28–29, 84, 153, 160–161, 162n4, 165–187, 188–203, 204–227, 249–250, 253–254, 257; eighteenth- and nineteenth-century Spain as colonized space, 148, 256; French, 168, 182n8, 182n10, 247; imperial nostalgia, 247; nineteenth-century Spanish, 120–146; North American, 74, 120, 248, 256; Roman,

204–227, 246; terms 'colonial' and 'postcolonial', 247, 254
Inca Garcilaso, 250, 252–254
Isabella I (queen of Castile), 211, 243
Italy, 149, 152–154, 156, 169, 171, 181n7, 229, 234–236, 240, 242. *See also* Sicily

Jefferson, Thomas, 256
Jews and Jewish cultures, 4–5, 30, 228–254
John of Austria, Don, 206
John of the Cross, Saint, 250–251
John II (king of Portugal), 240
Judah al-Harizi, 234
Jungk, Robert, 258
Juvarra, Filippo, 149

Kant, Immanuel, 166, 171, 181n4

La celestina, 252
La destruición de Numancia (Cervantes), 204–227
Lam, Wilfredo, 257
Las Casas, Bartolomé de, 250, 253
Latin America, 42–64, 71, 75–76, 84–85, 110, 113, 246–259; pre-Columbian, 246–248, 251, 253, 257. *See also* Bolivia, Brazil, Chile, Colombia, Cuba, Dominican Republic, Mexico, Venezuela
Lazarillo de Tormes, 252
Le Corbusier, 257
Léger, Fernand, 257
Leïla, 26–27, 29
León, Luis de, 250, 254
Llull, Ramón, 251–252

Madariaga, Salvador de, 222
Maetzu, Ramiro de, 249
Maimonides, 240, 251
Malevich, Kazimir, 257
Mali, 90–97, 101, 103–104
Man dos países, A (Rivas), 105–119
Manso de Contreras, Cristóbal, 190–200
Mariátegui, José Carlos, 258
Marinetti, Filippo Tommaso, 257
Melilla, 1–2, 5, 16, 18, 24, 27, 29, 32, 35, 40
Méndez Ferrín, X. L., 106, 110–111, 118n3
Mendoza, Bernardino de, 207
Mendoza, García Hurtado de, 207
Mengs, Anton Raphael, 149, 154–161
Menkes, David, *I Love You, Baby*, 47–49, 51, 55–56, 59, 60n9
Mexico, 188–203, 257. *See also* US-Mexico border
migration, 17–19, 23–27, 31–40, 42–86, 90, 96–97, 100, 105–119, 228–245
Minorca, 168, 182n9
modernity, 20, 249–250, 255–258
Mondrian, Piet, 257

Montalvo, Garci Rodríguez de, 213
Montemayor de Cuenca, Juan Francisco de, 192, 196–198
Montesquieu, Charles-Louis de Secondat, baron de, 148, 151, 174
Morales, Ambrosio de, 204, 208–209, 216
Morisco rebellion, 206–207
Morocco, 1, 3, 15–41
Morris, William, 258
Morvilliers, Nicolas Masson de, 148
Moshe ibn Ezra, 229–235, 238–239, 243
movida madrileña, 250
multiculturalism and *convivencia*, 65–104, 247, 253–254, 257–258; in al-Andalus, 229, 235, 243
Mumford, Lewis, 258
Muslims and Islam, 25–26, 30, 32–33, 72–76, 97, 101, 229–230, 233–234, 239, 243, 246–247, 249–253

nation-state and national identity: contemporary perceptions and concepts of, 18–19, 22–24, 44, 57, 105–106; Jewish national identity, 228–245 (esp. 237, 242); Mexico, 199; Spain, 1–5, 26, 32, 39, 59, 60n8, 106–110, 112, 117–118, 147–164, 204–227, 249–250, 257. *See also* nationalism
nationalism: Europe, 161; Philippines, 120–127, 135, 139–140, 144, 145n7; Spain, 3, 44–46, 59, 60n8, 65–89, 107–108, 117, 209–210, 249, 255
Nationalists and National Catholicism, 28, 49, 61n11, 249, 255
Nebrija, Antonio de, 253
Newton, Isaac, 255
Niemeyer, Oscar, 257
Nietzsche, Friedrich, 258
Noli me tangere (Rizal), 120, 122, 126
Núñez de la Peña, Juan, 184n20

O'Gorman, Eduardo, 257
Olavide, Pablo de, 255
Orlando furioso (Ariosto), 213
Ortega y Gasset, José, 249, 254

Paine, Thomas, 256
Paz, Octavio, 248
Perejil, *see* Leïla
Philip II (king of Spain), 204–206, 209–210, 216, 224n5
Philip V (king of Spain), 147–149, 152–163, 169–170, 183
Philippines, 120–146, 168
philosophy and intellectual life: medieval and Renaissance Christian, 242–243 (*see also* St. Augustine); medieval and Renaissance Iberian, 229, 234–243, 243n3, 251–255; philosophical

limitations of Hispanism, 246–259 (esp. 255); Spanish Enlightenment, 249–250, 254. *See also* France, Enlightenment
Pi i Maragall, Francisco, 256
Picasso, Pablo, 257
Pizarro, Francisco, 249
Poelzig, Hans, 258
Poniente (Gutiérrez), 96
Ponz, Antonio, 156, 159
Popol Vuh, 248
Portugal, 28–29, 110, 117, 175, 183n16, 205, 209–210, 213, 239–242, 246–249, 255
PP (Partido Popular), 32, 61, 71, 74
PSOE (Partido Socialista Obrero Español), 74

Queizán, María Xosé, 118n3
Quental, Antero de, 256

Ribeiro, Darcy, 256, 258
Rico, Vicente, 106
Rivas, Manuel, *A man dos paíños,* 105–119
Rivera, Diego, 257
Rizal, José: *El filibusterismo,* 120–146; *Noli me tangere,* 120, 122, 126
Roa Bastos, Augusto, 258
Rodríguez, Simón, 250, 254, 256
Rousseau, Jean-Jacques, 158
royal palaces: El Escorial, 162n9; La Granja, 153; Madrid, 152–156, 158–159; in medieval Jewish exile memory, 239, 241
Rulfo, Juan, 252, 257
rural spaces: Basque country, 79–81, 84–85; eighteenth-century Spain, 150

Sabatini, Francisco, 149, 162n5
Sánchez de las Brozas, Francisco, 255
Santo Domingo (city), 168
Sarmiento, Domingo Faustino, 250, 254–256
Sartori, Giovanni, 67, 86
Scarlatti, Domenico, 149
Schiller, Friedrich, 255

Scipio Aemilianus, 204–225
Sefer Ha-Zohar (Book of Splendor), 251–252, 259
Shaul ha-Cohen, 239
Sicily, 149, 153, 168, 240. *See also* Italy
Simmel, Georg, 258
Spanish Civil War, 28, 73, 98, 110–112, 117
Spinoza, Baruch, 255

Tehuantepec: rebellion, 188–203; Isthmus of, 199–200, 202n9, 202n10
Teresa of Ávila, Saint, 250–251, 253
Tiepolo, Giovanni Battista, 149, 155–161
Tonantzin-Guadalupe, 250
Tönnies, Ferdinand, 258
Toro, Suso de, 106, 111, 118n3

Unamuno, Miguel de, 249–250
urban spaces: contemporary Spain, 40n3, 96–98, 102–104; eighteenth-century Spain and Canary Islands, 150, 173
Uribe, Imanol, 43, 96
US-Mexican border, 17, 22–24, 109
Utrecht, Treaty of (1713), 147, 162n3, 168, 182n9

Vasconcelos, José, 249
Vaz de Caminha, Pero, 252
Vega, Lope de, 250
Venezuela, 256
Vieira y Clavijo, José de, 165–187
Vilas, Neira, 110
Visigoths, 211
Vives, Luis, 250–251, 254–255
Voltaire, 165, 181n5, 181n7

White, Blanco, 12, 250, 254–256.
Winckelmann, Johann Joachim, 154–157, 159, 163n12

Yanomami (ethnic group), 247, 257

Zapatero, José Luis Rodríguez, 1, 62
Zapotec (ethnic group), 188–189, 193, 247
Zizek, Slavoj, 65–67, 86